UP TO ME

Memoirs of a year in South America

by Jort Vanderveen

For them that obey authority
That they do not respect in any degree
Who despise their jobs, their destinies
Speak jealously of them that are free
Cultivate their flowers to be
Nothing more than something they invest in
Bob Dylan

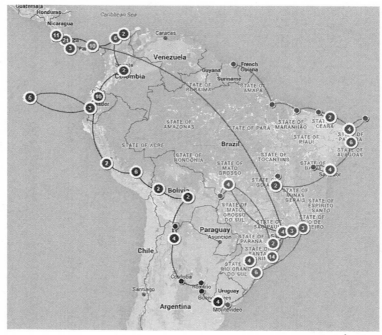

travel map

INDEX

Author's Note   p1

Prologue   p3

Chapter I   Suriname   p5

Chapter II   Brazil   p9

Chapter III   Uruguay   p75

Chapter IV   Argentina   p85

Chapter V   Bolivia   p105

Chapter VI   Peru   p113

Chapter VII   Ecuador   p127

Chapter VIII   Colombia   p163

Chapter IX   Panama   p197

Chapter X   Costa Rica   p213

Chapter XI   Panama II   p279

Chapter XII   Brazil II   p281

Epilogue   p381

Words of Thanks   p383

List of Accommodations   p387

AUTHOR'S NOTE

"If I'd thought about it I never would've done it, I guess I would've let it slide
If I'd lived my life by what others were thinkin', the heart inside me would've died
I was just too stubborn to ever be governed by enforced insanity
Someone had to reach for the risin' star, I guess it was up to me"
Bob Dylan

I've started writing this manuscript two months after I've returned from a yearlong travelling in South- and bit of Central America. During my trip I did not keep a diary, and my only notes were the monthly Facebook posts, in which I tried to share a part of my trip with my friends and family, by sharing some photos, and some words on the progress. When I was organising my nearly 42.000 photos I had taken in these 366 days it struck me that these photos aren't telling the entire story and in order to keep my memory alive I wanted to write it down, for my own recollection. During the process of writing, I've been telling some friends about this project, and some seemed interested in reading it, or at least some parts of it. For those interested a great selection of photos can be seen on www.jort.eu.

I immediately started writing my document in English, which is not my mother tongue. I chose this language as it was the language I had been travelling with mostly during my twelve months. Whenever I had to translate something to or from Portuguese or Spanish, I had always used English, and not Dutch. English is a richer language, in my opinion, even though I barely know its exact wealth.

Another reason to write this, is so I can make a book out of it. When I wrote down my dreams some years ago, somewhere at the top of the list was 'write a book', and now I finally have a story to tell, even if it's only for myself. A physical book, on my shelf, with my name on it, would fulfil this dream already.

Whoever might read this document, I hope to inspire them to travel, to see the world, to meet new people, to help them, and also follow their heart in their own journeys of life. It's all up to them. It's all up to you. And this, this trip? It was up to me.

PROLOGUE

I've always been attracted to 'the road'. To explore, to travel, to meet new people, to be free in wherever I go, and also in whatever I do.

Travelling was where I charged my battery whenever I went. I would get energy from new destinations, to meet new people, to make new friends. And mostly, I had liked to do it alone. My first ever trip abroad alone was a three week trip to Australia. When I would hire my first employee I felt great responsibility and I thought to postpone my holidays for a while. In a wave of excitement, a month before this person would start, I sent out emails to all the people I knew around the world at that time. Those weren't many, but I sent out an exact same email to Mexico, the United States, Germany, France, Spain, Italy and Australia. I had done it at time during the day the most likely persons to respond were the ones in Europe, but within seconds I had gotten a reply from the Australian girl I had met in London three years earlier, who I had barely been in contact with, but who told me I would be totally welcome. No words, but deeds, as the slogan of my favourite football team is, and without further consideration I booked a flight to Adelaide, with a return from Melbourne. Three weeks would be between arrival and departure. My parents first response was that Australia is way too big for a three-week travel and flying so long for only three weeks would be nuts. They would tell me you need at least three months there and this was what they would be thinking of themselves. There was no stopping me anymore and one week later I already was sitting in my plane to Singapore, where I had a short layover, before landing in Adelaide, over thirty hours after I had boarded in Amsterdam.

It became my first step of solo travelling, and many other trips would follow, such as the road trip around Scandinavia and the Baltic states, and the trip to Athens with a car, visiting all the Balkan. The United States had been my favourite country to road trip, and numerous times I went there, rented a car, and just drove off. My only other trip to South America was also one I took by myself and again only lasted three weeks.

I was very involved with my job, for which I felt great responsibility through the eleven years I worked there. It was my family, and the connection to it was deep. I had overcome some storms there, and had closed my eyes for its flaws, and also my own future.

In 2013 I had received a phone call from my two friends, who had started this company and who I had been working with for a little more than ten years at this moment. They informed me they had sold the company to a competitor and that in the next months the situation would be changing. I remember gulping for a bit, but immediately thought this new, bigger, company, would be able to teach me things I would never come across in the same old setting.

Back in the Netherlands things indeed changed, and however I was never negative about the new company, I did not mind them choosing others over me for the available positions, at the point the reorganising started. I immediately felt this could be my moment to break free, and do what I like most: travel for a serious amount of time.

Once the smoke had cleared I booked my ticket to South America for a three-month trip, flying into Paramaribo in Suriname, and leaving from Buenos Aires, Argentina. I would come back for a surgery on a painful inguinal hernia, and to continue afterwards Down Under, back to Australia. On January 21st I take off and that same day I land in a jungle of anonymity.

Chapter I

SURINAME

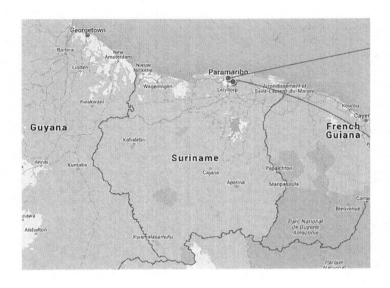

Suriname - Paramaribo, Paramaribo

On January 20th I fly to Suriname with KLM, a nine-hour flight, which is comfortable. I get to know a friendly woman who is sitting next to me and we chit chat during the whole flight. She gives me tips about her country and later offers me a ride to my hotel, as at midnight's arrival there's zero to none taxis.

The hotel is quite nice and centrally located. The next day I walk through the town. I think it is shit. It is small, it smells, and it is way too hot. Most people move slowly. They don't seem to do much with their time. I understand this is caused by the high temperatures. Too hot to get something done.

My biggest annoyance is however the thousands of mosquitoes, who seem to love my blood. Even though I use protection with deet they are drawn to me like a bee to honey. It drives me absolutely crazy. When I was in Argentina five years ago dengue was all over the news there, and together with the malaria pills I'm taking, the thought of that makes me believe every mosquito will bring me one of these horrible diseases. At night I stare at my arms and think tomorrow I will be in a hospital. Just after two days of travelling it can all end already.

I don't sleep well and the next day I wander around like a zombie. The sun makes my face turn the colour red, because the sun block isn't helping me much either. A red head zombie. How weird is that.

Even though people here are mainly black, there's a huge number of Dutch interns. Girls between 18 and 22 years old all come here to finish their studies. And it also seems the people that do really live here, are older than 50. I feel like I'm floating in the middle. And maybe this explains while even though they should be used to white people, they stare at me. Later I will find out this is only the beginning: in Brazil gazing will get a whole other meaning to me.

After these days adapting to the new time zone, getting bitten by mosquitoes, and burnt by the sun, I decide to actually do something, and I rent a bike to see a former coffee plantation. I dress up with long sleeves and long pants, as I think I will go into the jungle now.

I have two options to cross the river: a 6% steep bridge, or a ferry. I decide to take the bridge, even though the bike rental advices me to not do that. An hour later I know why and I regret my choice. I share the road up with cars and with this heat every paddle up makes my head tingle. When I finally reach the top I nearly faint and I throw all the water I carry over my face. For fifteen minutes I think I stare to the nothingness of my own eyes. The cars that were applauding me while I was going up, keep doing that when I sit there absolutely devastated. I need more water and climb my bike and let the road down do its work. With high speed I get off in maybe a tenth of the time that I used to get up. At a little supermarket I buy candy, coke and lots of water. I sit down in front of it and let my heartbeat return to normal again.

When all seems good again I continue my way and get greeted by many locals. I feel at ease now and soon I reach my destination. There's a trail through the natural section of the park which I can access with my bike and I decide to see this instead of the plantation itself. It's well worth it with many birds, salamanders and later even monkeys. I'm so happy to see monkeys in the wild. My first time ever since the semi wild monkeys in Japan five years ago. I take out my new Nikon D7100 and try to take some photos. I'm new to this type of photography and it takes time to make some proper photos. I stand for quite some time observing these monkeys make their ways through the trees. I finally see Suriname's beauty: the pure wild nature. I'm loving it. The park rangers talk to me and inform me about the different kind of animals here, and even tell me at times you can see jaguars here. I can't believe it: when I decided to go to South America, I read some books about the countries, its nature and its wildlife. One animal caught my attention and I got eager to see it: the elusive jaguar. Hearing about it first hand from these rangers fills me with excitement and my hunt for the animal has started.

The park will close soon and the rangers tell me how I can close it, as they will already leave. I'm happy with their trust in me and leave the park an hour later, locking it the way they explained it. I bike back, heading for the ferry: I'm not going to die twice today. After some negotiations I board a boat and easily get to the other side. If only I had done the same this morning. At the hotel I take a shower, flushing away all the sweat. I feel new-born. At night I find a super nice restaurant and the food is delicious. Oh Suriname, maybe I misjudged you the first days.

The next day I regret my positive thought, as trying to move on seems almost impossible: there is one city in Brazil you can fly to, Belém, and the flight I booked was postponed due to a lucrative deal the company took: fly to Miami instead. Communicating information seems impossible for them and their relaxed way of thinking doesn't make me feel it will all turn out fine. Oh well. Eventually all works out and I do get my flight, at an insane time: 03:30 at night. Another zombie night.

Chapter II

BRAZIL

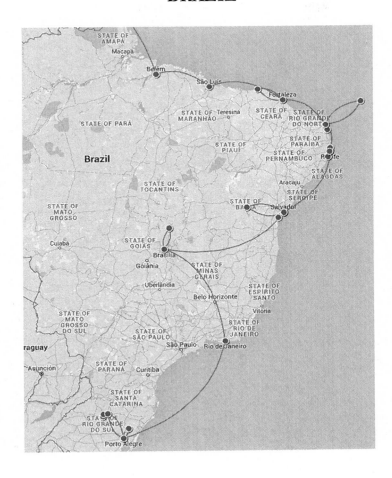

<u>Brazil - Belém, Pará</u>

At the airport I get in touch with a group of Dutch people, who introduce me to a word that will later control my diet: acai. They have a plantation in the Amazon and truly believe this will be a success for them. I listen to their ambitions and even get curious to this berry.

I sleep during the flight and upon arrival in Brazil the only thing I want is continue doing this. I have to find a way to my host's home however and this is a challenge. Where in Suriname all people speak my mother tongue, I am now confronted with a language I don't understand, at all. And the worst thing: even at an airport, people don't seem to speak English, at all. I use my hands and feet and finally get a cab to the housing complex of Raquel. The taxi driver doesn't speak English either and I'm trying to follow his route on Google Maps, to make sure I do not get kidnapped in my first hours here. The last meters seem to go through a favela, and then we get to a fence with security: the entrance to the community. There the house is easily found and I meet Raquel and her two roommates for the first time. They welcome me with all their hearts, and immediately make me feel at home. They also serve me the best tasting fruits I have ever had: so much taste in a small banana, I can't believe it. Their house becomes mine for the next days. They help me in every possible way and take me out whenever they have time.

The community is indeed surrounded by some kind of favela and my first steps through it alone were kind of wary. I feel the eyes of the people stinging in my back, but also when I get eye contact, I see their eyes grow bigger. I am white, with a red sun burnt layer, and I have bright eyes. My hair is not thick and black like theirs, but grey, with bits of blonde, and thin. Even though I'm small in Europe, here I'm tall. I'm different. And I realise this because of these stares. I get to a bus station to take a bus into town and all eyes are on me. I feel like I can get robbed any second. Shady looking men are in my mind robbing me with their eyes. Women are undressing me with theirs to see a milk white body. I don't know where to look. I feel intimidated by all these eyes on me. As the bus moves through the streets all I see is poverty. I don't dare to take out my iPhone. When I get out at the central market, the same ritual is happening. Looking over my shoulder I see heads turning to see me. I'm their walking tourist attraction, but all I think of is I'm their new robbery victim. I keep breathing. And walking. I don't stop too much, avoid empty streets. I don't know what is happening. I do not feel at ease, at all.

On my bus ride back something happens however, and all changes in a good way. I try to talk to a girl standing next to me, first in English, later in my two-word-Portuguese combined with arms and legs. I tell her how I feel, and she tells me she is very curious to where I'm from, why I have come to Belém, and what I do. She turns to her friends giggling and confirms they are all curious. I look around, and the eyes of all people express curiosity. I confused it with danger, after reading the stories about Brazil. This girl takes away my feeling of unsafety. A game changer. At the house I share my experiences with Raquel and she confirms what I've found out. I feel more confident now.

My idea to go to the local football derby is however strongly misadvised. It is known to be surrounded by violence. It's my first game in South America, and even though the teams play in 3rd and 4th level, the Remo and Paysandú teams are known to have an enormous rivalry and now I'm here, I want to see it.

Before the match I head to the mall with the new friends, where we have lunch. Way too early they decide to find me a cab, which appears to be very difficult: the first four drivers don't want to take me there. For them, it's too dangerous. I can't believe how dangerous driving me to a stadium can be. After finding a cab, who also agrees to pick me up after, I soon find out the dangers of this derby. Kilometres away from the stadium fans of both sides are fighting along the roads, chasing each other over the highway. It's complete anarchy here, and there's no police present. The cab driver seems to be anxious to get me at my destination, and keeps rattling. I don't understand much of it. When we do get to the stadium I see the police: thousands and thousands of them, most of them fully dressed in riot outfits. And the danger? Fans having barbecues at the parking lot. I don't think I ever saw a bigger police presence at a football match. And the police taking it seriously, makes me take it seriously. Maybe the warnings were not that exaggerated.
I decide to walk a bit around the stadium, and see fans of both sides walk criss-cross through each other. It's not that bad after all. As it's

Remo-Paysandú, I think the home team will have the biggest support, and even though I have an option to pick a side until the last second, I pick the home side, believing it will be more safe there. In the stadium, with a 42.000 capacity, I find out both sides get half the stadium, and I see the light blue of Paysandú making a wall on the first and second tier. In my stand there's people with instruments making music and amazingly many women wearing their club colours. There are surprisingly many beautiful women doing this. For me a totally different sighting, as in the Netherlands another type of woman seems to be attracted to football.

The fans chant, jump, make so much noise, that I finally start understanding the South American passion for football. I get into it, and am eager for the game to start. The level is very poor, but I'm totally loving the atmosphere. Passion is oozing from the stands. In the end Paysandú wins 1-2 and my cab driver picks me up as agreed. The adrenaline is rushing through me as I try to express to him how I felt. He was mainly focusing on getting away safely and started buzzing again. In no time we are back at the house and I rave about it to Raquel and friends. They only seem to be surprised I came back in one piece, with my camera not stolen.

I spend the following days exploring the city, and also hanging out in the house. Belém as a city is not very interesting to me: it's dirty, it stinks, and it's shady in many ways. The people I start meeting however are on another level. They are so warm and friendly and willing to share so much, even though they don't seem to have a lot.

Another thing happens during my strolls through the city, making me realise the world is a bit different here: upon strolling the streets I see a stand selling illegal DVD's. The covers are printed, and there's no case around the item, that is being sold for 1 to 5 euros per piece. From my left I see two policemen approaching, and I assume the stand holders see this as well, and like the gamblers on Las Ramblas in Barcelona, they would grab all their stuff as fast as they can and run away. I've positioned myself across the street to observe what will happen, but as they move closer, nothing happens. My amazement even grows when the two of them start browsing the discs, looking for some new stuff to add to their collection. I've heard about Brazilian corrupt ways, but had not imagined things would happen like this in the middle of the street.

After observing this strange new ritual, I get back to my bigger concern: the mosquitos are still hunting me, and every one of them is my number one enemy. Not a day goes by without me thinking of getting malaria or dengue. The idea of getting into the Amazon jungle is quickly set aside: I would not feel comfortable doing it right now. A shame, as I read great things about an island nearby.

I decide to move more south, and book a flight to São Luís, in the state of Maranhão. Booking the flight gives me headaches, as my credit card does not seem to be accepted, so eventually I end up buying the ticket at the airport, for much more money than it costs online.

Brazil - São Luís, Maranhão

Raquel and her friends were so amazing to me, that it set a bar I thought could not be easily matched. However, in my second Brazilian city, on my second couchsurfing address, this already happened, when I was picked up at the airport by Ana, who is a doctor in the army. Originally from Belo Horizonte, Minas Gerais, she was placed to serve her country here. Her English is super and I don't have to struggle with my lousy Portuguese. In her apartment I get a room for my own, just like in Belém. I'm feeling blessed for these things and happy couchsurfing makes it easy. Ana has a map in the guest room for guests with all places of the city marked. I study it and decide to check them out when she's working the next week. In the evening we go to a bar with another girl she met on couchsurfing and who is from Rio. Her English is so-so and I'm practicing more Portuguese with her. The next day is a Sunday and together with Sheila we drive up to a town where they have some amazing dunes. There's a storm though, and the rain and wind make it hard to enjoy. The boat trip is nice and the view of São Luís very far away is amazing. We walk over the dunes, laugh, and take lots of photos. On the way back we buy fruits and they are as tasty as in Belém. Brazil, fruit heaven. Sheila cooks us lovely dinner at night and we talk forever. At night more friends come over and it's a super nice get-together.

The next day is spent chilling and doing nothing. It dawns on me that I'm free, and I don't have to do anything. I have time on my side. No rush. It's all good. I'm loving it. The feeling of guilt I sometimes have in the Netherlands, when doing absolutely nothing, or even on other trips when you spent a day being lazy instead of doing things, "enjoying" your moments, is not there. What a big contrast with the rush of life.

I decide to see the city and take a bus. Walking in the heat, with the usual stares, gives me a smile. And the movie star moment comes that day, when I walk at the bus station and a group of girls want to take a photo with me. "Olhos, lindo olhos", is what they say to me in slow Portuguese. When I speak back in my basic Portuguese they get even more excited. They don't stop giggling until they enter their bus. I think I can get used to this. When I arrive in the centre I stroll the streets, which are a bit cleaner than Belém, but have the same shadiness around it. Very poor people, beggars, dirt. Brazilian cities don't impress me much. Not like the people do, again. The people are so warm, so kind. I find it unrealistic and often I don't feel I'm grateful enough.

One night Ana takes me to a concert of Maria Menezes. A singer who apparently is famous in one of the billions music genres of Brazil. I'm not really someone who enjoys parties too much. I can't even remember the last time I went out in Amsterdam. But I'm open to try: new country, new chances. When I enter the club one thing immediately catches my eye and the ground under my feet sinks away: all men are dancing. And not only dancing, they are dancing superbly! Their hips don't lie, as Shakira would sing. In the Netherlands guys normally stand at the sides until they have drunk enough alcohol, but here, it is a different world, and I'm an alien. I shyly stand at the side, with Ana and her friend politely talking to me. Every now and then a woman comes to asks me to dance, but I refuse, as my hips don't lie either. Eventually I try to do some moves, but even though it's a different world here, my feeling of rhythm is still non-existent. My eyes are drawn to a girl who dances elegantly all night, with a huge smile on her face. She is with a huge group of friends. I don't know if she's looking at me, but her eyes are certainly pointed to something or someone around me, at times. I decide to ask Ana what she thinks and she says Brazilian women don't want to talk, they just want to walk. I'm surprised, as I don't think in that way. At one point I stand close to the dancing girl and I try to ask her something in English. She doesn't understand a word of it, upon which she yells to her friends that I don't speak Portuguese. I correct her by saying all Portuguese words I know in the following minute. She laughs even louder and we share our numbers to meet the next day. Then within a blink of an eye she and her friends are gone, while the artists on stage are singing about iPhones. Later I find out this catchy tune is about "Ai fone". I'm loose now, as all people are drunk at this moment and don't see how bad I dance. I talk to numerous people, who all seem surprised a tourist like me comes to visit their city. Some girls want to meet me again and I'm the last one to refuse that. The night is great and the party awesome. I'm again super grateful with Ana and try to express it as often as possible.

She works the next day and I text Nadna, the girl from the night before, to meet up. She says she wants to meet up and agrees to pick me up at night, at eight. I do nothing during the day and I'm totally ready to rumble at 20:00. Nothing though. At 20:15 I text to ask if she's on her way. No response. At 21:00 I get a message that she, and her two friends, is almost on her way. My Dutch sense for time already makes me feel annoyed and I don't know if I want to wait much longer. I have the text ready to cancel it all. At 22:00 I still have not sent it and I get a message they are in the car to pick me up. At 22:30 I finally get picked up, and I don't know if I'm happy it happens. I ask them why, in a more aggressive way than I realise, and they say that I have to calm down. Nadna, Selma, Jequi and me go to have some food at SubWay, and after we go into the city for a pre-carnaval party. It's massive and all people are drinking and partying on the streets. I almost get pick-pocketed when I get pushed in the back by a fat tall man, pretending the crowd is pushing him too. When I look over my shoulder I see an old tiny woman in between me and him, whose hand is in my back pocket. Wow. Sneaky bastards. My heart beats in my throat as I try to speak, but the only thing I manage to do is get her hand out. With a blink of an eye they are gone. Professionals. I express myself to the girls and they say it's normal here and that I really stand out as a target. All in Portuguese, because none of the three girls speak one word of English, even though they are teachers at an elementary school. Late at night they drop me back at Ana's.

My Portuguese is improving these days, a lot. I use Google translate while whatsapping with all the new people I meet, and this makes me aware of the language and that many things are quite similar to the languages I already do know. In the next days when hanging out with others I put it into practice and they seem to understand me more and more. Ana helps me a lot, and I also get invited by Nadna and her friends to places where really only Portuguese exists. There's some funny things about the language I find out, and one is that Brazilians add 'ie' at the end of all English words, making them sound funny: WhatsApp becomes WhatsAppie, Facebook Facebookie, and good, goodie. In other words, they leave the last letter out, like in Instagra and even Amsterda. It just ends. And even though they don't speak the language English, a lot of people I meet sing English songs fluent, but when they leave me stunned by knowing the lyrics, they have no clue what it is about, or how to use these words to speak the English language.

While visiting the city of São Luís I of course walk into plenty of stands, and even regular shops, selling the illegal range of items (CD's, DVD's), but here another thing catches my eyes, and ears: the shopping streets with all their shops have not only plenty of personnel in it, but also someone with a microphone screaming, speaking, and even singing, about promotions in their store. It's a cacophony of people getting louder than their neighbour, and it's quite annoying.

I try to organise a trip into the dunes of the famous Maranhão desert, but I fail, due to prices and lack of apparent organisation. Besides that, the time of the year isn't perfect to see to pure white dunes and amazing blue lakes the rain leaves there. It's not my moment and I decide to look further and before I know it I book a flight to Fortaleza and transport from there to the hippy village Jericoacoara, in the middle of nowhere, about three hours north of Fortaleza, with no roads connecting and therefore only accessible with 4x4 transport.

Brazil - Jericoacoara, Ceará

Jericoacoara, commonly pronounced as Jeri, is one of the landmarks I had written down to visit when I was thinking of my trip. It's known for its emerald sunset (three seconds of green light at the moment the sun hits the horizon), its relaxed community, dunes, and wind surfing.

At Fortaleza airport I'm being picked up by my organised transport and I share the ride with Simone and Felipe, who are from Porto Alegre, in the very south of Brazil. Simone's English is fluent, but Felipe doesn't (want to) speak in another language than Portuguese. He's a youth trainer of Grêmio, and shy. We talk non-stop all the way, while our driver manoeuvres the car over first the highway and later the dunes and beach. It's a lovely landscape.

The hotel I booked with booking.com was one not too far away from my new travel friends. They have booked a buggy tour the next day and ask me to join them. I had no plans, so I accepted their offer. After checking into my lovely hotel, I rush to the beach to see only the last second of the sunset. There is a huge dune right at the beach and hundreds of people were descending as the party was over. In the next days I will find myself on top of that dune during every sunset, enjoying the view, meeting new people.

At night I stroll the sand streets, where's no cars allowed and soon get as calm as everyone here. What a paradise.
I find plenty of good restaurants and after some days also locals who know me, greet me, speak Portuguese with me. Among them two ladies who work in shops and who practice Portuguese with me all day. One of them introduces me to what would become my "song of the Northeast": 'Vai no cavalinho'.

The first day trip in the buggy of our guide brings us to beautiful coast, some amazing dunes and landmarks. The guide only speaks Portuguese and is super friendly. Simone translates all I don't understand. The better I listen, the more I understand. And gladly nature often speaks for itself. We get to know about how the dunes are moving, sometimes covering entire villages. The famous dune in town will probably be replaced by another in the next ten years. Nature is also very cruel.

I take so many photos that my memory cards can't keep up with it. I'm also Simone's personal photographer, and whenever she proposes to take a photo of me, I know she wants one of herself in that exact same position. We laugh a lot and have a great time.

We do another day trip the next day, seeing nice dune lakes and having great food. We even play football with a group of locals in the thick sand, and I get super exhausted by only taking one sprint. I have no stamina. Felipe has a great technique and I can see why he trains. He also involves everyone in the game, even the guest. Brazilian style!

There are many small examples of the kindness of the Brazilian people, but on my fourth day in Jeri one of the most outstanding happened. I had booked the guide for a private tour and we had a great time searching for animals. The day after I decide to chill in my hotel, but around midday the hotel tells me my guide is there. I walk up to him and ask him what is going on and he says I have to get in the buggy. I take my bag and off we go. I ask him where we're going but there is no clear answer: either he is avoiding giving me one, or I just don't understand. For fifteen minutes we drive over the beach, until we cross the dunes and zigzag along small sand roads to a little town, where all the local people (Indians) live. The fancy Jeri is too expensive for them to live and they have sold their property to business people and nouveaux riches. The guide says he will bring me to his home and there my mouth falls open: they have prepared a huge lunch for me and invited all their family and friends. My eyes get watery out of gratitude and I can't remember how many times I said "obrigado" this afternoon. These poor people take me to their home and share all they have with someone they don't know. I'm blown away by this kindness and will forever rave about it and will be forever grateful. Everyone wants to know everything about me, and again many photos are taken. The best surprise I could ever think of, and when I tell my local friends at night they are not surprised, but very happy, that I got to have this experience.

On one of my final nights in Jeri I meet an Argentinian dance teacher on the beach, whose English is non-existent, her Portuguese is very mediocre, and so I find myself speaking Spanish all of a sudden: again a language I don't know. But I manage. She asks me to join her to a samba party at night, and although hesitant, I agree to go. I tell her about my dancing experiences in São Luís and after laughing, she tells me everyone in the world can dance, no exceptions. She says she will teach me. Now, this gets me even more nervous: going to a party knowing I will dance? Ehm, no way! Around midnight we head for the party, which at that time had not even started, and therefore we enter as one of the firsts. As soon as the band starts playing it gets super crowded, and I see I'm not the only tourist anymore. I mean, almost everyone here is a tourist, but most of them are from Brazil. European tourists, not many, but here, at this party, I see people who dance as bad as I do: they can't be South American, can they? My teacher starts to move and explains me what to do and I'm hopeful and confident this can work. Two hours later nothing is left of this feeling and she tells me maybe there are exceptions: maybe not everyone can really dance. I'm cracking up and agree. My feeling for rhythm just doesn't exist and on the fast moves of samba, I am a donkey preparing french fries. The night however is great and the music contagious, even for me. Another memorable night.

The day after is just relaxing and I organise transport for the next day back to Fortaleza.

Brazil - Fortaleza, Ceará

I'm getting picked up at 06:00 in the morning. I wake up at 05:00, as mornings still aren't my best moment of the day. In the dark I see a huge pickup and the woman who helped me organise the transport to Jeri, now helps me to get out of there. She speaks English, and I'm happy she does, as I'm so tired I can't think of any Portuguese right now.

We drive over empty roads, seeing the sun beautifully come up, and have breakfast at some kind of trucker restaurant.

It is here, where my heart almost stops beating because I get terrified by a mosquito...

Ever since I hit South American soil the mosquitoes are everywhere, but in Jeri I hadn't thought about it too much. Now I see the vector mosquito of dengue in the car, against the window, flying around me. I recognise the black and white striped back, exactly how the images I studied in Suriname looked like. Oh my god, this is the moment I will suffer from dengue. I start sweating like hell, and I tell the driver to help me get rid of this fly. She is totally relaxed, even laughing at my panic attack. I agree, looking back at it, it was quite silly, but it just grabbed me. Within 24 hours I will know if I have been bitten, and if I did, if the mosquito was carrying the virus. The next 24 hours were not my most pleasant ones on this earth. In the hotel in Fortaleza I could not think of anything else, while doing nothing but lying in bed.

The 24 hours passed and I did not suffer of any dengue. This was the turning point of my fear as I realised I was behaving ridiculously. First I had to learn to deal with the South American way of time, all is more relaxed, then their amazing hospitality, their feeling for rhythm, and now with their diseases. Just like the other things I started accepting how things are. Life and travelling got much better after this.

In Fortaleza I take a cab for my second match of the trip, some unimportant local game. I'm wary again though, because football generally does not attract the most proper crowds. Less police here than in Belém, and also way less fans. The away team here do have a smaller section in the stadium, but everything is more calm. The level of play is however as bad as in Belém, and seeing this makes Feyenoord a wonder team all of a sudden.

I buy the ticket at the box office at the stadium, but here for the first time my Portuguese is insufficient. They sell me a ticket for a stand where all the VIP's sit, along with the player's wives. Now, sitting next to those women was not bad, but the price on the ticket was only five times as much as the normal tickets. Bastards.

After the match I meet up with a friend who is playing Brazilian pool with some friends. I play with them and have some great hours again. After that finding a cab on the deserted streets in the middle of the night was less great. The memory of a friend being kidnapped in South America by an illegal cab, was coming back to me. But also with this, you have to get used to it. I find a cab and I talk about football and politics in Portuguese for the twenty minutes the drive takes; I do track the route on Google Maps however...

Walking in the city of Fortaleza is quite nice, even though I don't find many interesting landmarks. It's more like how I imagine a city than São Luís and Belém. It feels safer, more touristy than the others. I like the skyline, the beaches. The people are faster here in many ways, almost Western. I have lunch with Simone and Felipe again, whose last days of their trip are spent here, and I meet up with other friends I made in Jeri; one of them is a Brazilian living in Copenhagen and points me to some differences in culture.

I also organise my trip to the archipelago of Fernando de Noronha, with the help of an independent website, yourway.com.br. I book a flight to Natal, and from Natal my flight to and from Fernando de Noronha, an island one-hour flying from the coast.

Fortaleza is nice, but it's time to move on. Move on to Paradise.

Brazil - Fernando de Noronha, Pernambuco

I had read a lot about the island of Fernando de Noronha, but never thought it would be as beautiful as described. After a one-night stop in Natal, near the airport, I fly to this island, in a pretty small plane, which is not totally full. I have read that pilots could make a touristic route to the island, so I pick a seat on the left side. As we fly I get more excited every minute. As soon as we break through the clouds and I can see the ocean, I believe that every white head of the wave is the result of dolphins or even whales popping up above the surface. The more I try to see it, the more I do see it. Unfortunately, I did not see any from high in the sky. Then the island comes near, but there's no touristic route: the landing is quite immediate and we only see some fragments of the island through our narrow windows.

The airport is one building, with one landing strip. Small. The luggage is rapidly taken out and brought to an open area, where you can pick it up easily. Then outside to find transport to my Bed & Breakfast. All taxis are taken, so I wait for the bus, or others taxis to appear. It takes a pretty long time before I find a free taxi, and then I have to explain where I want to go. Apparently housing here does not work with numbers, so I have received a description from the girl arranging it all. The taxi driver however seems to know my hostess Fatima and within ten minutes he is carrying my heavy twenty kilo bag over his head over some grass field, over a small wooden bridge, to a property where there's a lot of green, and a small red brick house. I get welcomed by my hostess, who lives here alone and makes money by renting a big room. In a small common area is a kitchen and stands a couch. She sleeps in one small room, the guests in a slightly bigger one. It's all I need and I'm happy to be where I am.

I drop my stuff, and start walking to a beach nearby. Here I see and photograph the small black lizard, that only lives on this island. I see the big waves crash and am impressed by the colour of the ocean. It's a beautiful blue colour with layers of emerald green. The sun shines high up, it's hot, and I walk the rocks to see what there is to see, until the sun sets and I get thrilled by the sight of the shifting of colours, from bright yellow to deep red. And then it gets dark. So dark you can't see anything anymore, so I decide to walk back, over the big main square, that is on a quite steep hill. I return to the house, and head out soon to find dinner.

The next day I make a new friend, Fabio. He's also a friend of my hostess and he pretty much defines my time on the island. He knows everyone. And everyone knows him. He's like a Brazilian me, so we get along just fine. His English is of course non-existent, but we do understand each other very well. My hostess pushes him to guide me, this second day. And so we take off, hitchhiking, jumping in the back of a buggy and being dropped off some kilometres south. We are heading to the famous Bahia do Sancho. In the morning Fabio sold me access to the national park parts, which is about 70% of the island. With this ticket I can access all beaches. I also had to pay a price to enter the island, so the price per day climbs pretty high if you only stay some days. I was happy to have booked eight days.
We walk an easy trail over wooden flounders and then arrive at the most breath taking beach views I have ever seen. We stand high up the cliff and under us appears a bay with a beautiful beach. The ocean here is even more beautiful than it was yesterday. All the bay is surrounded by the green of trees. Hundreds of birds nest these trees and fly up and down, making sounds that fill the air. The beach is almost deserted and it is absolutely breath taking. We walk around and through two very steep stairs which lead you through the rocky cliffs, we end up at the beach. It is as beautiful here as it was upstairs. The sand is soft and with every step you sink into it. The water is warm, when the waves come they tickle your soles. We sit down on a rock, and I'm just speechless. I've never been someone that in the recent years loved spending time at beaches, or visiting them, but this if from a different world. Spontaneously I write 'paraiso' in the sand with my heel. It is paradise. I feel like I am in paradise. And I never want to leave.

Fabio hands out the snorkel equipment we have been carrying and we walk into the water to see the most beautiful fish flying around us. The colours are amazing again. The tide is stronger than I'm used to, so I have to be careful not to be smashed against the rocks, and try to constantly be in motion. And then something magical happens: we see a sea turtle. It is calmly being carried by the current, being brought to the ocean. Fabio signals me to follow it and not much later I am super close to this turtle, jointly swimming to the shore. I let the current carry me now and I feel alone in the world. A moment

24

of pure joy. Paradise is getting a different meaning to me. Then the turtle has had enough and with some firm claps he is off, back to the deeper ocean.

We also get out of the water and Fabio wants to show me Bahia dos Porcos, the next bay. We find out the path to it is closed, due to fallen rocks, and the warning signs tell us to stay back. Fabio says we can walk around the cliff and so we start rock jumping, climbing, crawling, jumping. Until the moment we hear a big whistle. A boat arrived and is waving to us that we have to move back to the beach. I ask Fabio what is up. He says this is a natural reserve and we are not allowed to walk over these rocks. He doesn't care and says we will continue. I try to discuss with him, but he just continues. I say I might be thrown off the island, but he says it's all good. So we continue. Few steps later I slip and my back is cut open over a sharp pointy rock. The blood comes out like water in a mountain river, it's a stream of red fluid falling on the black rocks. No time for pain, and we continue over these rocks. Wherever we appear hundreds of crabs disappear. After somewhat like thirty minutes we arrive at the other side, seeing it is quite blocked by water. We decide to jump in and swim, and after the effort, it is a cool welcome. We snorkel a bit and then decide to head back. When we walk around we again see the boat, and the people are making the same gestures again. We get to the beach without any problems, and there was no police force waiting to arrest us. We climb up the ladders and walk over the pathways to see the Bahias from above again. Bahia dos Porcos is also very beautiful from the top: no big beach there, but more rocks. And in between these rocks we see a shark from high above. And not a silly small shark, no, a serious big shark. The cliff is about fifteen metres high and the silhouette of the shark is clearly visible from our position. Fabio starts screaming to the people who are about the go snorkel, to warn them. Although they first don't understand, later you see them all grab their cameras and take photos of this big fish. We continue our way to the Baia dos Golfinhos, a bay where you might be lucky to see dolphins. At the time we arrive there is none, although there are people sitting to observe and count them whenever they appear. On our way there we spot a giant iguana, with beautiful black and white colours. I chase him for a bit to take some photos. After this Bahia we head back and take a bus back to the posada. At night I invite Fabio to dinner to thank him for the tour. After dinner we head to a bar, where apparently all island parties every night. I get introduced to many of his local friends, and to many girls he sold tickets to before. I think I made the right friend at the right place! We party until late and when I finally find myself in bed, I sleep in seconds.

I'm still in a tourist mood and try to make as much out of my days as possible. So I wake up very early, have a small breakfast of fruits, and then head out to visit the other beaches of the island. I head south to see the Tamar project, where they study, protect, and help, the sea turtles, and to the Bahia de Sueste, where I actually get to see a turtle that has been stranded on the beach and then taken into observation for a while, before being released again to the water. At Sueste I stay for quite a while, strolling the strand, sitting down, and swimming. In the late afternoon little sharks are all along the waves breaking at the beach. I see so many. It's a beautiful spectacle to see these animals hunt for little fish. There are so many of them, that I can't believe this is really happening. The island keeps amazing me. Together with a tourist couple I meet, we photograph them through the water and share our excitement. There's nearly no one else on the beach, so this kingdom is ours for these moments. At night the same ritual of dining and later partying. This continues all week.

One of the days I head back to Porcos, but this time I bring an underwater camera I rent for fifteen euros per day. I snorkel there for hours and hours, but the magic of the first visit underwater is not there. The current is very strong today, and the sky is cloudy. The fish are hiding from the upcoming storm, it seems. At the moment I decide to leave the water, I think it's nice to play with the waves and swim along them to the shore. The waves are big however, and I think it's nice to be a human surfboard for a bit. I swim using my flippers to gain extra speed for some waves, until I see a big wave coming. Just when the wave is at its highest points I try to swim along moving my flippers as fast as possible. The wave breaks in a second and my body is squeezed in the power of the ocean. I feel helpless, and broken. My toes almost hit my eyes in this enormous squash, and some people at the beach who saw me doing it rush to the water to help me out. They first talk in Portuguese, but as they see I can hardly breathe the guy switches to English. They help me to their place where they let me catch my breath. I feel like I almost died. I recognise the group from when their buggy had stopped in front of a supermarket where Fabio and me were having a drink earlier, and we start to talk. Luzer, Simone, their son Gui (amigo), Luisa, her daughter (nicknamed Buddhina - little Buddha) and the brother of Simone and Luisa, all welcomed me in their middle with enormous joy. They invite me to come with them for a lunch, which turns out to be really amazing. In the afternoon we head to the north of the island and visit the museum there. Again I feel blessed by meeting fantastic new people.

Manolo is another guy visiting the island and he also stays in the house where I'm staying. These days Manolo sleeps in the bedroom, and Fatima moves to the couch. Together with him and an Argentinian couple, we have a great barbecue with fresh salmon prepared in a giant coca leaf on a fire of wood. Delicious. Later Fatima and Manolo fall in love. So romantic.

A dream for me is to see the dolphins around the island. Every morning at 6am it is possible to enter the park and walk to the Baia dos Golfinhos and try to see them. So one morning I go there with my new friends, but the ranger doesn't get there on time. So the people there wait for thirty minutes and then decide to climb over the fence. Arriving there just before 07am seems to be too late, as the observing Tamar employee tells us: the thirty dolphins has already left. Quite a bummer for all who came this early.

The next day we try again, and together with two other new friends from Porto Alegre, and Fabio, Manolo and the Argentinians we head out there before 6 in the morning. We arrive there also before 6 and decide to immediately climb through the fence this time. I hurry myself ahead of the group, as I don't want to miss one single dolphin. When I arrive at the viewpoint I see the Tamar girl looking through her binoculars and she immediately tells me to look, because I'm right on time. I look down at the blue ocean and see little spots moving high speed towards us. Dolphins! They rest here in this bay, float around for a while, before continuing their journey. I'm not aware all the others have arrived too by now, as I'm totally captivated by this heavenly event happening right in front of us. I see the dolphins playing, jumping, swimming, coming and going. For one hour I look focused and fascinated to these godly creatures. Others leave after thirty minutes, but not me. I can look at this forever. Around 1500 dolphins passed us in a little bit more than one hour: one thousand five hundred. 1500! Spot on one of the most beautiful moments in my life.

Noronha is an island full of highlights for me, and beauty keeps coming. A hike brings me and a group of other tourist to yet another bay, where there is a piece of ocean separated by rocks, giving it a lake like surface, with a unique chance to snorkel with fish and sharks. When standing at the shore you can see all of it already in the shallow water, but laying in the water (not allowed to use your feet, only move with your hands), makes you feel you are part of it. You can't stand on the rocks, so everyone is just floating around, enjoying the hour you have to its fullest. After stepping out I immediately would want to go again, but as it's all based on reservation, I have no chance this day. And the next day I leave. I think I have to go back one day.

The archipelago is said to be one of the best scuba dive places in the world, with a view of thirty metres under water. Even though I was tempted to do it, the price for a thirty-minute dive was a bit too high for me. As I don't have any previous experience with diving, I could not just rent equipment and go out, unfortunately. I did enough snorkelling however and loved that. Another thing I missed out on doing the entire week was going on a boat trip. I don't like boating too much, so I postponed it to the last morning of my trip. I take off early in the morning to the harbour, hoping to find a boat that will take me out to find dolphins. After walking in and out stores, I find someone that wants to help me and for a fair price I get to rent the boat and crew for as long as need to see dolphins. We see them straight away, just outside the harbour, a couple of dozen, moving through the ships that are anchored here. Sometimes they jump out of the water, giving me the goose bumps I had before when seeing them for the first time. I'm amazed by their playfulness and beauty. The group moves away quite fast, so we go more north, to see the landmarks, some cave that make an impressive sound, and get a view to all the surf beaches from the sea. It's pretty. And at this moment I feel sad I know I have to leave in the afternoon. The boat drops me back at the harbour and I hurry myself to the B&B to say farewell to Fatima and get to the airport, as the plane leaves in an hour. At the airport I meet a lovely girl who also spent some days at the island as a solo traveller and we exchange details for me to visit her later in her hometown of Florianópolis. Friends are easily made, but harder to keep.

Brazil - Natal, Rio Grande do Norte

The plane takes me back to Natal, where I have another couchsurfer lined up to host me for some days. I arrive here in the afternoon and get picked up by my host Cristina and her friend Ítalo, who immediately take me to a lovely restaurant to have a wonderful dinner. After all the warm welcomes I'm getting everywhere, you should say I would get used to it, but I don't. And I don't think I ever will. It's amazing how much people give to others. How many good people exist in this world? I'm happy I can say I always try to give travellers the same in the Netherlands, but I also realise the Western world is generally more selfish than what I'm experiencing here. Family above all, friends close to that. I moved out of my parents' house at age 21; here they generally stay much longer. Both has its pluses, but in ways I feel people here care more. They live now, they don't live for tomorrow. I like it.

The following days Cristina has to work and Ítalo takes me to a park in the dunes to let me photograph cute little monkeys. I see many of them, and take some good photos. I also see a tarantula and bullet ants. When we take a tour through the dunes (some of them are as high as the corporate towers in the city), we are warned not to stand still too long. The ants crawl up your leg and bite you, leaving you in a pain as if you were shot. That doesn't sound too pleasant to us, so we, among a group of tourists from São Paulo, are constant on the move. We are guided by a soldier, as we apparently walk through a very protected and restricted nature park. And with the likes of these São Paulo tourists, who are loud, not caring, rude, I think it's better this way. The tour is quite interesting and we learn a lot about these dunes. Between monkey spotting and this tour, we had a good lunch in a restaurant in town.

At night we meet up with Cristina again to have an awesome bowl of acai, and after that dinner at her place.

The next day I take a buggy tour through the dunes north of Natal, which is pricey, and looking back at the same kind of trips in Jeri, not really worth it. We did some nice touristy stuff on the way, like gliding off the dunes on a slide, and visiting a museum. I share a buggy with a lovely family: a couple and their bright young daughter. We have a great time together, all in Portuguese again of course.

In the evening yet another great dinner, before crashing into the night: the next day I have been set up to drive to Pipa with one of Cristina's friends!

Brazil - Pipa, Rio Grande do Norte

Early in the morning I am picked up by an old car, driven by a cool guy. We talk all the way to Pipa, during the 80 kilometre drive, which we did in little less than two hours. He drops me off at my hotel, where I am welcomed by a good staff. My room is good too, so I made yet another good booking.

Pipa is a village which is obviously used to having loads of tourist over. It's an invasion of people not living there, all walking along the cute little stores, and having dinner in the wide variety of different restaurants: there's something for everyone. I miss the intimacy of Jeri, but I do find some cool places.

The first day I visit a small natural reserve, on top of the cliffs. To get there I walk for over an hour, slightly uphill, in the burning sun. I almost finish all the water I carry before I even get there. The park is a maze of little small trails, with lots of trees, and therefore there's shadow everywhere. My main goal is to see the little monkeys again, the same as in Natal. I walk all the way to the end to finally see a huge group of them, jumping over my head. They get closer than they did in Natal and I manage to take some good photos. The cutest are the baby monkeys who curiously stare at me. If it's not for the people, it's the animals that stare, gosh. I spend hours and hours here, observing these little animals. A fascination for monkeys is born here and during the rest of my trip I will always be on the lookout for them. The park offers some great viewpoints over the beaches of Pipa. I find it hard to see the beauty of these beaches after seeing the top notch ones in Fernando de Noronha, but nevertheless I enjoy what I see. A floating turtle makes the view extra nice, and when I get to another viewpoint I meet a dolphin watcher. He points to the ocean, and yes, I see three dolphins swimming in the sea, fishing their meal in the waves. I also see many people on the beach trying to spot them, but their viewpoint isn't as good as mine. The student tells me years ago there was a group of around fifty dolphins swimming here, and that there are now less than ten. The tourists scare them away, they come too close. Even though there is a law to keep boats at a distance, they come much too close. I'm witnessing that some minutes later when a boat full of tourist almost run over the dolphins, while the guide on the boat enthusiastically points to them so all his customers get the good photographs. The respect for the animals on these boats seems to be zero and is again in huge contrast to the way my boat on Noronha showed me. The student reports the incidents, but he tells them there's not much done with it. He thinks within five years there will be no dolphins swimming so close to the beach anymore.

The next day I head to the beach myself, to see if I can spot the dolphins from there. Early in the morning the waters are already crowded with swimmers, who mainly stay in the corner, close to the rocks and beach. It's said dolphins appear there the most. Not that day. I also enter the water, swimming in the warm waters. I don't know how long I am already in the water, when suddenly two dolphins appear from the water some one or two metres from me. I stop breathing. This can't be true. So close. I see one eye looking at me before it disappears again under the surface. If my face wouldn't be wet, my eyes probably would have been. This same ritual repeats a couple of more times, and when I look at the shore I see people photographing my position, as well as the mass moving to me. That's the moment for me to leave, and obviously for the dolphins too. They are only seen slightly deeper into the sea after this. I look at yesterday's viewpoint and the observing student lifts his thumb to me. I lift mine in response. Yet another blessed moment in this magical trip.

In my last full day in Pipa I first head to Love Beach, very touristy, where I swim for a while, and after lunch walk to a village close-by, ruining my feet because of the distance. On my way I stop on several beaches, enjoying the peacefulness and silence. At the village I watch the sunset together with two Brazilians girls and after that we have dinner there together.

My taxi to the airport in Natal brings me to my last unseen monumental viewpoint of Pipa, and then takes of the 1.5 hour to the airport. My flight to Recife will depart in the afternoon.

<u>Brazil - Porto de Galinhas, Pernambuco</u>

Carnaval is about to happen and I've decided I want to spend one of these days in Olinda. I have heard this is one of the best places in Brazil to celebrate this nationwide party explosion, so why not? But before I head there, I first explore Porto de Galinhas, together with a dear friend I had met before.

I stay in Recife one night, before taking a taxi to nearby Porto de Galinhas, a city with a slave history and now a tourist hotspot. I have a central hotel and this town is, like Pipa, used to tourists. But what I experience is insane. It seems like everyone in Brazil has come here. The streets are so full of people that I can barely walk amongst them. The restaurants are so full, you have to wait in line for people to finish their wining and dining.

Interesting here is the tide. Like in Noronha, at low tide, the sea leaves pools of water in which also fish are cut off from the wide ocean, and you can therefore see them up-close and easy. Another dimension is that it's so shallow you can see people walk in the sea 50 metres off the beach. It gives a surrealistic image. Everyone has become their very own Jesus.

The downside again is the amount of people. I don't see any grain of sand during my three days here, as every inch is occupied by people. People everywhere. Especially families with children. Everywhere. Everywhere.

On the third day I want to escape and try to book yet another buggy tour. Generally it was already necessary to bargain with the Brazilians, but now it got even worse. I ask for a tour and they say it's 400 reais, about 125 euros. My mouth falls open. In Natal a same kind of tour was 150 reais, in Jeri 100. With my mouth wide open I walk away, but before taking two steps the guide says he wants to negotiate. I say I will take the tour for 50. He says 300, I say 75, and in the end I have to pay 125 reais. A drop of 275 reais within 2 minutes. Interesting. The tour itself is quite nice. I visit some popular beaches, as well as Praia dos Carnes, a really gorgeous beach.

Brazil - Recife & Olinda, Pernambuco

A taxi brings me back to Recife, where I get a hotel nearby the infamous coastline of the city. The ocean here is dangerous. Shark dangerous. I am told there used to be a meat factory near the river and all the meat garbage was dumped in the ocean, attracting hundreds of sharks. Now the factory is closed, but the sharks are still here. In 2013 a female was torn apart and the video of the incident went viral on the internet. When walking along the beach, every 25 metres there are warning signs to not go too deep into the water. I did go in one day, and came out harmless.

I visit the ground zero of Recife, as well as the synagogue where I meet some great people who tell me all about the history of both the city as the building. The same day I go visit my third football match in Brazil, Santa Cruz versus Salgueiro. Again I am warned to go there and my even my taxi driver thinks I'm out of my mind. When I arrive I think I should charge all the people looking at me, as I'm again a walking attraction: the white tourist who visits the coloured neighbourhood. As if they never saw a gringo before. It doesn't take long before some fans try to talk to me, but I can't understand much of their Portuguese. So I just tell my own stories, with the words I do know, and soon I have an audience. They all pat my shoulder and wish me a great game. Santa Cruz is big, they say. The stadium is, I must say, but even though some thousands of fans were there, the atmosphere was dull due to the size of the stands. Santa Cruz wipes the floor with their opponents, crushing them 7-0. The fans are happy and so am I. I don't want to experience what will happen here when they lose. It seems it's their only joy in life and many eyes sparkle aggression. I get along just fine with them and I am dragged into a bar after the match for some celebrations. Drinking water doesn't make me popular, but they all respect it. They help me get a taxi back and safely I arrive back in the hotel.

In the Netherlands I associate Carnaval with people getting insanely drunk while being dressed up. In the province I come from we have fares where the same is happening without costumes. I've attended many and alcohol is a big factor here. I had different expectations of the Brazilian Carnaval, where I believed the parades, the dancing, and the music would be bigger influences. And yes, in certain parts and on certain days, this is absolutely true. But when I start walking in Olinda, I soon experience this is not one of the days or places. It reminds me of Queen's Day in Amsterdam, but none wearing orange. A lot of colours are present and the historical streets are decorated. And everyone is drinking. Continuously drinking. Arriving there by cab was already hard because of all the people, walking the streets even more difficult. There are so many people. Olinda is built on hills and the streets go up and down. There are areas where you can use a toilet, but the later it gets the more people just pee wherever they want. Because of this the descending streets turn into rivers of pee. Yuck. I walk around on my flip flops, and every second step I have to make an effort to get them loose from the streets. It's really gross. And of course it starts to smell like it as well. I seem to be the only person that cares, as the partying continues and everyone is dancing on the music of the little bands that also move through the streets. 'Bloqas' move through the street, letting everyone know that they are there, nice and organised. It's nice to observe and to get dragged in the crowd, being patted. Everyone is happy. Everyone is drunk. When the night falls it gets less crowded on the streets and I decide to go back to Recife and see how the party is there. My idea is nice, but far from reality: I'm not the only one trying to get back to Recife and all the people wander the middle of the road to get a hold of a taxi. I walk for at least an hour before I finally get one. The driver of course tries to get a fixed price, but I persuade him to drive on the meter. I arrive in Recife, where the streets all are still filled with people. It's cleaner here. There are stands everywhere that sell fresh made food, and of course drinks. There's more police here. It's not a Carnival wild west like in Olinda. My feet don't want to carry me anymore and are begging me to go back to the hotel. After a while I listen to them. I haven't had dinner yet, so I ask a cab driver to take me to a good restaurant. I end up in a quiet place, that probably belongs to his friends or family. The food is good. After dinner the driver takes me to the hotel, where I can already see the blisters grow. Carnaval in Olinda: without alcohol it's the same shit as in the Netherlands, and I will stay away from it next time.

Brazil - Itamaracá, Pernambuco

When I was saved from the waves in Noronha, I met new friends
who live in Recife. Luzer takes me on a trip one day, starting at his
parents' home in Olinda. I see Olinda without Carnaval in the streets
and absolutely love it. It's a beautiful town with small streets. Many
houses have pretty colours and the view to Recife and the sea is
stunning. There's Dutch colonial influences here which still can be
seen in some fortresses along the coast more to the north. The father
of Luzer is very kind, smart, and well-read. He, like me, reads a lot
about World War II and we have an interesting talk about it. In
Portuguese. The mother creates beautiful vases and art. Again I'm
welcomed in their midst as if I'm one of theirs. Typical Brazilian is
the presence of other family members and the children happily
introduce me to the turtles that wander around in the garden.
We continue our way to get to the family vacation home in
Itamaracá, an island just north of Olinda. The route is pretty scenic
and gives a good idea of what the coastline is like. We cross the
bridge to Itamaracá and it gets greener and greener: nature taking
over control. I like it. The house is very close to the beach and it
seems like a good place to chill during holidays. We continue to a
former Dutch fortress and I take some photos here. What if the
Dutch would have kept Brazil, and I could talk Dutch with the
natives like in Suriname? Luzer negotiates at the beach with a boat
for a trip to the reefs. Not long after we head out and like in Porto de
Galinhas there's shallow water miles outside the coast. This is
however so much deeper into the ocean than there. I'm surprised.
We snorkel there and I can do handstands in the middle of the ocean.
How weird and unique. At one point Luzer and the boat man lost
sight of me and got panicked as it happens that the tide rises fast, or
sharks get a hold of you. I was just searching for and looking at fish.
They are relieved when I show myself again and not much later we
head back to the shore. There we take another boat to a nearby island
to have very fresh fish with fries. Accompanied by of course delicious
fresh coco water. Back at the main land we see the sun set and when
the orange ball is gone, we get in the car to drive back to Recife.

On my final night in Recife I am invited to Luzer's, Gui's and
Simone's home and we enjoy pizza together. A perfect ending of a
great stay in this part of Brazil.

Brazil - Salvador, Bahia

I take a plane to Salvador from Recife and book a hotel nearby the famous historical centre. The taxi to the centre from the airport is very expensive, but throughout my trip Salvador was the city I am warned most for. Crime capital. Upon arrival in my lovely hotel I directly get the advice to not wander the streets alone in the dark. It's even better to not leave the hotel at all at night. However confident, I decide to follow up the advice for a change. I find a cosy restaurant just next door and have it all to myself. I'm treated like a king, and I eat like one too. The next day I wear my walking shoes for some serious exploring of the city.

I reach the famous Pelourinho quite fast, from where my own made tour starts. I walk in and out of every church I encounter, and there are plenty of those. Some of them are really spectacular, decorated with gold and have great sculptures and paintings. It's the first city I visit which has an actual interesting historical downtown. It's bigger than the other cities I've seen and I feel like I'm exploring a European city for the first time. I like it. My feet however, hate it. Maybe it's still the aftermath of the Olinda Carnaval, but they hurt. I sit down more than I would like to. Near a viewpoint over the harbour I find a tree with cute little monkeys and together with two children I observe them for a while. I take a huge elevator down to that harbour later and get information on a boat to Morro de São Paulo, a tropical destination only to be reached by boat (or expensive 4 seat flight). I get the information, talk to several people and learn that the boat ride can be very rough. Just like I like it... Not. I really want to see it however and not much later I buy my one-way ticket to the peninsula, departing tomorrow. After this I walk back to the city, have a lunch, and then continue sightseeing. At the end of the day I think I've seen more than regular tourists do in a week. And when I meet two girls at breakfast the next day, I get that confirmed. I also learn I have only seen a very tiny piece of the city and there's so many more place to visit. I keep that in mind for a next time. Now I'm off to the boat!

Brazil - Morro de São Paulo, Bahia

The ferry that takes me to the island is a speed boat in the shape of a catamaran. There are a lot of seats lined up, as in a plane, but no real storage for the luggage. All big suitcases and bags are therefore stowed at the front of the boat. All people sit inside, because the outside seats are very limited. On every seat there's a plastic vomit bag, ready to be used. It's so hot inside as there's no fresh air, people complain loudly, or fall asleep. I'm among the sleepers as I pass out before the boat even leaves. I took a special pill to calm my stomach during the rough ride and I am happy I did. I wake up due to the sounds of a guy puking. The smell can't leave the cabin and it's very gross. The boat is jumping from wave to wave and there's no calm moment at all. And as one sheep crosses the dam, more will follow, and I see more people reaching out for their special bag. I don't hear the sound of the waves smashing the boat anymore, nor the talking of people: the sound of vomiting is taking over, one after another. Upon arrival I think 30% of the people puked. Everyone tries to leave the boat as soon as possible, because it really is unbearable. At the pier locals await you with wheelbarrows, as cars do not exist on the island. I think I will be fine, so I ignore them and move to the entrance gate where you have to pay a fee. After this it is a walk through the cute small cobbled streets with shops and restaurants everywhere. The problem is the road going up, and my bag does not roll on these stones very well. I don't know how much further this torture will go on for and therefore I give in and ask one of the wheelbarrows guys to help me with the bag. I was already halfway to my posada, but the five euros I have to pay in the end, are well spent. I have a room on a big property, surrounded by trees, houses separated, totally different than what I've seen in the village. I like my place.

After checking in, dropping my luggage, I walk to the beach, passing the unique crab species that only lives here, and in northern Colombia. The beaches in town are very crowded, so I try to walk to the ones a bit further away. The so-called 4th beach is the one I like most and I spend some time here swimming and relaxing.

What I immediately notice at night when looking for a restaurant is the enormous amount of Argentine and Israeli people. Most of the food places have signs to lure those tourists in. The longer I walk around, the more I notice this. In the end I believe there's actually no other tourists than these two groups. I walk in some stores and travel agencies, and instead of buying stuff, I'm making new friends.

During my stay here I get to know a lot of people, mainly from Argentina. When I get to talk to some Israeli people, they tell me most of them came here because they've served two years in the army and are now free to go anywhere to party hard. And they do indeed party like crazy. They tell me South America is a very safe continent for them to travel as they really blend in. I think they are quite right about that, except for their language of course. I feel like I'm on the Israeli version of the Dutch coastal towns in Spain: young people gather here to party non-stop.

I do party there too, and the beach parties are indeed quite nice. They sell fresh cocktails with the purest fruits. Yes, also non-alcoholic cocktails, so I have my thing too. The music varies from hour to hour and in the last hour, almost before sunset, all 90's classics come by and the crowd goes absolutely insane.

The days after the parties I hang out with the people I've met there. I keep postponing my trip back to the mainland, because I have no clue where I want to go. I'm travelling without a set plan and keeping flexibility as high as possible. It's not only this of course, because the idea to be in a boat going back to Salvador among the puking people is not very tempting as well. Because of this I outstay most of the tourists and I really get to know some locals.

One of them is a friend of a friend, and before I arrived I was introduced on Facebook. She brings me more uphill, to the part of town where there's much less tourists, and much more locals. Two of the nicest parties I attend are there. One in a sort of theatre where I move to the rhythm of reggae, and another in a very small amphitheatre, where children and later adults dance to the sounds of samba.

The sunsets on the island are pretty astonishing as well. I try to see them from all different angles. The fortress and the mountain are my favourite places. At a bar where they play live music I also see it one day, but I got in a discussion about an entrance fee that I refused to pay as he wasn't clear about it before. I unfortunately end up paying it.

One morning I decide to walk to a beach a bit further away. The tide is important to get there, as when it gets too high, you can't walk anymore. My hotel gave me the tide times and I think I can just manage. So I walk over a little hill to end up at a small beach. I ask the people I encounter if it's still possible to make the walk. None of them knows really. So I just start walking. The worst that can happen is that my camera in my backpack gets soaked... Oops. It's my first time to walk through an incoming tide, and it goes much faster than I expected. Soon I'm walking along the coast, over, under, passed huge rock formations, with my backpack over my head. My shirt is totally soaked and my flip flops can't be worn under my feet anymore. I have to swim at one point, and with this backpack over my head, I can assure that it's not easy. I'm of course the only madman trying it as this time, and when I finally reach the other side, I get welcomed by people who knew it was too late for them: they will have to take a boat. The sun is strong and I dry pretty quick. As I walk along the beach I pass a typical rock with a little waterfall coming out. The dirt from this rock is supposed to clean you and I see two girls under another small waterfall totally covered in this mud. I ask them to help me get covered too, so I have my cleansing as well. They help me and I make friends with them, upon which I'm invited to their table a bit further down the beach. While walking there I see a boat dropping tons of youngster who will attend a little beach club techno party and they all seem thrilled. I'm happy to just chill with my new friends. One girl's sister is waiting for them and the four of us share some french fries before taking the boat back after a couple of hours.

Another adventurous walk happened some days before, when I just decided to continue walking until I could not continue. I started in the early morning, passing my favourite fourth beach, and then continuing for hours and hours. At the first river I'm wary to pass, but I try anyway. It does get very deep in the middle, but I manage to pass relatively easy. At the second river I meet two women from Argentina and we decide to walk together. And we go on and on, until there's no people anymore. The only thing we see is forest, a very small beach strip, and ocean. It's desolate and pretty nice. I use Google maps and gps to determine position, and in order to get to another famous beach, which normally can only be reached by boat. We make calculations, and decide it's probably better to head back than to continue. Not much later we see a horse drawn taxi and we ask him about the estimated time to that other beach. He says it's probably more than another five hours. We look at each other and know we made the right decision in walking back. When we do finally get back to the town we are exhausted. We split our ways and later at night meet again for dinner.

I have dinner with them some more nights and one evening, when the pouring rain lasted the whole day, they introduce me to a salty ritual, in which they make a cross of salt in order to make the rain stop. I laugh of course, but it's funny people do these kind of things. The next day the rain was gone.

After six days I make up my mind and decide to go to Chapada Diamantina, a rock formation deep in the state of Bahia. This means I have to take a boat back, and then either a bus or plane to get there.

<u>Brazil - Lençóis, Chapada Diamantina, Bahia</u>

I book my boat back at a local agency and the next morning I'm due to leave. My stomach is already upset before I enter in the much smaller private speed boat. Fewer people, less stable: this will be my worst nightmare. I take an extra pill to calm my stomach and the two of them knock me out pretty quick. I dazzle while we crush the waves. Actually, the waves crush us and the little boat is thrown from wave to wave. Poseidon does not like me. When I open my eyes I see some people already being pale, yellow, and green. I'm happy it takes a long time before the first person throws up: we already see the harbour of Salvador when a woman fills a bag. In this even smaller space it could end up worse, but the open sides at the back bring fresh air and they steal the smell quickly. Me and the others seem very relieved however when we set foot on shore again.

I have booked the same hotel as before in Salvador, for just one night. There I meet some new people, among them an elderly couple who say they want to be me, two women from Sweden, and a very lovely girl from the United States. We all exchange details and hope our paths may cross in the future.

The next day I leave early to catch a plane to Lençóis, Chapada Diamantina. I have no bus experiences yet in Brazil, but when I saw them before I didn't really have a good feeling about them. Another reason I decide to take the plane is that flying isn't that scary anymore. Whenever I used to take a plane from Amsterdam I was sick hours before departure, but in Brazil it seems like taking a cab from A to B. It's easier, more relaxed.

When flying over Bahia we don't get too high up and I can see the landscape changing. It's beautiful. When my eyes catch the mountains of Chapada I get excited. I have no clue what will be waiting for me there, but this is already pretty cool.

I have reserved another posada. Last minute of course, so I have no idea how to get there. I decide to take a taxi to the town of Lençóis, and let it drop me off there. On my way I let the driver pick up a hitchhiker, who seemed totally lost. He tells me about his experiences, and offers me money later. I refuse. Upon arrival in the town I walk around with my luggage hoping to find my posada. I give up quickly as the roads are pretty bad, and my orientation is zero at this point. I walk to the bus terminal and decide to ask there. At the table outside there's a man drinking and we start to talk. He's a teacher and at the point of getting pretty wasted. He still manages to help me call my posada and some fifteen minutes later I'm being picked up by a huge car. The guy tells me he runs the hotel with his German wife and his English is outstanding. The posada consists of little yellow houses, spread out on a nice property. It's quite a walk from the cute little centre, and going back is a steep road up, but the accommodation and especially its owners make me feel perfectly comfortable.

The posada is at the start of a trail to a natural waterslide and on my first hike I decide to go there. Through a gloomy landscape I make my way through easy pathways, until I reach the roaring river. From there I walk a bit down until I reach a reasonable big pool. The smoke of weed welcomes me, and I find some people chilling there. I start to talk to them: two locals and two girls from São Paulo. One local shows how you can take the waterslide. He swims to the side and climbs up there before going down... not on his bum, but on his feet. This looks too dangerous to me. As he's very high, he doesn't seem to care. He says he's got plenty experience doing this, when we ask him about it. Then it's the girls' turn and I shoot some photos for them. Next it's my turn and I climb over the slippery rocks to the starting point. Then I sit myself down in the stream and push myself down. The water flushes me down, and I have a good path over the smooth brown rocks. I end up in the pool with a big cheer, and immediately go again. And again. I repeat it five times until my bum hurts too much. Later at night I find out my bum is totally purple. Nasty. We hang out until the sun starts setting and head back quickly: in the dark it will probably be impossible to find the way back.
At the front-desk I start discussing with the manager about my itinerary for the upcoming period. He says a trekking is the best thing to do, but I refuse to do that, with my hernia. If I get in pain, I'm far away from anything. So we think of day trips in the area. He knows a guide who he can set me up with, so I don't have to deal with the tourist agencies. I pick some places and then he discusses it with the guide.

For the following days there's no plan with a guide, so I decide to take a hike to a waterfall. This waterfall is supposedly situated upstream from the waterslide, so I can start the hike near the posada. The manager says it's recommended to go with a guide, but this, of all trails, could be done solo as well. I take off and soon I walk in the burning sun, uphill. At this point there's not much coverage from the trees, so I'm fully exposed. I use a lot of sunblock, and sip my water regularly. Here the trail is quite confusing, because it is a rocky area. When I'm more up, in the forests, the trails are found easier. I walk through a gloomy forest, with down on my left side the rushing stream. I go up, and up, and up, over big rock formations, farther away from other people. I meet some people coming back from the waterfall and say I just have to keep walking. I do as I'm told and continue for quite a bit. Then I walk into a young German couple who are apparently also on their way back, and like me, without a guide. I ask them how much further it is, but they don't know: they say they came to a point from which it was not possible to pass. With this in mind I continue and think it is wise to climb the side cliff and maybe this way cut off this difficult point. I climb up with my hand and feet, holding on to hanging grasses, until I reach the top. It's pretty steep and a fall would mean I would break something for sure, but I manage to get there unharmed. I search for a route, but the bushes are too thick: there's no path here. I try pushing myself through, but it's really impossible. After a few tried routes, I decide to go back, and slide of the steep side down to the river bed. Here I continue to walk the path the German couple did, and soon I come to the enormous rock they also faced. I try to find a way past it, but there's absolutely no possibility. When I turn around to walk back I see the German couple coming back and they spoke to someone who advised them to go under the rock. I look at it, and indeed see a possible way, but it doesn't look very safe. The three of us however do try, and we quite easily do get to the other side. Then the rock jumping really begins and we seem like a bunch of freestylers hopping from rock to rock. We think the waterfall can be behind every corner, but hopes are crushed for a long time, until we finally face the beautiful waterfall. We take off our clothes and jump in the cold water. It's so lovely. We go under the waterfall and let the water fall on us with its enormous power. It's forceful and soon we swim again. We take some good photos, eat some cookies, and then turn to go back. It's quite a hike and we don't want to be here in the dark. Knowing our way, we move easier now and soon we get to the easier part again. We take another swim in a place with enormous invisible holes under the water and have fun doing so. Feeling fresh after this we finish the last part easily. We get along quite well and I ask them to come on a day-tour with me the next day, together with my new guide Toni. They say they would like it, so two days later we start a trip together.

The next day I do a hike by myself up to some other rock formations. A trail that was marked, but of which I lost track as soon as I didn't see any other people anymore. I do hear them however, and I decide to climb straight up the river, from river bed to river bed. What I'm doing is not without risk and when at one point my foot slips away, I realise I should not be doing this climb. I say this to myself while standing halfway up. Down is probably more dangerous, and I still hear some voice above me, so I continue, despite the risks. I raise myself with my hands, throwing my backpack first over ridges, not caring too much anymore about my camera or stuff. When I finally reach the people, I see they are practicing rock climbing, with professional equipment and a lot of ropes. As soon as they see my head appearing from the river bed they run to me and reach their hands. They can't believe I came this way. What the hell was I thinking? I play it cool, and don't worry too much. It is how it is, and it went how it went. I'm safe, no worries! We talk a bit, before I continue my way up. Within minutes I can't see the group anymore and I feel lost right away. There is no trail. I walk back to them to ask, but they don't know that route. I go back and push myself to climb higher and I make the right decision, as pretty soon I come to the marked waterfall. Here I see another guy, whose hand is bleeding badly. He cut himself by doing the same things I was doing: finding an own path. We get to talk a bit and decide to continue going up. This is much easier as we now have a trail to follow. We reach the top of the plateau and it's nice here. Wide view, less trees, tranquil lakes and streams. We take a swim in the fresh water and make some jumps from rocks. His hand doesn't stop bleeding however and we decide it's better to head back. We reach a viewpoint where we meet four other people, who tell us the true trail and this makes the descent much easier. We come to another part of the river which is incredibly crowded by locals, who also seem to do their laundry here. Interesting sights. Then we reach the village and I take my new friend to the hospital. This hospital is more like a concrete building which seems not to be cleaned in the last decade and I can't believe the hygiene can be very good here. A group of medical students take him in and stitch the wound in his hand. I stay in the waiting room to see a football match while the flies are buzzing around my head.

It's interesting how Brazil's politics seem to work. I discussed a lot about it in the northeast, on how the government builds huge football stadiums for the world cup, while good hospitals don't exist, while there's lack of a good and accessible education system, while people are starving from hunger, while corruption is everywhere, and so on. No, Brazil does it like the Romans: give the people bread and games, and they will be happy. In a way this certainly works for the 200 million inhabitants of this giant country, but this seems a short term politic. Investing in education will indeed not help right away, but in generations these people will have more chances, and will also realise a country can only do well if you also invest in the long term. The small hospital in Lençóis is maybe not the perfect example, but in the cities of Fortaleza, Natal, São Luís and Recife it was already clearly visible.

We leave the hospital and get to town to have some acai, before saying goodbye. I go back to my posada, let the experiences sink in, and prepare for the next tour day, with my German friends, Phil and Bianca. I go out for dinner that night and meet some nice new friends, who I go party with and dance until the break of dawn. I'm tired, but so pleased. All the girls are super nice and they drag me into the oblivion of dancing. I don't care anymore, and just do it. I even enjoy it, a bit.

Toni picks me up in his 4x4 and we then pick up my new Germans friends pretty soon after at their hostel. We drive towards a couple of caves, and then to a viewing point. When driving in this area, and later walking, it does not seem to have any caves. It's just flat farm land. Not everything is what it looks like, and as soon as we've parked the car at a private property with some basic tourist needs, we get our flashlights and start walking. Soon we reach a sort of entrance of a bat cave. For me it seems totally out of place. The mountain seems to go inside the ground and the rock formations we're seeing are quite impressive. As if an alien landing ship crashed and created this big hole. We descend into the darkness, seeing some interesting plants, trees and animals along the way. Then we step into the darkness. The flashlights are our only guide and it's quite chilly under here. The cave seems to continue endlessly and our second guide stops us every now and then for a viewing of stalactites. Some formations become shadow monsters when the light shines on it, others are just impressive because you know it took thousands and thousands of years to create them. At one point we have to turn off our lights and be quiet for one minute. I can't remember silence being so loud. We stand in the absolute nothingness and soon only hear the quiet breathing each other. The minute seems to last hours and it's beautiful and frightening at the same time. My eyes are wide open, but I don't see anything. Absolutely nothing. Wow. When our lights are turned on again we are all speechless. From nothing to nothing. Soon we start sharing our thoughts on it and we're back in the real world. The cave also ends not much later and we get back to the car. We then drive to a lake where the water is stunningly blue. I also spot some monkeys here. The water in the cave is also light blue, but the sun's not shining perfectly to light it as it could be. We have lunch here and go for a swim. After this we take the car for a drive to a viewing point. We park it at the end of the road up, and the last thirty minutes we have to hike up, until we reach an enormous plateau. From here the view is stunning. We have a 360-degree view over the entire area, with its gorgeous mountains and forests. One rock is perfect for some great photography and we have fun whilst taking many. I see a falcon as well and try to take photos of this animal as well, even though the distance is enormous. Too bad the world has night and day, because we could have stayed there for a very long time. We have to go back though and walk down back to the car and then drive to Lençóis once again. Toni was very knowledgeable about everything and I would like to have him as my guide for the other tours as well. After some negotiations we come to terms for at least the next day.

In the evening I meet with my Brazilian friends from São Paulo again and we sit down on the curb of a silent street. One plays the guitar, the others sing. I sing. I sing horribly, but I still do. Bob Dylan, Guns N' Roses, and songs from artists I can't recall. It's a beautiful get together which I cherish very much.

The next morning Toni picks me up again and we head for a long hike to an 800-metre-high waterfall. It is quite a drive around the Chapada to one of the other access points of the park. When we arrive it is cloudy and rainy. We write our names in the book, so the park knows we are entering, and we see a long list of names already. We are late. Toni warned me before it is very hard to climb the first thirty minutes when the sun is too high up: you could burn alive. Because of this I'm quite happy with the partially cloudy weather. We start the track and it goes steep up right away. I feel like a cyclist of the Tour de France going up Mont Ventoux. I'm suffering. When Toni sees a snake I'm happy I can stand still for a while. Holding the camera is another story, as I'm already shaking. We continue and there's some plateaus every now and then, where we walk on a flat piece of land. After the final ascent we reach the big plateau and from here on it's only a straight walk. Not entirely straight we will find out later, as the trail is destroyed by heavy rain on many places. We have to avoid puddles and our feet get soaked. Near the end of the trail we have to cross a river. There are robes so it's a piece of cake. Then we arrive at the waterfall. The fall of the water is so deep and steep that it flies back up. It's a marvellous sight. And it gets even more divine when the sun starts to shine and creates rainbows. There's an outstanding rock where people can hang over to see the depth, and I slowly crawl there. Toni holds my feet. The wind blows so hard that I'm afraid to be blown over the edge. I only manage to get at 10 centimetres distance of the edge, let Toni take some photos and then crawl back as soon as possible. This height is scary. I take some photos of three Canadian girls and they are even more scared off the altitude. Me and Toni leave this popular spot, where more and more tourists arrive now, and walk a little more down, around the waterfall, to get a clear view from the other side. It's stunning. All the people we now see from below are so tiny, while the small strip of water falling is making an impression. After this we leave to head back to the car. The hike back is easier, although descending always troubles my legs and feet. We arrive back at the car and from there on drive to another waterfall which is much easier to access. We climb down some rocks and end up at a pool with a big rock wall where the water is endlessly falling down over a wide area. The waterfall itself ends up in a pool where we swim. From here I climb up the slippery rocks until I reach the brute force of the water falling down and I let it fall on my head for a while. The power is enormous and the water is quite cold, so I only manage to stay there for a few minutes. Then I walk back, almost like an ice skater, sliding from rock to rock and almost falling every now and then. I meet an Israeli girl and we talk for a while and I take some photos. Another guy sees what is happening and asks if he can use her as a model in the stream. She refuses. Her moto taxi brings her away after some time, and me and Toni swim around for a bit more. Then we take off back to Lençóis and he drops me at the posada. I take a shower and then have dinner there too, being helped by a lovely staff member who is cook as well as waitress. After that to bed, as tomorrow I will do another tour with Toni.

Toni's car is early at the property again, and I load myself in, still tired from the hike yesterday. My legs are quite sore and my shoes have killed my toes. Today I walk mainly on flip flops, as we don't really go on hikes: we go see some caves with blue water. Two days ago I saw my first, which was not that impressive, but Toni assures me today's going to be different. We drive for a while and then arrive again in a place where I can't imagine there will be any cave. There's just two small buildings. In one I get instructions and a big blue helmet with a light on it attached. Right behind it I see stairs going down, and it does remind me of the day when we descended into the other cave. We walk down and soon enter a dark cave, where we have to climb down in with a robe as our help. The path is marked on both sides with robes all the way to the viewing point. What we see is breathtaking. The water is spectacularly blue and for a while I think it's man-made, fake. It really isn't and my mouth almost drops to the floor due to this wonder of nature. The pool is very deep, about 80 metres and the cavern has a big opening on the left side through which the sun can shine on the water. We don't see a ray of sun directly reaching the water unfortunately, which I am told is the most spectacular, but I get the idea. I stay to take some photos, before sitting down in silence to just observe the beauty. Toni eventually disturbs me, as the clock of the day is ticking and we have yet another cave to visit. Walking uphill is tiring, but in the car I can take my moments of rest. We drive to the next cave where we park the car just before a river. We have to cross it by foot and the water only reaches knee height. One beautiful thing I see here is hundreds of yellow butterflies who rest in a sand area and fly up when you come very close. The colours are truly amazing and when they dance in the air I can just observe and tell myself how beautiful nature is. We continue to walk to the property of the cave, where we first have a really delicious lunch, amidst a dozen other tourists. I see life vests being handed out at the entrance, so this means I can swim in a cave, hurray. After lunch we line up for entering, together with three

Canadian girls and their guide. These are the same girls we saw on the hike yesterday, so we get to talk and exchange some details. When another group comes up, it's our turn to go down and through a series of wooden stairs we reach a platform from where we see the water in the cave. It is absolutely stunning. I can't believe it's real. Here I do see a sun ray reaching the water. It is a floodlight moving extremely slow over the water surface. I am told to hurry myself in the water and after closing my life vest I am given a snorkel. I step into the cold water, just when yet another group leaves the water. The girls are still in preparation and for some minutes I have the water to myself. I float on the top and feel the sunshine on my face for just some seconds. Then I keep floating there for a while, as Toni is taking some great photos of me. These are among my favourites of myself in this trip for sure. Then the girls enter and the still water turns into sparkling. They swim around, and I start doing the same. Legend tells there's a monster in the back of the cave, but we are superheroes and not scared at all. We taunt the beast, but it's not coming out. Who's the man now, right? After some thirty minutes we are directed to go out and even though we really don't want to, we are summoned. One by one we leave and I try to take some good shots before leaving, which is quite difficult as the lighting in a cave is far from ideal. We take the steps up and then take a shower before going back to the car and driving back to Lençóis. There I eat, read, and sleep, as my common nightly ritual here.

Last morning in the Chapada and it is pouring. My plane back to Salvador leaves in the afternoon and I hired Toni just one more time to see another waterfall. The entire world is a waterfall right now however and the wipers are set on maximum speed in order to see where we are going. Again we have to enter private property and pay the landlord a bit. At a viewpoint we stop to see this huge waterfall. It's not Iguazu, but waterfalls are magical to me. Small ones, big ones, I love to see them. When we later park the car a bit further up-road the rain finally stops and we head out, put on our walking shoes and start a hike down. The rain has made the surface dangerously slippery and our hands grab anything possible on our way down to not fall and die. We do manage to get there unharmed and the sun now also starts to shine. The waterfall is now a few steps away and it is enormous. The rainwater makes the stream flow faster and at times water from the fall shockingly increases. I try to see a pattern, but it seems to be completely random. I take off my shirt and head towards it, while Toni stays behind to shoot some photos. I stand under the fall and believe it's the best shower I ever have had. Again the power is brute, but as long as it doesn't give me a headache it's fine by me. From under the water I see another group arrive, three people and their guide. As usual the guides start talking to each other and the tourists hang around amongst themselves. The two guys stay behind, while the woman also approaches my shower. It's a woman from Argentina and she tells me she hates her group. She starts to see if she can join me, but I tell her my tour is already over after this trip. She is pouting. The guys don't make any effort to feel the water. The woman tells me they didn't bring swim shorts... As if underwear can't be used for the same purpose. Her guide summons her quite quickly and I join her walking back, helping her over some of the rocks, before splashing in a small pool where the others are waiting. They leave shortly after while Toni and me sit there for a while observing the power of water, and talk about how great the last days have been. Then we also start climbing back up again, and the rained down trail is not too easy to ascend. Toni drives me to the airport where I say farewell to him, and then queue up in line. After the luggage is dropped I only have to wait for the plane. Waiting takes a bit long, and the plane isn't arriving. I meet a German couple and we share experiences. No one knows when the plane will come and we wait for two hours until we finally see it come down from the clouds. A delay is not a problem, but there was no communication at all. A two-hour delay for an hour flight is also a bit much, we all think. We get to Salvador safely though, and I stay there one night before taking a plane to Brasilia, Brazil's capital, situated in the middle of nowhere.

Brazil - Chapada dos Veadeiros, Goiás

When I arrive in Brasilia, the city itself is not my first stop. Upon arrival I am picked up by Cassia, a good friend of mine who I got to know in Amsterdam in 2009. She was an au pair in Den Bosch for one year and we got to hang out a lot when she came to Amsterdam. We have a lot in common and she is one of the few people I know that understands my passion for Bob Dylan, as she also loves his music. We pretty much like the same kind of music and this is a great connection. First we drive to Cassia's home where I meet her lovely mother and father and get offered a great lunch. A tad later Cassia's boyfriend Ismael and his friend Cid join us on a trip into my second Chapada: Chapada dos Veadeiros in the state of Goias, upstate of Federal District. Before we arrive there we have to drive for some hours and the night is falling soon, so I don't see much of the scenery on our way to Alto Paraiso, the town from where we will explore the mountain range. Alto Paraiso seems to be a quiet small town and Cassia has arranged a lovely hotel. After checking in and freshening up we head out and eat in a lovely restaurant. We go to bed early: tomorrow is hiking day!

We have a very good breakfast in the early morning, and decide what trail we want to walk. Cassia and Cid have been here before, so we do have some expertise. I did some research on the internet and of course also have an opinion. We drive to another small town, Sao Jorge, where the main entrance to the park is. From here it's a short drive to a ranger station where we apply for entrance. A guide is mandatory, so we have to wait until they know there is one available for the trail we want to walk. It is possible, and not much later he arrives on his motor. It's only a short drive to the trail's start, and there we take off on the walk. The guide only speaks Portuguese, and I don't understand much of what he is saying. My three friends translate for me, so it's not a problem. The first part of the trail is on a normal level, but soon we are going up and down. I have a lot of experience with walking on my trip so far, and this is finally paying off, as it seems I'm the mountain goat of the group, while my friends are puffing and having a hard time moving over the rocks. We encounter the first small waterfall with also a pool of ice cold waterfalls in front of it, and before everyone knows it, I'm already in. There's a great view from here over the Chapada and when we're all rested we continue down the mountain for a bit. When hiking, going down is always harder than going up, as you use your muscles in a way they are rarely used. I'm aware of this, and try more to jump than to walk. After going down, we have to make the final trail up. This is quite easy, as we know we close in on the viewpoint we are aiming for today. And when we do arrive there finally, it is up to the nines. Wow. Breath-taking view over a big valley with at the horizon a series of three big waterfalls. Now this is photo material. So I find myself shooting photos for a long, long time, until I think I have captured it all. The forest at our feet is not accessible, but houses groups of monkeys. The guide tells us he went in there a couple of times with other guides, but that it is off limit for tourists. Now I'm the one pouting. We turn and start walking the same way back. My friends are struggling now, while I keep going and going. Of course we eventually all get back safely, but I see in their eyes they only think of one thing: beer! We drive back to Sao Jorge where we consume a nice lunch, in a kilo restaurant. These kilo restaurants are amazing and whenever I find one I try to eat here: it's very good food most of the time, for a very fair price. And you only pay for what you eat. Oh Brazil, how great you are.

After lunch we head back to Alto Paraiso where we take a shower and rest a bit, before heading out for dinner. We find another little nice restaurant and we have a good meal. After this we all think it's party time and we try to find a place where this is possible. We end up in some kind of open house where all modern day hippies seem to have gathered. There's a band playing live music and for a small town like Alto Paraiso this is probably one heck of a party. We observe others going absolutely crazy. Cassia and Ismael soon go back to the hotel and Cid and me stay and finally get to talk to the locals here. And I must say, these locals are really louco, crazy. I do meet a lot of people in my travels, but here we find an entire bunch is on a search for spiritual freedom. They tell us the town is on top of a crystal and this crystal sucks out the bad energy from people, and inject them with a positive one. We hear stories about them dancing naked in front of the waterfalls, and when they drank some more beers we are also invited for this. I call the people crazy, but I mean they are unique, and they have their own visions and opinions, which I deep inside myself respect and appreciate. It's in many ways just far from my own me. They want to introduce me to a certain herbal tea, for which they are organised in a special church, so they can use it legally. When I hear the stories about this tea it seems like a combination of acid, cocaine, heroin, xtc, and weed. It sounds like one of the most intense drugs ever. And they all seem to love it. Cid also leaves for home and now I'm the crazy one in the middle of the crazy bunch. The more I hear, the more interesting it is. I stay until the party's over, get involved in some more interesting discussions, conversations and meetings, before I am dropped off at the hotel, and try to sleep with a spinning mind.

Brazil - Brasilia, Distrito Federal

Even when I wake up I feel I am still on yesterday's trip, not believing how weird it all was. Me and Cid now have many stories to tell, and this continues the entire day. Before heading back to Brasilia, we have one more hike planned, and this time we go to the moonstone valley. We can park the car nearby and then walk the last couple of hundred metres to the river which indeed is surrounded by spacey rocks that look like they came straight from the moon. Their grey colour and the curvy curly shapes are very interesting to see. We walk a bit up and down river, exploring. I take off to check the lower falls, while the others stay and discuss the meaning of life, I think. My other thought is that they are too tired to take one more step, so when I see they are barely moving, I come back so we can head back to the car. Then the drive back to Brasilia starts and this time we do it at daylight. At a big barn we stop for lunch, and after that the only stops we make are at a gas station, and at a place where Cid takes a funny picture (it has something to do with the name). We arrive back in Brasilia when it's dark, and they drop me off at the house of another friend I know in the city, Renata. After a good time waiting she comes down, and before following her up, I say goodbye to my good friends.

Renata stayed at my place in Amsterdam quite recently and we had some good tours through my city and its surroundings. When I told her I would come to Brazil, she immediately invited me to her place. And now I'm finally there. She lives with her mom and sister in a big spacey apartment, where I get her room. Even though I object, she insists on this. During the upcoming week this house becomes mine, as the family also grows to be my own. I'm again surprised, grateful, on how a stranger like me gets welcomed so warm. They put everything aside for my wellbeing. Hospitality ++.

Some days I don't do anything in this city, and some days I take up the challenge to see its beautiful and famous places. When you think of beautiful places in Brasilia, you immediately have to think of the great architect Oscar Niemeyer, who pretty much designed the city and all its important landmarks. The city is built in the form of an airplane, with two big wings aside a bit tall middle. The idea is pretty nice, but naive at the same time: it's too small for the amount of people working here, or coming here to find a better future. The slums build up outside the city and the prospected amount of people that lives here is much more. Brasilia is clean and organised however, in comparison to what I've seen before. And yes, it's much more modern and western than the entire Northeast, where I have travelled up to now.

After some days of chilling and not doing too much, I decide to go on a sightseeing tour. My first stop is the impressive cathedral, of course designed by Niemeyer. I absolutely love this piece of modern architecture. I try to take photos from all angles, but never catch it in its full beauty. The inside is wide, spacious, light, it's different than any of the thousands of churches I've visited in my life before. Part of why I like it so much is probably because it is different. I spend some good hours here, before walking down the central avenue to a museum and a library, both from the same famous architect. I like both buildings, but they don't come close to the cathedral. For lunch I meet with Cassia, who, of course, works for the government. In Brazil everyone can take a test to work for the government. If you are the one with the highest score, you are hired. It does not matter if you are blind, handicapped, white, black, annoying, bright. Anyone can become a civil servant. There's no interviews, just a big important test, for which you have to study very hard, and which is not as easy as just the four letters of the words: test. Renata's parents also work for the government and she's considering doing the same thing. What else to do in Brasilia?

I do find enough to do in this city, as the nightlife is also pretty good. All my friends take me to several bars on different nights and especially the cover bands here I can appreciate very much. I find myself screaming along with Coldplay and Oasis on one crazy night, meet great other locals too, and on another I suddenly sing along with an Eddie Vedder lookalike on how his ex will find a beautiful life one day, that she will be a star in somebody else's sky, and he wonders why it can't be his.

Renata takes me to the presidential palace, and to some other government buildings (it seems all of Brasilia's buildings are owned by the government), and to two museums in which you can learn the history of the city. I do learn a lot here, and understand more and more about the history of the country and its people. We also visit the point from where a priest saw the place in which the new capital had to be built one day. This story became truth, and when I read about it, it actually sounds pretty crazy.

Besides this I'm being taken out on lovely lunches, dinners, in the best places in town, and I often come to the lake to eat acai. Renata's brother and father try to infect me with a virus for Botafogo and together we watch a game in front of their huge screen all dressed in jerseys. One former Feyenoord player is now player for Botafogo, so I do feel sympathy for them, but nothing comes close to what I feel for my Dutch team.

Time is flying in Brasilia and I feel very much at ease. I stay here longer than I would have thought, because seeing Brasilia can probably be done in a couple of days. Being surrounded by so many great people however makes me want to stay here so much longer. The road is calling me though, and I book a flight to the tourist capital of the country: Rio de Janeiro.

Brazil - Rio de Janeiro, Rio de Janeiro

From thinking about going somewhere and actually going there is a matter of a day during my trip. When I want to leave, I book a flight, and leave the very next day most of the time. I arrive in Rio de Janeiro for the first time and in the cab to my Ibis hotel in Botafogo I'm already surprised by the apparent chaos. The traffic seems to be crazy here. I arrive at my hotel after some time, and then take a rest for the rest of the day.

I go to the Maracanã directly after breakfast to see if I can buy a ticket for today's classico: Flamengo versus Vasco da Gama. Before I came to Brazil I read about Brazilian football and attending a match of Flamengo was on the top of my list. The people in the hotel have told me that it is not safe around the stadium and that the fans hate each other and they will fight. I have left my phone and bank cards in the hotel and only bring my digital camera with me. Getting a ticket is easy, even though a bit expensive. I wonder how Brazilian people ever can afford a ticket for this match. I chose a seat in the lower section in the middle of the stadium, where I am told there's a mixture between Flamengo and Vasco fans. Before I enter the stadium I am stopped by a young woman who works for Globo, a big national news channel. She interviews me and says she will put it up their website. Getting into the stadium brings me past some security checkpoints and like outside the stadium, there's enough police force inside as well. I find my seat easily and then wait for the stadium to fill up. It does not matter how long I wait; it never gets full today. It's a ghost atmosphere to be in a 70.000 seat stadium with barely any fans. I think the attendance is about 25.000 today, and it gives a miserable look. The match itself is almost as bad, as both teams don't really know how to play football. Maybe there's too much pressure as this is the first leg of the final of the Carioca state championship. Flamengo ended first in the group phase and needs two draws, or a draw and a win. Vasco really needs to win if they want to be champion. They play more offensive but it's not enough for victory. On both north and south side of the stadium, the fanatical fans are standing and make noise accompanied with drums. I've been in Brazil now for quite some time and I know these drums fit better here than they would in any other football stadium in the world. The drum is connected to the culture and the music. When European clubs introduce drums, it feels fake: this is the real deal. At the final whistle it's 1-1 and the sun burnt my face the same colour red as the jersey of Flamengo. The entire match the sun was eating the flesh from my face, inch by inch. I take some photos and a bright young woman with one of the most gorgeous smiles takes one of me, and I one of her. Outside the stadium I walk into her again and as she says it's not that safe, we walk to the metro together and talk and laugh non-stop. The force is with us. We can easily enter the metro and as she also lives in Botafogo we can leave at the same stop. There we say goodbye and she tells me the direction of my hotel, as I have no clue where it is, and I don't have a phone. I walk in the direction she points and about 1.5 hour later I'm still circling the quiet shady streets. I have no clue where my hotel is, and I can't find it anywhere. I nearly panic because the people I keep running into don't seem the curious types. Eventually I get some help by a woman who even walks me all the way to the hotel. Thank god. I'm in one piece. I rush to the room and hide under the blankets for the rest of the night.

I wake up with a spirit for sightseeing and decide to go to Sugar Loaf mountain. I let a taxi drop me off in front of the cableway that will bring me up. First I stand in line to buy a ticket, then to access the cabin that brings 50 people up to the first out of two stops. Even though the sun is burning that wait is not too bad and before I notice, I'm being lifted over Rio. The first stop gives me already a wonderful view over the city, and it has some monuments and restaurants. I stroll around and take many photos. Then I take the second cart up and there the view is even more stunning, and 360 degrees. At the back of the view to the city there's also a small forest where monkeys jump from tree to tree, not being bothered by all the tourists around. There's clouds moving in the sky and the shadow falls over the city. When the sun breaks through it seems like God is sending a positive message to his people. I get to talk about this and many other subjects with a Mexican woman who lives in Salvador and is on a tourist visit to Rio. We speak a lot of Portuñol (the mixture of Portuguese and Espanyol) before we go our separate ways. I feel even though language differences are inevitable, it is a way to connect, and not to disconnect, if, that is, you try your best. When I get back to ground zero I take a cab towards the centre where I will meet Renata for lunch: this Renate also stayed at my place with two of her friends a long time ago through couchsurfing and she had invited me to have lunch with her. We meet near her work and she takes me to a cute kilo restaurant where we have a great lunch and have a good time catching up. After lunch we walk into a church and monastery nearby, before she takes off to work again. After this lunch I first take a metro, and later a cab, towards Cristo Redentor, the enormous statue of Jesus looking over the city, arms wide-spread. I buy a ticket at the booth and then wait for the cable train to bring me up. It's a pretty long wait, and when I finally in, I take a window seat. Next to me, and on all seats around me, a class of some kind is taking seats. I have no clue what they are talking about, but they seem to be having a good time. I can't really put my finger on who's the teacher and who are the students. When we are five minutes underway the girls next to me ask where I'm from, after I was laughing at some of the things they were saying. We get into an animated conversation in which soon the entire class is involved. They nearly applaud for my Portuguese and it seems I'm more interesting to them than the Christ monument. They are all following an intense course to become a guide and they are here to learn. I get to take many photos with all the guys and girls and make a whole bunch of friends. We stay up as long as the sun is set and in the end are firmly asked to leave by security. On our way down the talks and laughter continue and we only separate after handing out our details. I'm in a hurry as I also agreed to have dinner and feel pretty bad when I arrive at the restaurant much later than planned. The dinner was great though in a place on the curbs somewhere in Botafogo. Hurray for Brazilian dinner times!

How lazy can a person be? I don't usually sleep in, as I wake up early, but I manage to not leave my room until some hours after. The climate in Brazil is perfect to take everything easy. I take all my time to have breakfast and then take the metro to Ipanema and from there walk along the boulevard. First on this relative quiet beach, and then to the famous Copacabana one. It's a bit busier here, but nothing as I expect it to be. I move my feet through the thick sands, passing about a dozen typical Brazilian bums, that are just laid out there to catch the sun. There are some bodies attached, but that's not what is catching the eye. The waves are breaking very hard, and the red flags that are continuously placed along the shore indicate this is not the best time to take a swim. Only some people walk in to escape the heat at the beach. I stop somewhere to eat acai and then start heading to Maracanã. One of my new friends works there and I can come for a free tour. Another friend from the guide group yesterday will join me on it and we meet outside the stadium. We are indeed on the list and are quickly welcomed with open arms. Ingred shows me and Lilian around in the stadium that will soon be the host of the world cup final. In the dressing rooms there are all jerseys of the Seleção and when walking around you can not only see 'now', you also walk through history. Once this stadium held 120.000 people, and now, after modernisation and renovation, it is still a pretty big venue. Now I'm here, I also try to get a ticket for the Copa Libertadores match of Flamengo that is being played here tomorrow. Students get a 50% discount so I ask my friends to help. We unfortunately find out it's sold out. We leave Ingred now to work in peace and head back to Botafogo where we have a nice dinner.

Sold out my ass, is one of the first thoughts in the morning. I can't believe Flamengo will draw a full stadium after it was so empty last Sunday. Prices are simply too expensive in my humble opinion, so I decide to go to the stadium hours before the match to see if I can find something in the black market. I try to find the people hassling tickets and soon I'm surrounded by plenty. Now I'm the gringo of course and everyone tries to rip me off. I meet some other tourists trying to get tickets too and they have not been very lucky. I decide to talk to some locals and see if they can help me. They hear some lower prices, so I let them do my negotiations while I look at the dealing from a little distance. I eventually get the ticket for the official price, so that seems to be a fair deal.
I head back to the hotel, have a lunch/dinner at a restaurant and then head back to the stadium. It's rush hour in the metro and soon I'm pressed down in a corner, almost fainting because of the heat and lack of fresh oxygen. A dad and his son stand next to me in Flamengo colours and I start talking to them to distract myself from the conditions. We get in a great conversation and before I know it we exit at the Maracanã stop. All people in the metro now are Flamengo fans and when we exit the first songs are being sung. It's a huge contradiction to what I saw Sunday. My new friends arrange a shirt for me and then I'm also really ready to go. I first walk them to their entrance and then continue to my own. Today I sit in the second ring, in a cheaper section, and I expect a bit more fanatic fans around me. As I enter the stadium I get sucked into the passion of all the people who are singing and jumping. The stadium is packed tonight, except for the huge stand the about twenty fans of Leon, from Mexico, have gotten. The stadium is bloody red and black. And no one is sitting. All stand and dance for all 90 minutes. This is a cup

atmosphere and this is what I miss so much from the tumultuous crowd in De Kuip, the stadium of my team Feyenoord. The game is open, the level higher than Sunday's, and the goals keep coming. Flamengo has to win to hold a chance to reach the knockout phase, but when the dust settles down after the match, it's a 2-2 draw. Not enough. The fans leave the stands in disappointment and I get back to the crowded metro. It's past midnight when I get back to the hotel, knowing the passion of Flamengo fans is closed in my heart.

Some days I really do nothing. The longer the trip lasts, the more these days happen. There's no rush to see everything right away, and after seeing so many beautiful things at times I am saturated. Cities in Brazil also are not that captivating to me so far and I can't really form an opinion about Rio just yet.

On these empty days I keep in touch with new and old friends over WhatsApp and sometimes Skype with my family back home. Not many days are passing by without me leaving some notes for my dad on Skype, and so I'm thousands of kilometres away, but still not too far. I follow all the news on a daily basis and therefore am well informed most of the time.

At night I'm exploring Lapa with a friend and we walk around in the crowded streets where a band is playing samba in every bar. There are lines in front of the clubs and people drinking on the streets. Walking towards Rio Scenarium we pass many shady people and these streets don't seem to be among the safest in town. There's a lot of police though and I don't feel unsafe at all. We enter bars, have drinks, and talk vividly. Rio Scenarium is a number one place to go for samba. It has three floors with bands, music, food and drinks and the lines outside in the weekends, and also on some weekdays, are huge. Lapa is the district of sin, the Amsterdam of Rio. No wonder I feel at home.

I get back to the hotel very late and then sleep like a baby.

I'm heading to the Maracanã today again to get a ticket for the second leg of the Carioca final, and have asked for help from another guide-to-be, so I can get student discount on the ticket. Before I meet up with her, I meet another fanatic Flamengo fan, Maiara, who also just bought tickets for the important match on Sunday. I talk for quite some time with her about the passion for Flamengo and it is amazingly cool to see how fanatic she is.

Then I meet with Juliana and she helps me get the ticket. This time I decide it's time to bring up the game and I get a ticket in the middle of the torcida. Of course this is strongly discouraged because those people are really too crazy. I will see.

After getting the ticket we get a metro and two stops later exit at a shopping mall where we eat acai together. Ever since those Dutch people introduced me to acai at the Belém airport I'm slowly getting addicted to this sweet pulp, which I mix with granola and banana. I heard it is also very healthy, so I can't eat enough of it.

Back in Botafogo I chill in my room, have dinner in the hotel and sleep quite early. Tomorrow I want to go to Floresta da Tijuca so I need some rest as this means I will hike uphill.

In the morning after breakfast I head out in my hiking clothes, with my hiking shoes, being even more gringo than I was ever before. I don't want to take a crowded bus with all my camera equipment, so I decide I will take a cab. Again the idea of a cab kidnap is playing in the back of my head. When my friends in Peru stopped a taxi they were taken to a cabin in the woods, blindfolded and then the kidnappers took off to withdraw as much money as possible with all the bank cards they had taken. In the books I have read about Brazil, I've seen this also happens in Brazil and you always have to be careful. Eventually I find my guts again and I enter a taxi and let him bring me to the park entrance. I keep track of the route on my phone, which leaves the battery on a low percentage pretty fast. He is going in the right direction and our talk, about football and politics of course, gives me a confident feeling. I put the phone away, while we drive through neighbourhoods that look like favelas. Some actually are favelas according to the driver. The road slowly winds up and after a while I'm dropped off in a little park from where you can enter through a gate into the park. I walk up over an asphalt road, as the visitor centre is situated in the middle of the park. There I buy a ticket and get information on where I can see monkeys. I of course ask to see monkeys, and jaguars. No jaguars here, according to the ranger, but monkeys can occasionally be seen. He has not seen any this week though, so I should not get my hopes up. I take the trails pointed out and walk under high trees in the shadows. The trails are marked quite well, so I find my way easily. There's a little stream, and

I pass little waterfalls. Sometimes I meet other tourists, mainly families with children. I sit down at one waterfall to have some cookies I have brought and drink some of the water. I'm heading to a restaurant where maybe I can see the monkeys. The trail goes up again, and I end up at the asphalt road again, but much higher up. Here's the restaurant and immediately I see movement in the trees. I slowly move there and get my camera ready. They are here and it's a big group. They are throwing down fruits in order to break them and eat them. They are curious to me and sometimes gaze perfectly in the lens. I haven't seen this type of monkeys before, so I can now cross them off my fictional list. I show the group to other tourists passing, and tell cars that are stopping what is happening. Some get out, cameras ready, others ignore the cute animals. After some hours I continue my way to see some other trails and here I am startled by little animals running away over the leaves. I had the idea to go all the way to the top, but the sun is not planning to stay up the entire day. It's setting already and the darkness comes to the forest sooner than in the city. I'm trying to move more quickly now, back to the ranger station or the road. I'm far off and the idea of walking here in the dark is not very tempting. I speed up and feel like Legolas chasing some orcs. I keep a close eye to my feet to avoid branches, holes, and hopefully also snakes, who are known to be here in good numbers. I pass a little candle that is lit in the middle of the forest and I decide to extinguish it, before the entire forest will be my candle. It would be easier to have my path lit, but this is a bit too much. I wonder who lit it in the first place. Now I can see lights of a building through the trees and I try following the path to there. When I go down steeply I know I lost the trail, but I'm now just determined to get to that building. The adrenaline is building up when I start using my iPhone to give a little more light than what the sun and moon together are providing right now. I finally get to the building, which I recognise being close to the visitor centre and from here I can follow the road down. When I get to the station I'm the only one left and only a few cars are still at the parking lot. Time-wise I'm right on time, but light-wise I certainly was not. I continue to the exit of the park and there another adventure starts: finding a taxi. There's absolutely no taxis passing, and if they do, they are full. I can't walk back, so I have to wait. The battery of my phone is long gone by now, so I'm quite cut off from the world as well. I see buses passing by, but I don't see a bus stop. I start asking people, and they point down the road. I have no clue what bus I can take anyway, so I place my bet on finding an empty taxi. When finally one passes I almost throw myself in front of it, and his honking makes clear I might have pushed my luck. He passes, but then parks at the curb a bit down, alarm lights on. I think this is my signal so I hurry there. He opens the door, I get in, and let him drive back to Botafogo. Now I can't follow the road on my phone, so I try to do so by landmarks. If only I left little stones on my way here, then I would be sure it will be all good. The driver is a student and incredibly friendly. I feel at ease now, and we talk all the way, in English. He hands his business card to me when we arrive at the hotel and this actually is the last time I worry about getting in a cab. All the worries are just not worth it.

Match day. Today is the final of the Carioca state championship and I support Flamengo. I am quite excited to be in a fanatic mood today, and finally support a team again. I miss the atmosphere of De Kuip so much and every time I hope something will come close to it, and today my hopes are up high. I dress neutral on my way to the stadium, but do bring my jersey this time. In the metro I meet Dado, and we get to talk about the match. He will meet with a friend at the Maracanã exit and he invites me for a pre-match party. I agree to it. We meet with his friend Alex and I introduce myself as 'gringo louco'. We laugh a lot on our way to this party, which seems to be a lot of barbecuing in some streets not too far from the stadium. As my ticket is for the right stand, but not the right area, we discuss a way on how to get me inside the middle of the chaos. Just thirty minutes before the match we head to the stadium, after them slamming one beer after another. I get some attention from the fans, as apparently it's not very common for a tourist to come here. We enter the stadium through different gates, but inside we meet again easily. Then we enter the stand, and it is absolutely packed. We don't even try to get to a seat, because there's none; there's way too many people inside. We stand behind a plastic fence which separates us from the area where my ticket is actually for. There's people around me everywhere, but I stand in a good way. Then the thriller begins and the crowd goes absolutely wild. There are few empty seats in the stadium and the atmosphere is superb. It stays superb until Vasco scores the 0-1. The crowd calms down, afraid to lose. That is something they never do against their arch rivals: lose. They commonly say Vasco always gets second, Vice Vasco. The second half is even worse than the first, and the level of play of Flamengo is horrible. They don't create any chances, and Vasco solidly defends, while trying to score from counters. Even though Vasco plays on the second level this year, they are the better side today. The last thirty minutes the people around me almost fall completely quiet and are mostly biting their nails. The tension is enormous. I do feel the same tension, and also the frustration of my team Feyenoord never winning anything. Now I'm finally supporting a team in a final, and they're going down. I also can't stand the silence when the team needs the support, so before I realise it, I scream "Meeeeeeengoooooooooo, Meeeeeeengoooooooooo!" Dado and Alex first laugh, but then scream with me, and then everyone else follows. They soon get back to themselves though and the tension is building up again. Every now and then I try to make some footage with my camera, but there's not much to film. As usual I film with free kicks and corners. At the 90th minute, when all hope seems to be gone, Flamengo gets a corner kick. It is easily cleared but then the ball is brought back in and via the post it gets to a player who nets the ball in. I'm filming the entire thing and the eruption is bigger than the Vesuvius has ever had. All people fall over each other, people run up and down and when everyone is standing again I see dozens of people crying. Grown men, crying, women, crying, boys, crying. Everyone seems to let it go and the tears of happiness are flooding. The main chant of before the match is sung massively now: "Nos queremos respeito, e compartimento, isso aqui e nao Vasco, isso aqui e Flamengo, wooo, hoo hoo hooo hooo", on the melody of the White Stripes' Seven Nation Army. The other side of the stadium is knocked out, and rapidly the stand of the Vasco side empties. The players of Vasco are devastated by yet another loss and they don't even seem to try anymore in the last minutes of stoppage time. When the final whistle blows everyone is cheering again, happy, chanting, and many seem to want give me a hug. One guy tells me I'm their mascot now. Dado and Alex now nickname me 'gringo pika', which literally means that I'm a dick, but in Rio it also means someone beyond cool in the slang of the city. The neutral blue light that was lit in the stadium during the match now turns red, like when Flamengo doesn't play another Rio opponent, and the trophy is handed out. The players celebrate with the fans who stay in the stadium to do this. For quite some time we stay here, and when we finally do walk out the people continue singing and it echoes through the concrete of the stadium, and then infinitely in my ears.

I walk back to the metro with Dado and Alex, in an asylum of joy, and there we part ways. I arrive at the hotel quite late and can't sleep for many more hours due to the adrenaline.

The adrenaline keeps rushing through my body the next day. I spend my time meeting a friend, and booking my flight to São Paulo, the next stop. Tomorrow I will leave for Brazil's economic centre, and biggest city.

Brazil - Porto Alegre, Rio Grande do Sul

I never get to São Paulo, because of a change of events, which starts at the Rio airport. I go to the federal police there upon arrival to see how long I can actually stay in Brazil and if there's options to extend this period. I hand in my passport and they walk away with it to not much later come back with the news it's a maximum of three months, and there's no options to extend, at all. I have only read a little bit about this subject, and now all of a sudden I have a deadline. My list of places to visit in Brazil was still long and now I don't seem to have the time for it anymore. I reach out to my friends Simone and Felipe to see what their schedule looks like the upcoming days, and also to Fernanda, a girl who I met through couchsurfing and helped me throughout my trip with a variety of things. She lives in a shithole in Rio Grande do Sul and I was determined to visit her and thank her in person for all she has done. I run between the desks of TAM and GOL, in order to get my ticket changed and skip São Paulo and see my friends. I manage to do so, and the journey takes a sudden twist to the south.

I arrive late that night and Simone and Felipe pick me up from the Porto Alegre airport and then drive me to the old stadium of Grêmio, the club Felipe works for. We drive around and I take some photos. They welcome me to their city and home without blinking their eyes and once again I'm grateful. We eat sushi in a very fancy area of the city, with many restaurants and bars. When we get to the house I fall asleep in the guest room.

The next morning Felipe brings me to the stadium again and I get to see the first team's training and the club's facilities. It's amazing how it all breathes football here and all the people I meet are extremely nice and welcoming. Felipe's working with video analyses of youth teams and it's a new insight for me to how things are done in a football club. Around lunch I get to meet Simone and with her I visit the federal police in Porto Alegre, to once more try to look into possibilities of staying in Brazil for a longer time, and now specifically trying to use the world cup as an excuse to do so. No one seems to know anything about the rules for visiting the matches, and we even get to call the headquarters in São Paulo for information. We leave the bureau without any new information unfortunately.

Simone brings me to a place where I can take a hop on and hop off bus that will show me the city of Porto Alegre, and I spend the afternoon seeing the city from the top of a bus. It's the same old story for me with the cities in Brazil: they don't appeal to me too much. It seems chaotic, dirty, dangerous and too crowded. So far cities here are not my cup of tea. The tour however was a good thing to do to get some general idea of this city.

In the evening I meet with other friends I've met in Fernando de Noronha: Mariana and Vivian. They take me to that nice area of the city again and we dine in a place where they play live music. Later we switch to another bar and continue talking all evening. Then I'm dropped off again.

Next day's afternoon I have lunch with yet another friend I've met in London the year before. She shows me around her neighbourhood and we have lunch in maybe the best kilo restaurant I've been to so far, and most certainly the cheapest. We walk around a bit more after this lunch and then I move myself to an old factory in another part of town where I will meet Mariana again to visit a famous photo exhibition, which is very inspiring to see. All photos in black and white, of the most beautiful places and the most amazing animals.

It's Easter now, and for Simone and Felipe the perfect day to take me to Granada and Canela, two towns in the nearby mountains which are very popular locally. We drive there and quite soon head up the mountains. A lot of towns have German names here and the influence is inescapable. Before we get to Granada we visit a gondola that brings us to a marvellous viewpoint of a waterfall. Granada has many houses that look like they have been imported directly from the European Alps, and so does Canela when we finally get there. It's weird for me to see it here. Also, the mountains are gloomier here, and less steep. It's less rough here.
From driving in to Granada one thing is clear: they do love Easter here. Everywhere you look are small and big Easter bunnies in all kind of colours. It's an Easter Disneyland and it attracts many visitors. I snap some photos of it, and walk around grinning at these customs. I've been to the Alps numerous of times and they've copied it quite well. The sound of Portuguese just does not fit the image, at

all. We have a massive lunch here, fondue, with a dozen different sauces and for dessert even a chocolate fondue. I'm so full afterwards my friends have to roll me from place to place. We visit some markets and take some photos of all the nice spots. In the evening we drive back 'home' and arrive there when it's already dark.

I quickly book my flight to Passo Fundo, which is a small city in Rio Grande do Sul, from where Fernanda will pick me up tomorrow. At night I say goodbye to Simone, Felipe, and their cute little princess dog. In the morning they will be gone for work when I will leave the house.

Brazil - Não-Me-Toque, Rio Grande do Sul

I get to the Porto Alegre airport by cab, and then it's only a short wait and a less than an hour flight to Passo Fundo. This airport is so small that I'm surprised it even exists. Nanda awaits me here with the car and it's a warm welcome. We take off to a pet shop, to buy dog food, and then to a mall. We walk around a bit there before going to a sushi restaurant. The rain welcomes me while we park the car, as it starts pouring. In the restaurant the music is unconventional, the staff lousy, but the food tasty. We then head out to drive to Não-Me-Toque, where Nanda lives with her parents and sister. Não-Me-Toque means "Don't Touch Me", and is a town with huge Dutch influences and many agricultural companies that still have Dutch names. There's not much here, but the new family is great. I get to talk them quite a bit this first evening, but then we prepare to leave to meet some of Nanda's friends. We go to a gas station in Carazinho to buy some drinks and then meet with them at a bar. We only stay a few minutes as we head out to the apartment of another couple. Here we have to wait a bit as they don't open the door right away, but eventually we get in, sit there for a while and then head off to a club called Hipster. The cars are parked in the parking, then tickets are purchased, and we are in. It's not that busy as we arrive and the DJ is spinning some mellow records. Some of us start talking to the owner and use me to get a VIP table: bringing in a gringo apparently counts. Later I get to have some nice conversations with this controversial owner. More and more people drop in and all are just sitting and drinking. This all changes when two female DJ's take control over the booth and get the party started. It's getting more packed now and the dance floor is quickly occupied by a whole bunch of hipsters. The set the DJ's are playing makes everyone wants to move their feet and eventually we leave our table and go wild. Everyone's drinking, talking, dancing, having a good time until some get hit by the booze and we all decide to go back home. I'm not really done with the party, but travel days make me tired, so I don't protest too much when we leave. It's late when we get back to Não-Me-Toque, and the visit to the middle of nowhere has started perfectly!

The next morning we leave to visit a lake house of the family in a town about an hour away by car. It's nice to see the landscape with its gloomy hills, acres of agriculture and lots of green. Cars appear as aliens in this setting, not really fitting in, and it makes it extra nice.

The lake house is on a private property among many other houses and it's a perfect getaway. The lake is beautiful and we are lucky to have a lot of sun. Nanda and me walk around, take many photos and talk about life. It's all relaxed and all the things that I've been experiencing the last three months fall into place. I see one of the most amazing sunsets with all the family from a campsite nearby and I feel once again blessed to be experiencing life in all its beauty.

At night we go to a party where we meet a lot of Nanda's friends, and end the evening with two of them, Téo and Tete. We sit in a bar with a Dutch owner, where many bikes are used for decoration. I get along very well with Téo and at the end of the night we start a bromance: we seem to be brothers, just with many kilometres between us, and with different parents.

With them we do a hike the next day on a property near Téo's family's farm, somewhere in between Carazinho, where they live, and Não-Me-Toque. The sun is shining again with all its might, to make the day very smooth and bright. We see the most beautiful scene right at the start, when two horses are drinking from a mirror of water. The very small lake is at the start of the trail, and I walk around it to see if there's more life. There's none and then we continue to walk past streams, until we get to another lake. In between we do some adventurous jumping over the little river and I climb some tree trunks. It's a perfect day. At the lake we meet some of Téo's relatives and chit chat a bit, before we head back. Then Téo makes a beautiful big bonfire in the garden of an abandoned house, where we have a great picnic.

The day after is a day of chilling around the house, uploading photos, and thinking of a next step. In the evening we go to have sushi and then to a nice bar where we listen to Bob Dylan and philosophise about life.

I spend a week in the middle-of-nowhere, but absolutely love it. It's the first time I'm not pacing around to do as much as possible and everything's sinking in. My tries to stay in Brazil longer haven't worked out however and I now have three days to leave the country. I did however postpone my flight that's supposed to bring me back to Amsterdam, and pushed back the date to the end of June.

I book a plane back to Porto Alegre, and from there a plane to Montevideo, Uruguay. Nanda and her sister bring me back to the Passo Fundo airport and we say farewell. I board the plane and within an hour I'm in Porto Alegre, where another friend picks me up to have sushi. The next day I have a flight to Montevideo.

Chapter III

URUGUAY

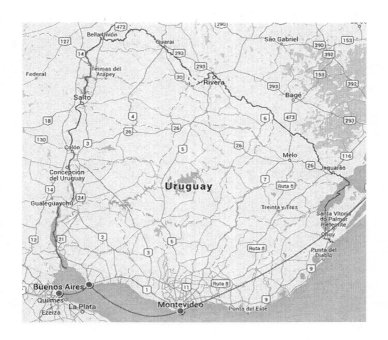

Uruguay - Montevideo, Montevideo

I arrive at the airport and have to stand in line for customs for quite a while. I'm the last one tonight to pass the officer and get my stamp to enter Uruguay. Then I get a taxi at a counter to bring me to my hotel. It's quite a drive to get there, but eventually I do. I'm confronted with a language barrier however: just as I've learned enough Portuguese to manage, I have to switch to Spanish, yet another language I've never had any lessons in. I speak Portuguese and with hands and feet I manage to make myself clear. The people in Uruguay fortunately seem to understand a bit of my 'Portuñol'.

The hotel is quite nice and the staff very friendly. I get some recommendations for some bars, and I head out to walk around a bit to check them out. I pass many monuments, old buildings, and a gorgeous theatre. I find the bars, but they don't seem to be my cup of tea, thus the night out ends early.

I start the next day with a good breakfast and then a long walk through the city. I explore the main street, the 'Avenida 18 Julio', and turning on it I bump into a Nikon store. Here I finally buy a cap to protect my lens; the original one fell from the walls of a fort into the ocean in Morro de São Paulo. In Brazil I had not found any place where I could buy it, and here within minutes I'm successful. I continue to walk to the big Olympic stadium, where a classic match will be played this Sunday: Peñarol versus Nacional. At the stadium I ask the police where I can buy the ticket and they point to a long line. I enter the line and it looks like it's going to be a long wait. After about fifteen minutes I start to notice it's mainly women and young girls in this line, so I decide to ask why they also want to go to the game and why there's so few men. They laugh at me when I ask and they tell me I'm in line for tickets for some band called One Direction... After some laughing they point me to the right counter and I walk pass the line to see some booths where's there's no people waiting. I manage to get a ticket easily and buy a seat in the Peñarol section. The opponent is the former club of a player I don't like, Luis Suarez, so I'm definitely not supporting them. After buying the tickets I buy entrance to the stadium's museum and also get inside, to see how old and rotten it is. All the concrete is falling down, and it seems it really needs a renovation. I try to get into the stand of the fanatic fans, which is called 'Amsterdam', just for the fun of it. Officials however stop me when I try to get there, saying it's not accessible for public right now. When I get outside again I take some photos of the outside of the stadium and then continue my stroll through the city. On my way I walk into shops, have some tea, and grab some lunch. I find out there's also a match tonight, so after a short stop I walk to that stadium, buy a ticket, and take a seat. This stadium is mere an amateur complex and its state is even worse than the big one. I can't believe it. Then another thing happens: the referee enters the pitch protected by the shields of military police. There's no threat in the stadium at all, and I can't even see fans from the away side, nor a section with fanatic fans. All seems peaceful and then still this protection. When the match is well underway more and more people fill the stands, but an atmosphere stays out. It can be the cold, as it's around 5 Celsius, and I'm nearly freezing. The level of play is horrendous and it's more about how to hit the leg of the opponent than it is about kicking a ball. It's a tough match and I start to understand why the referee is protected. The audience doesn't appreciate any decision he makes and he's being targeted with yells and screams throughout the match. At the final whistle the score is 1-1 and I walk back to the hotel through dark and empty streets. I don't feel unsafe. It's a big step forward from the abandoned nightly streets of Brazil.

I again wake up early the next morning and decide to make another walk, more north. Here I come across some government buildings, and finally find a church that was marked as being worth visiting. It's closed however, but its architecture is impressive nevertheless. Then I hear shouting and it sounds as if there's a football match going on. I follow the sound and enter another amateur complex where two other top tier teams are playing. This time I don't have a ticket and because the game has already started I don't want to spend my money on it. Instead I find a fence from where I can see it all happen after I climb in it. Other people soon hang next to me in the fences and together we see an atmosphere, and also another rough match. The away team is supported by some thousands fans and they have some pyro and sing throughout the 90 minutes. The home team wins though, 2-1, which leaves the biggest crowd happy. In the meantime I've met a guy from France, Nico, who I walk back to town with. He's been travelling for a long time already and provides me with some tips about other Southern American countries. We pass the old train station, which is now totally abandoned, but still impressive as a building. Eventually our paths separate and we exchange details for maybe a future meeting. I head back to the hotel and chill the rest of this day.

The next day is a big day: derby time! I wake up with excitement to see yet another important match. When I walk on the main avenue I see a lot of black and yellow, the Peñarol colours. People carrying flags, wearing jerseys, it looks like it's going to be a big day for them. When I reach the park near the stadium I see a parade coming from the city, with the people carrying banners, singing and making a lot of noise. I'm of course standing out as someone who's not Uruguayan, but there's no hostile approach. When I reach the stadium everything is black and yellow. I don't see any fan of Nacional, until I try walk around the stadium, and walk into perimeters, which totally separates the two groups of fans. A massive police force is present to separate the sides. I try to get into the Amsterdam stand with my ticket, but am refused and directed to another entrance. I thought it was worth the try, even though I was a bit nervous in what mess I would end up in. Later I find out it was better to not be there, and I was right where I was supposed to be. I make some rounds through the stands, before taking a seat, not too far from the fanatics. This is how I think, but even in the pre-match, between two senior teams of the clubs, I see there's almost no difference in fanaticism: everyone is going crazy against Nacional, and for Peñarol. Everyone is wearing black and yellow, and I'm happy I brought the same colours. I sit next to three girls who tell me more and more about the rivalry, about Peñarol, while the kick-off is coming closer. One of them used to have a season ticket for Amsterdam and she tells me about the continuous smell of marihuana there, about the craziness and how it's not safe to be there as a gringo. Most of the conversation is in Spanish, but fortunately they also speak English. From the moment the teams enter the pitch until the final whistle it is absolute chaos. The fans and players of Nacional are being sung to as whores and whatever more. It's crazy. It's madness. And it's not even Sparta. The atmosphere is amazing and I haven't seen this for a long time. This is equal to De Kuip, with the difference my heart doesn't beat for Peñarol and my emotions are therefore different. I get dragged into the Peñarol support though and I do sing along with the chants, which the girls are teaching me. On the pitch, history is being written, as Peñarol is humiliating the opponent. This is Celtic outplaying

Rangers, Barcelona punishing Real, Feyenoord crushing Ajax. Peñarol is everywhere, and Nacional is nowhere. The 1-0 is greeted with tears of joy, and so is the 2-0. At the 3-0 the people get melancholic, and at the 4-0 the fans almost feel sorry for their opponent. This is a historic win. It gets even worse at the 5-0, when all above emotions are mixed and people look at the pitch in disbelieve. The Nacional fans, who are having an entire stand for themselves, and are there with tens of thousands, were silent for a long time, but at 5-0 they start being ironic and sing on how they are the best, and lighting all the flares they have brought. With the sun setting over the edges of the stadium, the red flares, together with the smoke they produce, is giving it all a fairy tale layer. I'm being hugged and kissed by random people that just run around finding people to share their joy with. Everyone tells me how I will never understand what is happening here, but they are probably unaware my team hasn't won a thing in years and that even a 2nd place is nowadays celebrated as a championship. I'm probably more aware than anyone of what it does to people when beating the arch rivals in a superior way. The party is contagious and I'm celebrating as one of the fanatic Peñarol fans. When the final whistle blows, people gaze in disbelief at the scoreboard, which indeed is telling them: 5-0. Down at the Amsterdam side some fans rush to a stand which was kept empty and some climb the fence. It's one big delirium. The fans can't leave the stadium yet due to some safety restriction, but even if they could, they would not: no one wants to leave just yet and they all keep celebrating and singing. This continues when the gates do open and the stadium empties quickly. I walk with my new friends back to the centre and I drop them off at their apartment, agreeing on having drinks the next day.

I meet with another friend, who I met the day before on my walk, to play billiard at night and we have some drinks, also with other friends. Getting to sleep at night is hard, because adrenaline keeps rushing to my head and my memory keeps replaying the scenes in the stadium.

I don't sleep a lot, some four hours, and wake up still sleepy. Normally when I wake up, the high level of energy is immediately present, but now it's not. I feel like a zombie. I have promised myself to go to the Brazilian embassy however, as it was closed when I got there on Friday. So I drag myself there to see if I can return to Brazil right away, or that I really have to wait three months. I take a number and then have a seat and wait until I'm being helped. Nico's also here for his search for a long stay in Brazil, in order to make a documentary. We talk about possibilities and options, until it's my turn; a lovely girl helps me and says she will try to do what she can do. I spend some hours here, and even the ambassador comes out to have a talk with me. He's called with Brasilia and São Paulo to learn about the rules during the World Cup. Renata's brother in Brasilia has offered me tickets for one match in the capital, and I'm trying to use this as my leverage to get in the country. Despite the calls there's no news for me right now. They say I have to be patient, but as I'm not planning to stick around in Montevideo forever, I leave them my email address. One month later I will finally get my answer, when I'm already far, far, away.

The rest of the day I walk around this lovely city. I really like Montevideo. There's many historical buildings, beautiful churches, and the streets are always filled with people who give it a great vibe. On corners there are vendors selling food, clothes, and whatever they can. I feel safe here and at ease. The people I meet, from the waiter, to the vendor, to the randoms, to the strangers, they are all nice, friendly. They seem a little less "happy" (outgoing) than Brazilians, but instead more sophisticated, more to themselves, more thoughtful. I'm sure not all is what it looks like, but it leaves me with a feeling Montevideo is certainly a city I would want to return to.

My final afternoon in Montevideo I go to a mall, to do some shopping and get the taxi to see some sights a bit farther than I wanted to walk to. The taxi driver seems to be a friend of the hotel, which works in my advantage as it's cheap and the guy is used to showing around tourists. We visit the harbour and the market there, and some other places. Back at the hotel I have to make a tough decision: either go to Punta del Este, or to Colonia del Sacramento. Renata's brother is in Punta del Este, so it's tempting, but a Google search shows me a skyline of hotels, tourist attractions, beaches and more of what I've already seen plenty of in Brazil. The only thing I would really want to see there are the whales in front of the coast, but, as I find out, this is not their season. And another good reason to choose for Colonia, is all the good stories I have been told to by almost everyone I met in my three-month trip so far: if I really want to see a town from the colonial times, with great historic value, go there. So I book a bus and the next morning the same cab driver drops me at the bus station and I'm taking my first long bus ride of this trip...

<u>Uruguay - Colonia del Sacramento, Colonia</u>

The bus is not as comfortable as the buses in Argentina in 2009, and the time moves slowly. The bus stops a lot, and the people come and go. I thought it was a two-hour drive, but it seems to be around four. This is not leaving me in the best of moods when I finally arrive at the bus terminal of Colonia. From here it's a small walk to my hotel, but the road is made of cobblestones and my bag on wheels is not really suited for this. I do get to the hotel and the style, decoration, and feeling of this, makes me change in a good way: it's really amazing and after checking in I get to a lovely room with maybe the best bed of my trip so far. If this is an introduction of what Colonia will bring me, I'm very happy to be here.

The next hours I spend searching for what the people were raving about when they recommended me going here. I'm also trying to match the fantastic words I read in travel books and magazines, that all tell me great things about this town. I don't find any match, at all. It's the biggest disappointment I've experienced in travelling so far. I decide to chat with my dad at night over Skype and he was here too, left in the same disappointment as I am now. This really is a shit town. And I can't imagine how people like this. This has to be pure propaganda. The power of the press. The power of words. There's no ancient atmosphere here. There's no cute small streets lit by cosy coloured street lights. There's no amazing ceilings inside the buildings, there's no square where people come together. There's nothing here. What a bullshit town. I head out at night to find a restaurant and when it's dark, you are happy you can't see all the crap of this town. The restaurant I find is nice though, like a living room, with good food and friendly staff. It's such a big contrast to what I see and experience outside though.

Before going to bed I reread some articles on the internet, thinking I might have missed something, and I fall asleep with the idea to explore more tomorrow and see if I maybe missed something.

I try it with all efforts the next day, but it's the same disappointing story. After walking the same streets over and over, I know it's time to leave as soon as possible. I rush to the hotel, tell them there will be no other night, I grab my stuff, and rush over those stupid cobble stones again, to the modern ferry terminal. Here I buy a ticket for the ferry to Buenos Aires, a city I know I loved back in 2009. Up to civilisation, to culture, to history. As long as I can leave this shithole, as nothing can be worse.

Chapter IV

ARGENTINA

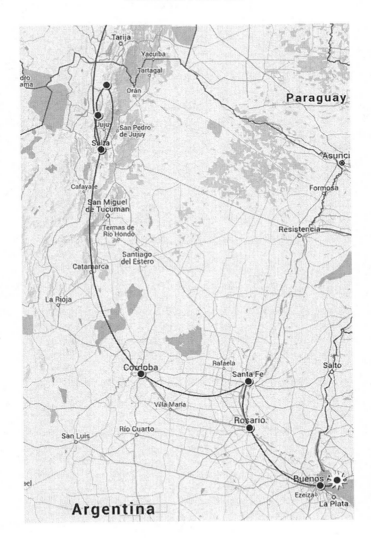

85

Argentina - Buenos Aires, Distrito Federal

Boat trips aren't my favourite, but the one hour cross from Colonia to Buenos Aires is a piece of cake. It's a huge boat, with chairs like in an airplane, and a television showing some Champion's League match. I make some friends here, and they ask me to join them for a party later tonight.

Leaving the ship and finding transport is chaotic, as there's too many people, not enough taxis and many people trying to get something from you. I fortunately get in a cab who just dropped off another passenger, and ask him to bring me to my boutique hotel in the area called Palermo, from what I remember is great for its restaurants and nightlife. While being driven to the hotel however, I notice a kind of sadness around the city. It doesn't seem to be maintained too much and it is dirty. More homeless people stroll the streets and from what I'm seeing I'm not getting the same vibe as I did five years ago, when I told myself I could see myself living here. Of course I had read about the economic problems in Argentina, but I never imagined it would be so visible to me. I talk about it with the cab driver, as there is heavy traffic and the time to talk is plenty. He tells me about how he has to be a teacher before and now makes crazy work days of sometimes 18 hours a day to pay his bills and support his family. However, the situation in the northeast of Brazil is probably even worse, I'm shocked because I did not expect this, at all.

The hotel is nice, and the staff supporting. Most of them are from Peru and are studying and working here. My room is spacious and booking.com's reviews have not let me down once again. At night I walk through Palermo until I find a nice sushi restaurant where I wine and dine, and meet some nice people, by whom I'm invited to their table and we talk until I nearly fall asleep at the table. I walk back home, and vastly fall asleep.

I'm enjoying a good breakfast before I get picked up by my dance teacher from Jeri, who's living here and I kept in touch with throughout the journey. She's offered to drive me around in her car and show me the sights I want to see. I'm seeing the same sadness as yesterday and through talking with Gaby, I realise this country is in a world of shit. Nearly bankrupt and the economy is going downhill with a high speed. And there's no hope at the horizon...

We start the tour in La Boca, where the stadium of the famous Boca Juniors is situated and where the tango is everywhere on the streets.

In 2009 I visited a match of Boca Juniors which was a great experience. Today I only see the stadium from the outside, and we walk around the neighbourhood, visiting some stores. There's many fan-shops with even more different kinds of jerseys. In 2009 I felt like the only tourist there, and now they move around in swarms. I can hardly see any locals. We take the car to drive from the stadium to the other touristy area of La Boca, where we see the tango, street artists, graffiti and many restaurants. I get to eat a very nice cookie here, which is typically from here. We walk until we reach the river and then head back. Then we take the car past other historical sights and even see yet another huge demonstration moving through the streets like a snake. They are obviously protesting against the government, and from what I know now, I can't blame them. We continue our way and I'm surprised how many sights I've already seen five years ago, and how clearly I remember them all. Because of this we rush by a lot of things like Japanese tourists: drive, stop, photo, drive, stop, photo, repeat. We decide to get to the other side of the city and visit the stadium of River Plate, Boca's arch rivals, and the club Gaby is a socio of. It's situated in a wider area, a bit north of everything. The stadium is huge and we walk around to see as much as we can. We can't enter unfortunately, even though I do an effort by climbing in the fence. At night we have a dinner in Palermo and then I'm dropped off at my hotel. I've seen enough of Buenos Aires and decide I will move forward much faster than I would ever have imagined. I book a flight to Rosario, which is due the next day.

Argentina - Rosario, Santa Fe

I've never been in Rosario, but a family from this city has visited me in Amsterdam. I'm invited to stay at their place, and I'm picked up at the airport of Rosario. In the plane I was sitting next to the squad of Estudiantes, another famous Argentinian football team. The home of the family is situated near the Rosario Central football stadium. The jersey of this team was given to me in the Netherlands, and my research told me the fans of this club are amongst the most fanatic. And it happens there will be a match tomorrow... I'm in, of course I am.

The first night we have dinner with Liliana (mother), Mariel (daughter) and Ricardo (father) and we talk about our mutual experiences and my findings of Argentina so far.
I get my own room in their big house and it's perfect. Without realising it, whatever I gave them in Amsterdam, is given back to me here, and more. I fall asleep happily.

The next day is another match day: Rosario Central will play Olimpo. The son of the neighbours will take me there and I don't have to worry about the ticket. In the morning we go to the centre of the city by car and pick up some stuff from Lili's pharmacy, and then also visit a monument. We also have to change the car's tire, as it's pretty much done. After a lunch at the house I get picked up by the guy next door. I've left my phone and bank cards in my room, and have my grey blonde hair covered under a cap. I also bring my sunglasses. All in order to be not recognised as a tourist. In Argentina you can only buy tickets as a member of the club and all is strictly regulated. There's also no away fans allowed in the stadiums, as brutal violence was very common, with many fans dying from riots and shootings. I get a season ticket with a photo of some other guy in my hands and instructions from my new friends on how to behave. We have to get past at least four checkpoints before we get into the stadium, three of which are military police ones. Even though I'm not that worried, I feel my heart beating in my throat when I walk past the first checkpoint. They don't look at me, as there's a mass of people moving at the moment. The second and third check are also easily passed and when some club official finally quickly checks the card I'm showing him, I'm inside. This was a piece of cake. There seem to be no rules inside the stadium, as I see zero officials and no more ticket checks. We can go wherever we want from now on, and we walk to the second floor, through clouds of weed. The smell of Amsterdam is welcoming me once again. We find a place and there meet many other people my friends know. It's a big group. Surprisingly again many women dressed in the colours of the team, without being accompanied by guys. Some get the giggles when they find out there's a gringo in their midst. We wait until the players get to the field and then a massive banner is being rolled out while the fans continuously sing a song which I have no clue what it's about, but after hearing it for fifteen minutes it sticks in my head non-stop. There are fans standing on little fences with a bandana wrapped around their body, jumping up and down like crazy. The entire stand is actually jumping and fanatically singing. The passion is all over the place and this continues throughout the match. What happens on the pitch is very poor, and my attention is mainly focused on the fans. It feels like a big get-together of friends and they discuss things beyond football. They realise they're not here only for the football, but for the bond: to cheer, and to suffer, together, to create a band, a band of brothers. The match ends as it started: 0-0. I believe the support in this section was amongst the best I've experienced so far in South America, and better than what I saw in my other Argentinian match in Boca Junior's stadium in 2009.

Leaving the stadium is much easier than getting in, and together with two of my new friends we walk home. There we say goodbye and I enter the house to rave about my experiences.

I slept early the previous day, after having a nice dinner, and many nice talks again. Today me and Mariel will go on a bike tour through the city. Mariel is one of the people trying to get Rosario to become a bike-friendly city, and is doing very well at this, as the bike lanes show in the centre later that day. It's a nice and sunny day to pedal through the Rosario streets and see some landmarks. Mariel's parents join us for a great lunch, before we bike back. Then Lili and Ricardo take me in a car to see all the other sights of the city and we spend great times at the big central monument, the synagogue, and finally the Ché Guevara monument, as Ché was born here. We also pass the Rosario Central rival's stadium, the one of Newell's Old Boys, known as Lionel Messi's first team. In between all the stops we have a stop at a very neat bar where we have a drink. Just outside the bar we witness an accident and see a guy laying on the ground after being hit by a car. It's quite disturbing to see, and we're happy there's police at the scene.

At night we have yet another delicious dinner and I try to organise my photos and upload them.

I continue doing this the next day and I don't even leave the house. It's nice to just chill for a day, and hug the dogs whenever they come to ask for attention. In between I'm being treated on a great lunch and dinner. I can't wish for anything else and my stay in this city has been great. When doing nothing though, it always makes me think of where to go next, and I decide to move more north, to Santa Fe, where some friends live that I've met in Morro de São Paulo. The rest of the day I spend puzzling about my itinerary for the upcoming days, weeks and months, as my good friend from Amsterdam, Eduard, is planning to join me when I go to the Galápagos. As he also needs to buy a ticket, I have to tell him some dates and this is cracking my brain: I have to let go of the go with the flow attitude and my last minute decisions and actually plan something, which seems to be a big challenge. Keeping in mind someone wants to visit me on my journey is making it well worth the efforts though.

Next day's breakfast is the final one in Rosario and I say farewell to the dogs, before being taken to the bus station by Lili and Ricardo. Mariel works near the bus station and she comes out quickly to say hi. We meet another family friend there and the three of them end up waving goodbye to my bus. I'm in the second floor of the bus, all alone, on my way to Santa Fe.

Argentina - Santa Fe, Santa Fe

I have never been to Santa Fe before, nor have I ever read anything about it. The only thing I know is I'm touch with a great friend who has invited me to her city. The ride is fairly short and easy and I arrive in the city in the afternoon. I struggle a bit in finding my hotel, but eventually I do. It's a very old fashioned hotel, which is stuck in the 1950's it seems. My room is small and noisy, but it has a bed and private bathroom, which is all I need. I rest a bit upon arrival and then go out to find a place to have a late lunch. I find a place in some kind of sport's bar in the main shopping street, which is very close to the hotel. Here I chat with the staff and watch some old football flashes on the screens.

During making plans in Rosario my hosts recommended me to visit the north of Argentina and after hearing their stories I'm eager to go there. There's just one slight problem: it can get very cold there, high in the mountains. In the shops of Santa Fe I search for warmer clothes, as I will probably not manage in the clothes I brought for my three months in Brazil. It's expensive however and I don't really succeed in finding what I want, despite walking in and out many of the shops. I head back to the hotel and then find myself walking to the hospital where Luciana works as a doctor later that evening. She's invited me for dinner at her parent's place, so after she's done seeing some patients and showing me the hospital, we walk there. The hospital is by the way in a quite poor condition, and I can't figure out yet how people are being helped in the chaos. But they manage it seems, and in the end it all looks better than what I've seen in Brazil. And, like in Brazil, all the people I meet are amazingly nice and friendly.

We walk to Luciana's home through a mall and past some buildings that are being lit in nice colours. The house we enter is very nice and again filled with amazing people. They serve the best food and it tastes like it was prepared with love. The talks are numerous and the laughs plenty. Luciana has a great family and they've welcomed me with open arms.

After dinner I walk to my hotel, which is a fair distance. The streets are quite empty and the people that are on the streets all look a bit shady. I'm cautious of what might be, and speed walk to my hotel to fall asleep there in a snap of a finger.

When waking up I'm just in time to grab a lousy breakfast. The food tastes as old as the building looks. Something is better than nothing though, and I eat some croissants and drink some orange juice. Then I head out to explore the city. I've made some screenshots on my phone of websites telling me the cool spots and with that as my guide I soon am striping things off my list. The city has numerous old buildings and some nice churches, but it lacks a concentrated centre with a historic heart. Some school children start talking to me in Spanish and I'm quite lost in translation, as slowing down is something they don't seem to know, despite my request. I buy some fruit from a street vendor and sit in a park to eat it and look at the life passing by. Then I walk to another church and chill in another park. It's nice, but it's not making me thrilled. I rate the city itself as average. Its people however are ace again.

I walk to Luciana's home where I pick her up for a walk in the afternoon and we cross the bridge into a very nice natural reserve, where we see some nice birds. Rain makes some trails inaccessible, but nevertheless we get to a viewpoint at a lake, not far from one of the universities in the city. We continue to the river shore when we exit the park and sit on a bench there and hear the water splash calmly to the shore. Dogs are running by and their owners peacefully following. We talk a lot, about past, present and future and have a good time doing so. When the sun starts setting we head back of the bridge and walk on the boulevard on the other side, where now many people are on an evening stroll or run. I'm extremely thirsty and the first bar we find I rush in to get a banana milkshake. Delicious. Then we walk back to Lu's home and talk with the family there until we are being picked up by one of her best friends for dinner.

The restaurant is very nice and the food delicious. The company is of course even better, as always. We talk for hours and I don't notice the clock ticking and the time passing. Working people have to go home however and we are taken back to Lu's home, where I say goodbye to everyone. Tomorrow I will continue to the city of Córdoba by bus and my stay in Santa Fe turns out to be another short one.

I sleep in for a bit, have my breakfast and then walk to the bus station, where I arrive much too early. First I walk around a bit in order to find some fruits, which seems an impossible mission. When I finally succeed I head back to the station, sit down and let the wait game begin. My three bags stand in front of me; my big 20kg, one backpack with all my cameras and electronic equipment, and one small bag with foods and extra clothes for the road.

The terminal is busier than when I arrived in Santa Fe, two days ago. The seat left and right of me do not remain empty for long. A woman seats herself next to me, and soon a girl does so on the other side. After a while this girl turns her back to me, and not much later she turns and taps my shoulder, asking where the toilet is. I point her the way, and she walks off. Just when she does so, I see she left a bunch of keys on her seat. Me and the other woman try to call for her, but she is already too far off. I decide to pick up my stuff and do a good deed, and follow her to give her the keys back. She is paying at the counter for the toilet when I reach her and hand her back the keys. She answers with a warm and well meant "gracias". I don't feel like walking back to my other seat and take a seat on a bench near the toilets. Not much later the girl exits and smiles, nodding to say thank you again. She takes place on a bench not far from mine and focuses on her two phones.

Just then a guy walks by and drops his wallet, without noticing, and continues. Me and another guy see it and try to call him. He does not respond. The other guy picks up the wallet and runs after him. The guy is happy when he gets his wallet back and even offers the finder money. The offer is refused. I look at it and think me and the other guy are good persons. The girl in the meantime has bought some chocolate and is eating it. She looks my way. I look back. Then she walks to my bench and sits on the other side. I turn around and ask her where she is from. We talk for a short time. She tells me she is going to Córdoba. I tell her I'm going there too. While talking to her I think I am the first foreigner she has ever talked to. Her eyes gaze at me as if I am an alien. Not much later her phone rings and she stands up, and she moves as if she walks away. Then she comes back and sits herself next to me. I turn my head to the left so I can talk to her, while my bags are a bit to my right. At one point I turn my head to the right, because I saw movement and a guy stands with my backpack in his hands. I grab it and pull it back to me. He shows some keys, pretending he was looking for those. My adrenaline level goes sky high. I however calmly tell him to fuck off. The girl says I should put my bag in between my legs, in order to prevent such things from happening. I tell her I have to go to the toilet, and grab my stuff to go there. She states she will wait for me. Five minutes later I return and she is gone. I get suspicious. But my bus leaves in ten minutes and I still need to buy water. So I search for a place and run into the girl again. She calmly says she went anyways because it took me so long. Then she walks me to a place where I can buy water. My heart is beating fast and I don't trust her, and suspect her in having a part in the attempt of the theft of my bag. I quickly say bye and walk to my bus. There I talk to a security man, who says he can't do anything and that these kinds of robberies are very common here, and then I enter the bus and take off.

Argentina - Córdoba, Córdoba

For the entire ride the adrenaline is rushing through my body. I still can't believe all this was happening, and can't wrap my head around it yet. Upon arrival in Córdoba's bus station, which I know due to my previous visit in 2009, I'm not trusting anyone except myself. Therefor I also decide to walk to my hotel, instead of taking a taxi. According to Google Maps it's less than thirty minutes, so it should be doable. I'm conscious about all people around me and more than once I look back seeing if I'm being followed or if I see someone suspicious. I realise my behaviour is a bit over the top, but can't seem to help myself right now. It feels like a natural consequence of the things that went down earlier today. It's already dark when I reach my nice hotel and check in. I feel like sharing the attempt of robbery and it helps in my advantage as I get an upgrade for my room and have a free choice of room. The staff is thoughtful for helping me out this way. After leaving my stuff in my room I head down again and head out for a night walk and see all the squares, old buildings, churches, beautifully spotlighted. As I've been to Córdoba before nothing is new to me, but this city is still a historical gem to me. In one of the churches I see an announcement for Faure's requiem the next day and tell myself to go there tomorrow. Then I sit myself down in a nice restaurant where I have a pasta dinner. I get back to the hotel past midnight and struggle with falling asleep for a long time.

Even though I have a perfect room, my night of sleep was not that great. The movie of the Santa Fe bus station was replaying in my head for a long time. I have my breakfast whilst my eyes keep closing and I'm yawning non-stop. The food gives me energy fortunately and after this I'm ready to head out and explore the city once more. I visit the same buildings and enter the churches to see the beautiful decoration. In between the touristy things I'm shopping for warm clothes. This morning I've booked my flight to Salta and the cold is now coming closer. Once more I don't succeed. I also find time to visit a barber and have a haircut. It's not one of my favourite activities, especially abroad. In Brasilia I had my last one, but I was assisted by Renata who translated all my wishes to her befriended barber. Now I am all alone and in my basic Spanish explaining what I want. The woman helping me understands everything perfectly though and soon the three hairs on my head are retouched.

After this I spend a decent amount of time in the university complex and get in touch with several students and professors, who all think it's pretty nice I'm having such a big trip all by myself. In between these acts I observe the cats sunning on the patio. I head back to the hotel for a dinner in the hotel's restaurant and then hurry myself to the church for the requiem of Faure. This classical piece is my uncle's favourite and the first time I've seen this was on Omaha Beach, at D-Day's 60th anniversary. Back then it gave me goose bumps throughout the performance as the setting was haunting. Now I'm amidst depressed Argentineans in a church of Córdoba awaiting what it will be. And again I'm getting touched by this piece of music. It's short, around an hour, but intense and when looking around at the faces of the audience, I'm not the only one thinking like this. To my left a woman is continuously wiping off her tears, and at my right a guy can't keep his mouth closed as he's gasping all the time. Even though the surrounding isn't as special as Normandy in 2004, the evening finds a place in my heart and memory. After the final notes there's a long applause for the performers and I'm one of the last people leaving the church. In a trance I walk back to the hotel and quickly fall asleep.

In the morning I have time to take a morning walk before heading to the airport and boarding the plane in the late afternoon. It's only a short flight to Argentinian's most northern big city and I arrive there when the sun is still shining.

Argentina - Salta, Salta

I take a taxi to the centre of Salta where my hotel is situated. It's a very nice hotel once again with an uttermost friendly staff. The room consists of one big bed and a separate bathroom. It's all recently modernised and perfect for my two nights here.

I then take a walk to the centre, where all important buildings are highlighted and I see a lot of history in a few square metres. I can't enter any of the buildings, but obviously this stuff is old. I circle around for a while, drift off to some side streets, but always come back to the main square. I try to retrieve money from an ATM, but the machines aren't very cooperative. As I need money to pay my tour in two days I'm getting desperate to find a bank that will work, but tonight's isn't my lucky night. After giving up I find a nice restaurant where I have dinner: as often on this trip it's chicken, salad and french fries, accompanied by a fruity milk shake. After dinner some chit chat with a small group of French tourists and then back to the hotel to sleep.

I'm walking around to see all important buildings from the in- and outside from the moment I wake up and finish my breakfast, so I can say I've at least got a little bit of everything. I also visit two museums, which aren't exactly extraordinary to me. Main focus today is to find some warm clothes and to get cash. I finally succeed in the first objective, but the second again fails. Instead of buying a winter jacket or ski pants, I decide to buy thermal underwear, as I can easy carry this with me in my luggage. It looks ridiculous though, with my long sleeved shirt and especially long underwear, that reaches until over my feet. All is white too, which makes me a milky man. It's about being practical however and I don't expect to be undressed when standing in the cold.
The money issue is giving me a headache however, because I run from bank to bank, ATM to ATM, without finding any that is accepting my debit card. I call the company that will take me on a tour the next day and they say they can stop at a bank a bit further from the centre when we leave the city tomorrow. This message relieves me a bit, and I can continue my sightseeing tour through the city, which I keep doing until late at night.

Argentina - Purmamarca, Jujuy

The day starts incredibly early as I'm being picked up by a van, filled with tourists. I check out, pay my hotel with my final cash, leave my big bag in this hotel for when I come back in I-don't-know-yet-how-many-days, and only bring what I think is necessary for my upcoming mini trip. There's already other people in the van, and I take a single seat a bit at the back. There's no interaction yet between the groups, and I'm the only one travelling alone. Before picking up the last people we stop at an ATM from which I really have to get some money. It finally works, and I'm happy as fuck. I get back in the car and off we go. Our guide firstly explains all in Spanish and then takes some time to also explain it to me in English. All other come from Spanish countries, like Colombia, or other parts of Argentina. Our first stop is at the start of the railway that goes the same way: up into the mountains, to Purmamarca, but takes a lot more time. Then we continue to a river bedding from where we see the railroad bridge and beautifully sunlit cactuses. I take the camera out and here the first interactions in the group happen. I get to talk to the woman from Colombia who's visiting, and now travelling with, her daughter. Her daughter soon joins the conversation and tells she lives in Buenos Aires and this trip is family quality time. In the van we can continue our conversation while we get to higher and higher altitudes. I've started to chew on coca leaves, what supposedly should help when you get on high elevation. My head starts hurting, despite drinking a lot of water. I take a paracetamol, as a placebo. Maybe that will wake my body up. We get into a little town, at around 3500 metres. The tire of the van is flat and now we have to wait for alternative transport. The wind is blowing hard and we get into a building where a lunch is served. I sit myself down at a table with three Argentinian friends, who are on a break of university too. We talk and eat, but the pain in my head is getting worse and worse. I feel like I'm floating and my mind is flying and my body being punched by every sound or move. We then go for a walk to the railway station, which is not that far, but on this height every step seems to be one too much for me. I'm trying to be persistent, as sitting myself in sorrow probably won't help either. I start to feel like throwing up, but nothing happens. I'm sick. All the group is there to help me fortunately and they all try to take care of me. This give me some power to continue and when we finally get into the other van I'm feeling slightly better. I keep chewing on these gross leaves, which are one of the main ingredients of cocaine. One should think this would give me energy, but it's not helping a single bit. The landscape is beautiful with some steppes, low grass, thick singular bushes and llamas. These animals walk in herds and eat the green. Every now and then there's also donkeys, horses and cows. At the horizon we now see white shimmering flats, meaning we are getting closer to our main destination. The road thinks differently as it winds around the area in a huge bow before we finally get on the road that cuts the flats in two. We stop at a building, where there's some facilities, and then get out to walk on the white soil, made of salt. It is absolutely freezing right now and I think far below zero. The wind is cutting and making all of us suffer. Some flee back in the van after just some five minutes. My clothes don't do any work, and don't keep me warm. I'm nude and being exposed to the torture of Mother Nature. The flats are quite impressive; however, the signs of industry quite ruin the view. There's machines and small buildings with chimneys, both close to us and at the horizon. Eventually I'm the last man standing and everyone is ready to continue the trip. I make a run back to the transport and upon arrival I feel like I ran a marathon: I'm totally exhausted. Now the spirit is high in the van when we continue going up and up. Music is playing and people are clapping and singing along. I have no clue what it is all about, this music, but it puts a big smile on my face. We make one more stop, at the highest point of the trip, at 4170 metres, where we take some photos before blending in the darkness of the night. All passengers are being dropped off at their accommodations in the town of Purmamarca and I'm among one of the first leaving and I'm shaking hands with everyone. Again I've made many new friends. The check in at the hotel is smooth and the room is perfect. Then I walk to a restaurant where I have a good dinner before taking a very long hot shower and falling in a deep sleep afterwards.

I've not had such a good sleep as this night in a long time. I wake up feeling reborn and when I step out the room the sky has an amazing blue colour and the sun is shining brightly. I have a great breakfast and get to talk with the staff for a long time. Then I head out and bump into my Colombian friends, who are already waiting for being picked up for the next trip. I talk to them and they point out where the three Argentinian guys are residing. I walk to their hostel and find them getting ready for a hike. The four of us not much later make a first small hike behind the village and see the most amazing colourful rock formations. Then we head to the other side where we climb upon a cliff and have a marvellous view over the small town, and the absolutely stunning colourful mountains surrounding it. Supposedly there are seven different colours, but for me that is just a number. The view is breath-taking. Soon I have to catch some air though as I get to talk to two girls who are also enjoying the view. They are also from Buenos Aires and for an indefinite time on the road. We exchange details and agree to have dinner with all of us at night. Then we continue our path and walk over a very small trail over the top of this hill, where soon we meet the other two guys again, who were far ahead whilst we were chatting with the girls. We now continue with four again, over a dry river bed, uphill. We don't know where this will lead us and after having to climb through small caves we decide it's better to turn back. We descend now and see things from a different perspective. We discover some fossils and observe them for a while. Upon arrival in the village the three guys decide to help a very old woman, who was begging for some money. Instead of giving money, the guys run into a small grocery store and buy her some stuff. I find this an amazing gesture and the woman without teeth seems to be very grateful. We have a good lunch in a quiet restaurant and then we hang out a bit on the market on the central square where rugs are being sold in all colours of the rainbow. After a while I head back to the hotel to chill a bit there and later in the evening we all meet again for a dinner.

The restaurant where we meet again is near my hotel and I meet the guys there. The girls however arrive very late. Argentinian punctuality? The guys disagree as this seems to be exceptionally late. For the girls it seems quite normal and while we listen to a guy playing guitar, we order our food and talk. The talking continues later on a big rock in the middle of town, which is not supposed to be climbed. Oops. The Argentinians smoke some weed, while I sit myself a bit from them and gasp at the bright stars. There's a police car structurally patrolling the streets and we see it move through town for the next hours. Then I get tired and leave them up there. Going down past little sliding rocks and cactuses is much harder than getting up there, but I find my way and soon lay in bed once again.

Argentina - Iruya, Jujuy

I look for a way to get to Iruya the next day. This starts by going to the bus station, where the counter is closed. I ask some people and they say you can just buy the ticket in the bus. I get my stuff from the hotel and then wait for its arrival. It's as easy as they say and I'm off to Tilcara, from where I have to change into another bus which will bring me to Humahuaca. There I will have to take another bus to Iruya. Tilcara is quickly reached and I have some time to explore the cute town before getting into my connecting bus. I walk the quiet streets and see many remarkable faces. They're so unique in my eyes, drawn by the grooves of the sun, that leaves its mark in the skin of the people here. I sit a bit in a little before and then head back to the bus station where I'm right on time to get in. It's another short drive to the next town, which is much more touristy than the previous one. There's an enormous monument in the centre of town, with a big Indian on top of it. Many steps lead to the top of the statue, and at the bottom there's many market stands, who sell original clothing, bags, toys, and all other things tourists would want. There's big groups of tourists coming and going, and most of them are elderly people. I don't see many youngsters. I walk around town, explore the little streets, shops, markets, squares and churches. Then I sit myself in a park to enjoy the sun. I sit there for quite a while and then walk back to the bus station, to grab my bus to Iruya. The two previous buses were modern touring ones, but the one I have to get in now is something from an ancient history. It doesn't look and sound that trustworthy, but there's no other choice. The bus is quite full and mainly brings back school children, and locals, to their houses and villages along the way. There's few tourists, and they are all spread out in the bus. The bus climbs out of the valley, up into the mountains and we reach high once again. The landscape's beautiful once more and the road winds its way through it. I'm glad I don't feel sick like on my other trip, and I'm listening to music while the bus gets more empty the further we get. The sun is also setting and the road gets smaller. We pass steep cliffs and I'm a little concerned we might fall in. The driver seems to know what he's doing, so I'm not too worried. The sun going down brings stunning sights in these high mountains. The shades create an entire new world. All tourists have their noses against the windows, if they're not sleeping. It seems to take forever and ever, but finally we get to the town. We're dropped off at a road and immediately are jumped by people who are renting out rooms. I tell them I already have a reservation and ask for directions. I have to go up a very steep road, and will then find it there. I'm struggling on my way up, as I once again underestimated the impact of the altitude on my body. When I finally reach the hotel, I'm totally devastated and out of breath. The staff immediately gives me some water and I sit down before I can start the check-in. I get another spacious room in this quiet and luxurious hotel. Dinner is also served here and it tastes delicious. Back in my room I fall asleep quickly.

The next day I start observing the condors that are circling high above the hotel. Then I have a breakfast that mainly consists of fruits. I take up my walking shoes, pack my camera bag and then start my hike to San Isidro, which is supposedly a 1.5-hour walk. The sun is high in the sky, the birds are chirping and the path is winding down past other houses, until I reach a point where two valleys come together and the rivers from both mingle. I follow the sign saying San Isidro and basically walk over a wide river bed, with a small stream in the middle. I don't see any other people, and therefore need to find my own way, as the trail itself is not marked and the horse road is too windy and also leads through the rapid streaming water. I catch an elder couple who I've seen at this morning's breakfast and start talking with them. They're both super friendly Americans, from Colorado, and I decide to walk with them, until they get tired and turn back. We agree to talk later in the hotel. I continue my way, and am surrounded by colourful mountains once again. Every step I start feeling the altitude again and after a while it seems like my feet are stuck in the mud and every time I have to drag my shoes out of it. It's becoming a struggle more and more. The curiosity to San Isidro, and what there is to be seen behind every next curve of the valley, is what keeps me going. I take a lot of breaks, sitting down, drinking water, and enjoying the complete solitude. I'm getting problems with breathing, although it's not as high as it was in the trip to Purmamarca. Being alone in this situation is not very ideal, I realise, but I still go on. Then I finally see San Isidro. I should be happy, but I'm not, as it's situated on a steep cliff and the road to it is insanely steep. I sit down and observe the road from quite a distance. In my current shape it seems impossible and after hesitating for quite some time, I decide I have to return and not to make these final 500 metres. The way back is downhill, and goes a bit faster. I'm taking enough breaks now, and drink plenty of water, some of which comes from the river, as my two bottles have run out. The final part of the trail is up again and I walk as slow as someone behind a walker. It's really inch by inch movement. Yesterday I arrived out of breath at the hotel, but today is even worse, and I'm happy my heart is still working when I arrive. I quickly go to my room, where in seconds my body seems to surrender to the conditions. I hurry myself to the bathroom and I have to throw up continuously until I'm completely empty. I thought this would give relief, but I keep feeling miserable, as if I can faint any second. I lay down, try to drink water, and take some more placebo, aka paracetamol. After a while I drag myself to the restaurant, where I had a reservation for the dinner, and ask them for some fruit. They immediately see I'm not doing very well, and give me a dozen apples, and some oranges, as well as six bottles of water. I go back to my room and don't leave it anymore until the next morning.

When I wake up in the morning, I feel the altitude nearly killed me yesterday. I'm still not hungry, and I'm wondering how I have to proceed from here. I decide to have some dry bread and more fruits for breakfast and there meet the American couple again. I tell them my situation and without a blink of an eye they invite me to join them in the car back to Humahuaca. This is great news for me, as I could not imagine myself going into that shaking bus right now. Not much later I sit in the back of the rental car and hear about all their amazing travel experiences. They are birders and we stop every now and then to spot them. It's so much better to get through this landscape in a car, instead of a bus. It gives the freedom to stop wherever and see whatever seems interesting. This road trip can't last too long as it's great and I don't see any age difference between me and these retirees. When we finally arrive in Humahuaca it is kind of sad. They leave me right at the bus station, where I buy a ticket to the bus and then walk around with them for a little bit, before they move on to Purmamarca. I have some time to kill and fortunately get to talk to some locals, who tell me more about their life here. They aren't influenced by the West and popular music is non-existent to them. It seems they have all they need and are very happy in this way. Materialism is not known to them and it makes me wonder. Being a collector of many things, like books and movies, it surprises me how unimportant they now seem to me. I'm on the road, collecting my own memories, and realising this is what really counts for me.

The bus back to Salta is a direct one, and takes some hours. I nap in the bus, listen to music, while I try to ignore the horribly bad movie they have put on. From the bus station in Salta I walk back to the hotel where another room awaits me, as well as fresh and clean clothes. I walk into town and decide upon a 'safe' dinner in the restaurant I was before. The staff recognises me and gives me a table in the over-crowded place. I eat chicken and rice and feel better after that. It was only yesterday I was sick, and I'm happy I recover so quickly.

Chapter V

BOLIVIA

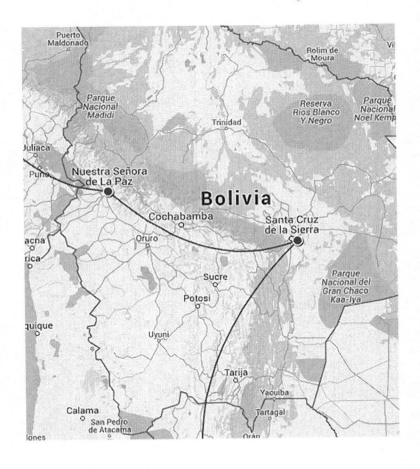

Bolivia - La Paz, Departamento de La Paz

I wake up feeling up for the challenge of going to La Paz and landing at one of the world's highest airports (4061 metres). The flight leaves very early and breakfast is not even officially served when my cab comes to pick me up. It's a fairly short drive to the airport and I'm well on time. I have to make a stopover in Santa Cruz, Bolivia, for some time, leaving me focused on the travelling all day. The Santa Cruz airport seems to be quite new and big, and I find out this city is the upcoming city in Bolivia and many companies are moving here from La Paz, as it's much easier accessible in all ways than the capital. The stopover is smooth and soon I fly towards La Paz, world's highest situated capital city, at around 3640 metres. The view from the plane is crazy, so beautiful. I see the gigantic mountains of the Andes with snow white peaks beneath me and try to take some impossible photos of it. Then La Paz itself shows up in a sort of crater in between mighty rock formations. It's like a hidden fairy-tale city from this high in the sky and I'm the angel descending to it. I've bought a pill at Santa Cruz airport that should take care of altitude problems, and I've taken it right after take-off from Santa Cruz. I see almost everyone falls asleep upon approach of La Paz. The landing is smooth and with a blink of an eye I'm at the small airport of Bolivia's capital. I take a cab outside, which brings me to my hotel in the city of La Paz. It's a new hotel, with all modern facilities, opposite of the impression the city has given me so far. The drive from the airport down to the city is a gorgeous one: the airport is situated some couple of hundred metres higher than most of the city and thus gives me a great view. The hotel staff welcomes me with a drink and then lets me fill out some forms, before bringing me to my luxury room. It's a great place and soon after I have a late lunch at the hotel bar and chat with the staff there, practicing my Spanish and getting familiar with the Bolivian accent. For me it's not much different than from what I've heard in Uruguay and Argentina, but I'm sure people who actually know the language will notice a difference. I then go check out the mall and cinema which are in the same building as the hotel, and walk around a bit there. Surprisingly I don't have that much problems with the altitude here, like I had in northern Argentina. I return to the hotel, have another small meal and ask the staff to help me with planning a day trip for the next day. After deciding what I want to see, they find me a taxi that will drive me around the entire day. I get some special coca teas before going to bed and falling asleep.

The cab picks me up right after breakfast the next day and the guy is a nice chap, who, of course, doesn't speak any English. I had asked for a cheap ride, and cheap means no English. The staff in my hotel all speak fluent English, this is a requirement for getting hired. I later will find out that a lot of young people in Bolivia speak English very well.

The taxi brings me first to Valle de la Luna (Moon Valley) and leaves me there to explore it, while the driver takes a nap. The park of Moon Valley is quite amazing, having rock formations which seem to be, logically, from the moon. The spires rise up in different variations, colours, shapes and height, making it wonderful to walk around it. Here it's up and down again, and I move slowly, eager to avoid any breathing problems this time. I see different kinds of birds and am captured by some hummingbirds, who feed themselves on the flowers. It's my first try to photograph these speedy tiny birds, and I think I succeed at least one time. I continue walking around before getting back to my taxi and consult the driver on what to do next. We decide to see the Muela del Diablo (Devil's Tooth), a single rock standing out over the city and according to tradition this was the tooth of Satan. We head back to the city first and then go into some neighbourhoods, and I get the idea my driver has no clue where to go, or that he has never been here before. He stops to ask several times, and we then get onto a very bad road, that winds up the hills. We get higher, and soon rise above the city, giving a great view, which is different from the one at the airport. Now I can see the snow topped mountains surrounding the city again, the ones I saw from the plane as well. It's a very impressive sight and these Goliaths seem to be the protectors of the city from my point of view. The Tooth also comes closer now and we pass a little valley, which used to be a crater of a volcano, and now has a very small living community, including a school, and a sport's field. Further up the road we see a van standing still, and soon we find out the van can't drive up the hill because it's too steep. We try to get up, but fail as well. This means the car is parked and I have to continue by foot. I'm above 3800 metres now and walking is tough again. I'm taking it easy and stop for every bird I can photograph, having an excuse to go slow. On top I find a parking, meaning decent cars should be able to get up here. I walk a bit up to the Tooth, but it's steep and the trail is over high rocks, so I soon decide to not go further by myself. I turn back and calmly walk back to the taxi. We start the descend and wave to a big group of tourists that we saw walking up before and who now are descending as well, not being bothered by a winding road, and just walking down in a straight steep line. After this adventure we go see the football stadium of the city, which now can't host any international official games anymore as its altitude makes it almost impossible to play at for opponents of the Bolivian teams. I don't manage to get in, and only walk around it. The taxi then drops me off at the hotel, suddenly surprisingly charging me more than the agreed fee. I feel like I'm being ripped off, as the fee was set, but now the guy, who was my friend-for-a-day, tells me going up the road at the Devil's Tooth took a lot from his car and this costs extra. I ask him why he didn't inform me before, and his answer is that he informs me now. For me a moment to frown, but he stoically looks at me, wondering how this moment would be the wrong moment. Reluctantly I pay him and then nod goodbye, feeling a little bit pissed off about it. Soon I calculate the difference and for me it's not even that much money, so I easily let it go. I wonder why my principal reaction was so annoyed, and conclude I feel I was being treated unfair. For the cab driver it was very normal however, and for a moment I felt lost in translation. The staff of the hotel is also surprised by my story and immediately calls the taxi company, even though I try to prevent making a real situation out of it. During the call they seem to understand my gestures and later explain me what was discussed: in the future fees will be communicated in advance to the taxi clients, so situations like mine will be prevented. I eat dinner in the hotel restaurants and get to talk with Tony and James, an American and a Brit, who are also travelling by themselves. We have some good conversations and when James leaves, Yolanda, from Nicaragua, replaces him in the conversation. We all have dinner together and talk until bed time.

I have breakfast with Yolanda, as all the others already seem to have left for tours or whatsoever. I will go to the historical downtown today; to which I decide to walk right after breakfast. Soon I give up the walk though, as it's uphill and I hate uphill. A taxi is cheap and less effort and soon I rush through crazy La Paz traffic and let the taxi drop me off at the main church. From there I walk through the small streets filled with activities. Shops are open, vendors sitting or sleeping outside and there's many tourists here. There's rugs and hats in all possible colours again and the typical Bolivian faces can be seen everywhere. The old women wear bowler hats and this is how one would recognise someone from Bolivia. These hats once were imported by the Brits, but the heads of the Bolivian men were too big, so the supply of hats went to the women and it's their protection from the sun now, and their tradition. I walk over the witches' market and see the most disturbing things, like dried frogs, animal bones, and dried llama foetuses, yuck. This is Bolivian ritual tradition, and attracts many tourists.

I walk into a travel agency to get some information on climbing one of those white topped mountains, which is advertised a lot on signs on the streets. I talk with the ladies inside and soon find out this is not for me right now. It's cold, hard and you need to be in better shape for it. I can't handle any of this, so I take a folder and get out. The next stop is more my cup of tea: I see an agency advertising with the jaguar. I walk up the stairs and get in an office where two girls are working. I ask for information and I receive a presentation about Madidi park. The girl who's helping me loves it there and without trying to convince me to book anything, we get into a vivid conversation about wildlife. Apart from with some of my guides in the northeast I have not had many conversations like this. I get excited to see the wildlife of Madidi, and tell her I will come back later to pick up the prices, as she has to check them, among the availability. After strolling the streets a bit more, I come back and find out I can't go to the park within the next 48 hours, but that the next week could be an option. It's tempting, but I decide to not do it, as I don't want to pin myself down yet. I leave my details and then continue my walk. I get in touch with a group of people wearing blue vests and who are there to help tourists find their way in the city. It's a great initiative which goes both ways: the people can practice English, and the tourists are being helped. We talk for quite a while. I later meet them again at the church, after our roads separated before. There I take some photos with and of them, and also get requested to be in the photo with three ladies from Santa Cruz, and who think my eyes are worth being photographed.

My new tourist guide friends tell me about a zebra story I read about in my hotel: people can go on the street in a zebra outfit and help pedestrians safely cross the streets. I find it hilarious, and can't stop laughing. They also think it's funny, but also point out there's even a waiting list for it, and that the help is quite effective: there's now less accidents and people are more aware. When their work is done I walk with my new friends to their office and visit the gallery there, before being escorted to their other work place. Here we say goodbye and I walk back to my hotel, downhill. On a square about five minutes from my hotel I stop at a very little supermarket, where I buy some drinks and snacks. When I have to pay I can't believe it's so cheap and I ask for a recount. The girl working there confirms the price is right and her sincere smile and laugh upon my reaction is wonderful. We get to talk and she tells me she helps her parents out with the shop, while she is still studying. My Spanish apparently is hilarious as it cracks her and her friend up. Her mom seems to understand me so-so, and when we switch to English, she totally backs out the conversation. We continue for a while and this very cute little shop with the friendliest people becomes my bar for the night. I arrive back at the hotel much later than expected, where I have a dinner and then go to sleep.

During my stay in La Paz I have also been organising my next step in the trip: Peru, and more specifically the famous Machu Picchu. I'm trying to find out how to get there, what the requirements are, and if there's room for going there on the flow, as the area became restricted some years ago. I also book a flight from La Paz to the historical Peruvian city of Cusco, which is also base 'camp' for the trip to Machu Picchu. My flight leaves today with Amazonia Air, and is scheduled around 11:00 in the morning. James from England has the same flight, as he has a connecting flight the next morning from Cusco to Lima, and that same day from Lima to Iguazu and then to Rio de Janeiro: a very tight schedule. At breakfast he already comes to me to say we can take a cab together, and I totally agree with him. At 07:30 he's ready to go and asks me when we will leave. I tell him I've received an email from Amazonas that we have to be at the airport one hour in advance. He frowns, as it's an international flight. I'm not even doubting a second that the information in my email is wrong. Two hours and fifteen minutes in advance we take a taxi. I say goodbye to the staff and off we are. There's crazy traffic and the clock is ticking. I ask the driver how much longer it is, and he says about thirty minutes. It takes us 1.5 hours before we finally get to the airport, just a tad later than the one hour that was mentioned in the airline's communication. We run the last metres to the desk and immediately are told we can't board anymore. I ask them what the problem is and they say we had to be there one hour and fifteen minutes ago, as boarding closes two hours in advance. I'm shocked, and furious at the same time. I show them my email and now they are shocked. I'm demanding we can board the plane. The manager is called and even though I'm smashing my fist on the desk, we're not allowed to board. I'm explaining them James will miss his entire itinerary if he misses this flight. They say they can't open the passenger's list anymore due to security procedures. I'm not doing this anymore for myself, I do this for James, as I feel horribly guilty following up the email, and not his words, nor my own sane thoughts of having an international flight. I'm cursing and demanding a solution. The only thing they can do is move us to the same flight the next day, but arrival in Cusco is later than James' flight from Cusco to Lima. I tell them to go fuck themselves and head to the counters of other airlines, hoping they have a solution. Most desks are closed as they only open when there are flights arriving or departing, but at one desk they can help us. They come with a perfect flight, but with the costs of 2000 US dollars. We can forget about this option. I'm walking through the airport, trying to find any help, but don't find any. James stays calm the entire time, and eventually I find my brain back as well. I tell James I have an idea that could work, but it's not the ideal one: taking a nine-hour bus in the evening. He's open to it, as missing his consecutive flights would be an even bigger disaster. I head into a phone booth and start making phone calls to bus companies and find one that offers a spot for less than twenty bucks. After taking the option on it, I head back to the shitty airline and start a conversation without emotion, but with the facts. They admit they are wrong and offer a complete refund for our flights. We just have to send an email to them and all will be good. I can reserve the flight for the next day on the internet and pay online, and then I can fly out La Paz tomorrow morning. I ask them if I need to bring anything special for tomorrow's flight, and they answer all I need is my passport and the electronic ticket. Easy, I think, and I'm happy it will be all good.

Me and James again grab a taxi, now back to La Paz' centre. We find the travel agency easily and before we let the taxi go I walk in to make sure everything is alright. The ticket is ready, the price still the same, and James can leave in the afternoon to Cusco. James is very happy I put so much effort in helping him and this is when we say farewell. A burden falls off me and I take the cab back to the hotel I just checked out some hours earlier. They are very surprised to see me, but also have a painful message: all rooms are booked... I sigh and ask them what they can do. They say there's one room under construction and I can take that one for a special price. I agree on this, tired of arranging more today. I drop my stuff there, and sit myself down for a lunch. The hotel staff brings me delightful news just a bit later, saying they have an executive room now, which is way bigger, and I can have it for the cheaper price as well. Hurray for Bolivia! I take a nap in the room and then head back to my new local 'bar', which is probably the best thing of staying one more day in La Paz: meeting my new friend in the local shop. We talk until they have to close the shop, and this time other family was there to talk with too. Then it's really time for a farewell, and I'm hoping to cross paths with all these nice new friends soon again.

Back in the hotel I enjoy one final meal for real, and meet another nice guest whom I dine with. A business woman, who's from California and is taking care of some cases in Bolivia. A job that you can travel for: seems ideal! I head to bed early however, as I don't want to miss another flight.

Chapter VI

PERU

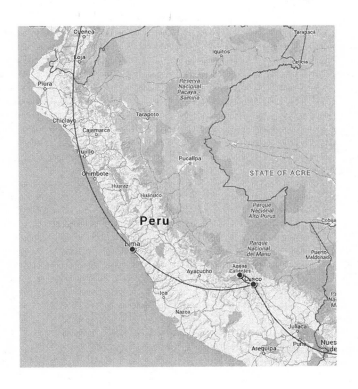

<u>Peru - Cusco, Urubamba</u>

I'm awake very early and have barely slept. Fucking Amazonas! I'm eating a quick breakfast and then take a cab at 07:30, as I want to make sure I'm on time. The traffic is less crazy than yesterday and three hours before take-off I'm already at the airport. I'm one of the first people to check in and the people behind the desks recognise me immediately. I'm asked for my email with my ticket, my passport, and the credit card I paid my ticket with. Wait, what? I have to show my credit card? Yesterday I was told I only have to bring the first two things. I tell them I can't show the credit card physically, as I used my dad's card: my own credit card got blocked in Brazil already because of some shitty protection service, and I haven't been able to use it for several weeks now. I show them a photo of my dad's card, but they demand to see the physical card. I tell them I can't do that; upon which they reply I can't board the flight. I feel I'm going absolutely crazy. What a retarded flight organisation! In what year are we living? In what year are they operating? Oh my gosh. I try to not lose my temper, but the steam coming from my nose and ears probably betray me. The manager comes once again and tries to explain it. The more he tries, the more annoyed I get. They must be the only organisation still wanting to see a physical card. They can only offer me to buy another flight ticket and refund the other one to my dad's card. I don't see any other solution than to follow this up and use my debit card to buy a new ticket. Despite their desperate tries, they can't do any good to me anymore. Worst airline e-ver.

What's left is over an hour wait, and I enter border control area, where I'm summoned to open my carry-on luggage. When they ask about my trip so far and see my iPad, they want to see photos. The two guys ask if I have taken many photos of beautiful girls and are eager to see them. I think they're joking, so I look at them with a smile, but they don't seem to take my hesitation as a signal to not do it. I take my iPad out, and quickly show them some animal photos. They start scrolling too and I'm frowning at this situation. It's kind of intimidating as I can't really speak out my thoughts in Spanish and I don't want to be stuck in Bolivia for much longer. Abuse of power, I guess. After this awkward iPad affair, I can enter the waiting area where I sit down and count down the moments I can leave the mess of this airport.

I have to admit the flight itself was good and the staff on board were doing a nice job in handing out our drinks. Cusco is reached within two hours and the flight had some nice scenery. Entering Peru is much easier than leaving Bolivia and I get my entrance stamp after a very short interview. Then I pick up my luggage and head out the airport where I'm offered a taxi on every inch. I wait for a ride my hotel has organised for me though and refuse politely. My driver shows up after a little while, holding a sign with my name. We walk to his car and in less than thirty minutes we manoeuvre through very small streets to the hotel, which is situated a little bit on a hill, and looks super nice from the moment I step in. The staff immediately warmly welcomes me and give me a very smooth check-in. It's recently opened and freshly renovated, and my room still has this new smell all over it. I change clothes, and then head out with my camera to enjoy the lovely day. I'm having lunch in a restaurant close-by which serves delicious food. I sit on a table with a British couple, who provide me with some tips, as they've just visited Machu Picchu yesterday. They have also travelled Colombia and Ecuador, and give me their experiences of these countries, and also of their trip to the Galápagos, which are very useful to me. After lunch I'm heading down to the Machu Picchu tourist office to pick up my reserved tickets. I pass some crowded streets where police are organising traffic. I ask them for directions and they friendly help me on my way and the female cop also wants to know where I'm from. Amsterdam is always something that opens doors, and she gives me a look that my city is a cool thing. I continue my walk and don't find the office very easily. First I'm drawn to a football match, being played on the most awful pitch I've ever seen. It's school teams playing each other. I can't believe how they keep going and running all the time. We're over 3000 metres here and they seem to have five time as much lung capacity as me. I get to talk to a group of fans, students who don't participate and they say they feel honoured that I'm seeing their games. I ask them for directions to the Machu Picchu tourist office and they give me different directions than the police officers earlier. I'm heading out the ground and trying to find my way and after some circling around I finally find it. I tell the attendant that I'm there to pick up my ticket. She replies that a reservation is only valid for 24 hours and that mine is long gone. Oh. But, she says, I can just buy my ticket here now, for tomorrow, as there's still plenty availability. Some minutes later I walk out with my entrance ticket to Machu Picchu and to Machu Picchu Mountain. The famous Huayna Picchu mountain, where you climb to the top of an actual temple has been sold out for months, as it only allows 200 people per day. I continue to walk through the historical centre of Cusco, which is actually very amazing. There's churches, museums, and a lot of cultural heritage. There's also women and children walking in traditional clothing and for a small fee you can take a photo with them. Sometimes they also have lamas with them, which is kind of awkward to me; seeing these animals in the streets. I continue walking for quite a bit and end up at a very large market, where some boy band is performing and the audience is clapping to the music. My next stop is the ticket shop for the train, as now I need transport to Machu Picchu itself. I buy a ticket from Ollantaytambo, as it is sold out from the closer stations. To Ollantaytambo I will have to take a bus or taxi, but my hotel already told me they could help me with this.

The sun has been shining all day, but when it's gone it's actually quite cold. I hurry back to my hotel, ask them to set me up with a cheap taxi, and then head out again for dinner, which I consume in a nearby empty restaurant. I'm the only customer and as the staff has nothing better to do, they spend their time talking to me, which eventually leads to singing and later they even dance. I'm having great fun with these crazy people. It's a short walk back to the hotel and the front door has already been closed when I get there. Some knocks make the night staff open it and I hurry myself into bed.

Peru - Aguas Calientes, Urubamba

I don't sleep too well and wake up early. I leave my big bag behind in the hotel and after breakfast my taxi picks me up to drive me to Ollantaytambo, which is about 65 kilometres away, and will take about 1.5 hours. It's raining today and it doesn't give the best of views along the way. My driver is a father of two children, of which he speaks highly throughout the journey. We go up the mountain, to a plateau, which is beautiful. The rain falls down slowly now and we're surrounded by green. Every now and then we make a stop so I can take some photos of the landscapes. The roads winds through the agricultural lands as we slowly get closer to the destination. Then the road goes down the mountain with a lot of hairpins and a bigger town shows up in the valley: Urubamba. We stop at a parking to take some photos and then continue the final miles down, through town and then through the valley to the station of Ollantaytambo, which is a small city, with some Inca ruins. I let the taxi bring me directly to the station, even though I have plenty of time. I pay him, say farewell and get myself to the main building of the station, where I sit myself on one of the benches and await the train arrival. I'm the first passenger taking place, but soon more and more tourists appear, mostly in groups. When some sit themselves next to me we have conversations, but they are mostly focused on their travel companions. Then the train arrives and we can board. It's a train with windows on the sides, but also the roof is one big window. My assigned seat is at the window, and across me sits a Peruvian guide, and next to me two guys from Sweden, who I talk with the entire train ride. We get a snack and drink from the cabin crew and then move into the mountains, while all windows are being covered by rain drops. It's hard to see the beauty of the surroundings because of this, but the view is good enough to get the idea. Through the train speakers a voice in first Spanish, then English, tells us things about the surroundings, about the history of the train, about the history of the towns we pass, and much more. We're unlucky with the weather and everyone is praying for better weather tomorrow, when most of us will go to the sacred Machu Picchu site. Upon arrival in Aguas Calientes the rain has stopped, leaving the streets empty, and the river flushing. Leaving the train station brings me into a big market, where I'm being asked to buy things every two metres. I finally get out and as it's getting dark, and it's a new town, I have no clue where to go exactly. First I find myself an ATM and then ask a couple of shop owners for directions to my hotel. I walk up to the main street, with a lot of restaurants, who all have a pusher to get me inside, until I finally see the sign of my hotel in one of the side alleys. I check in and am brought to a small room, where the towels are folded in the shape of love swans. Apparently I'm the romantic couple. I place my bags in the room, change my sweater and shirt, and then look online for a good restaurant in this town. From all I've seen so far it's super touristy, so it should not be a problem finding a place. I find a traditional restaurant, which actually serves very good food and I enjoy the meal, and later also the conversations with other guests. I do head back to the hotel early though, as tomorrow I want to be in one of the first buses going up to the sacred site. In my hotel bed I can't catch sleep easily, as I'm too excited to head to what is supposedly one of the most beautiful places in the world. My expectations are high, and tonight I will only dream of what there is to come.

Peru - Machu Picchu, Urubamba

I leave my small bag with clothes in the hotel, and only bring my camera back pack, in which I have put a plastic rain-cover for myself, which I've bought last minute last night after hearing the weather forecast: more rain.

I enjoy a breakfast with many other people, who all will go up today. Then I walk some hundred metres to the bus stop, and buy a ticket at a desk there. Then I stand in line as small buses pick up the people. I have to wait before I can get into mine. It's small, and there's nearly any leg space. Bags are placed in the small storage room on the top, and off we go. This road goes up steep and is small and very windy. We cross ledges and some people think we might fall into one of the ravines, especially when another bus comes down and two buses pass each other. The driver seems to be capable as he keeps going up high speed. Within thirty minutes we are at the entrance, where there's another huge line in order to get into the park. I step in line, and directly after it begins to rain, making all people reach into their backpacks to get their rain coats, and umbrellas. Soon it's a colourful line with people covered in red, yellow, blue and white rain covers. Mine is see through plastic, so I stay black. The line goes pretty fast and while holding my breath I take my first steps into the old Inca ruins. I'm so excited to finally see this praised sight, that my walking pace has at least doubled. I walk into a mist, and only see five steps ahead of me, therefore only seeing some rocks here and there. I'm supposedly in the middle of world famous ruins and don't see anything of it. I walk up the steps, until I reach an old building, in which I can take a bit shelter from the rain, together with five other tourists. They are complaining about the weather and are hugely disappointed. I'm not giving up yet, and continue going up, to some kind of Inca bridge. I reach some top floor, and then move my body to where it is said the ruins should be. As I look into the mist I see the clouds moving and there, through rays of rain I see the mighty Machu Picchu. Wow. I'm impressed, despite the horrible weather and take my camera out, despite the rain. A woman joins me and we both gasp at what lies at our feet. The rain is not ruining this moment for us, but is giving it an extra dimension, one of mystery. We take some photos for each other and then continue our own ways and I follow a very wet track around a mountain to that bridge. On the other side of the mountain the view is clearer and I can see the clouds slowly crawling to the top, as if they're white ninja assassins. I observe this ritual for some time and take some photos and videos of it, before heading back to the main site. The weather there has slightly improved giving a bit better overview, but it's far from ideal. I decide to start walking up Machu Picchu mountain and head to the entrance of this trail, where I have to write my name, age and country of origin in a book. I see quite some names on this day already, meaning I won't be alone. The woman tells me the trail will take about 1.5 hours and that I should bring enough water. Duly noted. I start in a positive mood, but soon find out this is like steep long stairs I'm walking on. It goes up and up, without getting flat for a second. My breath is getting heavier soon and my memory gets dragged back to my walk in Iruya. After fifteen minutes I already feel exhausted and I take a rest on a rock. A big group of Americans is just before me and they don't seem to be prepared at all. They laugh all the time, even though they severely struggle every step. One of the kids is running up however and ignores the warnings of his father that the road will be long and harsh, and he should not waste his energy. I get caught up by a young couple, Kathy and Foek. Foek is Dutch like me and Kathy from Texas, USA. The three of us all have about the same pace and we walk up together, making numerous stops to take photos of what we see below us, the mighty Machu Picchu. The clouds have mostly moved away and we make sure we take enough photos at every stop. Because we are walking up, and our back is to the view, we have plenty of time to talk about live, past, current, future and mostly about travels. We all seem to love taking good photos and whenever we get the chance we act like super models. Kathy is, Foek maybe too, but I'm just a drenched little cold bird. The steps are getting bigger and bigger and I can't believe these small Indian people thousands years ago could make these steps at all. We get higher and higher, through forests until there's no more trees and we are fully exposed. The rain fortunately has stopped and we can continue with only our clothes wet. The rocks are not that slippery from the rain, so we can continue in the same pace. Then we meet some people that are already heading down, having reached the top a while ago. We ask every person that comes down how much longer it is to the top, and all of them convincingly tells us it's about fifteen minutes. I believe we still walk at least forty-five minutes before we reach the top, after walking on crazy steps with deep abysses on the last part. We get to 3082 metres, meaning we have ascended over 600 metres in our over two-hour climb. The view is breath-taking and I'm so happy to be on the top. Together with about dozen other tourists we are taking photos and eating some snacks we've brought. We forget the pain in our legs and also take a group photo when the American family's reached the top just moments after us. The view is not only to Machu Picchu, but also to other sides, as we have a 360-degree view here. Top of the world. After some thirty minutes on the top we decide to go back and we take the steps down. There now are now trains of people ascending and we have to stop a lot of times to let them pass. They all ask us how much longer it is, and we consequently say about fifteen minutes. We're using different muscles in our legs on this descend and it hurts like hell. All of us are feeling shaky on our stops and feeling pain in our hamstrings. Going down is actually much harder than our way up, and our stops are again plenty. When we finally do get at the end of the endless steps we sit ourselves down and try to catch our breath again. While we're doing this other familiar faces show up and we all sit there to rest. Then we start exploring the rest of the ruins and get a great impression of how this once was a stronghold for the Inca culture. And when the sun finally breaks through, we see it in all its glory. I'm sweating like hell now, as I've been wearing all my warm clothes the entire day. We take some scenic photos and at a photo-generic rock I also get to talk with two Peñarol-fans: a father and son, both Uruguayan, but living in Canada. They are on a road trip to Brazil, from Canada and I listen breathlessly as they tell me about their fantastic experiences. Foek, Katy and I then continue our exploration and are some of the last visitors to leave the sight, when the sun has already set behind the surrounding mountains. We take a bus back to the town and say farewell there. I walk back to my hotel to pick up my stuff and then head to the train station to see if I can still buy a ticket back to Ollantaytambo. I get a seat and inform the hotel in Cusco if they can arrange transport from that station back to the big city. They set it up and I get into the train about half an hour later. It's dark now, and the night is blocking the view, instead of the rain. There's some folklore taking place in the train now, as traditional clothed people, perform an act, and also invite people to dance with them. I'm glad to escape an invitation for this. All people are happy, clapping, and smiling, and the way back seems to be much faster than it took getting there. I exit at the station and walk to where I expect a taxi to be, or a car with my name on it. Nothing. It's dark, and I get approached by many men, but politely refuse their transportation offers. When thirty minutes have passed and I still don't see anyone looking for me, I try to call my hotel, but the pay phone is not being cooperative. I wait another thirty minutes and then start worrying: how the hell can I get a safe transport back to Cusco? I start walking and talking to people, trying to figure out what to do. Then, when I don't expect it anymore, a car comes driving with high speed and immediately asks for a Mr. Vanderveen. I'm relieved and hop in the car and together we drive back in another 1.5 hours, reaching the hotel after midnight. The hotel pays me a little bit back due to the inconvenience and I crash in another room than before on my comfortable bed. My legs are sore and my mind exploding from the great experiences of the day. Machu Picchu was beyond my expectations and is truly divine.

Peru - Cusco, Urubamba

My night's rest didn't cure the pain in my legs and I'm still incredibly sore. I drag myself to yet another lovely breakfast, with lovely conversations with the staff, who are practicing their English with me.

After breakfast I head into town, to find some better walking shoes, as my Nike's are horrible for walking and at least one size too small, leaving my toes purple. I find some great shoes in a shop that is specialised in trekking and buy them together with a new pair of hiking pants. The rest of the day I stroll around town, visit two museums, sit in the sun, have lunch, and eventually of course have dinner. Dinner with my friends of the empty restaurant of course, where we end up singing again. It's very late when I finally head back at the hotel and I knock the door as I did before. I don't hear any movement and I knock again. Again, no movement. I peek through the slits of the building and don't see anyone. I continue doing this for thirty minutes and then start to feel cold. I see a police officer walk the empty streets and I decide to ask him, but he shrugs his shoulders and ignores my plea for help. I go back and start knocking very loudly. The neighbour sticks her head out of the window because of all the noise and supports me to continue doing so. Again there's no movement inside, and no sound indicating it will happen. I'm getting desperate and already imagine myself sleeping on the streets and getting woken up by the tongues of the lama's. Then I think of another hotel of the same brand, which is at the central square. I decide to walk downhill to there and after some time I finally find it. I knock and ring the bell and the door quickly is opened by a man and a woman, who let me in, hear my story and offer me a drink. The only thing I want is to get to my bed, so I ask them to call the other hotel, which they immediately do. They apologise for the inconvenience and after two tries the phone on the other side is picked up. The guy had been sleeping and didn't hear any of the knocks. My saviours call a taxi for me and I'm taken back uphill to my hotel. There I'm awaited by the sleeper himself, who is totally embarrassed and can't stop apologising. I'm petting his back to be calm and quiet, so I can finally go to bed and sleep. I'm deadly tired and immediately pass out in my room.

I wake up and get to the breakfast, where all the staff can only talk about my adventure last night. Even the manager of the hotel comes to apologise once more. I tell them the guy should not be punished, after she talks about certain actions, but that I hope the hotel will make a better system for guests who arrive late: a bell, for example. She takes notice and I have the feeling she's taking it serious.

My legs are a bit better today and I head out without a camera. There's a military parade on the main square and it's quite a Soviet parade, with the police marching. The rainbow flag hangs high in the tops. The flag of Cusco has rainbow colours, and is not to be confused with the flag that is often used by the gay community. I'm trying to explore new places and find some nice monuments, and later some view from higher up the mountain. At night I end up in a vegetarian restaurant where I share my table with a father and son from Belgium, who are absolutely great company. The son's lived in South America for a while and has plenty of stories to share, and I share mine in return. We also talk about world politics and world problems and all feel to be better off here travelling and collecting memories. It's very late when we finally leave the restaurant and I get to my hotel. The door is opened amazingly quickly today. I talk a bit with the night watch and then head to my room.

Peru - Lima, Lima

I begin the day with a good breakfast and then pack my stuff. Today I will fly to the capital of Peru, Lima. I spend quite some time saying goodbye to my new friends in the hotel and then let a taxi bring me to the airport. I board my plane and then fly smoothly to Peru's biggest city. At the airport I rent a private car to bring me to my hotel in downtown. It's not a taxi, it's a fixed fee, and I let him drive me past some of the most important sights of the city. I don't have much time here, as in two days I will fly to Quito to meet my friend Eduard, who will fly in from Amsterdam.

My first impressions of the city aren't that great. It's a huge city, widely stretched and the architecture and history aren't that appealing to me, in these first stops. I direct the car to the hotel and do my check in there. I get into a discussion with the front desk, as my fee through booking.com was slightly lower than what they charge me. It's not about the money, but the principle, and I get a refund for the difference. I chill a bit in my room and look for a good restaurant online. In a recent list I had seen that Lima hosts two restaurants in the top 25 of world's best restaurants and this makes me curious, even though I'm not a foodie at all. I find a very fancy place not too far from the hotel and decide to spend some serious money on a dinner for once. I take out my best clothes and walk through the dark streets until I find a newly looking building, where I'm welcomed with all respect. I'm being brought to my table, in the full restaurant, which has an Asian fusion kitchen. After a look at the menu, I decide to go for the chef's menu, while I try to ignore seeing the high price on it. My personal waiter comes to me and asks me if I have any allergies, and I reply I don't think I have one. The next hours are some kind of food bacchanalia and I'm licking off my fingers after every small dish. This food is godlike. The highlight however is the dessert, ice cream made of a typical fruit. I order two more scoops and slowly enjoy the taste of every bit. I feel I've gained fifty kilos after this meal, and I pay the bill with a big smile. I walk back to the hotel, where I fall asleep satisfied.

Satisfaction doesn't last too long however, as insane cramps in my stomach wake me up and I rush to the toilet to throw up. I feel so miserable. Everything seems to come out and I feel like losing 100 kilos. Normally one would feel relieved or better after this, but I continue feeling bad. I nearly faint and try to drink as much water as possible and also take some medicines to stop throwing up. Nothing seems to work and the entire day I hang over the toilet. My knees must get callus by the end of the day if this continues. I have no clue what to do, and I feel so weak, so tired. At this moment I miss my family in the Netherlands, who always take care of me when I feel bad. I try to reach out by WhatsApp, even though I don't tell them how serious this really is, as I don't want to worry them too much. Just a small food poisoning, I say. I can't remember feeling this bad though. At one point my water is gone, and I don't have anything to eat. I need to go out and buy stuff. It takes me some hours to get ready for this, but when I do, I walk the streets like a zombie. I'm moving slow, with the feeling I can throw up any second again. I'm a walking time bomb. I do manage to buy some fruits and lots of water, and when I get back to my room, I feel like just finishing running half a marathon: completely exhausted. My main goal is to be able to fly tomorrow, as I can't leave my friend there alone. When I keep the apples inside, I take some pills to stop everything from coming out and slowly my body seems to stabilise. I keep lying in bed, drinking water, and trying to sleep. This continues until the next morning, and I think I grabbed at least two hours of sleep in the end.

Chapter VII

ECUADOR

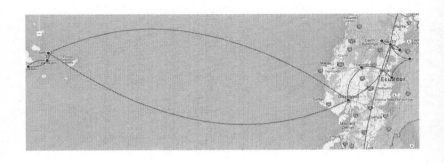

Ecuador - Quito, Pichincha

In the morning I take more pills, placebo's, in order to get to Quito without any problem. I'm shooting prayers in the air that everything will be fine. I order a regular taxi at the front desk, and not much later I'm on my way to the airport once again. I'm not paying attention to what I'm seeing outside, and just focusing on how I feel inside. It strikes me that I haven't enjoyed Lima at all, and have barely seen anything of it. Oh well, maybe another day.
At the airport I do my check in, drop my luggage and then wait for boarding. I visit the toilet regularly, preventively. Upon boarding time I really do feel good enough to fly and I manage to get into Ecuador without any problems.

At Quito airport I have to wait some hours before Eduard's flight from Amsterdam arrives. I talk to the tourist information centre for about an hour and exchange details later in order to get more tips for the city. Then I sit myself down in the restaurant and order a small salad, my first proper food since that 'star' restaurant. Eduard made a reservation for a hotel, and a guy will pick us up, holding a sign with his name. When Eduard finally arrives, I find him quickly, but we don't see our guy, at all. It takes quite some time, and even a phone call to the hotel, before he shows up and drives us to the old centre of Quito, to our little boutique hotel.

It's great to see a familiar Dutch face after about 4.5 months and I'm happy he can join me on a part of my trip. We do our check-in in the hotel, and get into a small noisy room, on the first floor. The building of the hotel is very interesting, and looks colonial. We're being helped with tips by the staff, and later have dinner in the restaurant that is enclosed with the hotel, where we are being served by friendly staff and have a good meal.

The next day we have a goal: finding a cruise on the Galápagos. A friend of us found such a trip last-minute when he went here, so we are inspired to do the same. We take a cab to the new centre, which is a horrible place to be at, with way too many (party) tourists, modern buildings, and bars and restaurants. It's a big contrast with the old centre, where we have wandered this morning and visited some very pretty churches and squares. In the old centre we could peacefully try to photograph hummingbirds, while in this new centre the animal most likely to be photographed is a rat.

Soon we walk in and out travel agencies that can offer us a price for a trip. The prices are sky-high, up to 1600 US dollars, and the best trips have already been booked. We continue our search as we both believe a cruise would be the best way to see the islands. Quality comes at a price, but this price makes me doubt if a cruise is really the best option. I've met many travellers that went there and booked day trips, and this is what I suggest to do as well, as we keep finding itineraries that are not ideal and overpriced for what they offer. We didn't think t it would be so difficult to find a cruise and it's a bit of a disappointment for Eduard. He eventually agrees to do some island hopping by ourselves and at night we book a one-way flight to, and a hotel on, the main island, Santa Cruz. Our flight will be in two days, meaning we still have one full day in Quito.

At night we dine in a theatre restaurant, which is a treat. Unlike walking the shady streets at night, which is a bit creepy. I'm wearing my hoodie though, and people are more afraid of me, than I am for them. Hoowah!

The next day we wake up after a proper night of sleep and enjoy a good breakfast. We have arranged a taxi for the day and he'll first bring us to 'Mitad del Mundo', the middle of the world, where latitude and longitude are both 0. It's a fair drive up there and I chit chat with the driver in Spanish, as English in Quito is also again nearly non-existent. When we arrive the sun is shining and it's warm. It's a big park, with several monuments, and lot of green. There are plenty souvenir shops, and places to buy snacks. We climb the main monument and have a nice view over the area. There's also again a lot of different kinds of birds, and I'm chasing them for a good photo, leaving Eduard laughing at me. When I've photographed every bird in the park we head back to our taxi and let him bring us to Pululahua, which is a former volcano and now a national reserve. It's cloudy and when we start walking it's a bit chilly. The cab driver tells us we can quickly walk in and out in an hour, so we expect a fairly easy walk. After the first corner however we already know we really are entering a crater and thus walking down, on a trail. After seeing the first people coming up, we know it's not as easy as it looks. For me, at least not. Eduard is in a far better shape and goes down like a pro, leaving me behind puffing and sweating. I try to find as many birds as possible to have an excuse to make stops. When we get into the valley the sun has chased off all the clouds and we walk a bit down the road, and ask people where exactly this all will lead. Supposedly there's a hostel with a nice restaurant further down the road, but we decide to return to our cab, as we don't want to exceed the hour too much, and we still have a hill to climb... Going up is easier normally, a bit more intense, but the legs can handle it better, as I've experienced recently climbing Machu Picchu mountain. The sun is burning now and I'm drowning in my own sweat. Eduard is like Marco Pantani, the famous cyclist who was ace (and on doping) in the mountains of the Tour de France, and goes up like a mountain goat. We do make more stops now, as the weather is clear, and the view over the valley very pretty. When we get back to the cab I'm exhausted. We buy some small snacks in the store and then take a well-earned seat in the car and let it drive us to our next stop, teleferiQo, a cableway going up to one of the volcanoes surrounding the city of Quito. We buy our ticket and get into our cabin going up. We share it with a couple and we talk with them for a bit, while we see the city becoming smaller and smaller as we reach higher. The station on top of the mountain is at 4100 metres and my memories immediately go to my altitude problems in northern Argentina. Nothing of this now fortunately, and we start walking some of the trails that are easily accessible around the station. We're taking many photographs. It's cold up here, very cold. From burning in the sun, to freezing above the clouds: it's quite a contrast in an hour time. When we have walked all trails, we take the cableway down again, where our taxi friend is waiting for us to bring us back to the hotel. We chill there a bit and then head out to find a restaurant, which is quickly found and we enjoy every bit of the first proper meal of the day, which brings a bit of life back to our exhausted bodies. Back to our hotel we fall asleep quickly and deeply.

Ecuador - Isla Santa Cruz, Galápagos

We wake up hella early and eat some of the bread that has been put
on a table for us. Then we head out where our friend the taxi driver is
waiting to bring us to the airport, which is quite a drive from the
centre. There's barely traffic on the road when we see the sun rise.
Both me and Eduard fall asleep every now and then, before awaking
with a shock. At the airport we check-in and enter the plane that will
first bring us to Guayaquil and then to the airport on the island of
Baltra, which is the biggest airport on the Galápagos Islands. At the
airport we have to get a special visa for entering the islands and
Eduard quickly figures out in what order we have to take all the lines.
In the plane I meet a female politician who is a representative for the
Galápagos Islands in the parliament and now on her way to spend
some vacation time with her family. She explains the political
situation in Ecuador a bit and she mentions a few of her favourite
spots on the island. When we finally arrive in Baltra, we have to wait
for our luggage, while customs walk around us with dogs, that sniff
the bags. They are very serious about what people bring to these
protected islands, where animals are kings and outnumber the people.
After getting our luggage we have to go through another bag
inspection before we finally leave the airport and have to get into a
bus that will bring us to a ferry. My new friend suddenly has private
transport and I don't manage to get me and Eduard into it,
unfortunately. Thus we sit in a packed bus for the next thirty minutes
until we reach the water, where a boat brings us to the other side. We
now are on Isla Santa Cruz, the most developed island of the group
of islands that together form the Galápagos. We're not quite sure
what our next step should be, about how we have to get to Puerto
Ayora, where we have a hotel room booked. First we think of taking
another bus, but then taxis are offering themselves for a fair price
and we hop in one. It's a fairly short drive to the town and we get a
general idea of this island when we cross it. The cab driver tells us
some stuff as well, and we are well informed when we get to our
hotel, which is quite a new building, with even a small pool. We have
to find the staff ourselves and then get a spacious room and some
offers for day tours. This is our main headache: finding good day
trips. This first day we don't worry about that, as we head out to get
last minute into the Charles Darwin Research Station, which is a
research centre, where they have numerous animals on display, and
was also the last resort of the world famous land tortoise, Lonesome

George, last of his kind and now extinct. It's basically a little zoo, where we face our first turtles, iguanas, birds and pelicans. In the zoo we also meet our first locals, two of them being inhabitants, and their friend from Quevedo, who's visiting them. The local couple are guides and work on a cruise ship together. They confirm us all trips are pretty much booked and that the good cruises need some in advance planning. After our walk in the stationary we have some drinks with our new friends, and then head into town to find ourselves some day trips. We get a lot of information, and prices, but they're quite alike. We do have to make some choices though, but postpone this for the next day. In one of the offices we meet some girls and we first have dinner with them and then go out to a bar to have a drink. Far past midnight we get back to the hotel and fall asleep after discussing the trip options.

Next morning starts with a breakfast in an establishment next door, which serves a decent breakfast, which was included in the rate. Then we get ourselves to the few ATM's on the island to withdraw cash to pay for our day trips, as almost none of the agencies accept a card. The ATM's aren't very cooperative either, as they don't always respond too well to our withdrawal requests. I finally have a new credit card, as Eduard brought mine from Amsterdam. Now I don't want to use it, being afraid my bank will block it again. When my debit card gets rejected, I have to use it though, and it works like a charm. With our pile of cash, we head down to the agency we've selected for our trips and get welcomed with Ecuadorian kisses by the owner, who's now our friend. We get a receipt with the three trips on it and have to be ready tomorrow early morning for our first one. Then we have a lunch and after that Eduard decides to go to our room, as he's feeling very bad: stomach problems. I know the deal, so I don't give him a too hard time, and get geared up for a hike that I can do from the village, to Tortuga Bay. All I need are flip flops, swim shorts, a shirt, water, and my camera bag. I head out and quickly find my way. I walk up some stairs, register myself in a small office and then walk for quite some time over a straight trail of wooden footbridges. It goes up and down every now and then, and I'm walking in silence, hoping for some decent wildlife. I see many salamanders, and some birds, but it's no big game, unfortunately. There's few other people walking and some are heading back. Eventually I reach a white beach with a stormy ocean, with wild waves that break quickly and give a nice view. I follow a pelican fishing and shoot too many photos. I head to a black rock formation where I see a group of young tourists. They are looking at something, and it takes me a minute before I see what: giant black marine iguanas sunbathing. Wow. I can get very close, with respect to the animals and observe them for a while. With a smile I continue my walk over the beach, with left of me the roaring ocean and to the right sand dunes, with different kind of birds circling above it. I walk until I reach a small pool of ocean that is slightly separated from the ocean because of the tide and rock formations. I see a blue footed booby, yes this is the name of the bird, hunt for fish and crash into the water like a rocket. Some pelicans do the same. The booby gets under water entirely, while the pelican's body and wings are too big and therefore only its head and big beak disappear under water. Some people are also snorkelling here and they come out of the water, pointing at a shade moving. It's a small shark! I also walk into the water, with my big camera, and try to make some photos, which, of course, is nearly impossible. After a while I give up, and stop trying, as well as my observing the fascinating fish hunt by the birds. I continue and take the path to the right, and end up at a beautiful beach, with white pristine sand, and incredible calm water. This is a small bay, with rocks protecting the waves from coming in. Again I see a shark and get quite disturbed when two tourists try to touch it. I ask them to stop it, which they immediately understand. If they were not red from the sun, they would get red from embarrassment. I leave this shark and walk the entire beach, to the far end. Here I enjoy the view for a while and then go in for a swim. First the water is quite clear, but later it gets turbid because of the alga. There's trees hanging in the water on this side of the bay, making it some sort of mangrove. Also here I see some small sharks and they seem to swim with me. After some swimming I get back to the beach and let my body dry in the hot sun. I see people doing yoga, snorkelling, playing beach tennis, and mostly sun bathing. If I would narrow my eyes and forget about the serene surroundings this could be any tourist beach anywhere in the world. I'm not, and looking at all beautiful nature surrounding me makes me aware of that. The soft white sand sticks to my feet and finally there's something whiter than my own skin. I sit down for a while, observing the beauty of nature, eat my cookies, drink some water, and then slowly head back. Coming back to the big main beach I almost stumble over the big black iguanas, who I totally did not see, as I assume it was dried black wood. One of the iguanas is heading to the water, gets in, and is a marvellously good swimmer.

Amazing! None of the others follow however and I sit on my knees looking at them sleep deeply. I continue when there's no movement and walk back talking to a tourist couple. Back at the footbridge trail I suddenly get some pain in my stomach and I decide to sit down to let it pass before making the walk back to the hotel. Then I see people surf, and I walk into the water to take some photos. One boy offers me his board, but I refuse politely: I've never surfed and am probably very bad at it. I later get to talk to his mom, who also lives on the island. After a farewell I start the hike back and cross my name off the list in the little office when I arrive there about an hour later. From there it's a short walk to the hotel, where Eduard just went out for some food. I dump my stuff, and take a shower and then head out to meet him. We meet at a terrace and have some dinner together. The bed is hit early, as tomorrow morning the trip starts early too.

We walk to the agency the next morning, after an early breakfast. A van comes to pick us up a bit later and off we are, to pick up more people. It's a good group, of about fifteen people, with who we head to the harbour north of the island; where we had to take the ferry the first day. Now we are picked up by a small rubber boat and in three fares we are all brought to our ship of the day. It's quite a big boat, with a big cabin. Here we are instructed for the day to come. First we will pass a singular rock in the middle of the ocean, where we can see our first birds, and then we head to Isla Bartolome, which is some hours away. The rock is seen quite quickly, but it takes longer than expected before we reach it. Eduard and me sit ourselves at the front deck and make a German friend, who we talk with for a while. At the rock we see some boobies again, as well as our first sea lions. Then the boat continues over open sea for a while. We sit upfront, talk, and stare into the abyss. Then something huge jumps from the water and we are all wide awake. What was that? We ask our guide and he comes forward to explain it is most likely giant manta rays. Soon we see more of them jumping high up, sometimes over a metre. Incredible. We also spot giant sea turtles swimming down into the darkness of the ocean as soon as the boat comes closer, and when we are closer to our main destination also another sea lion. When we get our first stop, a small bay with another pristine beach, we are being brought there in the small boat. There we have time to snorkel and see the underwater world of the Galápagos for the first time. The water is a tad cold, but what we see there is amazing. The water was already heavenly blue, but the sun rays that get through and give a colour boost to the already colourful fish is amazing. We see them in all forms and colours and are truly blown away. Me and Eduard keep seeing extraordinary things and our fingers nearly get sore from pointing. We are amongst the last ones to get back to the shore and don't have time to walk the little trail up there, because the boat is already transporting the people back. Back at the boat we dry ourselves and we head for the next stop, just around the corner, where there's a big exposed rock formation. We move slowly and the colour of the water is a mixture of blue, green and turquoise. It's stunning. The little boat puts us ashore once again and wooden footbridges and stairs form a trail to the top. Our guide is explaining how this island came into existence by volcanic eruptions thousands of years ago. When we follow the trail we see the desolated rock formations all around us. Then, we see a bird hanging over our heads, praying. It is floating on the wind and it's a beautiful sight. It's a Galápagos eagle, a juvenile. It circles right above our heads, not being afraid for us humans. It's is an amazing sight and seems to continue forever. I take many photographs, which is quite difficult with the sunlight hanging just over the bird. It won't move away from us and then it takes a dive down, and lands on the wooden rail of the trail, and splits our group in two. Amazing. This means close-up time, as the bird seems as curious about us, as we are about him. It sits there for a while, organising its feathers and observing us, moving its head in all awkward positions. Then it takes off again and circles a bit above our heads before landing on a rock not too far away again. I want to bring this beautiful bird, with its yellow beak, light brown colours, its spots and sharp claws, home. This animal makes my day. We continue the last steps to the top and there have a marvellous view over the area and again the colours of the water are great. At the top we listen to our guide once more and then head down, where a seal is chilling in the middle of the path at the pick-up point. After a while our guide walks to him to pet him away, and so the sea lion hops to a nearby rock. At the Galápagos animals are totally not afraid of humans, due to their preservation through the years. It's great to see. We return to our ship to pick-up snorkel gear and then head to another beach for our second time snorkelling. On our way to the beach in the small boat I spot a small bird sitting on a rock and after looking at a zoomed-in photo it appears to be a penguin. I ask to go there and not much later we are floating in our boat in front of a penguin. My first ever penguin in the wild. I always have associated penguins with the south pole, but now I see it here, sunbathing. It's an interesting shift of mind. Upon reaching the beach I see another, or maybe the same, eagle sitting in the sand. While all the others a putting on their equipment and entering the sea, I try to approach the bird while walking on my toes. I get fairly close and shoot some photos before returning to the group and entering the cold water. The sun is hiding a bit now and the colours aren't that beautiful as the first time today. Maybe I'm already spoilt. We swim for quite a bit and highlight are the big red sea stars that are numerous here. After about an hour we get back to the boat, get a lunch served and then head back, and spend our time talking to other people. Americans want to have my email address and learn everything about my trip. Big birds follow our boat when we come closer to the harbour again and we observe their chase and take photos. When we arrive at the island we are awaited by the same bus that brings us back to town. It was a long day, but we are back earlier than we thought we would be. We chill the rest of the day, having dinner in the middle of the food street again and head to bed early.

Ecuador - Isla Isabela, Galápagos

The next day we go on a tour to Tintoreras, on the biggest Galápagos island: Isla Isabela. We leave our big bags at our hotel, saying we will be back at one point, and head to our agency. There's two Chilean girls there waiting for transport to the other island, and the four of us are being walked to the pier downtown. We wait on a little square and have absolutely no idea what's going on. We feel like we've been abandoned, but every now and then other people are being added to our group, and so we grow in numbers bit by bit. Then suddenly we have to move and we enter a small boat that brings us to a bigger boat, for the 1.5-hour trip to the big island. There's just enough room for everyone. I've taken a stomach tranquilliser, dramin, in order to prevent getting sick. The waves are high and the ride is rough, and I'm just counting down for someone to start throwing up. A guy who's been big mouthing and joking at first, is now the one getting in trouble and bag after bag is brought to the small bathroom. Another guy sits on a crate and it's funny to see him balancing the entire time. Sometimes he falls, but mostly he keeps steady. The rough sea throws the small boat from wave to wave and our steersman keeps searching for the ideal line for not getting smashed down. In exactly the expected time we manoeuvre into the small harbour of Isabela, and then the confusion starts again. Most of the group is being taken off the boat, and we, together with the girls from Chile, are left behind, with no clue what will happen. No one talks to us, nor has answers when we ask them. We wait for some kind of transport, we think, and ask everyone that arrives if they are there for us. Then a big war truck comes, a bus, and we are told we can sit in there and then we will be brought to the hotel. We are indeed brought to our hotel, but there's still no one that really seems to know our group of four. We get to our rooms, and me and Eduard get some dorm, but then for just the two of us. There's no facilities, and four single beds. It's all been recently decorated, but it totally lacks atmosphere. We drop our stuff and then head back down to wait for our tour. There's not much happening and we talk to the Chilean girls a bit. Then a guy comes to pick us up in the big bus again and we hop in and head to pick up some more people. Then we head to the little harbour again to board a boat there. It's cloudy and there's a hard wind. Right after embarking we already pass some sea lions who laid themselves down in open boats and are sleeping there. They are very cute and huggable. The boat stops for a bit and then continues, where we see a penguin. Again we pass slowly, so everyone can take a photo. Then we already arrive at our destination and climb from the boat onto the rocks. We cross the rock wall, to a pool of ocean water, which is, when the tide's right, protected from the big sea waves: it's a lagoon of sea water. We get on snorkel gear and splash into the water. The guide will this time show us where to go and we move as a group. Yesterday it was free for all. Within some minutes we already see the highlight: a huge sea turtle resting on the bottom of the ocean. Wow! We all float above it, and it's not moving at all. Then some of our group dive closer to it, to take selfies with their GoPro cameras. First I'm annoyed by their behaviour, but when I see the turtle doesn't care, and the guide isn't correcting them too much, it's okay. It's not something I do myself though. I'm slowly getting behind the group and taking my own route. The guide is mainly speaking in Spanish and only sometimes pointing out stuff. There's more giant sea turtles, but none as big as the first one. We dive down to see some sea eagles, and fishes that look exactly like plants. At one point I get in the middle of a school of big fish who are going along with the stream and I let myself float as well. I get too close to the reef though and have to use quite some effort to get away from there. There's some other small schools of fish as well, and it remains a marvellous sight. The Chilean girls haven't gone into the water as they don't know how to swim, so they handle my camera to do at least something. When we get out of the water, we get back to the boat, dry ourselves and head out to the ocean, to a volcanic rock formation, where we do a hike over a very easy trail. The guide is rushing us a bit, as I think we are a bit behind schedule. I'm not here to be rushed though, and I take my time to take all the photos I want. Therefore I'm way behind the group, and not hearing any of the explanation, unfortunately. First we see the blue footed boobies, which I think are very funny birds, with their big blue feet and their beak making weird noises. The rocks on the island are very black, and it's clearly volcanic. We see thousands of the typical black iguanas. They are everywhere. They lay on top of each other, over each other, in any possible position, taking in the heat of the sun. Next to the first heaps of iguanas, there's a small canal with seawater, and in it are two big sharks. They're resting on the floor and it's a marvellous sight. Every now and then they make a circle and then get back to their original spot. These sharks are much bigger than the ones I've seen on Santa Cruz. We pass some other big groups of bigger black marine iguanas, and then head back to the boat. We are brought back to the main island shore and there we enter our transport again and head for a turtle preservation centre. Here we learn more about the small land turtle's behaviour. I don't like it too much as it is basically a turtle zoo. They also breed eggs here, but nothing very interesting to see, especially because it's not the wild. After this stop, which takes about 45 minutes, we head to a little lake a bit further down the road, and there we see beautiful flamingo's, in the wild. Too bad the sun is setting, as we arrived quite late, and taking photos, especially from the distance we are observing them, is nearly impossible with the lens I have. My eye's recording it however, and it mostly likes the taking off into air of the dark orange birds. When it's dawn we head back, and we're dropped off at our hotel again. Here we freshen up and down at the reception we get to hold some harpoon and pretend we're pro fishermen. My first time to hold such a weapon. I'm happy I don't have to fire it. We head to a restaurant where our Ecuadorian friends, the ones we met in the Darwin centre, are eating and we join them just as they are finishing. We order our plates and enjoy a fine dinner with great company. After dinner we go for drinks and my still water is as good as it gets. The rest is filling themselves up with booze, and coco water. It's not that late when we head back to our hotel, which is, like everything, within walking distance.

We have a good night's sleep and in the morning start with a decent breakfast. Then we are picked up again, as we go to 'Tuneles' today: some rock formations south of the island which appear to be tunnels. It's all in a name. Again we go with a group, and by boat. We have to go by boat for at least an hour, but the waves kick in the right way, and therefore we don't get too sick today. The coast stays on our right and is as untouched by it as they were before. We see sea lions resting on the rocks, surrounded by penguins and boobies. Maybe it would be better to see a penguin with boobies instead, but that was out of the question. Then we see what is supposed to be our destination. We start a very difficult manoeuvre to get in and our steersman has to find the right wave to get us in safely, and not let us crush on the waves and rocks. This requires skill. We all hold our breath when we go full speed ahead on top of a wave, and sigh with relief when we get to the other side. Then we get into very calm waters and put the ship at bay. We get ready for snorkelling, but today there's doubt in everyone's eyes as soon as the first person gets in: the water is absolutely freezing! With no wetsuits, this will be a hell of swim. I quickly adapt, while I see Eduard turning blue and then purple. The water is quite shallow here and we go search for sharks. This is where they are supposedly resting. Our guide leads the way, followed by the ten of us. At one point, where we think there's no entrance he suddenly moves quickly forward and then comes back, telling us there's at least five sharks in a small cave in front of us. One by one we go in and out, holding our head down and our breath in, to get into it as long as possible, while our feet are still outside this small cavern. And indeed, we see five semi big sharks laying there, in peace. Wowsers. We're all so excited we forget about the cold for a moment. When everyone has seen them we all start exploring caves and every now and then we get a signal there's a shark to see and we hurry over and under rocks to see it. It's so amazing to see this. Our highlight still has to come though, and it's me who is the scout. Alone, lying outside the caves, in pristine white sand, under sky blue water, lays the biggest shark of them all. Upon seeing it, I stop all my movement, just gasping in excitement. I quickly move my arm up, and try to signal Eduard, who's with me within a minute. A father and his son follow Eduard and the four of us observe this fierce hunter, feared by many, until it moves away with high speed. In Brazil I would say "ai meu deus", oh my god, after experiencing such an epic moment. I could have cried from happiness if my eyes weren't wet already, and I was a bit more emotional, I think. I continue my search to see if I can top this moment, but I unfortunately can't. When I look up from the water I see the guide making some gestures and I hurry myself to where the group partially is: now we swim with a giant sea turtle, who uses his fins to move slowly into the wide ocean. We swim with it for a while and then let it go. Amazing. After this I see that most of the group is already back at the boat, and now the steersman gestures that I also have to go back. Okay, okay, and I'm out just a bit later. Now we all share our experiences in excitement, while we head for a stop on the land, where we can walk on top of the tunnels. While going there we see many heads of turtles coming out of the water every now and then. It's a great sight. When we make our landing at a pier, we climb out one by one, and see a sleeping sea lion within ten steps distance. Two blue footed boobies are standing just in front of him, and everyone is taking selfies with them, while they fiercely pose. I haven't been this close to these birds, and only now see how extremely blue their feet really are. We all walk the islands, and in the little basins we spot fish and also smaller turtles. Then we face another two boobies and these are doing a pairing ritual, by doing a specific dance with each other. It is hilarious to see how they try to impress us with their moves. Animals and humans aren't that different after all. After observing this entire ritual two times, I continue and then spot a very big cricket, which is blending in perfectly with its colours. I try to snap it with my camera, but it jumps high and moves fast. I follow it for a while, until I'm satisfied with my photos. I'm again gestured to move my ass back to the boat, as we're leaving again. I don't like to be on a timer, but I obey to the command. We have one more stop to go before heading back, and this is another snorkel event. We sail for a while and then get to some rock formations in the water, where we jump out. Penguins are not only on the rocks here; they also swim around. Seeing them swim in the water is truly amazing. I try to follow them from a distance and for a while, and can't get enough of it. Our guide also shows us some other animals more on the bottom, making us dive in to the deep, plopping our ears. The sun has started to shine and the water gets a bit warmer here, so we stay in longer than before. I'm the last one to leave the water again, after having searched every slit, crack, and cleft, in the rocks. On our way back to the harbour we can only wish for orcas, whales, and dolphins, but unfortunately not get to see any of those on this Galápagos trip. Back at the island we are transported back to the village, where we change clothes and then head out for a lunch. Then we rent bikes, with our new friend, who's from the US, and joins us for our afternoon activity. The bikes are cheap and soon we are off to get to a former prison that was once built on this island, and later used by the US army, when they had to set up barracks here. We have to bike slightly uphill, and as expected, I'm quite out of breath soon. Another tourist who's going downhill is in tears after falling and her boyfriend helps her get back on her way, but she's done with the biking and wants to go to mommy. We continue and finally reach the big wall, where we park our bikes and continue on foot. We climb stairs that leads us to the top of a hill, where we have a view of 360 degrees all over the island. It's stunning once again. We can go down quickly and we inspect the ruins before getting back to our bikes and make a stop at every point of interest, seeing what it is all about. We see a mangrove, abandoned beaches, lonely turtles, another viewpoint from a mountain, and a very creepy long cave. Near this cave is a breeding area for my marine iguana friends. We see plenty of them again. It's late and near sunset when we return our bikes to the rental company. A quick dinner is all what we do the remainder of the day and then head back and into our beds.

<u>Ecuador - Isla Santa Cruz, Galápagos</u>

We have no plans for the next day, except from getting back to Santa Cruz, with a boat that leaves in the afternoon. In the morning we stroll through the village, climb a viewing tower, to observe more iguanas, and pelicans fishing. We enjoy a lunch and then walk to the harbour to await our transport back. There's the usual chaos and for a while we don't know what boat we have to board. Eventually we get in, of course, as we left our worries days behind, and start our journey back. My anti sea sick pill helps me again, while at least one person breaks and pukes. Gladly there's no domino effect here, as I've seen in my trip to Morro de São Paulo, in Brazil. We set foot on Santa Cruz safely again after a two-hour trip and head back to our hotel, where we get a new room. Here we relax a bit, and at night have dinner again in the dinner street, this time joined by our Quevedo friend, Diana. After that we check out the bars, but not much is going on and we split our ways again and Eduard and me go to our hotel to sleep.

On our last full day on the islands we have one final tour, to North Seymour, the island just north of the island of the airport. We know the route now, and pay less attention to the surroundings, and more to the talking. The Chilean girls are also on this trip and it's good to see some familiar faces again, even though their English is non-existent, and my Spanish just enough to manage. After the drive we embark another ship and set sail for the island of North Seymour. When we arrive we see other people gazing at the water, and there's some movement. We just get there too late to see a couple of sharks splashing in the water. The first animals we see at the land are two spotless clean bird, lava gulls, with a grey cap, white chest and a very bright orange line around their black eyes. Their feet are pinkish and they scramble over the rocks for food, while they ruffle their feathers over and over again. In the meantime there's again some splashing, but it's no sharks, but a school of yellow black fish that hit the ocean's surface. After observing this for a bit, we start a tour, as now all people from our boat have hit the shore. The guide explains a lot, but nature speaks mostly for itself. There's big Galápagos frigates flying over, with a big pounded red chest, that sometimes is bigger than a football. Another familiar face we see is that of the giant yellow Galápagos land iguana, which we first saw at the Darwin Station. The ones we see here are much bigger though, and we learn they can weigh up to 25 pounds. One of them is moving slowly, and eating plants. It's quite amazing to see how he opens his mouth and we see his giant tongue curl around the steel of a green plant, crushing it and then chewing it only shortly before swallowing it entirely. We then pass two sea lions who are sunbathing, whilst throwing sand over their bodies. Then more and more frigates, and their red chest is getting bigger and brighter as we move more on the island. The guide explains us their chest is part of their mating ritual, and the female lures a male with putting it out as big as possible. A male will then fly down and they will spend some time getting to know each other, before taking it off, it there's a match. Incredible human behaviour, I think, and observe one pairing with a big smile. We also come across blue footed boobies, one of which is sitting on its nest with two babies in it. The mom is feeding them with whatever it has in its beak and their little beaks reach deep into mom's. It's a big spectacle and we all look in amazement. The trail continues to make a circle around the island, but suddenly the guide tells us we better head back. I see other groups make the entire circle and ask if we just can continue. The guide has a list of excuses to not do it, but I believe time is not on his side. I propose to make the circle by myself, but I'm not allowed, as you can only wander around with a guide. I'm frustrated and annoyed, because from my point of view I'm still the one paying for a visit to this island, and not only for a visit of the main strip. Screw them! I follow the leader however, but with a big distance now, taking my time to take my photos. Things turn in a better way though when I regroup and Eduard suddenly spots a very small snake, the one animal I wanted to see very badly. However, we see it only in a flash, but I'm grateful and happy Eduard saw it. Yet one other animal from my check list. I now can also forgive my guide, because this is part of the butterfly effect: if we would have continued the trail, we probably would not have seen this. When all the people are boarding the boat again, me, Eduard, and our guide, explore a little of the trail to the right of our embarkation point and see more big yellow iguanas. Back at the boat we are served a good lunch and we enjoy our sail back to the harbour. Before getting back into our van, I watch the pelicans hunt for fish once more, and try to snap some photos. Back in the hotel we chill a bit, and then have dinner in town. After this we go to our Galápagos friends' home, where we are invited for karaoke. Me and Eduard must be amongst the best singers in the Netherlands, so this is exactly our piece of cake... Not really. We are probably the worst ever, but tonight I find out Eduard's tone is at least better than mine. I suck balls at this karaoke game, but we have a great time, with laughing until the tears roll over my cheeks. We all sing along with the Beatles' yellow submarine, and the more the time passes, the more hilarious it gets. Tomorrow we have a flight though, and when everyone seems to be tired from laughing and singing, we head back to our hotel, which is a stone-throw away. At the hotel we already pack a bit of our stuff and then fall asleep shortly after.

Ecuador - Guayaquil, Guayas

In the morning we take a taxi back to the airport of Santa Cruz and there do a checkout of the island, declaring we didn't take any animals or plants. We sit at a table, snacking and drinking some things, before we can walk to our plane, that will bring us to Guayaquil, Ecuador's biggest city. The flight is short and smooth and Diana's daughter, Karla, has promised to pick us up from the airport and then do a little sightseeing tour with us. We head to the Malecon, together with Karla's aunt, Jenny, who is by chance the same age as her niece, and Karla's boyfriend. At the Malecon there's a huge sign saying Guayaquil and being as touristy as we are, we take some photos with it. The Malecon is a big strip with entertainment, and monuments, and is guarded by big fences and security guards. We are told this is the safest tourist attraction and that the rest of the city is shady and dangerous. We walk up and down the strip, also visiting a nice little park inside. It's warm here. After the little walking tour we head back to the car and they want to show us a park with big iguanas. They don't seem to know exactly where it is and we get lost on the way, seeing more from the city than we expected to see in the first place. It's a wide and modern city, and booming for the Ecuadorian economy. Traffic is crazy, but not as bad as in Brazil, and buildings don't seem to be too well maintained. When they notice they are driving the wrong direction, we make a U-turn and head back to downtown, where we suddenly do find the park immediately. There are big iguanas everywhere here and they wait for the people to feed them. Little boys are pulling the tails and the animals just let it happen. I'm not that shocked, after seeing how the animals on the Galápagos were used to people. I'm the only one out of us five that really takes interest it seems, as I try to take the perfect iguana photo and am fascinated by the colours while they bath in the sun. We take off not much later and drive to the hotel we've reserved. Its entrance appears to be right at that same central square, so we drive some blocks before we arrive there in the right way, as a lot of streets are one-way-streets here. Me and Eduard say farewell to our new friends, who were so nice to us by picking us up without meeting us before, and giving us a great day-tour. After check in we move into our spacious room and order a lunch to our room, as room service seems to have decent prices. When the night falls we prepare to go out, to find a restaurant in the famous area of Las Peñas. We walk here from our hotel, through the Malecon, and see many young people hanging out in the streets. As both Eduard and me are quite stubborn, we have a little discussion about the directions when we finally reach the foot of the hill that hosts a big lighthouse on the top. I say go right, Eduard says go up, and we first walk to the right, where we find out there's nothing there. I'm too tired actually to walk up the stairs we saw earlier, and I think my idea of going right was with the hope to find an escalator, or elevator at the least. We find none of that, but we do meet a group of women walking with their children. First we are asked for some photos, and it seems like Japan all over, where girls also wanted to take photos with the tourists there. We play and dance a bit with the youngest children and then say farewell again, to follow the path up the hill, up the stairs; Eduard's way. It is the right way, but my legs disagree all the way. They don't like to climb these stairs. On the hill there are a lot of bars and there seem to be a lot of parties going on. We keep going up though, to see that lighthouse. As we didn't bring our phones, we can't take any photos. When we reach the top of the lighthouse, I ask a mother and daughter to take some photos of us, and then later mail them to us, so we at least have some pictures of our night out. Then we walk down again, finally trying to find a place to eat. We don't see anything decent, and end up strolling the Malecon again. The restaurants there are now closing and we can't order any food. We head back to the hotel, and find that the restaurant is still open and we hurry to eat a meal there, being the final guests.

In the morning we have breakfast and then Eduard checks out, as he's going back to Amsterdam again. We've ordered a cab for him and we hug farewell when he's being picked up. I'm a bit worried if he will make it, as the driver of course only speaks Spanish, and Eduard's skill of this language is even worse than mine. He texts me an hour later that he's arrived safely at the airport and is now waiting for his flight. I get another room, as I only need one bed now, and spend some time there thinking about my own next steps, and reminiscing over the last weeks. I don't do anything that day and only leave my hotel for a short exploration walk in the neighbourhood, my lunch, and my dinner. This week the world cup starts and I'm eager to see some matches on the television. My first few days alone in Guayaquil are spent with the same walks, some shopping, and in the end watching all this week's football matches.

Diana's come back from the Galápagos and together with her niece Jenny we spend some time walking in shopping malls, having dinners, and picking up Karla from school, which was quite an operation. My week in Guayaquil is very peaceful and like in Não-Me-Toque, I get totally de-stressed. One thing is on my mind though: how to continue my trip? Where to go next?

Like many answers in life, my answer came spontaneously, as Diana offers me to drive with them to their home town, Quevedo, which lies north of Guayaquil, and where Diana's family has a palm-tree farm. At the Galápagos they were already talking about this, and this could be a chance for me to see such a farm myself. I decide to take the offer, although my research doesn't show any tourist attraction in this city. The good thing about travelling the way I do, is that if there's no expectations, things won't be disappointing, and every day is another surprise. I'm loving it.

Ecuador - Quevedo, Los Ríos

After a final sushi meal in Guayaquil, I'm picked up the next morning for our drive to Quevedo. Today the Dutch team plays their first match and I'm dressed in orange, and upon my request, so are my friends. I see the kick-off in my hotel, and the rest of the game in a little market along the highway, where I see my fellow countrymen write history by crushing the defending world champions with 5-1. I can't believe it, and my friends are now totally sucked into the orange fever. As I can't stay at their place, my friends leave me in one of the few central based hotels of the city, Hotel D'Barros. Even though it's a bit old-fashioned, after a short inspection of the room, I decide to take it, also knowing there are not much alternatives. I have no clue how long I will stick around here, so I first book the room for two nights. I find myself a lunch in a restaurant close to the city, and eat at the same place later at night. The rest of the time I'm hanging out in the hotel lobby, talking to the hotel staff. It's a family owned hotel, and it's a coming and going of cousins, aunts, nephew, uncles, fathers, mothers. More family members work in the shoe store at the corner. From what I learn, everyone is family here.

The next day I'm looking for activities in Quevedo, but there's none. So I talk more with my new hotel friends, and have great fun with them. I'm advised not to walk into the centre, as they say it's dangerous. After being around the hotel for too long, I decide to go anyway. It's not dangerous, in my opinion, although I'm looked at with frowns: what the hell is a gringo doing here? I'm standing out once again, and it's Belém all over. Later in the afternoon Diana and Karla pick me up and we go to their house, where I meet Diana's mother, and her other, younger daughter. They just got some puppies and they're cute as hell. I get to hold them a bit, and they seem to be so vulnerable, that I'm afraid to drop them. I hand them over quickly again. Then we go for a dinner and dessert to a small organic restaurant, which is actually close to my hotel. After dinner I walk back to the hotel, while they take off in the car. Back at the hotel I talk a bit with Jose, Roxi, Silvia and Grace, the ones I know best now from the Barros family. Later a small niece walks in and I do some kind of hide and seek game with her. I find out my Spanish is more this little kid's level, so I might be better off making friends at a kindergarten next time.

It's match day for the Ecuador team, and as I don't have any jersey, I take a blue shirt. I'm going to watch with the Cruz family, and they're all dressed in yellow blue. We go into a bar and see the team of Ecuador lose, unfortunately. It doesn't seem to matter to anyone, as the party continues nevertheless. Participation is more important than winning it seems. They have the Olympic spirit going on here. After the match I'm dropped off at my hotel and watch there the second game of the day. Then Jose and Roxi tell me they are going to a party, and ask me to come with them. I'm totally game and not much later we drive to the outskirts of the city and later into a neighbourhood, that first seems a bit sketchy, but later appears to be very welcoming. We go to some kind of community centre, where a DJ is spinning some records, and people have watched the match on a big screen. It's mostly family again, or friends that go way back. Some are already pretty drunk and I'm being welcomed as a hero. A lot of them want to talk with me, or even dance, and I get introduced to everyone. As I want to escape from the dancing, I head to another area, where there's pool tables, and I start playing. I'm winning most of the games, and even teach some people who have never played this game. There are many children here, and I can talk with them on my own level of Spanish. The party is kind of dead, but we enjoy the games of pool. Then some of us go for some food downtown, and we drive off in the car. We head for a small restaurant where I can eat my daily portion of chicken. The restaurant is pretty packed, and everyone walking in wears the colours of Ecuador. We sit there for a while, talking, chilling, laughing. A great time, with great new friends. Then we head back to the hotel and continue the chilling part in the lobby. When everyone's gone, I head to my room and go to sleep.

Today I go to the palm-tree-farm and it's quite a drive. I've never seen so many palm-trees together, and we first pass thousands of banana trees. I'm told there are many snakes in this area, and I'm hoping to see one. My guides of the day don't really agree with me, and want to stay as far away as possible from these animals. The only animal we end up seeing is a baby bird, who's fallen from a nest and has no chance of survival. My trip continues and I get a general idea of how it all works here. On the farm ground there's a little house where the ground keeper lives and it all looks quite primitive. I learn the dependency on a good harvest, which is very dependent on the weather conditions in a year; thus uncontrollable. The tour is pretty short, as it seems to be more like a field trip for work, and soon I'm back in the Cruz house to have yet another great family lunch. Then back again to the hotel, to think of my next destination. I'm quite stuck in this town, and for now I can only see a bus exit. Buses aren't my favourite, so I'm thinking of another way, and soon come up with a road trip idea with maybe some of my new friends. I start messaging with Roxi, and talking with Jose, to see if they're up for it. I get positive reactions, even though they all seem to be tied to obligations. I inform how much it will cost to rent a car, and the rental companies' prices I get, are crazy. I ask them if they know any alternatives, and via via, they seem to know someone that could rent us a car. When I have the price, my considering starts, while I'm still discussing options with my friends. Roxi seems to be up for the trip, and she later brings up the name of her nephew, Xavier, who would also like to join. Late at night I decide to go for it, and both of them are soon confirming to join me. We will leave in two days, to see one of the more popular tourist towns of Ecuador: Baños.

My last day in Quevedo I spend walking down the centre once again, eating fruit salad at my favourite fruit-salad-bar, having my daily fruit juice at the KFC, and of course talking with my Ecuadorian friends. The hotel became my home for these days, which I had not foreseen when I first came in here. This is mainly because of the great staff and all the amazingly friendly people, who treated me as one of them. I also have a final meal with the Cruz family, which took me in and welcomed me as no one else could have done. Quevedo is now certainly on my map of the world. It is also the greatness of being on the road, without a plan, ending up in places I would normally never get to, and leaving having met many great people. Being treated in such warm ways, it's beyond my mind, and I'm often asking pinching myself if this is all really happening. I'm blessed once more.

Ecuador - Baños, Tungurahua

The next day we aren't in a rush to leave, and it's the first time I meet my travel companion Xavier, who's a chef at a beach town in Ecuador, and a very laidback and friendly chap. He also speaks a little English, which is useful in some occasions. The car isn't spectacular, but it seems to work, and that is all what counts. We first head to Roxi's home to say bye to the family. I also meet Jacob there, a beautiful dog: a Siberian husky. His blue eyes are amazingly contrasting the black and white of its head. He doesn't like me too much though, as he continuously barks and even sometimes shows his teeth. I assure the family the trip will be fine, and nothing will happen, so they don't have to worry. Not much later we take off and head for the road out of Quevedo. We pass one of the bridges over the river and then start heading more landward. The road goes through valleys, with a lot of green on the mountains surrounding us. We go uphill and soon are on windy asphalt roads. I start to think Xavier is driving weirdly as he doesn't seem to shift gears in time, but later find out the car capacity is not really sufficient for this kind of steep roads. We slowly crawl up, and up, until our ears clog. Trucks moving up go even slower, and sometimes I can hardly see them move. Passing other cars seem to be free at will. There's not much traffic though, and we mostly have the road for ourselves. Then the inevitable happens: smoke from the engine. I look at Xavier and Roxi, telling them I have no clue what is happening and my knowledge of cars is far below zero. Xavier seems to know what we have to do, and asks for one of my bottles of water. He opens the hood of the car and opens something to pour water inside. More and more smoke now comes out and I believe the engine is overheated and will explode any second. I hand over all my water and he slowly keeps pouring it in. In the meantime I look into the valley below us, which is beautifully spread out at our feet. The white clouds are circling around the mountain tops and the green is almost fluorescent. I take photos of the scenery and later see the damps from the car disappearing. Xavier starts the car again and says we're good to go. Even slower we now move on and both Roxi and me think we can stop any second again. All our funny worries are for nothing though as we close in at the top. Then, at a straight piece of road, near the top, we think we see a nice viewpoint and we head out, over a fence, a little down a hill, through the high grass, to where a group of horses is quenching water from a small pool. We climb up a small hill and from there take some stunning photos of the valley below. The white clouds are making it heavenly here, as we stand above them. Here I take one of my favourite photos of my trip, when I press my shutter being close to one of the horses, who is descending into a sea of foam. Me and Roxi then head back to the car where Xavier's waiting for us, protecting the car with his life from all the attacking wild animals, drunk truck drivers and invading aliens. We speed away and are now high up in the mountains, and reach up to 4000 metres. We reach a big plateau, where there's not much vegetation anymore. I'm not dazzling this time, for two reasons I think. Firstly, I have no clue we are this high, and secondly my body is used to all these altitudes by now. We pass a small town, and then the descend starts, while we already see the contours of the bigger city of Latacunga, far away. The road winds down, and the sun starts setting. By the time we finally reach Latacunga, there's no sun to be seen anymore and we continue on the badly lighted highway. We drive south now, and follow the signs to Baños. It's still quite a drive and it's already late in the evening when we finally arrive. We don't have accommodation yet and I'm using my phone to search for some cheap hotels with three beds and availability. We end up in a good hotel on the outskirt of town, just within walking distance of the centre. Xavier has been here before and says it's a good location. We unload the car and get into the hotel room, where three good beds are waiting for us later. First we head out into the centre to find a place to eat, which we eventually find and attack our plates like hungry animals. After dinner we stroll around for a bit, and then head back to the hotel, into the bed and sleep like babies.

In the morning I see Baños for the first time by light, and I see it is surrounded by high mountains. From our room's window I see a waterfall and a school where there's a puppet master giving a show. We head down for breakfast and then walk into town. We visit a church and then head to find some bikes that we can rent. We want to see the famous waterfalls here and don't plan to do it by car or bus. The idea I get is that these waterfalls are only reachable through bad roads, and bikes are the best way to get to it. Later I find out all can be reached by car and that the waterfall trail is just along a main road, and cars are passing fast, and bike lanes, of course, don't exist. We take off and we mainly go downhill. It is nice for now, but I already fear the way back. It's good weather to be on a bike. At first we share the road with cars. Later there's parts where cars can't get and we can go safe. On one of these parts we take our first stop, and then have some fun riding under water falling from the rocks, which can hardly be called a waterfall, but is enough to make you soaked if you stay under it long enough. We just get a little wet and then continue going down. To our right, deep below, is a little river and the waterfalls are coming from the mountains into this stream. At the first big waterfall there's enough tourist facilities and even a sort of cableway that can take you to the other side, and close to the waterfall. We decide to just observe it from the road side. Here we also see some hummingbirds, which I, of course, obsessively try to photograph. We continue to the next waterfalls, which are the furthest we will get on the road, and are also the falls we get closest to. The bikes are parked, a small entrance fee paid, and some snacks bought. We have to descend a small trail, over suspension bridges, until we nearly reach the bottom of the valley. Here we are getting soaked by all the water fiercely falling down. It's one big white continuous stream of water, and certainly one of the most forceful waterfalls I've ever seen. The roaring sound is scary, and this is a place you don't want to get in. We take photos, and Xavier and me take our shirts off to run under the waterfall, where the stones of the trail are completely wet. Our bodies get soaked in seconds and we run back to Roxi the photographer. We head back up, where we again have to crawl under rocks, as it's a very narrow pathway. Then we walk to the other side of the falls, of another suspension bridge, to have a wide angled view of the coming together of two rivers, and we now see the waterfall in all its mighty power. We then head back to our bikes, as the weather is weary. Some raindrops are falling down. Not enough to worry us, but enough to slightly annoy us. We pedal back and struggle with the road going up and through dark tunnels where we share the road with fast moving honking cars. I'm far ahead from the other two at first, and we meet again at a pit stop, where we eat something and mostly drink a lot. Then for our second half of the trip we move slower and slower. Roxi's already started to walk when we finally reach the outskirt of Baños, and soon I join her. My legs are sore. Xavier stays on his saddle, pedalling like a mad man, but hardly moving forward. Other cyclists we see are also wandering. We decide to just finish it on our feet and an hour later we get to our bike shop to turn in our bikes. We then head back to our hotel, to freshen ourselves up, before we go out again to have some serious food. When we get back to our hotel at night, we are all extremely exhausted, but fulfilled from our performance of today.

Ecuador - Quito, Pichincha

Waking up is hard, the next day. We plan to drive to Quito, and I suggest the scenic route, past the Amazon forests in the east of the country. It's a further drive than the direct way, and neither Xavier or Roxi have ever driven this road. I'm pulling them into my adventure and convince them at breakfast. We gas up and head out of Baños, to the east. The road is small and soon we already see a change of scenery. The mountains are on our left, and to the right tropical rain forest spreads itself out. The trees are huge and from the back of the car I'm shooting prayers for wildlife. I use my phone to navigate, and it's all fairly easy. We drive calmly and focus our eyes on the trees to see parrots, which are supposedly often seen here. In the village of Puyo we see all travel agencies advertise with parrot tours, so we shouldn't be able to miss it. From Puyo we head north, towards Tena, and we keep the Andes on our left side. Giving it a great contrast with our right, where we see more and more thick jungle vegetation. Whenever I think to spot a special bird we stop at the side of the road and I aim my camera for what I see. Mostly I spot the condors, which I've grown really tired of. Ever since my first day in Paramaribo, these birds seem to be everywhere. At another stop I see a small eagle, but it's too far to take some clear shots of. I try to approach it like a thief, quietly moving foot after foot. In this process I get disturbed when one of my footsteps next to a dirty ripped off head of a doll. It's not far from an abandoned house and this situation gives me a little bit of chills. I imagine to be in a Child's Play, and turn to wave at my friends, but they are out of sight. Some more steps before I am at my ideal position, but the soils under my shoes sinks. Swamp area. Before I get stuck I move my feet quicker now, making too much noise, and the bird flies away. Damnit. I walk a bit further down, to a small smelly water, where a swing hangs on a big tree. This entire scenery makes me think I'm in a horror movie, and I head back up, unable to express these ideas in Spanish. We get back in the car and continue the drive. All villages we pass are small and primitive and it's nice to see the other side of Ecuador. Not soon after our last village we start heading up again and slowly wind up the mountain range, eventually reaching up to 3400 metres. It's changing to a rough mountain range, and we continue over a road that's under construction. It's quite an adventure when we finally reach the end of the pass and see the city of Quito at our feet. It's a stunning view. We now get totally lost however, as neither Xavier or Roxi exactly know where their uncle, in whose house we will spend the night, lives. We head north, west, east, south, ask people, use Google, but without result. Then, we finally get to find it at a map and find it not much after this. Quito seems like a maze this time, and is much bigger than I thought it was after my first visit some weeks ago. We are welcomed by a lot of family in the house and straight away make a friendship with the little girl, Valentina, and the small dog. Children still seem to understand me better. The entire family is extremely welcoming again and I feel at home straight away. I get to share the guest room with Xavier, in this big house, which also seems to be a maze of its own. I settle for finding the living room. Here we have a great meal and talk until late.

What to do next, is the question once again. I had assumed Xavier and Roxi would have to return the car, but they seem to stick around a bit longer. We decide to go to Mindo, which is a birding paradise, and about a two-hour drive with the car. We mobilise more of the family and in two cars we finally head out north. I share the car with Roxi, Gaby and her boyfriend, while Xavier, Endor, Vane and Valentina are in the other car. It's a nice drive up there and I pass some familiar points of interest that I had already seen with Eduard. Now we continue north of the middle of the earth though, and soon wind west, into the forest. The road is winding and it's quite busy. Slow cars hold up the others, and lines are formed, with people impatiently waiting for opportunities to pass the slow ones. We aren't in a hurry though and just move with the speed that is given to us. Then we take a hairpin to the left, which is the way down to Mindo. It's beautifully situated in a valley, which seems to be a sort of crater. The town is small, has a lot of small stores, tour agencies, and ho(s)tel accommodations. We park the car to get some drinks, and at the small park I spot some yellow birds. Every bird I see here, I assume is rare. Even though I'm not a birder, I like to see what is rare, and I like to practice my photograph skills. On these moving and flying animals I find my practice for the moment I will ever encounter a jaguar. I have to be prepared. We take the car then on a small dirt road up a hill, through the forest, up to the start of a trail that leads to some waterfalls. Here I see my first toucan, high up on a branch. My friends all wonder what the hell I'm doing walking to this desolate tree, but when I later show them my photo, they wish they would have done the same. The trail immediately goes steeply down, and at one point there's a short cut with ropes. Roxi and Xavier take this way, while all the others follow the main trail which leads to the same point eventually. Then there's a sort of open space with a swing hanging on a huge tree. We all take turns swinging. When it's Roxi's turn, she all surprises us with a true circus act and she climbs above the seat and hangs in the ropes as a trapeze artist. We give her an applause like an audience in a circus would do. The road continues a bit more down, where we meet the river, which we follow downstream, until we reach a basin. Here we see more people, and also a big slide, that I had only seen in city swimming pools before. I'm not exactly a daredevil, but I decide to check it out and me and Xavier climb back up the trail, where there's some tough guys discussing tactics on how to come out the tube in a cool way. Some put on life jackets that are laying there for people's use, others just go without. When all these guys are gone, it's only me and Xavier, and looking down I'm having some second thoughts. It's quite steep, and the water must be freezing. I take a deep breath and take my seat in the slide and seconds later I push myself into eternity. That's what is going through my mind at least when I go down this concrete tube super-fast and almost move out in one corner due to my velocity. The slide is quite short, but it launches you at the end at some two metres altitude. I totally move all ways but the right one, and hit the ice cold water on my side. Ouch. The water however makes you soon forget you're alive at all, and I'm rapidly swimming to where my friends await me. Brrr. I'm hooked now however, and do the same thing three more times, eventually also dragging Vale's boyfriend with me. The other times I slow my speed along the way and make sure I'm launched with my feet going down first. The water gets more pleasant the more you get into it, and I start recommending others to at least take a dip. None are willing to, and I can't really blame them, remembering my own first dip today. I change my shorts into drier ones and then we explore just a bit more downstream, before going up again. I'm fresh now because of the water and for the first time I don't struggle climbing up. Xavier and me also explore another corner of the meandering river, but don't find any animals. Then it starts raining and we try to get up to the car as fast as possible. The huge trees are our umbrellas and we barely get really wet from the few drops coming down. I even find time to photograph some tiny birds who are on a search for fruits. Back at the cars the rain has stopped already and we share some of our snacks, before heading back to the town of Mindo. I request one more stop however, as we pass a hostel with a garden full of hummingbirds, so I have read online. It's easily found on the way back, and while everyone sits themselves down on benches, I go wild on photographing the many hummingbirds that are indeed present in this garden full of flowers. There are also special hummingbird feeders, thus it's easy to see the clapping of the wings right before your nose. It's not that easy to photograph this, and even though I try, I don't think I've taken one good shot. The others return to the car and I make some last efforts for the perfect photograph. I give up when the rain starts falling down again and join the others at the cars. Now we drive into Mindo again, park, and find a restaurant for a very late lunch. We find an empty establishment, where we are quickly helped and served. After this good meal we start our journey back to Quito. Back at the family's home, I teach Valentina how to use my big camera and full of enthusiasm she starts running around and taking photos of everyone. Catch them young, so they say. We talk and chill until there's another dinner served, this time prepared by Xavier, the chef. It tastes delicious and it is a perfect ending of yet another great day.

The next day is a relaxing day. I hang around the house, talk to the family, have my meals, and play video games with Roxi. The day after is mostly the same, even though we have one field trip to a viewpoint to see a great view over the city of Quito. Xavier has left us with the car now, and Roxi stays behind, as she doesn't have to do much back in Quevedo anyway.

Ecuador - Papallacta, Napo

We think about making another trip, and this time we decide to try to find bears in the Andes, in a national park, near the town of Papallacta, where they are spotted frequently. Me, Endor and Roxi pack some clothes, and head out, planning to sleep there one night, so we can start a hike into the park on an early morning. We take Endor's car and drive up into the mountains, the same way we've arrived to Quito a few days earlier. There's still constructions going on the road, leading to slow traffic. The higher we get, the cloudier it gets, leaving the sun only to warm the valley. Upon arrival in the very small village we drive around to find an accommodation. First we drive all the way up, to the park entrance, which is situated at a luxury hotel, way out of our budget, and then we return towards the town centre, stopping at every hotel possible to inform for options and prices. Eventually we get a room in a nice hotel in the middle of the centre, as far as you can talk of a centre, as the village seems to contain only a few houses. We drop our luggage off and then find the last open restaurant where we quickly have a bite. It's very cold up here, and I hope tomorrow's weather will be better.

Waking up and a quick look out of the window prove yesterday's hopes were false, as it is drizzling outside. We are awake very early and the first to have breakfast in the hotel. Yesterday a tour guide from a renowned bear spotting travel agency has told us it will be incredibly difficult for us to see a bear today, but I keep my head up high and am positive that we can see one. After breakfast we all wear our warmest clothes and then go in the car to the park entrance, and drive through the luxury resort to end up at a small road, that winds up more into the mountains. It's dry now, so we don't worry about the weather conditions. At a ranger station we park our car and look at the map that's hanging there. Then our hike starts, going uphill straight away. I haven't seen this kind of scenery on my trip until now, with green yellowish bushes along the side. I head off the main trail to see a small waterfall and walk through blubber and mud. I think to see a pile of bear shit, as the pile reminds me of my first bear encounters on Vancouver Island, Canada, back in 2012. It makes me feel positive and I report my findings to my friends back on the main trail. We keep going up, and walk around a lake. It's beautiful, even though the sun isn't shining, and we walk under a thick blanket of clouds. The trail keeps going up, and I think we've reached an elevation over 4000 metres. We see another waterfall along the lonesome trail. Every now and then I stop to look at the slopes of the mountains to see if I can spot an Andean bear. I don't see any movement of any animals, except for some occasional birds. I continuously walk ahead of the other two, as I've learned it's best to keep your own tempo while going up or down a hill. I stop every time the distance becomes too big, as sticking together seems to be a good idea. We keep passing little lakes, and the scenery is nice. The vegetation is all very wet because of previous rain and today's dawn. At one point we observe clouds capturing our view from a lake. It's pretty impressive to see the clouds move so fast and then blocking our view. The further up we get, the more this happens, until at one point we are walking in the clouds, or the fog. At five metres distance I can't see my friends anymore, giving it all a spooky effect. It's cold up here, very cold, and my clothes aren't protecting me enough. I keep moving to keep warm, but I believe it's better the trail would end soon. Even though I try to spot bears, I become convinced this isn't our lucky day, and my focus more and more shifts to how to keep warm. We continue the trail all the way to the end, to a little dam, where we take some final smiling photos. My smile soon is removed from my face, as on our way back, our worst case scenario becomes true as the first raindrops start falling down. Soon it is drizzling, and then raining, leaving us soaked. There's no shelter up here and we can't hide from this rain at this altitude. Now it becomes free for all to get back to the car as soon as possible. We've walked up for four hours and I hope we can make it back sooner. I barely make any stops while my soaked feet splash in the water on the trail. The mud makes it slippery and at times I'm a trapeze artist to overcome the puddles. Other times the puddles are too big, and the best way is to try to walk around them, off trail. I'm not waiting anymore for my friends, only look back at times to see if they're still moving. I'm so cold that I might faint. I'm not aware anymore of taking steps, all seems to be done on automatic pilot. At times I go up, but most of the time downhill, sometimes sliding over the path. The trail seems infinite and I can't recognise anything anymore. Did we really walk this far? I have my hoodie on, and the gloves I've bought this morning aren't any help anymore. My hands were first extremely white, and now the colour purple appears. This is not good. I'm also pushing my endurance while I determinedly tread. Then I finally recognise our first lake, which gives me hope for a second, which is soon replaced by a realisation it is still at least thirty minutes going down. I try to take a pee, but my body won't cooperate too much and this exposing isn't helping against the cold. I'm now far ahead of my friends, but instinctively I have to keep going. The rain doesn't stop for a second, and I feel naked, exposed to this force of nature. Then I finally see the car and the ranger station, but also a little shelter, a roof. I move there in the same pace and sit myself down, laying down my backpack, and drinking my last drops of water. Surprisingly the ranger at duty comes out his house and invites me in. I try to explain my physical situation, but I think he knows it's not good. He mentions hypothermia and puts an electric heater next to me. When he sees this isn't doing too much good, he gives me a towel and directs me to a shower, a warm shower. Undressing never was this hard. The hot water isn't warming me though, and I keep shaking, now that my body is finally at a point of rest. I'm trembling all over. When I finally feel my fingers again, I get out of the shower, and put on my wet clothes again, which were laid drying for the twenty-minute shower and thus are a bit drier. I get a tea, and the ranger tries to keep talking to me, which works like a bliss. We start exchanging animal encounters, and it makes me forget about my situation. Endor and Roxi then arrive, in much better shape than me, fortunately. They are cold, but not that cold, they say. I'm worried however, and stop thinking about my own state, finally. We all have a tea together and laugh. Finally, my smile's back. Then we get into the car and drive off, thanking the ranger for all his help. In the car we put the heater on, but it takes ages before it gets a little warm inside, which is probably mostly due to our wet clothes. In about two or three hours we get back to the house, and there we have a good laugh about our crazy bear adventure. We are served a very warm meal, and all fall asleep early.

Ecuador - Quito, Pichincha

The next day is all about recovery. My legs are incredibly sore, and I'm happy to hear my two friends suffer from the same problem. We spend the day in the house, cheering for the Ecuadorian team, which I now also support, wearing the nation's national jersey, which was handed to me today as a gift. Unfortunately, the team sucks, and doesn't get through to the next round. I also decide upon my next destination and book a ticket to Bogotá, Colombia, with departure in two days.

My last day in Quito is another quiet one. At a shopping mall I buy some gifts to thank my host family for their incredible hospitality, and the rest of the time we watch the World Cup. In the evening we do one final trip, to 'El Panecillo', which is the tallest virgin Mary statue in the world, and the only one, I think, that has given her wings. It's up a hill in the city, and I've seen it many times already from a distance. Now, in the evening, it is lit up beautifully. The closer we get, the bigger the statue becomes, until it is bigger than I could have ever imagined. We walk around, I take some photos, and we browse the market stands. My friends give me my warm hat, that I love, and a nice little statue of a hummingbird flying over the word of Ecuador, thanking me for my stay. I'm extremely grateful again, and absolutely love these people, not for their gifts, but for everything they've done for me, and their unconditional friendship. Emotionally I gaze at the millions light at my feet and hear the sound of silence. Valentina pulls me out of my moment and I start playing hide and seek with her, while we walk back to the car. We're laughing out loud every time she finds me. Now we drive to a park with monumental hummingbirds in all kinds of artistic colours, where we spend time in the nearby playground, before walking past huge stone birds there. I can finally take some good photos of the hummingbird. When we get back home I hand out my gifts and everyone seems to be happy, even though this is my last night in this house with great people.

COLOMBIA

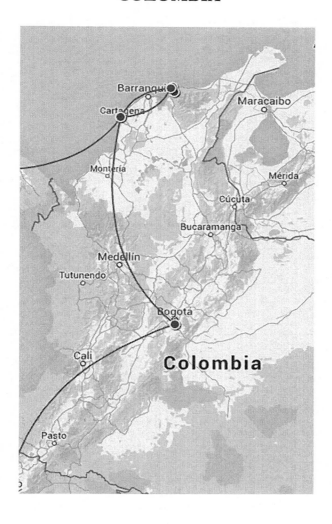

Colombia - Bogotá, Cundinamarca

Endor and Roxi drive me to the airport the next morning, the one I've of course been to before twice. We have a small bite together in the nearby shopping centre, and then they wait until I've dropped off my bag. Just before I go through customs we all hug farewell, and all speak out the hope to see each other again.

The flight to Bogotá is not too long and even entering the country is easy. Much easier than some of the other South American countries. At the Quito airport I considered sealing my bag in plastic, as slipping in drugs at an airport would be most likely in a flight to or from Colombia, I thought, but I soon got rid of these ridiculous thoughts. All the people at the airport are friendly and helpful. I get my taxi again from the airport office, which I always think is the most reliable upon arriving in a new country. The taxi brings me to the hotel I've reserved and it's quite a ride to find it. The street where the hotel is at, is totally blocked by construction works, and the taxi can't get to the entrance. He insists on walking me there the last metres, and even persuades me to carry my big bag. The hotel is very modern, and is situated in one of the better areas of the city, but is quite far from the historical centre. I do my check-in and then have a dinner in the restaurant, as I don't want to explore the city by night and it's already quite late. I sleep quite early, really not really aware I'm in a new country.

I kind of sleep in the next day, and hang around a bit in my room, before heading out to meet my friend Andrea, who's invited me to come watch the Colombian match at a popular square in the area of my hotel. We meet some hours before the match and first get me a jersey, as I need to be properly dressed she says. I agree, and soon we're bargaining for one of the fake shirts, and I get a nice yellow one in the end, for a proper price. Then we head to a bar where we see the other match of today. We can't stay there for the Colombia match as all seats are reserved. After paying we head out to the square and first get a sandwich, as we need to be well prepared for the game. Then we try to enter the square, where it's already packed. An enormous crowd is sitting in front of the big television screen. Around the people sitting in the grass, there's a crowd standing. I assume everyone will stand when the match starts, but everyone keeps sitting. We also manoeuvre ourselves into a seating position and are now totally ready for the match against one of Colombia's rivals, Uruguay. It is an ace performance of Colombia, and they totally outplay the opponents, with good football, and see the goal of the tournament, made by local hero James Rodriguez. 2-0 is the final score. The crowds totally go mental now and everyone's jumping, singing, clapping, partying. It's a madhouse. It's great to see how these people love and live football. Andrea needs to go, so I walk her to a place where she can get a taxi, and then head back into the party, where I meet many new friends. Late in the afternoon I head back to my hotel, where I have my dinner.

I haven't received so many text messages after a night's sleep as today. The Dutch news reported seven people died in Bogotá during the victory celebrations, and I'm often asked if all is okay. I didn't see anything bad happening yesterday, so I let the front desk inform me what happened. They also don't know, but they say it's quite common people die here when there's a party: cars hit pedestrians, people shoot in the air with guns, and sometimes bullets hit other people. The way they tell it to me, it seems a regular thing here and they just shrug their shoulders about it. I have my breakfast and then get ready for being picked up to see the match of the Netherlands versus Mexico. I'm wearing my orange jersey and like in Ecuador people seem to support my country to reach the final. Many people only rate their home country higher than Holanda. I'm meeting two Colombian sisters who I've met for the first time in 2009 while exploring Santiago, in Chile, and always been in touch with. They live in Bogotá and as soon as they knew I was coming, they were eager to meet up again. We watch the match in a mall, laying on poufs. It's a bad game, but in the final 10 minutes the orange machine turns the game around and wins it in the dying seconds. I release a primal scream upon victory and the other people watching excitedly applaud for me. I make a dance outside the mall and we then take a taxi to another mall to have lunch. There I receive many congratulations from shopping and eating folks. After lunch we walk to the area of my hotel, and there say farewell again. Investing in friends pays off as I've seen today once more. In the afternoon I see today's second match in the park again and then get ready for some nightly sightseeing with a friend I've met on couchsurfing, and who's making a living on photography, and I hope she can teach me some things. First we meet and have dinner in another area of the city, a big mall, where we have a great dinner. Just before we had seen two girls who are food sellers on the streets, got in a big fight, and I was wondering if this was a common thing here. We continued to walk around a bit, and it was quite a nice area. The restaurant is better than everything else though, and the food delicious. Later we go our own ways, and I fall asleep in my hotel.

I spend the next two days walking around in the shopping mall, seeing a movie in the cinema, sitting in the casino playing roulette, and having a spontaneous dinner with a fellow gambler. I'm making some money like I've done in Las Vegas before, putting small amounts of money on black/red, and odd/even. My patient tactic works here as well, and I believe I can fly. I also see all the world cup matches, mostly in the park, amongst businessmen who are on their daily break. One afternoon I go on a quest to get my broken iPad screen fixed, and I'm helped by a front desk employee of my hotel, who accompanies me all the way to this technical centre, and helps me bargain for a good price. It's during his work hours and basically his boss pays him to help me out. I think it's a great deal. While we wait for my screen to be fixed we have a lunch in a small cafeteria, where we also see another football match. We get back to the hotel some hours later, and my iPad seems to be working fine again, which allows me to back up my photos on the internet once again.

On my final full day in Bogotá I meet up with my photographing friend, Layne, as she will take me to Cerros de Monserrate, and the historical centre, so I finally will see something of the 'real' Bogotá, instead of the modern and snobbish sites. We take a taxi to the foot of the mountain, from where a cable cart will bring us to the top. The entire way I nag my friend about how this cab driver could kidnap us, which makes us both laugh out loud. The cableway takes us to 3000 metres, and from there we have a brilliant view over the wide-stretched city. We first walk through a market to a viewpoint at the back, where I have my first master classes in photography. Then we head back, stopping at details which I would have overlooked if I would have been alone. It's all in the details, it seems. We have a typical Colombian lunch in one of the restaurants made for the many visitors of this city's highlight. After lunch we continue walking through the nearby parks, where we see hummingbirds, which by now has become the surrogate for my jaguar. We also make a very long stop at a sea of magical purple flowers, and try to photograph the bees buzzing from flower to flower. It's incredibly difficult to capture these small moving animals, and when I later see the photos, they have all failed. At the end of the park we chase a unique hummingbird, one I've not seen before, one with a tail that's twice as big as its body. It's tremendously difficult to photograph it, but I think I at least take one good shot. Then we take the cableway down, and walk from there to the historical centre, where we soon sit down for a drink and a snack. It's quite busy in some streets, and the safety is not guaranteed here, according to my friend. I only take my camera out when I take a photo, while she doesn't take it out at all. There's a big square, that in a way reminds me of Amsterdam's Dam Square, mostly because of the many pigeons, the historical buildings attached to it, and the street artists trying to make money with their performances. We walk by the palace, to a church and from the church back through small cobble stoned streets. Then we kind of leave the intimacy of the historical buildings to walk through very busy business streets, where I see a huge diversity of people. A severe headache then forces me to go back to my hotel, and thus we split our routes once more, now probably for a much longer time, as tomorrow I catch a flight to Cartagena, in the north of the country. I keep being lucky in who I meet on my trips, and Bogotá once more showed me this.

<u>Colombia - Cartagena de Indias, Bolívar</u>

Yet another travel day, as I keep being on the move. Today I fly
north to one of Colombia's oldest cities, Cartagena. I land here at
sunset, and during the flight I've had a good view of the sun slowly
moving away. At the airport I get in a line to grab a taxi, and then try
to talk to the driver, who doesn't seem to have a clue where my hotel
is. We have to drive into the walled historical centre, and my driver is
wary about it, and I can't understand why. I keep pushing him to go,
and use Google Maps as our guide. When we get to my hotel, he also
suddenly wants to charge me extra money, and I pretend that I have
no clue what he's talking about. The rudeness. I'm warmly welcomed
by the staff of my hotel, which has a nice patio, and my room is
directly accessing it, and is also right next to the breakfast area. I put
away my bags, and then head out to meet a friend I know who lives
here. She's invited me to have dinner and I gladly accepted this offer.
We meet up at the main entrance of the historical city and from there
walk to a very nice square, with an old church, where we have dinner
outside. Even at night it's warm here. The food's very good and the
staff thoughtful. I'm having great laughs about the weirdest things
with my friend, and it seems both of us are high or something. Not
that I know how that feels, but I assume it's about feeling light in
your head and being vague in your talking. Exactly how this night is
passing by. After dinner we walk outside the walls to a place where
my friend tells me are good bars. Now I see even weirder acting
people than me, and I'm not sure how safe this all is anymore. At a
little square there are indeed some bars, and it seems more like the
squatting area of Cartagena. The bar we enter is a very nice one
though, and plays some of the best music that I've listened to for a
long time. I keep using Shazam to look up the songs. After an hour
or so we walk back into the centre, where the streets now are
desolated, and only scum is crawling around, it seems. As I have no
orientation yet in this city, I'm walked back all the way to my hotel,
from where my friend takes a cab to her own family's home, as she
lives in Bogotá normally. Back at the hotel, the friendly night watch
keeps me up with some stories about things to do in Cartagena. Even
though I'm half asleep, it's quite amusing.

Sleeping next to the breakfast area is not ideal, as I find out. Around
six in the morning the ladies of the hotel start preparing everything
and thirty minutes later the first people sit themselves down there

and start their chats, which isn't very helpful for my sleep. I keep turning from side to side, hoping my brain will shut off and fall asleep again. I think I sleep about five minutes more, before getting out. I step into the shower, but no water comes out... Huh? I put some clothes on and sleep walk to the front desk. They tell me there's a problem with the water in the entire city. I don't understand why, but it comes down to it that I can't take a shower now, and it's very unlikely I can take one at some other point of today. Maybe tomorrow... Clean or dirty, today is match day! Colombia has to play the host nation, Brazil, and the entire country is free to see the match. Most shops are closed when I try to buy some water. At many places the electricity isn't working either, thus giving the town a hard time. I head to the entrance of the historical town once again, now to meet the niece of Jessica, the girl I had met during my first Flamengo match in the Maracanã. As she is half Brazilian, and half Colombian, she has some family here and gladly introduced me to Jennifer, daughter of the brother of her father. Or something like that. Jennifer, like Jessica, doesn't speak English, so I will use my 'Portuñol', combined with hands and feet once more. It's a funny first encounter, as I try to make sense, and she doesn't have a clue what I'm talking about. "O dios mio", is said very often those first minutes. We walk to a German bar, as the first match of today is that of the German team. It's packed with Germans, but we find a place at the bar. Jennifer kicks off with beer, while I slurp my water. It's getting more crowded, and while it was cool at first, now it's bloody hot inside. The German team is supreme against France, but only wins 1-0. The crowd goes nuts, so does Jennifer, but I'm a bit sad: the sooner the Germans are eliminated, the better. They have a tendency to reach finals and win them, and I rather have my country win the cup for a change. After the final whistle we walk back to the centre, eat some chicken in a sort of fast food restaurant, and then sit ourselves down in a boteco, a bar. I'm not allowed to bring my water in, but later find out the only drink they serve here is beer. Only beer?! I'm left thirsty for the next two hours, unfortunately. When the Colombian national anthem is played everyone stands and sings along proudly. I can feel the tension inside here, and just hope no one will pull a gun when they're happy. Colombia plays another great match, and their star James is better than any other player on the pitch. The referee however helps the Brazilians win the match. I expect a hugely disappointed crowd now, just like when the Dutch team lost the final four years ago, and everyone walked home in silence. The opposite happens here though, as the party continues, and people keep celebrating as if they just won. They are all so proud of the performance and of their team, that no matter a win or a loss, they are happy about it. The beers have put Jennifer in a party mood too, and we head to a bar outside the walled city once more, where there's a big crowd dancing to the sounds of Colombian music. I think all girls inside ask me for a dance, but I keep refusing politely, and keep fist pumping from my barstool. The crowd really goes wild, and things only get a bit nasty when we finally leave the bar and two guys get into a fight. Not over football of course, but over a girl. Jennifer sneaks out a glass of beer, and continues her party out on the street. I think it's best for her to go home now, and I manage to get her in a cab and send her home. Later she thanks me for doing so, even though her hangover the next day is massive. I walk back to my hotel and on my way find a restaurant for a very late dinner.

Another day, another match. Today's the day for the quarter final of the Dutch team, and they have to play Costa Rica, who have a Colombian coach. I've invited my friend to watch the game with me, and even though she says she hates football, she joins me. I'm first taken to a very nice restaurant where we have a great lunch, and we then find an Irish pub where they have many screens for the match. We sit ourselves in the very back, where we have the biggest screen. Just before the match starts a man and woman walk in with a baby, all dressed in orange jerseys as well. Not much later I find out the guy's Dutch too, and his wife Bolivian. Evert is here for work: importing used trucks from Europe to South America, and he's overseeing the arrival of a shipment. My friend Giseli is extremely bored by the match, and seems quite annoyed, while me and the family on my left totally get into it. The Costa Ricans withstand attack after attack and it's a miracle the orange machine isn't scoring a goal, nor in the 90 minutes, nor in the extra time. A penalty shootout will decide who will move on to the semi-finals, and a miraculous goal keeper substitute by the Dutch coach surprises everyone. The new goalie stops a penalty of the Costa Ricans and the Netherlands win their match once again. I don't have any nails left and another primal scream is released from my throat. We all, except for Giseli, are happy and make a little victory dance. Outside we take a photo together, and then say farewell. I walk to the city walls with my friend and there see the sunset. This is followed by a dinner in the centre, and then a discussion in a park, where we are surrounded by couples doing their marriage photo shoot. My friend then takes a cab home again, and I walk the few steps to my hotel, where I avoid the nightly talks with my friend of the staff, and directly head to bed to sleep.

Today finally a day without football and some serious exploration of Cartagena. I take out my big camera and start walking the streets with a different eye now. An eye for details. My hotel is in the same street as the former house of Gabriel Garcia Marquez, the winner of the Nobel prize of literature, and probably one of the most famous persons from Colombia. The house is surrounded by big walls however, and one can't see much there, unfortunately. I continue my walk past the colourful houses, getting lost in the infinity of alleys and streets. Sometimes I walk in circles, but everywhere I discover new things, new details. There's bright flowers in the planters of the colonial houses, and the Colombian flag waves proudly on many of them. Just when my feet are getting tired, Jennifer arrives to hang out with me. We sit down on a terrace and see the people pass by. One of them is a famous Colombian politician, who has a big entourage and is having friendly chats with the shop owners, most likely to win some votes for an upcoming election. We order a lunch and let the meal taste good. For dessert we have a drink at the second floor of yet another colonial restaurant, and make friends with the staff there, whilst even listening to some Bob Dylan music with the people at the table next to us. We then continue our walk over the walls, and see the sun set in the late afternoon. A husky walking by reminds me of Jacob, but I'm unable to photograph the beauty of its eyes. After some more walking and talking, my friend hops in a taxi once again, and I slowly find my way back to the hotel, trying to take some night shots of the city.

The following day is a very relaxing one. I'm less hurried to see things, but more and more enjoy just to do nothing, to meet up with people, and take it all very easy. In the morning I make a small walk to stretch my legs, and in the later afternoon I meet up with Jennifer. It starts to rain just then, so we take shelter in a bar and watch video clips on the big screen and just chit chat the entire afternoon. Then we go have dinner at the restaurant with our new friends that work there, and the food is tasteful, as it should taste at a farewell dinner. Tomorrow I have arranged transport to bring me to the town of Santa Marta, from where I want to visit Tayrona National Park. I walk Jennifer to a taxi after dinner and walk myself back to the hotel.

Colombia - Santa Marta, Magdalena

I wake up incredibly early to get a taxi to the parking of the company
that will bring me to Santa Marta. It's a van like I've seen in northern
Argentina, and there's many others joining me on this ride, all of
which we drop off in either Barranquilla, or in Santa Marta. It takes a
bit more than two hours for us to reach Santa Marta. I'm glad I didn't
decide to stay one night in Barranquilla, as driving through this city
made me see how ugly it is, and how extremely industrial. After
dropping most of the tourists, they let me out in a nearly abandoned
street, in front of a renovated building, which actually looks very nice.
I'm also welcomed as a king, and it's the start of a great stay. I ask for
a good restaurant and am pointed to a square nearby. I find a nice
one, where they also broadcast the world cup's semi-final of Brazil
versus Germany. I'm the only customer, and as the match is crazy,
the guys from the kitchen join me in what is history in the making:
Germany crushes Brazil with 7-1, it being the host nation's biggest
defeat ever. No one can believe what just happened, but all are
happy, because this team eliminated their beloved Colombia in the
previous round. I get back to my hotel and chill a bit, whilst trying to
upload my photos of Colombia. The Wi-Fi is very unstable and I
inform the staff about it. They can't find a solution right away, but I
get the private network key, which is already a significant
improvement. To my surprise later that day Evert also checks in at
the same hotel, which is one lucky coincidence. I'm having dinner by
myself that night though, and getting in the mood for the next day's
match of the Netherlands versus Argentina.

It's the day of the second semi-final of the Netherlands in a
consecutive World Cup. Now it's the tough Argentinians, with
world's best player, Messi, that is the last obstacle for reaching the
final. In the morning I'm chilling and enjoying my breakfast over a
long time, and in the afternoon I meet with Evert at a bar at the
central square. There's also a big group of Argentinians and later
some other Dutch people too, and of course Colombians. This is the
only packed bar on the square, it seems. Evert's mother in law is
travelling with him too, and she joins to look after Evan, the baby, as
is Anita, of course, doing. The match is like a game of chess, and
every move seems to be answered with a counter move. After 90, and
120 minutes it's still 0-0. Penalties. This time the Dutch lose this
lottery, unfortunately. The team's been so close again, so for a change

we all seem to have some pride in it. We congratulate the Argentinians, who of course are very happy. My new friends leave, and I stay behind talking to two Colombian girls, who also had hoped the Dutch would have won it. Then I also get back to my hotel, and notice the hotel hasn't changed my room into one with two beds, as Jennifer will join me to go to Tayrona tomorrow, and still needs a bed tonight. They organise it quickly, just before she arrives. We have dinner together and after Eduard I finally have a new roomie.

Colombia - Arrecifes, Tayrona National Park, Magdalena

The next day we don't move too quick, and after a breakfast we head out to find a bus terminal with a bus that will bring us to the entrance of the park. I'm happy I'm with someone who speaks the language fluently, as it makes things a lot easier. We buy a stash of bread and water before walking over to a big market, where they seem to sell nearly everything. Then there's a bus that has a sign of Tayrona, and this hippy bus will take us there. In the bus they play very loud funky music, which is quite awkward at the beginning, but later becomes quite nice. I even Shazam some of the songs. The road leaves Santa Marta and goes over a hill, before getting into a small village. Then it's only a bit further, until we reach our stop and we, among some other tourists, get out. We walk up to the entrance and get some information from one of the rangers, as we want to sleep overnight in this park, but have no clue about availability, and if those suggested hammocks are indeed a good way to sleep. We are told everything will be fine and we just have to walk to Arrecifes and get to one of the accommodations there. After paying our entrance fee we get into a little van, that brings us to the start of the trails. We start our hike in the heat and immediately go uphill. I'm very curious for the monkeys in this park, and I've read there's even a chance for jaguars here. Woohaa. The ranger had laughed at me, when I told him I'm here for that animal, but confessed there's a theoretic chance, which is enough for me to believe I can see one. Except for ants we don't see any animal in our first hour of hiking. We're bathing in sweat, and the recommendations of wearing pants to protect yourself from mosquitoes proves to be a bad one. When we leave the jungle for the first time, we see a mighty blue ocean, which is an amazing sight. We get down and walk through dry mangroves, through the sand. We re-enter the jungle now, which borders the beach. There are wooden footpaths here at times, to make the trail a bit easier. I see something moving in a tree from my left eye corner and immediately have my camera ready. It might be nothing, but I'm extremely focused on seeing at least one normal animal. I try to silently leave the trail a bit and get a bit closer to what I thought to have seen. The leaves crackling under my shoes probably scaring away all animals, but I'm hopeful and persistent this is a hit. And yes, high in the tree, hardly visible due to the shades, branches and leafs, there's a monkey sitting, a howler monkey. It looks at me and for a moment I feel it will come to attack me, but after some steps in my direction it slowly moves up and to another tree. I snap some photos and on them I can better see how it actually looked. I'm very excited and happily return to the trail to show my photos to everyone that passes by in the next seconds. Not much later we arrive in Arrecifes and start looking for a place to sleep. Jennifer asks for options and normal beds seem rare here. Then we meet a couple of friends who had stayed in small cabins a bit more down the road and we decide to check it out. We struggle finding it, but eventually do. We inspect the cabin which has three beds, and a fan, which might be useful in this weather. We decide to take it, and change our clothes into swimming gear, so we can take a dive into the nearby 'Piscina', which is a small bay with an even smaller beach, which is nice for swimming. I hadn't realised one thing though: Jennifer doesn't know how to swim. Oh well, she can watch my camera while I take a swim, fair enough. It's a little trail to this bay and we arrive here shortly after. The water is chillier than I thought it would be in this hot weather, but it freshens me after day bathing in sweat. Before sunset we return to the bigger beach near our campsite, from where we see the sun going down behind the hill. We walk back to the camp and have a very good dinner at a typical picnic table. One guy keeps walking around with his phone high above his head, obviously trying to get a signal. We can't stop laughing at his desperation, moreover because at moments that he does have a signal, the conversation is utterly useless. The next day holding the cell phone up high becomes our extra-terrestrial move. We get to our primitive cabin when it's late and extremely dark. I use my cell phone now as a flashlight and scare the hell out of my friend when I tell her there's a giant snake. I get the bunk bed, and Jennifer the normal bed, as it should be and then try to fall asleep while the fan desperately blows some cold air.

Colombia - Santa Marta, Magdalena

Four o'clock at night. I'm overheated and sweating like never before. The fan doesn't move anymore and the cabin has become a sauna. Jennifer's still snoring, probably used to this, but I can hardly breathe. I try, and try more, I try for an hour, but I can't get back to sleep. I decide to put on some shorts, take my camera, and head out, maybe there's some animals to be seen. I first walk to the beach and it's already getting light, even though the sun is still to come. I sit down in the sand and wait for things to happen. Soon a pale sun, as if it's the moon, rises up at the horizon over the ocean, and it slowly climbs higher and higher, changing colours along the way, until it is one fiery yellow ball that gives the sky a bright orange colour. This must be the best sunrise I've ever seen. A couple now enters the beach too and without them knowing I use them as my models for this captivating moment. Then I start walking into the jungle, all alone. I hear the jungle waking up and the silence is soon disturbed by chirping birds, and cracking leafs. I spot an agouti searching for his breakfast, and some small yellow-black frogs, which seem to be everywhere. I keep walking until I reach some kind of indigenous village which I don't enter, out of respect for the inhabitants. Close to there I meet a guy from Germany and he says he's seen some monkeys a bit down the road. I thank him and hurry myself there, but too late to see any of them. Some donkeys pass me on their way back to the park entrance apparently and this means I head back to the ground to get some breakfast and to wake up my friend. She's already awake when I arrive and even ready to join me for breakfast. We can leave our stuff here for a while, and after our pieces of bread we head out once more. First we pass 'Piscina' again, and then the trail leads us to Cabo San Juan, which is a wide open space, with two gorgeous beaches, separated by a big rock. Being all warmed up from the hike in the sun, I immediately go for a swim in the lovely water. My friend is lying on a rock to get a tan, while I'm making silly handstands and enjoying the scenery. We stay for quite a while here, and then walk back to our camp, to first have lunch, and then hike our way back to the exit of the park. When we pass the indigenous village again, I start my search for monkeys again: maybe they have returned. And yes, I see monkeys. It's a family of red howler monkeys: father, mother, and two babies. They are very high up, and protected from my camera by many branches and leafs. They slowly move in the tree top, eating the fruits they find. The babies every now and then are playing and hanging upside down. They're quiet, even though I'm sure they've seen me. I try to take many photos, and Jennifer sits herself down, realising this might take a while. Then something happens, as we hear many branches being broken in the trees a bit further in the forest. I look through my camera and see a big group of capuchin monkeys, closing in on the tree where the howler monkeys are. This big group is not hiding they're there, and within minutes they overtake the tree from the howler family, who slowly move over the branches hanging over the trail, to the other side. There they sit down for a while, looking at the capuchins throwing down fruits, branches, and whatever they encounter. The capuchins stay on their side of the forest and move forward rapidly, being led by one, who signals the other to move whenever needed. The group vanishes as soon as they arrived, but it was a fascinating spectacle. Now the howler monkeys continue their way, and I follow them from beneath. They again cross the path over the branches and then have some fruits before also being swallowed by the jungle. I've spent over 1.5 hours observing these wonderful animals, and thus also giving my friend her rest, so we can now go over the hill to the exit. The trail we now follow is the one of the donkeys and horses, and is basically use to supply the camps in Tayrona. There's shit everywhere and you have to pay attention not to be overrun when you walk up or down the small caverns of the trail, where only one person or animal can pass at a time. We make it to the other side safely; sweaty, but safely. Going gradually down here is quite easy, and the last part is on a flat trail. We arrive at the ranger station again, and await transport to the park's exit, as walking back these final kilometres is more than we would think it is, so we are told. The van arrives quite quick, and is completely full when it takes off and drives us back in thirty minutes. From there we wait for our bus back to Santa Marta, which all goes extremely smooth. Back in Santa Marta we walk back in some twenty minutes and are happy to be back in the hotel again, and have a good shower. Dinner is ordered in the restaurant, where we also get to talk to Evert and his family. We agree to join them the next day to Playa Crystal, which is also situated in Tayrona, but at another entrance, more to the west.

We share our breakfast with everyone, meaning with the six of us, then pack our stuff, and hop in Evert's big rental car. We take off and only miss our exit once, before getting on a bumpy road into the park. The road winds up and has many rocks everywhere. We're happy Evert's a good driver. Then we come to a big bay, which is marvellous from high up the hill. The road goes down until we get to a parking, where we station the car, get our stuff out and then head for the boats, trying to find one that will bring us to the designated beach. We find one quickly, and almost feel we're in some kind of amusement park; all is going too smooth. Fifteen minutes later we are welcomed on Crystal Beach by people renting tents, and we soon sit in a street of these little blue tents, with neighbours on both sides. Drinks are being served and we all sit, talk and chill here. I of course go for some swimming and splashing in the water, while the others drink their beers. For lunch I get back and the fresh fish is very tasty. After eating I help Jennifer to enter the ocean and make sure she doesn't drown. She even smiles, even though afraid. We don't last too long in the water, and while she overcomes the experience, I walk to a view point, north of the beach. I'm so stupid to forget my flip flops and my adventure on the rocks make me swear, as these rocks are awfully sharp. I bite my tongue though, and continue until I have a good point to take some photos. Then back and up the hill, where the small rocks are even more annoying and harmful. My feet start bleeding, but like a honey-badger, I don't care. From the top I should have had a good perspective, if there weren't trees blocking my sight. I manage to snap some photos and then hop back. I spend the rest of the time in the water, and in the waves breaking on the beach. The waves have quite some power and I let them drag my body to the sand, over and over again. I'm nine years old again. The others have packed their stuff, and then it's also time for me to get out of the water. The beach is already quite empty and we're among the last ones leaving. Evert drives us back to the hotel, where we all get ready for a night out. Evan and his grandmother stay behind, and the four of us go to the modern touristy part of Santa Marta, El Rodadero. We've heard of a nice restaurant with a great view of the skyline there, so we try to get there, which is a big adventure, as we keep driving the wrong way. We do find it though and then are seated an outside table, where we inspect the menu and then order. I'm the designated driver tonight, so the rest is continuing what they've started at the beach today: drinking. We're having a great time, and even though the people already have started to dance here, we decide to move to another club, which we heard is very good. Google Maps totally sends us in the wrong direction though and we end up close to our hotel, instead of the actual place, which was two blocks from the restaurant we just were at. We head back, find the club, enter, and see a nearly empty setting, with some couples dancing, but it totally lacks atmosphere, for now. We decide to head back to our restaurant and continue to party there. And we do party, as kings. And I dance, like a moron. Jennifer tries to teach me, and I must say, I do better than in Jericoacoara, but still, my body's not made for rhythm. Evert obviously has had more practice and it looks much smoother. Anita and Jennifer however, are the queens of the dance floor. When all the bottles of whatever-local-drink-they-are-drinking are finished, we get back to the car and I drive everyone back. We stop at a night market, for some food and this is when it becomes clear Jennifer really drunk too much, as she soon hangs out of the car emptying her stomach. The food arrives and off we are. The parking near the hotel is closed, so it takes a while before we find one nearby that is open, and also looks safe. Again we manage and we help my friend walk back to the hotel and I lay her in her bed, feeding her with as much water as I can, hoping to prevent a serious hangover. I lay myself in my bed and see her passing out right away. I reminisce over the night before also falling in a deep sleep.

I get out of bed early, to have a breakfast, while Jennifer has a huge hangover. She can barely talk and the only thing she's doing is hiding under her sheets. I give her some fruits and lots of water again, and eventually she starts feeling better. As she has to return home, this is quite good, as she'll be taking the bus back to Cartagena. When she is finally able to walk, at the start of the afternoon, we manage to have a little lunch and then she heads out, grabbing a bus which will bring her back to Cartagena in about four hours. We all say farewell to her and then my second travel friend leaves. I ask the staff to make one big bed again in my room and while they organise that I visit Evert's room, which appears to be a two floor apartment, on the top floor of the hotel. It gives a good sight over the town of Santa Marta, and also of its harbour. We talk until we see a beautiful sunset over the ocean and I snap some shots. We have dinner together in the restaurant and then go to our beds.

Evert and the gang leave the next morning, so out of six it's only me now. I've made friends with all the staff of the hotel, and they keep me company when I again figure out what I will do next. I visit a travel agency in town and get information about the so-called lost city (Ciudad Perdida), which is Colombia's Machu Picchu. I get in touch with other travellers, and some of them went there, and tell me to absolutely not go, as it is shit. It makes me reconsider it, and I ask around for other options. What I certainly want to do however is to revisit Tayrona, as I absolutely loved it there, and I still haven't seen the white-top tamarin monkeys, which only live here in Colombia. In the afternoon I meet with the third sister of my Bogotá friends, who now lives and works in Santa Marta, and my friends had told me to meet up with her. I have lunch with her at the same place where I saw Germany's match against Brazil. I also see her work and meet some of her co-workers. Her work is next to the travel agency I visited earlier.

The next two days I spend walking around Santa Marta, thinking of my next step, and taking it all a little easy. I get to know some new friends, and also meet up with my friends that I met at the football match of Netherlands versus Argentina, in a shopping near Rodadero. I also find myself a restaurant that serves a perfect chicken for a very low price, and thus a place I'm visiting more often. I decide to visit Minca, a birder's paradise, with some waterfalls. The front desk of my hotel are trying to contact a guide, but coordination isn't really working. I will go there nevertheless, and find my own way if needed. I find out from where the bus will go and the next day I'm going.

I wake up early, pack my hiking gear, and head off to the market, from where also the Tayrona bus leaves. Some blocks further up should be the bus to Minca. I keep walking busy streets without finding any bus, or any sign. I ask some police officers, but no one seems to know about this bus to Minca. I ask at a shop, and they then finally point me to where the bus is supposed to leave. I see a small sign and ask when the bus is leaving. They reply there's no bus, but there's a car, pointing at a small old car that's parked in the street. I'm confused. How is this a bus service? They all laugh. I'm told this car only leaves when there's enough people to go, and they hope it will be in the next hour. I decide to wait a bit, but there's absolutely no one even informing about this transport, and I'm seriously having second thoughts about this. I abandon my plan, tell the folks I'm going back to my hotel, and walk off. At the hotel I tell them my experiences, and they all laugh at and with me. David and Vanessa, the young couple running the nice hotel, suggest I go with Yurleidys, the girl at the front desk, and that she will know how to get to Minca. I of course embrace this idea and she is also up for it. I warn her that

I'm very annoying with my camera and that every bird needs to be photographed at least one hundred times. She doesn't seem to care though, so we confirm our trip for tomorrow. The rest of the day I chill in the pool, have dinner in my restaurant, and of course sleep when I think it's bed time.

My friend's arranged a befriended cab driver to drive us to Minca, which is about an hour drive, and goes up a small windy road. We are dropped off at the start of the trail, beyond the town of Minca itself, and from there on walk downwards, through dense forest. At the first waterfall we have some drinks and snacks, before deciding to continue over a trail which is mostly overgrown by green grass. Here I spot some hummingbirds and other bird species. At our right we see the stream flowing in the shades of the big trees and we think that would be a nice place to see. We inspect the abyss next to our trail, but it's very steep and there's no trails leading there. Determined we find a place which might do and we go down step by step, weary of the leaves, and branches, that could make us slip. We get to the river bed safely and it's even more beautiful here than it looked from above. We only hear the river crawling over the rocks, accelerating when it narrows, and keeping calm where it widens. Through the roof of trees some silver sunlight reaches us, making the moving water sparkle, like diamonds in the sky. Other people seem to walk both up and down the river bed, soon disturbing the peace. We are sitting looking into the water with infinitive looks, seeing past and present, and philosophise about life, death and beyond. I see a golden squirrel looking at us, and slowly pull out my camera to snap his flickering eyes, that sting me through the mazes of green. The squirrel runs off, and we decide to go back up the trail, where blooming flowers welcome us again. We keep walking up the trail, until we are face to face with a brown horse. He's blocking our path like Gandalf who's preventing the Balrog from chasing the poor little hobbits. Instead of fighting this wizard in disguise, I gently approach it, until it moves out of its way, so we can continue. The path seems to never end, and when we start getting tired, we turn and walk back, seeing the path from a different angle, and also spotting some toucans a bit further in the forest, unreachable for us. We get back to the river, and walk our way back to Minca, now walking up, which is tiring. Fortunately there are now many birds to photograph in a landscape that now looks like the Shire, after Gandalf made his entrance just a bit before. In Minca we go to a restaurant that has hummingbird feeders, and there's a couple dozen little birds swarming around them; they take some sips, then rapidly fly off and come back later again. It seems like an organised feeding fest. Our chairs stand just a metre away, and even though we're so close, it keeps being a challenge to photograph these birds. The only good takes are the ones when they rest on the branches. Then our taxi comes to pick us up, and first brings Yurleidys back to her family home, and then me to my hotel. It can't be a coincidence anymore that so many people help me on my travels, maybe I have something to do with it myself, and maybe not... Back at the hotel I directly take off to the town's beach to enjoy a sublime sunset: the colour of the sky turns from bright orange to soft pink, and I'm just aw-ing. Let nature be blessed. I take a dinner, and then walk to the hotel to rest a bit.

Tayrona National Park is today's destination, and I pack up my gear once again, for my second visit to this park, to see more of the wildlife. I walk to the bus once more, and find it all very easy now, and also know what to do and say to get me dropped off at the right place. Today I'm taking another entrance, the one at Calabazo, which is more secluded from the main entrance, through which most tourist enter. It's about ten minutes earlier that the bus now drops me off, and I immediately see signs that point out the way. I don't see any booth where I can buy my entrance ticket, until I'm called at after passing a house. It's a young park ranger who overlooks this entrance, and summons me to pay the fee. I happily pay, let me inform on the trail possibilities, which are minimum, but can be a world apart, in hours of hiking. After that I'm ready to go, and start the hike. The road passes some houses of locals, who have their own little gardens with vegetables, and dogs on the loose. Chickens are everywhere, and behind the barbed wire sad donkey eyes follow my steps. The main entrance hike's going over gloomy hills and isn't exactly hard, but what I'm facing here is a different category. The first few hundred metres felt fine, but it keeps going steep up. No wonder I had been offered to do the journey on a horse's back. I'm quite out of breath and in need of sugar when I finally reach a flat plateau, where there's a small indigenous village, where they sell some cold drinks. I buy one from the little girls, who, like all other villagers, are dressed in white costumes. Their black hair is rugged, and their faces slightly dirty. These people live in the wild. I walk by them after some friendly chit chat and continue my road, which is gradually going up now, and is easier than before. Then I arrive at a fork in the road, and have to decide to go either left or right. Left goes directly to the coast, to Playa Brava, and the right one to Pueblito, an archaeological site, which can be seen as a three house Machu Picchu, and is holy to the indigenous people. I take about ten steps to the left, but go back, following my intuition the right might be a more interesting route. Some fifty steps uphill later I'm already proven right: in two trees I see very small animals hopping around: it's the tamarin monkeys. I get my camera in position and shoot it like a machine gun. There's a whole group swiftly moving through the trees, stopping every now and then to take a peek at me. The adrenaline's rushing through my body as I try to get closer, but these animals are so fast that soon they're all gone deeper into the woods, unreachable from the trail. I wait for some time and keep staring into the bush, hoping for them to come back. The only ones coming back are some other tourists, who had spent the night at Cabo. I ask them how long it took them to come from there, and they say about two hours. Fair enough. I continue my steps, gazing at the size of the trees and the beautiful roof of trees and leafs. The path winds a little bit more up, and sometimes steep down, before going steeper up again. I'm alone with nature and alert for all the sounds around me. As I mainly try to spot monkeys, my eyes or mostly aimed high at the trees. This pays off, as in one of the big trees I spot a red howler monkey, and when I scan the tree with my camera, I spot the rest of the family too. They are laying on a huge branch, but soon hang down to reach for food. The family's very high up, which makes it difficult to photograph. I try to do it anyway, from different angles. I'm spending over an hour here observing these marvellous creatures, pointing them out to the few tourists passing by as well. Some are very happy, as they've spent two nights in the camp, and during their days here have not even seen one monkey. At one point during my observing of monkeys another magical thing happens, as one fiery blueish butterfly dances around me, sitting down right in front of me at times. It's the kiss of the butterfly. I badly try to take a photo, but its wings are moving constantly. The machine gun setting helps, and I might have taken some photos with the wings open. Then my focus goes back to the lazy monkeys in the tree top. They are sleepy and don't move too much. My patience pays off when a fifth monkey comes out from a hidden corner, and they all get a bit grumpy, breaking a branch loudly, whilst showing off their razor sharp teeth. Having this on photo delights me, and I take this as the moment to continue. I walk a bit more and then the trail goes a bit down, until I reach Pueblito, which is a little village, with emphasis on little: there's three primitive houses, and a ranger station. Also some Indians are selling some handmade stuff, as well as sodas. I take a rest by sitting down for a while, drinking some, and then trying to find my way out again, to Cabo. After a while I find the trail, which is a bit hidden, and goes up for some ten steps, before a long descend starts. It's only rocks now, and it seems to be a dry river bedding. At one open space I meet a very small stream, and I suck in the tranquil atmosphere, which doesn't last long, as I clearly hear an animal moving through the autumn leafs. I first think it must be a big snake, but when I zoom in with my camera I see an armadillo. I'm quite excited as it's the first time ever I see one in the wild, and as fast and silent as I can I try to get closer. This animal is on the move non-stop and it's extremely hard to take a good photo, especially considering it's big pointy hairy nose is under the leafs all the time, scrambling the earth for food. Every now and then it digs in the ground, and at one point it completely disappears out of sight. I wait for a while, but soon decide to continue again, as its movement is silenced too. The trail continues going down over big rocks for a long time, and then there's an arrival in Cabo. There's much more tourists here than my first visit, and after some quick snaps of the turquoise sea, I continue my way. I nearly stumble over a big camouflaged lizard on the camping ground and it rushes off in its typical run. I take some photos of it and then continue. On the way to Piscina, I spot a capuchin monkey, with a baby on its back. And again I point the monkey out to other tourists. Not everyone is here for the wildlife, as some teenagers stumble by, being insanely drunk, and also carrying more beer than they can handle. I continue my way and in the big forest near Arrecifes I again spot a moving group of capuchin monkeys. I follow them for a bit, and then continue my way back over the donkey trail to the park entrance. Here, somewhere near the hilltop, I spot one single very tiny tamarin monkey, and it's only because of my photo I can confirm it has the identical black and white colour. Upon reaching the van-stop, I'm deadly tired, and for the first time in this trip my inguinal hernia is hurting like a knife slowly pinching my left leg. I take the van and then the bus, back to Santa Marta, where I have dinner with a friend, and later hit a bar, which is insanely crowded. We manage to find some seat in the patio in the back and spend the night talking, laughing, and meeting many other people.

I can hardly get out of bed in the morning. My leg is painful, and my feet are sore. Despite my intention to go to Tayrona again, I decide to have a day of rest, also thinking of where to go after Santa Marta. I go to Rodadero to walk the beach there, and sit on a terrace to see the sun set. Then back to old town, having dinner in the hotel, and then to bed early again.

Today I think I can face the hardness of Tayrona again, and I do my same morning ritual with a good breakfast, and then the walk to the bus. I'm again taking the Calabazo entrance, and both the bus driver, the ticket vendor, and the park ranger, recognise me. I don't have to pay my entrance fee again, as he lets me through for free after a short talk. At the steep mountain up I get company from a cute little dog. I don't try to give it too much attention, as I'm afraid it will stick with me the entire way and thus scaring off all the wildlife. After some crazy gestures it finally backs off and lays down in the sand, waiting for a next victim. The trail is of course all the same, but I keep seeing new things, new spots, and I'm mostly hoping for new wildlife. I see another armadillo, or maybe it's the same, but now I finally get some proper sightings of it, as it's scrounging right next to the trail. Another couple is observing it too, and the tree of us are filled with excitement for having the animal this close. I can now clearly see its shape, its armour, its ugly face, and its pointy tail. When it disappears out of our sight, we all continue our ways: me going down, them going up. My leg's hurting again, and I'm biting my tongue to relieve me from it, as well as making more stops than I want. This way I get to enjoy the silence of the forest more though, as for a change I don't rush. I see some lizards crawling around, and some birds coming and going. Passing the trees, I'm always aware of animals, and also today I get a big group of capuchin monkeys passing me. Some are chasing each other, others are carrying their young on their backs, making amazing jumps from tree to tree. Other young monkeys find their own clumsy ways. I think I can observe these animals forever. It's just amazing. When the group has passed I get moving again too and walk to Cabo, then Piscina, and then the exit, without seeing any other notable animals. I take the van, then the bus, then walk to the hotel, and get back there with a feeling of someone pulling of my leg. This hernia better goes away soon... I take a long rest at night, only moving to get my dinner in the hotel's restaurant.

The pain isn't completely gone the next day, so I take another day of rest. This rhythm of walking, resting, walking, seems to be perfect, and I'm accepting the situation as it is. I was supposed to fly back after three months, and now I'm already out on the road for a bit over six, so I'm counting my blessings, instead of my curses. Besides that, I'm not dead yet, my bell still rings, and I'm keeping my fingers crossed like the early Roman kings. I spend a long time in the pool today, chilling to the max, only moving when needed. I catch up with friends and family through the magic world of the internet and chat with the hotel staff.

I take a deep breath when I wake up and feel if my body is still entirely there. I pinch myself when I find out I don't feel pain, and I'm actually feeling fit for another trip into Tayrona park. I send some messages out to all the people I've met before in my visits in Tayrona, wondering if someone wants to join me. Surprisingly I get word from a friend who's up for the hike, and I meet up at the bus station. I suggest taking my Calabazo entrance, but warn for the hardness. My friend says no challenge is big enough, so we hop out, get to my ranger friend, pay, and kick it off. I'm a bit overconfident and push my body to the limit by going up as if there's no pain. The pain does come back though, and I'm trying to shake it off by talking and focusing on spotting animals. Near the first small village I spot an eagle, and we approach it like hunting cats. It's standing on a free branch and we get a clear view of this grand animal. Another group of people is coming at our back and I gesture them to stop and then point to the animal. For a short time, it sits still on the branch and then flies off to a tree some fifty metres away. I do a high five with my friend and we continue our trail, up and down, as always. At the river bed past Pueblito we see the armadillo again, and I fascinatingly track it for a bit. While doing that suddenly all the trees around us seem to move and a big aggressive group of capuchin monkeys is coming as if they're storming the Normandy beaches. It seems like someone or something is chasing them, as they almost seem to move in fear. Seeing us seem to calm them down, and they now start eating and even drinking from the stream. They're incredibly weary for us, but we are in the middle of their family now. I see a mother breastfeeding her baby, I see young ones chasing each other and playing, and I see a male adult correcting others. It's the best viewing of these monkeys so far for me, and I can't get enough of it. My friend sits down on a big rock, more observing my fanaticism than the monkeys, and seems to be entertained doing that. A girl comes up from the other side and joins me in the hunt for the perfect photo, which I end up not taking, of course. The sights are burnt in to my brain though, and I hope my memory will help me stick to it. When the group has finally passed us, we also continue our way down over the rocks. We are joined by a couple and the four of us balance on the rocks, make our jumps, our slides, and get to Cabo unharmed. Here we take an extended swim, to cool off, and then march on. We pass another group of capuchin monkeys, but they're more shy, and to my surprise later we also bump into a single tamarin monkey, who's obviously seems to be too far from his group, as this is nowhere near to be seen or heard. The excitement of the wildlife has made me forget about my pain and only when we get into the small van bringing us to the park exit, I realise I might have pushed it too much, again. After walking through the market me and my friend split ways, and I head to the hotel for yet another good rest.

Something is keeping my head occupied: I've read on the official website how many mammals there are in the Tayrona park, but at the internet there's no list of which ones. I decide to go to the main office of the park today to find out. I ask at the desk how I can find out, and they say there's a library where there are many books that should give me the information I need. Only one problem: the library is closed, because the woman working there took off already, and the office only opens again on Monday. I get back to the hotel and I rest the remainder of the day, giving my body the rest it needs.

After these days of rest in between my visits to Tayrona I always feel new-born and ready to explore the park again. So there's no exception on today and with a good mood I head out to do the usual drill. Today I see a black cat on the hill of the Calabazo entrance, and I hope it's not going to bring bad luck. I can again enter without paying, as it seems my bracelet is valid for multiple days. Today the weather is way better than during my previous visits, with a clear blue sky and a bright shining sun. This also means I'm sweating like hell again while walking up the first hill. Not that I wasn't sweating the other days, I'm just more aware of it today. The dogs and donkeys along the way now all seem to greet me, as I'm becoming a regular here. Today for the first time I hear the howler monkeys yell. First I thought it was a helicopter, but then I find out it's the typical sound of the loudest mammal on this planet. If I hear it so clearly already, I can't imagine how it would sound if you are right next to it. Their sound gets lost in the forest and I can't really pin down from where it comes. The further I get on the trail, the louder it sounds. I see a big tree far from the trail, inaccessible from here, and I think to see something move in it. I take my camera, which I often use as binoculars, and zoom in. Yes, it's a monkey. Now I want to get closer, but I'm weary to go through the wild, as I've read there are different kinds of vicious snakes here. And you're not supposed to leave the trail, as that's in violation of the park's rules. I nevertheless take some steps towards that tree, but soon see it would be a hopeless expedition, as it's far, steep, and on rough terrain. I consider to walk around, and follow to trail down, and now I recognise being close to Pueblito. I take the trail from here to Playa Brava, hoping I might walk straight into this tree. I follow the track, which is obviously much less used than all the other trails, until I reach some kind of village. I hear the monkeys somewhere to my left, and apparently have already passed wherever this tree might have been. I head back and see a dry river creek. It's not a trail, but at least there's no big trees in here, and I decide to explore it for a bit, moving uphill. Some branches hit my face, rocks shave my legs, but I'm persistent in finding these noise monsters. The rocks become bigger, my route less accessible, and I'm about to give up, when I suddenly hear them again: right above me. I really have to close my eyes a little bit to focus, but then I see them. There must be at least ten of them this time, and they're far too high for my lens to photograph them, but I did find them. I get to the tree's trunk and then realise how high they really are. They follow my movement, and soon see I'm not a treat as I will never be able to come closer than this. I fight my way back through the bushes to the river bed and from the rocks there I look up, seeing what will happen. Not much, I realise, after at least one hour. Only some of them have moved, to different branches, but there's no action. The babies amongst them are more curious, but it's so hard to see any expressions from this distance. After some more useless photos I decide to find my way back to the trail, It's an easy find and from there just a couple of minutes to Pueblito, where I eat my dry bread, which I buy daily at the same bakery. From Pueblito I again reach my favourite place near the small creek, where I've always seen capuchin monkeys, and of course the armadillo. Today there's no monkeys however, but the armadillo is right at his place, sniffing around, scrambling anything he'd like to eat. I follow the path down, passing many tourists. I'm quite familiar now to this trail over the rocks, so more accustomed to getting down, as I don't need to find out anymore where it's best to stand. I pass a group of Germans, and talk to them for a bit, giving them tips from my experiences so far, especially regarding seeing wildlife, and the trails to wander. I'm just a bit ahead of them when the trail takes a right, around a big tree. In the corner of my right eye I see something move, and assume it's a little green-blue lizard, so with my camera in my hand, I bend a bit around the tree to see what's on the other side. I think this moment lasts less than a second, but what I see is phenomenal: a small green snake just attacks a baby lizard and when it sees me it rises up, scaring me with its skinny small body. I back off and then see the snake crawl away, with the lizard still in its mouth. It crawls up a little plant, and I now see how long it really is. Its tail is still on the ground when its head is already quite far up, and reaches out to the sun. I see the little prey in its mouth and it starts to swallow it. Someone told me to never disturb a snake while it's eating, and now I'm only some metres away from this process. I have my camera zoomed in to the maximum and I see up close how the snake is devouring its prey. I see the bulb moving into its body and am live aware of this processing. When it's quite deep in, the snake moves again. The three Germans now join me and I warn them for the snake and later help them take their photographs. I sense the snake doesn't like our presence and it can move pretty fast. How fast is what we see in the next seconds. It suddenly rushes forward, its body in the air, while just the back holds it up, until it reaches the ground and shoots over the trail, like an arrow from a bow. We all make a little jump back, not willing to taunt it towards us. We now see it move extremely fast under the leafs, deeper into the forest, until we've no sight of it anymore. I then continue to breathe and feel the adrenaline rush through my body once more. Even though the snake was extremely small and tiny, seeing it having a lunch, was quite spectacular. I hadn't seen a single snake thus far in Tayrona and I could now cross it off my list. I walk up with the three others, and while chatting my eyes suddenly catch another snake, which is crawled up at the side of a rock, in its thick vegetation. Wowsers. The two girls of the group now really back off, and I also first take some steps aside, before getting closer. Even though this snake is small as well, it's much bigger than the previous one. I don't have much knowledge about snakes, and have no clue if some of these in Tayrona are venomous. The camouflage of the snakes is excellent though and I'm happy to have spot them. I get closer to get some photos and then tell the others to come too. The snake is slowly moving up and manoeuvres silently through and over the little branches that cover the rock. When it's gone we are all excited to be so lucky in such a short time. They stop for a rest soon after and I continue towards Cabo. At a dry river bedding just before there's a gigantic rock and under it spot a giant toad. It sits there without moving, just chilling, it seems. I take some photos and just when I'm done my friends come, so I have one thing more to show them. They take their photos and I'm off again. At Cabo I walk the rock in the middle of the two beaches and take some photos of the Colombian flag there. I get to talk to two girls who ask me for some photos. My big camera invites others to ask me to take their photos, as this wasn't the first time. They go lay on the beach, sleep away their hangover, while I take a fresh swim and let the waves flush out my adrenaline. After calming down, I continue my hike. I leave the bush area behind, pass Piscina, and then come in the forest before Arrecifes. Here I get another unique experiment. There's an extremely hostile group of capuchin monkeys throwing branches down. Two of them hang high above me, and give me their meanest faces. They show their sharp teeth, and are brawling. They seem to be pissed off, or they suffer from severe rabies, making them completely nuts. Other people pass by, not interested, until there's two couples coming by, who are totally captured by the monkeys, their first monkeys on their three-day trip. It keeps surprising me how people miss out on all the wildlife. I haven't been on one visit here without seeing at least one monkey. Most of them seem to be too busy talking, instead of watching. It reminds me of a little tile my parents used to have at the front door: "A wise old owl sat in an oak // the more he saw the less he spoke // the less he spoke the more he heard. // Why can't we all be like that wise old bird?". There's certainly some truth in that, and it applies to this situation today. Together with my four new Colombian friends I follow the group of monkeys for a bit, until they get beyond a fence of a campsite. They now feel the adrenaline I felt before with the snakes and they keep raving about these great monkeys. I'm ahead of them after a while again, when I see a cotton-top tamarin in a palm tree on my left. I hadn't seen one this clear, but it is too far for a photo. The fence to my left is not stopping me this time, and I climb over it, approaching the animal as quietly as I can. It did move some trees further, but all these trees are quite open. The sun is finally also cooperating and giving me a good light for seeing its white, black and brown colours. There appears to be a group, as I soon spot others moving around. I

beckon the four friends as soon as they pass and make a sign with my
hand they first have to climb over the barbed wire, and mostly be
quiet. Now there's four humans creeping through the jungle, until
they reach my spot. I see their jaws fall wide open by seeing this very
rare monkey. Their cameras aren't really sufficient, but they still
manage to take some quite good photos and videos. I get some pets
on my shoulders and they now call me their guide. I'm honoured
with this new title, and totally blend into my new role, telling them
everything I know about this park. When they tell me they wish to
have met me before, I know I'm doing the "job" right. I gratefully
accept their cookies and sodas, which they offer me as sign of
gratitude. We just manage to see one special animal on the road to
the exit, a colourful bird, of which I don't know the name. We are at
the exit very late, and there's only one van leaving to the main road.
We are crammed in it, and then take off. When we get into the bus
back to Santa Marta it is already dark and we make some bus party on
the crazy music that is bouncing from the speakers. It's late when we
get to town, where our ways part, and I head back to my hotel where
I arrive with the biggest smile on my face: this day was perfect.

Although yesterday's trip was indeed perfect, my body is still far from
perfect. Today my hernia is playing up again, and I mostly lay down,
in bed, and in the pool. I just head out for a lunch with a friend and
the dinner I take at the hotel. After dinner I nearly fall asleep in the
pool, but just in time I find my inner life guard to save myself and
bring me to bed.

I'm stubborn and not listening to my body, as the nearby national
park works like a magnet on me. Today it's the second day in a row I
wake up with pain. The same pain that brought me to the doctor and
hospital at the end of 2013, and it's nagging. Despite the signals I
head out again. First walking, sitting in the bus, and then the walk
uphill. While walking I think to feel a relief of pain, but whenever I
stand still, there's a needle carving in my body top to bottom. At the
first stage I mainly see ants and birds, of which some I hadn't seen
before here yet. Up on the hill I walk by some fat worm, and try to
take some photos of this slimy animal, with its golden and black
stripes. Nearby I hear the howling of the monkeys, and from the
sound of it, it seems like a decent group. I try to follow the trail a bit
more, and then I see four of them in a tree uphill and off trail. I try to
walk off the beaten path, but soon find out this isn't the smartest

idea, as the leaves make it quite slippery. I head back to the trail and try to see if I can get a better angle from a bit back on the trail. I do see a big tree, with more than just the four in it, but it's too far away to take proper photos, even though I try for a while. I continue my way and before the descend to Pueblito starts I walk aside of a group of capuchin monkeys. They are moving slowly, but avoid me, and two other tourists, by climbing around us. We stay in our positions, only moving our arms for the photos. One of the monkeys beautifully hangs himself on his tail, trying to grab a branch under him. It's a great view, because the tree is free from leafs and therefor very clear. When the group's gone I move on as well, until I reach the dry river near Cabo. Here I see my toad friend again, and soon also a group of cotton-top tamarins. They are grabbing the fruits in the trees around and are hopping from branch to branch. They are very small and move very fast, which makes it fascinating to spot them and observe their behaviour. They use the branches as bridges to get to the other side of the dry stream, find a big tree where they spread out and search for more fruits. A group of some six guys now walks by and asks me what I'm photographing. When I reply I'm seeing a group of rare monkeys, they shrug their shoulders and move on. Why the hell are they here, I ask myself. I continue looking at them until they vanish and then walk to Cabo. I arrive there quite late, so I don't take time for a swim, and just continue the hike. Near Piscina I stumble upon my fiftieth group of capuchin monkeys and look at them with some other tourists. Because this species is so active there's always something happening and I like observing them, even though I've already seen so many of them. This time I see one cracking a coconut and protecting its meal from other hungry monkeys. Another monkey is sharing her nut with her baby, which is a cute sight. The sun is sinking, so I hurry myself over the donkey trail and just I think I'm done for the day, when I walk from the stables to the departure point of the van, I see a big black eagle sitting on a branch. I quickly take out my camera again, and try to capture this big black beautiful bird, with its yellow beak. The twilight isn't very helpful and my photos turn out bad. I jump in the van, get to the bus, hop in there, and get back to town. I rush to the hotel, get my meal and then lay down in bed, I'm tired and in pain.

Like most nights of sleep, the rest helps, and the next morning I'm up for my visit to one of the main sights of Santa Marta itself: the place where local hero Simon Bolivar, liberator of many South

American countries, drew his last breath. I have my local guide in Yurleidys and she tells me more about the history and the meaning of this to Colombian people. The park around the monuments is big and has many iguanas in all sizes and colours. We have a drink at a terrace and with Google I learn even more about this place and the importance of this historical figure. We return to town after this and have lunch there, before we head to the hotel, where she has to work the rest of the day. I go back to the park office of Tayrona now and hope to get access to the library. The same girl that talked to me last time, in English, is here again, and she helps me to get started. She's a journalist herself and writes articles about the Colombian national parks, and has quite some knowledge about it all. She can't give me the answer though to what mammals exactly live in the park, and first she enters the workplace of some guides, and bluntly ask around there. She gets laughed at a little, and I'm happy I'm not understanding much of their answers. We walk out again, and she says the answers only lay in the library. She leaves me there, and the librarian helps me out with the animal books about the park. I'm writing down all the mammal species I find in the four different books and still don't come to the 100, as being mentioned on nearly all websites: I only count 85, of which 41 are bats. I ask for clarification, but no one has the answer to what animals are missing on my list, or are counted in the official count. I have a quick vision of doing full time research in this park to clear up why the official count is 41 bat- and 59 other mammal species. It puzzles my brain. I have some more chats with Vanessa and her colleagues and am also given directions for a completely different subject: finding a certain kind of bag for a Dutch friend who's asked me to ship some of them to her. There's some replicas being sold near the big square and I'm pointed in that direction. After saying goodbye to the crew, I head out there and soon find myself comparing colourful handbags. I soon have enough information to tell my friend, and also inform my sister about these fashionable bags. The day ends with pain in the leg, which leads to my back and even to my knee and ankle. I have no plans for tomorrow, and think to keep it that way.

The next three days are a bit of horror, as the pain due to my hernia peaks. I feel so miserable that I seriously consider flying back to Amsterdam. Being in so much pain is no fun at all, and being in a distant country, far from caring family, isn't making it any better. I spend most of the time in my room, laying down, resting. Only a few times I head out, to meet some of my Santa Marta friends, and I always manage to disguise my pain with a smile. I don't feel like bothering others with my pain. I express myself on WhatsApp to other friends, far away. Complaining about it, and getting tips, helps in the process. The few walks per day I make are getting better daily, but I get a setback when I hear my room's booked for a night. I've always kept my room flexible, as I never wanted to be pinned down to one location, and now my own flexibility backfires in a situation of suffering, at the least desirable time. I reach out to the helpful hotel staff and they eventually help set me up with a room in a hotel just across the street. I move my stuff there, and in this new hotel I realise how good it was on the other side. I'm happy it's only for one night. I don't spend the entire day in the hotel, and visit the cinema with a friend to see Dawn of the Planet of the Apes. Here sometime hilarious happens. I buy my ticket for the subtitled version, because I probably would not understand too much of the movie dubbed in Spanish. As we sit through the commercials, the film starts, and the first voice heard is a bit unclear, and appears to be Spanish. I'm not entirely sure though and we wait for another ten to fifteen minutes until the first dialogue of the film takes place. Then there's no denial in it: we're watching the Spanish version. I look at my ticket and it clearly states it's the subtitled version. Against my nature I decide to walk out and ask the staff what's going on. I show them my ticket, they look at their schedule and soon they admit they've started the wrong version. They tell me to go back to my seat and that they will fix it. I ask them if they can continue from where they are now, but my words seem lost in translation. I walk back to my seat and as soon as I sit, the screen goes to black. Rumour immediately starts in the room, which is more than half full, with some hundred people. Then there's something playing again, and they have started the movie with subtitles from the beginning... I crawl deep in my chair, as people stand up and scream some things to who-knows-who. Some get out for a toilet break, other seize the moment to buy more snacks, and other just talk, until the movie is at the point where they had stopped it. I feel kind of embarrassed, but if there was any anger, it was not pointed at me. I'm relieved and glad I don't have to show my kung-fu moves after the movie against possible haters. The movie itself is not as entertaining as the prologue, but I like it very much. Upon my return to the hotel I walk out for dinner and then pass a bar where I see a Dutch friend sitting playing cards. I knew she was here, but we hadn't coordinated a meeting, yet. Upon this coincidence I walk in and sit myself down at the table with her, and her three Dutch friends, and we catch up for a bit. It's great to see another familiar face so far away from home. I leave them to their card game and head back to the hotel after a quick meal at my local restaurant. After this I spend one more day in the hotel, lying in the pool and on my bed, giving my body more rest.

Five days of relative rest have passed now, and I declare myself ready for one final trip to Tayrona, as I now have the chance to go with a park ranger, and I don't want to let this opportunity pass by. I meet my guide for the day at the main park office and together we walk to the market, get in the bus, and then to the main park's entrance. My guide knows everyone and when we get out of the bus we first spend quite some time socialising with everyone familiar we encounter. My hernia isn't hurting too much when we start a hike to the beach, which I haven't walked before. There's two little lakes here, and I search for American crocodiles, which supposedly can occasionally be seen here. We don't see one, but do look fascinated at the waves breaking on a rock in the ocean, at times totally swallowing it. We then head to Arrecifes, with many other tourists. The first group of monkeys we see are my favourite tamarins, and shortly after a group of capuchins. These capuchins aren't too shy and openly have their meal in front of us. The many tourists walking by eventually scare them and when they leave, we continue too. At Arrecifes we have a lunch in the restaurant, and then walk over the beach past the little lakes here, to again see if there's crocodiles. We again don't see them, and on our way back we focus on monkeys once more, with a big group of tamarins going over us at the trees near a campsite. I think I can look at them forever, and see how they live their lives in the trees. I'm taking many photos, while for my friend these are common sights and therefore less interesting, it seems. The monkeys are moving out of range of my camera, so I follow them as far as I can, before they're too far. I wave farewell to my little buddies. We take the donkey trail back, even though this is normally not a route a ranger can take, as it's a transport route, and officially not a park trail. I hadn't been aware of this and I tell him I've taken this path all the time. I'm told that's okay, unless someone had forbidden me, which has not been the case. Back at the parking, we take the van, the bus, and our feet to get back to Santa Marta, where I say farewell to my guide and friend, and I head back to my hotel, to start organising my departure.

I've decided my next destination will be Panama. I have been hesitating between Venezuela, and Panama, but rumours coming from Venezuela aren't very positive, given the revolt and recent violence. So I pick Panama, and from there I really want to see Costa Rica. I reach out to a lodge in Gamboa, where I've read there's a very famous wildlife trail, Pipeline Road. Ivan, the owner of the lodge, provides me with enough information for me to make a reservation. I then book my flight to Panama, and set up transport from the airport to the lodge. I arrange a spot in the van from Santa Marta to Cartagena, and book a hotel for one night there. Then a road of farewell starts, to thank all the great people that have made my stay in Santa Marta so great. A special thank you was for the hotel staff, as they've been excellent and have made me feel at home for nearly four weeks.

Departure is very early the next morning and I nap during the ride. I'm dropped off at the same parking from where I left 28 days ago, and from here I take a taxi to the walled-city, from where I easily find my little hotel. I check-in, get to my room, take a nap, and then go out for dinner and to run some errands. After dinner I make a final tour through Cartagena and say goodbye to one of the best cities in South America.

Chapter VIII

PANAMA

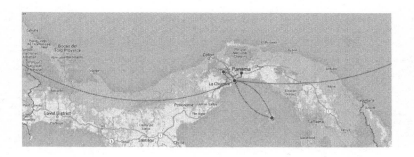

I take a taxi in the morning from my hotel to the Cartagena airport, where I still have to book my flight. After doing so I buy my exit visa at a booth, do my check-in, go through customs, and wait to board the plane. Like most of the time in South America I can walk to the plane and enter on the stairs. And like always I have a seat in the quite empty back of the plane. Today I see something new however: when we are high in the sky, an employee of Copa Airlines takes a seat behind me, takes some food out, and then a bottle of wine, which he opens and drinks a glass from. Maybe this is a Colombian policy? I keep wondering about it. The flight itself is fine, and the view beautiful. It is my first viewing of the world famous Panama Canal and I can see the big container ships slowly moving like ants. When we've landed I go through customs, which is a simple affair, and then off to the luggage. Upon exiting this area, I expect a driver to pick me up, and although there's many signs, there's none with my name on it. When everyone's gone, I'm the only one left behind. Some taxi drivers start offering their services, but I'm fine in waiting. After some thirty minutes waiting, I ask the guy at the tourist information booth if I can use his phone to call Ivan. Ivan answers the phone friendly, tells me to wait while he calls the driver. I soon get word he's on his way and soon will be there. Not much later I see a guy speed walking to the doors and he's the one looking for me. He doesn't have the sign unfortunately, but I later find it in his car. I think this was the first time my name was on such a sign. We drive about two hours to Gamboa, and soon after this metropolitan city, with an impressive skyline full of (small) skyscrapers, the trees start surrounding the road and within minutes we are already out, and into nature. I also get my first glimpse of the canal from the road, and from a distance I see a big freight ship very slowly moving through the water. Then we arrive in the town of Gamboa, which seems to be directly flown in from the USA: wide streets, big lawns, spacious houses. I learn this village belonged to the Americans a long time ago, and that this famous Pipeline road was where they trained for jungle fights. I'm dropped off at Ivan's place, and it's a huge house, also built in this typical style. He welcomes me warmly and after dropping off my luggage he starts talking about the house, the surrounding, and of course all the animals. His garden is being visited by many species, so theoretically I don't even have to go hiking to see some of the birds here. He also informs me at what times breakfast and dinner are served, so I know my time slots. After talking to this great man, I pack my stuff for a first exploration and to see if I can find the start of the Pipeline Road. It's already past 18:00 when I leave, soon seeing my first agouti in someone's garden. I follow the main road that leaves town, and by mistake take the wrong exit to the right, leaving me on a road going up towards a power station. Unaware of my mistake I just walk up and see a very pretty bird there, the black-throated trogon. Its yellow breast stands out in the serene green wilderness and his big black eye blends in the dark green and black around his hat. The black and white striped tail hangs down low. The trail has a dead end, and there's a big fence preventing me from going on. Here I realise it's not that simple just yet to reach my destination. I also think it's better to make this mistake now, instead of tomorrow, when the real deal will go down. I walk back to be in time for dinner and see some more of the cute town. At the house I'm served a delicious meal and I continue having amazingly great conversation with Ivan. It's already late when I get to my fine room and fall asleep directly.

Waking up early can be a problem for me, due to some stomach issues, but today at 05:30 it isn't one of these days. I'm excited to go walk this trail and at 06:00 I'm already out, before the sun rises. When I get to a little lake, I see the sun coming up behind me, giving it a surreal effect. The lens of my camera is fogged, because of the heat here. In my room it was very cool due to the air-conditioning, and the difference in temperature gives me some start-up problems. I try to fix it as good as possible, and then continue my way, neglecting the trail I took yesterday, and continuing straight on. There are now cars passing by me, with the first workers going to work in the nearby harbour, and construction sites. I keep walking despite being offered a lift, as I have no clue yet who they are, and what intentions they have. Soon I find myself at a fork, and I go to the right, and then see a sign indicating the road I'm looking for. It's much easier to find it than I thought it would be after yesterday's failure. At the start of the trail there are maps that give some information about the Soberania National Park, through which Pipeline Road cuts. The first part of the trail is just a road, where ranger cars drive over, and even visitors have a chance to go upon. This is quite a long way and then I reach another fork where I go right, avoiding the ranger station and parked cars there, and enter a bigger parking space that leads to the actual trail. Here I cross a bridge over a pond, where I see some small turtles swimming. It's so early that I'm all alone here. The humidity is crazy already and the path is often interrupted by big mud pools. The tropical rain showers come every afternoon and I hope to keep clear from that, even though deep inside I know better. I'm walking in a steady pace, my ears pricked up, and my eyes wide open. I soon see my first ever sloth, hanging lazily high in a tree. It's blending in amazingly with the trees and it's very hard to get a good view. I continue my way and at times this seems to be a paradise, when the butterflies in all possible colours fly around me, the sun beams hit my face and the only sound I hear is the wind calmly touching the trees. I keep walking though, as I want to see as much of this trail as possible, and hopefully also some black howler monkeys, which should be out here somewhere. At times I hear their howls, but it seems too far away, far from the trail. And one thing I know is not a good idea: walk away from the trail into this thick jungle. Suddenly I hear an animal to my right. I freeze, as I have no clue what it is, yet. I of course immediately hope for a jaguar, but Ivan already told me I would have to go in the night, and even then chances would be minimal. I then see a strange animal coming out of the bushes, and it starts gazing at me for some seconds. I recognise the animal as a coati, as I've seen the photo in one of Ivan's books. As the animal doesn't seem to be too disturbed by my presence, I quickly try to take some photos, but its moving and the light are making it too hard. It soon vanishes in the shadows of the forest again. I continue walking, seeing the sunlight marvellously lighting a big spider web. The trail goes up a bit, widens, and then narrows again. The trees in the valley below are very tall and there's no ending. There's bushes now hanging over the path and I have to literally push myself through. I need my hands to push away branches. I'm now fighting for progression. Then the path is easier again, but it's very obvious there haven't been many people here. Since the last sign I've at least walked another two kilometres, meaning I'm at about twelve kilometres on the trail. Being so far from anything, without a cell phone signal makes me wonder if I should continue, or not. This question is answered for me some thirty minutes later, as the trail becomes completely inaccessible as the fallen trees are blocking the road. I try to overcome them, but it isn't working. I sit on a trunk and eat some of the food I brought. Then I start walking back, descending, and again many branches are hitting me. Also the howling of the monkeys becomes stronger now, and it seems to come from everywhere. I'm hoping to see them, but as I can't really leave the trail, I have to be very lucky. Suddenly I freeze once more, for the second time today: in the centre of the path now lays a snake. It's brown and not exactly moving. Its head is blueish, and I estimate it on two metres. I believe it's sunbathing, because I stand there for at least fifteen minutes, taking some photos, before it finally moves out of my way. Relieved I continue my way, seeing colourful flowers, and birds. A group of big green parrots distracts me from walking for a while. They are high up in the tree and as green as the leafs, so it requires all my focus to see them. The trail's going down, winding around a hill, with the valley to my right. When I come back to the main forest trail, I suddenly hear a loud howling to my left. It seems close, but I can't see them through the many trees. I take two steps from the trail, losing my feet in the soft pillows of fallen leafs. What if there's another snake under here? I take my steps back, follow the trail a bit up and down to see if I can spot these monkeys, but no luck from this position. Then I take a deep breath, and without further thinking I climb the little sand wall to my left, and enter the dark forest. I'm not leaving breadcrumbs, nor any rocks, as it can't be that hard to find the way back later, right? The leafs on the ground make it impossible for me to move quietly. It seems to make the howling louder though, and I soon spot one small black monkey. I have more spider webs on my head than hair now, as I nearly crawl to move forward. I reach a very small open spot, whilst my eyes are more focused on avoiding snakes, than they are to look up in the trees. I call this open spot safe ground, and finally I can look up. I immediately see several black howler monkeys, and it seems to be a group of at least ten monkeys. My camera is now making extra hours, as I use it as a machine gun, shooting as many photos as possible. Then the howls start again, and instead of it moving away, the sounds come closer. My eyes search the branches, and yes, there's the causer: a big male, who's actually coming down from high in the tree, and is moving in my direction. What is his idea? I do one step back to show him some respect, but he keeps climbing closer. I get some good photos now, but I'm unsure what will happen. Within minutes I know though, and it is mind blowing. The monkey is now on two metres or something, and I've not been as close to a howler monkey until now, and when it's widen its mouth a devastating sounds is coming out, trembling nearly my entire body, and leaves my ears swishing. It continues and continues, obviously trying to scare me, which actually is working. I never thought it could be so intimidating. I do one extra step back, to let my friend know I don't want to hurt him or his family and I'm just here to take some photos. I don't think he understands as he continues making this extreme sound. He finally shuts up for a bit, still giving me some mean looks. The other monkeys in the meantime have searched for higher branches, or trees further away. This distraction seems to have worked, as they are 'safe' now. This is what the monkey now also realises and it turns its back to me and climbs back up the tree. I'm taking some steps forward again, and I see a capuchin monkey within the group of howlers, which for me, at this point, is awkward, remembering the hostility of these two species in Tayrona. After seeing this, and scratching my head about it, I turn to find my way back. I thought it would be easier, and my thought about leaving rocks behind would not have been a bad one now. How far did I actually walk into the forest? I assumed only thirty metres, but the trail isn't appearing. I take a steep left now, thinking it's there, but another couple of minutes walking don't lead me there. I don't recognise any of the trees, and this isn't one of the coolest moments of the trip. I take some rights, lefts, and then finally reach the road, exiting the forest at a complete different point as I had entered. For a minute I wonder if this is actually the same trail, but I put this thought aside quickly, as I look at the photos of the map I took: there are no other trails. I continue descending, leaving the dark forest behind me, which fortunately not became my Mirkwood, in which the famous hobbit and its companion of dwarves got lost in. To my surprise I spot another, smaller, group of howler monkeys some fifteen minutes later. These are incredibly hard to see though, and I don't spend too much time trying this time. I also finally meet another human being here, as a young German birder is also walking the road. I point him to the monkeys, but he's not interested; the only thing that counts are the birds. As he walks up, I continue walking down, seeing the same butterflies and birds once more. Then the fun is already over, as it starts pouring. It's not even 13:00, and the sky changes into an endless waterfall. The rain falls straight down, and even though the trees help a little bit being my umbrella, I'm soon totally soaked. I put my camera away, pull over the rain coat from my backpack, and stoically start walking back. My body's getting colder, and my shirt doesn't seem to exist after a while, but the only thing I can do is continue. That German was better prepared, as he had been wearing a rain outfit, which I, at that time, found kind of silly given the warm sun. I walk for hours in the pouring rain, passing the ranger station, then the entrance of the road, and then finally into the village again, soon arriving at my homestay. Taking off my clothes is the same struggle as in Papallacta. The warm shower, and the fresh clothes are so welcoming. I'm chilling a while, before getting to dinner, where I get another great meal, followed by great conversation with Ivan, and shortly with his daughter Natasha. I head to bed early, as tomorrow there's another hike up to Pipeline Road.

As I've explored the road extensively yesterday, I take it a bit easier this morning. I finally manage to drag my legs to the road at around 09:30. Today I'm not alone, as when I enter the path beyond the ranger station, there's a big group of Americans walking a bit ahead of me, with bigger cameras, bigger lenses, and, with a guide. I pass them, say hi, talk a bit, and then move forward, hoping to be ahead of them when it comes to seeing the wildlife. This illusion is soon shattered, when I hear cars on the track, and indeed, two vehicles come up the road, with the Americans in it. They stop ahead of me, I catch up, they board, I follow, catch up, repeat. The good thing about this ritual is that these cars stop when the guides spot interesting animals, and because of this I see more variety (of small animals) than yesterday. When we both reach an open space with little wooden benches, I continue, as I see they're getting lunch, and I now might be finally ahead for real. This pays off, as I walk into another coati, who's putting his nose in between the leafs and moving non-stop to find food. It strikes me again that I'm not a good photographer, as when I look back at the photos I take, they all suck. I also get to see some capuchin monkeys, who quickly move out of sight. I'm not planning to walk another 25 kilometres today, so I head back shortly after, of course walking into my American friends. I point them to the coati, telling he might still be scrounging around. They move on up road, and I go back, in a slow pace, trying to spot more insects, butterflies, and birds. One colourful bird gets extra attention, as it's sitting absorbing the sun on a branch, showing off its bright orange breast. I move on, and again get on the main road in between the ranger station and the road's entrance. About half way I suddenly see many black howler monkeys. Many, as in over fifty probably, who are slowly crossing the road in the high trees. I'm amazed. There's all kinds of them, small, big, ugly, beautiful, young, and old. I'm not even trying to take too many photos, as twilight's starting and they're too high. A family joins me in looking at them, and they appear to be Dutch. They've been here numerous times, so it's not all new, but it is to their two little children, who excitedly observe the troop with us.

The scene lasts over an hour, and then they have all crossed the road, and they keep moving more and more into the dense forest. While the Dutch family is walking to the ranger station, I head back to town and to a warm shower to wash off all today's sweat. There's only a short spell of rain in the afternoon, and I'm already inside, so not too bothered about it today. In the evening it's the same good ritual again: great food, great conversation, and another early bed time.

I have not seen the rest of Gamboa, so after breakfast I explore the town, and especially a big operational hotel, which has a great view over the forests nearby, as well as a huge garden where you can see a great variety of birds. It's hot today and I walk slowly, thus seeing much. I walk into the hotel fairly easy, no one is asking this gringo where the hell he's going, and I take a long walk in the park, mainly observing a couple of eagles who are flying in between two pines. I sit in the high grass for a while, enjoying the morning sun on my white face. When I feel the skin is getting red, I move out, getting back to my room, to pack my stuff, and wait for my ride to Panama City. I've booked some random hotel, again based on its user ratings, as I have done all the time, and when my driver's picks me up, I say goodbye to Ivan, we drive for about an hour, and get lost only once, before I get dropped off at the hotel. It's a new building, with good rooms. The staff's also very friendly. My legs are sore and my hernia is slightly bothering me, so I can justify a long nap in the afternoon. At night I've agreed to eat sushi with a Panamanian friend, who I have met on couchsurfing some years ago, when she was visiting Amsterdam with her boyfriend. There's a sushi restaurant attached to my hotel, so we meet there and it's great meeting again. We have a lot of things to catch up over, and time moves fast, while the food tastes great.

The next two days I spend chilling, not doing much, except for going for lunch, dinner, and cinema, with my friend, who badly wants to give something back for something she's got. She takes me into the city, shows me around, and Panama City at night is beautiful, for a city. These days of slowly moving have given my legs the rest they needed, and I decide to go on yet another hike the next day, into 'Parque Metropolitano' (Metropolitan Park), which, as I found out, is a tropical jungle in the middle of the city, with all the animals that come with it.

This park I go to today also has a good possibility to see the local tamarin monkeys. Family of the ones I've been tracking down in Colombia, although these once are not as endangered. I'm not sure what to expect from the park, so I go into a cab heavily packed. I had asked my hotel to fix the cab for me, but it's a new country, and thus new taxis. I keep my Google Maps open to see if he's going into the right direction for the first few miles and when I see it's good, I continue the talk with him in my Spanish plus hands and feet. At the entrance of the park there's a big stationary where I have to write down my name, and where I seize the moment to get some information and to ask where the jaguar is. Except from the laughs I get no serious information, even though the poster hanging in the office clearly shows one. I get a map of the park, including the trails available, and then head out. The animal I see most in this first trail is the spider, which is everywhere, with their big webs. I keep walking, through an open space, with some bunkers on my left, and later also right, side. I assume they are bunkers, as these huge concrete building don't seem to suit any other use. My eyes are not focused on these ugly grey things, but on the nature surrounding it. I focus high in the trees to see monkeys, but the first thing my eyes cross is a big furry hairball hanging in a tree some fifteen metres from the trail. I take some steps into the forest and quickly notice it is a sloth. I take some photos of this fun animal, which of course is doing nothing else but sleeping. I head back to the trail when my brain starts sleeping too, and head uphill. It's quite steep, much more than I expected. When I reach a fork in the road, to go left, down, or up, I do still decide to go right and see what is on the top of the hill. Now steep really gets its meaning and I'm out of breath when I finally reach this great viewpoint. I see the skyline of the city as a fortress laying at the horizon, with the ocean behind it. Every skyscraper looks like a modern tower of a medieval multi-tower castle, and the only thing missing is the banners waving in the wind. There's also no horse to carry me, unfortunately, so I ask my legs to get me down, back to the fork, so I can continue my round in the park. After some curves I get to an open space, where there's some cut down trees on the left. To my right I see little animals crawling in the trees. I immediately recognise them as the Geoffroy's tamarins. They are on a food hunt, of course, and moving from tree to tree. Some carry very little babies on their backs. They are still making huge leaps from tree to tree, and I'm surprised how they really throw themselves off a branch, and just grab whatever they hit first in the tree next or below them. It's a fascinating spectacle and I'm lucky there's quite a few of them, making it last long before they pass me and move further in the forest. I continue with a smile, having found what I was looking for. I get a little extra at the end of the trail, when I scout the area where I saw my first sloth today. On the opposite of the road now hangs another, or the same, sloth, and it's on the move. It moves slowly, but it's really amazing to see how it finds its way from tree to tree. I point the animal to a family passing me, and they're extremely excited to this animal. They're Colombians and very friendly. I spend some time talking to them while the four of us follow the sloth going down and up again, with both eyes and cameras. All of us leave the park; them being picked up at another exit, and me continuing to the station, from where I stand on the road, thumb up, hoping to find a taxi. A small yellow vehicle then stops and I hurry myself into it and tell my driver where I want to go. He's a young chap, and he's enthusiastically using his few English words to communicate with me. When we reach the outskirts of town, we leave the main road, to avoid traffic and we pass a decent neighbourhood. He then makes a stop, and let's a woman, who was doing the sort of thumb thing, in... For a moment I'm shocked: who's getting in my taxi? The woman is American and tells us she's going to the casino. I ask her why she got in my taxi, and she explains me that this is totally normal here in Panama. It relieves me, because generally other people getting in your taxi means trouble. We leave the woman at the casino, and then it's only a short drive back to my hotel. I walk to a nearby bakery and have a good late lunch there, before resting my body in the hotel, even having the sushi from downstairs ordered to my room.

I find another bakery the next morning to get a breakfast/lunch, as I wake up quite late. I'm having a lazy morning too, but in the afternoon I decide to head out to the park once again. Another taxi brings me there, and at the station they're surprised to see someone return for a second day in a row. I write my name down again, and head out. It's much sunnier and warmer today than yesterday, giving a good light on the flowers, and animals I see, like the capybaras, and the spiders. Today I see a big woodpecker, with a big red mohawk. And just before that I see a small group of tamarins, who were quicker than my shadow though and I lost track of them pretty quick. A big yellow beak behind a tree isn't moving too much, and I see a couple of toucans chilling in the trees. The colour of their beaks are amazing, and it's another magic moment. I'm disturbed by some movement down the road, and I hurry there to see a bigger group of tamarins, and now I can look at them for quite a while, jumping again from tree to tree. Then I take a different trail back, over another hill, steep again, and from there I have a great view over the city's skyline again. At the station I find a taxi pretty quickly and thirty minutes later I'm back at the hotel, to have dinner in a restaurant nearby, and then sleep early.

I have been mailing back and forth with a woman whose website I've found on the internet. She's an American and runs a tour company from Panama City, that focuses mainly on whale watching. For a long time I have been dreading looking at the price of such a tour, but two days ago I have confirmed her to join today's tour. I'm being picked up very early, as the first of the group. We have to pass some other hotels to pick up other people, before we head down to a harbour, from where we will leave with two boats. I've never seen a whale in my life, and although it's not guaranteed I'm pretty stoked. I'm sharing the boat with an English family, and a mother with her son and daughter. On the other boat there's a French family and one from Panama. Our speed boat goes at a very high speed and bounces on the little waves of the ocean. The city is on our left and soon its skyline looks like a vague silhouette on the horizon. Suddenly the engines seem to be turned off and we lose speed rapidly. Our guide tells us there's a whale right in front of us, together with a baby. I have to gaze a bit, and focus, as everything looks the same here, but then, closer than I expected I see the huge body of a whale. Wow! It's bigger than I imagined and it's just quietly laying in the water, the youngster close to it. Probably disturbed by the two boats with low running engines, the whale very smoothly, calmly, swims away. It's super-fast though and it soon has disappeared from our sight. We're all thrilled and the day is already a success now. We continue our sail to the Pearl Islands, which is the main destination of today's trip. When we see the first little rocks of the group of islands, there's also our second whale sighting: a big one moving with a lot of show off and jumping high out of the water and falling back in leaving huge white foam of the waves coming off like sparkles. Then we see it slap his tail on the surface and it's just brilliant to see this. A huge whale tail coming out of the water, rising like a mushroom, smacking it on the water. It's going on and on and on, and we're all gasping and gazing, while some of us try to photograph this in the unstable boat, that's dancing on the little waves of the dark blue ocean. After about ten minutes we all try to get a bit closer, and we actually do get respectable close. The whale then seems to sink like a submarine and we lose track. But then it suddenly jumps in between our two boats, clearly showing off, and it splashes back in the water, its waves wetting some people in the other boat, and then disappearing to not be seen again. At the horizon we see two other whales making the tail splashes, and the other boat goes there, at high speed. Our boat stays a bit, hoping the other whale will come back. It's not coming back though and we calmly circle around for a bit. Then our guide says what we've all been hoping for: dolphins! We all try to spot them, but none sees them, yet. The guide's eyes are superbly trained and we get the motor a bit running and then we all see them, about twenty dolphins who start following the boat, using the waves to jump from. It's marvellous as they're sticking to the boat's tail, and make high jumps out of the water. It can't get any better than this. Some dolphins nearly are standing on the water with the end of their tail, seeming to be some kind of Jesus' species. Others tumble and jump, until they all get a bit calmer. Then we are allowed to jump into the water to see if they also want to swim with us. The children head in first, and soon yell they're being stung by little sea creatures. Our guide tells us this is perfectly normal and there's nothing to worry about. I don't consider going in, as I rather stay on board to take photos. A wise decision, as the dolphins take off and are not to be seen anymore. Except for a floating plastic bag, that we save from the ocean, we don't see any other animals anymore, until we go on land at a beach of one of the islands. Two steps through the water and we're ashore. Here we have a nice lunch, all sitting at one big table, sharing stories, and laughing. Behind us are some hummingbirds who of course draw my attention, and I take some photos. When the food's been eaten, the bills are paid and the bathroom's visited, we head back to the beach, and climb aboard. It's late in the afternoon now and we head back to the city, hoping to see some more whales on our way. The only animals we see however are blue footed boobies, and some other birds. We are now at full speed racing over the water, as a flat rock being tossed on the surface, making little jumps from wave to wave. At full speed it merely appears to be a hovercraft, floating above the water. Soon we see the skyline again, with many big ships lining up for the Canal. It's a great view. Back in the harbour we have to wait a bit before the car drags us out of the water, and then are soon back in the van again. We start dropping off all people, and being the first at the start, now means being the last. There's a big traffic jam however and the last miles take forever. When we finally do get to the hotel I thank my guide for the great tour and tell her spending this money was worth every penny. Back in my room I take a quick shower and then head out for dinner.

Sitting in a boat for a day has an advantage, as I could rest my legs while still photographing animals. Now my legs are fine for yet another visit to the Metropolitan Park. I head there in a taxi around midday, and start my usual hike. Today is sloth day, as I see about seven different ones One ranger pointed three out for me at the very start. He told me they are at the turtle pond, but finding them there is still very hard, as they don't move and perfectly blend into the trees' colours. I also see two groups of tamarins, which always delights me, and a spectacular catch of a spider: a blueish mot, which he's eating right under my nose. The buzzing of the little insect is gigantic, while the spider approaches, soon tearing it apart, piece by piece. Badass spider. At my return I have a very close sighting of a sloth, which is slowly moving to another tree. I see two girls on the trail and gesture them to come see, and they're super excited about their first ever sloth. Like in Tayrona, I'm becoming a guide here too. Grabbing a taxi back today is a bit hard, as they all seem to be having passengers and I'm not the one who wants to intrude, whatever the custom might be here. Eventually I'm picked up and due to traffic brought back home in a record slow.

The next two days I'm resting once more, going to a shopping mall, seeing a movie in the cinema, having dinners, and mostly just lying in my bed, resting my body, while thinking of my next destination, which most likely will be Costa Rica. I also think of following up a tip I received from my whale-watching-guide to visit the locks of Miraflores where I can likely see my first crocodiles.

Miraflores it is, and I take another cab there. It's some thirty minutes driving and I'm being dropped off at the main road, as I want to walk over the bridge to see if there are some crocodiles. After my first step on the bridge I immediately see a huge crocodile lying in the mud. It's big and its point nose is halfway in the water, maybe waiting for an easy fish to catch. It starts drizzling and I quickly walk to the entrance of the locks, which are huge, to take shelter for the tropical rain shower. The sky only explodes shortly today and I exit the line for the attraction as soon as it's over. There are many tourists, but seeing a lock like this is not my cup of tea for today. I return to the bridge, but the crocodile's gone now. I see another crocodile at some hundred metres, and I can't get any closer, unfortunately. I walk back to the main road, stop a taxi and ask him to drive to a lake a little bit more down the road, and wait there for me while I explore the area there for more crocodiles. I don't see any there, just some toucans, which of course are as beautiful as always. I rush back to my taxi, as time now is money, and I head back to the hotel. At my hotel I schedule my flight to Sao Jose, Costa Rica, and also reserve a hotel room for the day after tomorrow.

My final full day in Panama City I of course want to say farewell to my favourite city park and I take a taxi down there to walk my round. Besides the usual animals, I finally see a family of black howler monkeys. They're loud and crushing branches, the trees not ready for their weight. I also see a cute deer and the end of my walk, and it politely freezes for me to take some photos. I walk all the trails for a final time, and then get back in a taxi in the late afternoon.

Chapter X

COSTA RICA

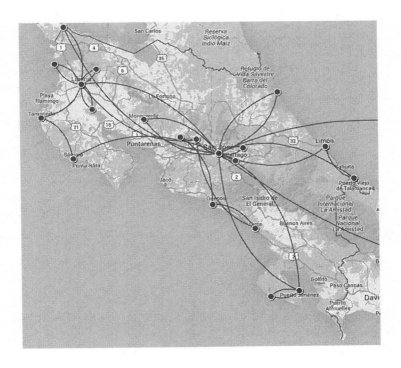

Costa Rica - San José, San José

I'm checking out as late as possible, as my flight is in the late afternoon as I don't want to be bothered about my luggage the entire day, and I can use some extra rest. The more I travel, the less I do. Maybe this is what vacation is all about. In the early afternoon I take a cab to the airport and surprisingly we don't hit any traffic. In less than an hour we get to the airport, where I buy a ticket from San José to Managua, Nicaragua, as it's obliged to buy transport out of Costa Rica as proof, or else you can't even get in. I'm early at the gate for a change, and I wait in the seats nearby, where I get to talk to a Panamanian woman and her baby son, who are on their way to Colombia to visit relatives. The plane ride is easy and short, and before I know it I'm setting foot at Costa Rican soil. It's already dark when I get into a taxi which drives me to my hotel, which I randomly picked, and appears to be in the middle of nowhere. The first thing that surprises me here is that houses don't have numbers, which is why the taxi ride takes longer than actually was needed: the driver has to figure out where it is, and even has to ask some people. I arrive in some American-style hotel, which from the patio's view looks like a motel. The room is very spacious however and the only thing lacking really is things to do. I eventually walk for some twenty minutes to a restaurant where I continue my habit of eating chicken. I get to meet a new friend in the small cheap restaurant who later drops me off at the hotel. Costa Rican friendliness has started on day one already.

For five days I keep hopping from hotel to hotel, until I finally find a place that I really like, and which is also well located. I also reach out to some car rental companies as I want to explore this country by car, as my dear friend Vera did with her boyfriend some years ago. My main focus is however to organise a trip to Tortuguero, a remote place in the northeast of the country, known for its turtles breeding on the beach, and, yes yes, for jaguars eating these turtles. There's recent footage of the BBC filming this ritual and it's amazing. People in Panama told me Tortuguero would be the place to be to see a jaguar. I would not be able to miss it, as they made it sound.

During these five days I also meet a lot of nice new friends, in shopping malls, in restaurants, all just random encounters. I seem to master the spontaneous meetings by now and my Spanish is finally also good enough. One highlight of these days however comes from far away, when I receive a message from my Turkish friends Aslihan and Selin, who send me a photo of them holding a sign saying 'Jort, miss you!'". It's such a warm and thoughtful message, which leaves me speechless. It's great to make new friends, it's greater to keep in touch with them who care. While I'm speechless, I write some emails to a guide in Tortuguero and also find a transport that can bring me there, without having the fuss of going by a maze of buses. It's all set up, I'm totally rested, and ready to go.

Costa Rica - Tortuguero, Limón

I pack all my stuff and load it into the taxi that will bring me to the van's pick-up point, the famous theatre. It soon becomes clear that near this theatre, on the main street of the city, there's more than one van picking up people and it takes a while before I figure out what's going on. I ask some people if they are also going where I'm going, but no one is replying positively. I wait a bit more and then finally get to meet the guys who'll be driving us. After stepping in, we head out to pick up other people, at their hotel, leaving me wondering why they can be picked-up and I had to take a cab. Anyway, I'm travelling with an organised group, and I'm the only one just on the transport. There's some nice people in the group and we soon kick off talking, also being helped by the guide who plays an introductory game with us, and keeps everyone involved. One of my first questions to the guide is how likely it is to see a jaguar in Tortuguero. His answer makes me believe I'm really close to my goal: in the past year 500 turtles were killed by jaguars. That is more than one per day, amazing! I might finally see the animal I've been chasing in all national parks throughout South America so far. The van stops at a crossroad, where there's a gas station, and also a restaurant. The group has paid for a lunch here. I haven't, so I cross the street to get some food at the supermarket. After the meal the road continues and we finally end up at a parking with a big tourist facility, from where the rest of the way will be covered by a long small speed boat. This is actually the first tour I do, and I take out my big camera. We see green iguanas, our first crocodile, and also some birds, while we cross the first small river, until we reach a wider open one, which eventually leads to the town of Tortuguero. Most of the group is left at a hotel on our way, which is really remote. Me and two others are the last ones to be dropped off. From here I expect to be picked up by my guide, who's also set me up with a room in a cheap accommodation. I ask some rangers in their office where my guide is, and they make a phone call to let him know I've arrived. He's already on his way and soon he arrives on a bike. There's no paved roads here, no cars, and I pull my big bag on its wheels through the sand. It's hot, and soon I'm sweaty. We walk towards the beach, and then to the right, where there's a neat ho(s)tel, where I'm welcomed. I say bye to the guide for now, and he tells me he will pick me up in the evening for the night tour. I now have some time to kill and I head to the beach, and walk there a bit, seeing some very obvious trails of turtles, and also many opened eggs. I then head into the forest, immediately seeing a group of capuchin monkeys. That's not all, as I suddenly see a monkey with extreme long legs and arms. I pinch myself and realise I see my first spider monkeys. They graciously move from tree to tree and soon are out of my sight. I'm full of adrenaline now, and continue on the well maintained trail, where I soon walk into the third monkey species: the black howler monkey. This must be my lucky day. Realising it might be, I take every trail to the beach to see if there's a jaguar. I take the same trail back to the main path and repeat this at every beach exit. In the meantime I see many more capuchin monkeys, who are feeding themselves on the fruits. I now get deeper into the forest and am actually already past the ending of the official trail. Here I walk under higher trees, and the trail is often overgrown with weeds. My attention is drawn to noise in the tree above me and I see my second group of spider monkeys. The baby hanging right above me is missing its right arm, and it's a pitiful sight. She still manages to fly through the trees though, but it still leaves me kind of sad. Nature's laws are cruel, and if they will encounter an enemy, this monkey is probably the first to die. I follow the troop for a bit, and soon I know this must be my favourite monkey species so far. After losing them, I decide to head back and again see many capuchins. I also walk by a huge shell of a dead turtle, which will be a reference point for me in the upcoming days of walking here. When the sun is slowly going down I head back to the hotel, from where I quickly go grab a bite in a restaurant near the main 'square'. At 19:00 I'm back at the hotel and ready for my pickup. Right on time my guide arrives and we head out to pick up some more people and then start walking away from the village, along the beach. There's spotters on the beach, and they inform the guides whenever there's a turtle nesting. We're not the only group, and when we arrive at some covered waiting area, we sit ourselves down as last in line. It takes a long time before we get called up, and I accidentally took a little nap, missing out on some of the information that was being shared. Now I'm wide awake again though and in line we walk to a beach entrance. There's another, bigger, group, in front of us and we patiently wait, while using our flashlights to search for other animals. Then it's our time to storm the beach, and we can't use the lights anymore. It's so dark now, and I'm still surprised how we all managed to get fairly close to the turtle. One of the rangers is lighting it and we see a huge turtle in some silent modus resting, breeding. It's amazing, especially because we had waited so long for this. It had to be good. Upon walking back to town we see some small frogs, lizards, and bats. I'm exhausted by the time I arrive back in my room, which contains two single beds, and is entirely made of woods, with some top 'windows' which can't be closed, or opened, and only some mosquito nets are in between me and the outside world. Even though this makes it quite noisy, I sleep like an angel.

"Doink, doink, wake up, wake up!", is the first thing I hear when I open my eyes the next morning. Did I miss my tour?! It's before six in the morning, and my guide is knocking on my door like a mad man. I open the door, putting my sleepy head out and ask what's going on. "A turtle! There's a turtle on the beach near the hotel, move move move!". I dress like lightning and then hurry myself to the beach with my camera ready. It indeed is a big turtle, that is lying in his hole at the point where the sand meets the bush. It's forbidden to enter the beach before 07:00, but we are going anyway. From a respectable distance we observe the turtle waking up, and then starting his crawling to the ocean. It must be one of the most beautiful sights of my trip, as I stand looking at the turtle making its way, while the sun is coming up, and the sky is like a Van Gogh painting, light blue, dark blue, orange, pink, it's just like an etching, covered with all pastel colours. The turtle is slowly moving, and I'm shaking, not sure whether it's because I got abruptly woken up, or because of the sensation of this moment. When the turtle is swallowed by the ocean, I return to the accommodation and there is a big group of howler monkeys in the tree. In the thirty minutes before the boat tour it's a good moment to see these loud animals having their breakfast, while I also eat some dry bread. Then I'm being picked up again and with some oars we walk to the spot where I first arrived in this desolate piece of world. There's another couple joining us in the boat, and they're from Argentina. The four of us head out for a tour where we might see some serious wildlife, like a tapir, or a jaguar. My guide now tells me there were only 100 turtle kills last year by jaguar, significantly lowering the number the other guide had given me. But still, one hundred... If I stay here four days I should be able to see at least one, right? We're not the only boat which docks at the ranger station to buy our licences for the day, and we're only one of the few paddling. Other have little motors, but these boats are also over crowded, and, make noise, which of course might scare off wildlife. We paddle over the big wide rivers and enter some small ones, seeing a wide variety of animals, especially some nice bird species. We get up very close to the caimans and it's great just seeing their eyes coming out of the water. At one point the other guy in the boat wants to touch its tail, and the guide is letting him. I'm totally against this though, and make a protest, which is honoured, to my satisfaction. Here I lose a little respect for my wise cool guide. We see two monkey species and observe a nice ritual when a mother capuchin lets her very tiny baby find its own way, and make some dangerous jumps. The baby barely makes it, and the mother then comes pick it up again. If the monkey would have fallen, for sure one of the caimans would have torn it apart. Our arms get a little sore from the peddling, but here, in the wilderness, it's amazing how silent everything is, and how we can hear all the sounds of the jungle. We slowly paddle back to town, and about three hours after we had started we now get back. We jointly have a good breakfast/lunch in town, and then I walk back to the hotel, where I see the same group of howlers still in the trees. I now walk on the neighbour's property, to which I'm invited by the girl who's working in the hotel, and where her family is living. There's a cute baby that likes being photographed and makes funny gestures to me. His mom observes its happiness and smiles throughout. I focus on the monkeys above me and see how they move from branch to branch, and let the fruits drop around me, giving me a feeling of a bombing. I move out before I get hit, and decide to walk the forest trail once more. I soon see capuchins, howlers and spider monkeys. One of the spider monkeys is drinking from a tree, which fascinates me, because I don't understand how he's doing it. Cutest are the small baby ones, who really are adorable. While walking the trail I run into a couple I had met in the transport to Tortuguero, and they're walking with a guide. He shows me a very pristine frog, lying on a leaf, and it's truly amazing. Its white-greenish colour and his red eye which has yellow veins running through, it's superb, and I never thought a frog could be this pretty. Rumours are also confirmed by him, when I ask him about a nearby boa constrictor, one of the deadliest snakes. I ask him politely to show me, and the couple agrees to walk me back there. And yes, hidden in a little bush, there's a baby constrictor, wrapped up, but clearly identifiable. It's my first ever boa constrictor and its colours and pattern are amazing. It's small however, only two or three metres, and obviously digesting a prey he has consumed. It will probably lay here for some days and then move again. I'm very grateful and when they leave I keep observing this symbol of evil. I then continue walking the trail to its end, seeing a family of three red squirrels and a huge black cricket. When the evening is falling I head back, feeling satisfied with what this day had brought me.

Yesterday's morning ritual of seeing a turtle was that amazing, that today I wake up before six again, and walk the beach myself in search of a turtle. There's no beautiful sunrise today, but a turtle I do find. It's amazing to see how it's dragging its shell back to the deep blue ocean, leaving a distinguished trail. I return to the hotel over the trail, seeing some spider monkeys and I of course pass the big snake again, which didn't move overnight. I then head back to sleep, as in the afternoon I've hired the guide I met the other day for a private tour in search of the jaguar. He's less positive than the other two guides and nearly laughs on the numbers they had been telling me. He doesn't want to destroy my dream though and politely guides me through the forest. We first start at a private property where I see some amazing spiders, frogs, birds, as well as snake eggs. At the ranger station we have a very clear view of a group of howler monkeys and they walk over a rope in the sun, making them very visible for the very first time here. Then we head back to the main trail, which we walk extensively, without seeing anything new. I do finally get some explanations and information on all the animal's behaviour, which makes it a worthy trip anyway. At one point the guide thinks to see a jaguar foot print, but I think he's just giving me hope, as I don't really see the pattern. Back at the hotel after a five-hour hike, I still haven't seen this damned jaguar. Where art thou, mighty animal? The evening I spend uploading photos and enjoying a good meal.

My alarm clock is waking me up early again today, as I plan on doing a canoe trip today by myself. I had seen others doing it with a guide's company, and I thought I could do this by myself. When the ranger station opens at seven I'm almost first in line. While waiting for my turn, I see a leaflet hanging there, with an official count of turtles killed by jaguars. I'm shocked by the guide's lies, as it states less than 30 kills last year. My hopes are kind of shattered for good now, and Tortuguero might not be the perfect place to see them after all. I get my permit, walk back to the canoe rental company and within minutes I'm peddling the rivers. I have a little map with what rivers are advisable, but I stick more to my own plan. It's harder to take photos while sitting in a canoe by myself. The backpack is laying in front of me, between my legs, and when moving to the left or right, everything seems a bit unstable. Just being free in the nature here, going wherever I want, keeping still whenever I want, is just what I like about it. I don't spot too much wildlife, and the more I paddle, and the further away I get, the more the clouds are gathering above me. I'm holding my breath it won't rain, as I'm totally not prepared for that. There's very few other boats today, and it's been a long time since I've seen any for the last time. Then my fear becomes reality as I first see some drops falling in the brown river, and then they fall by the thousands. It's pouring. My first thought is that this kind of rain will sink my canoe, and thus I take shelter under huge hanging tree with enough leaves to serve as some kind of umbrella. I expect the rain to pass over, like it did many times before, but it keeps coming and coming. There is water coming in my canoe, and I'm worried the big camera in the backpack will be totally wet, even though I put the rain protection over it. I'm continuously looking at the time and hoping there will be a boat coming to pull me out of this mess. Nothing is coming, and after over an hour and a half I think it's better to take a chance, and go back as fast as I can. The rain soaks me within seconds, and I lose my orientation, as my forces drain due to the heavy paddling. This isn't looking good. I come at a fork and instinctively take a left, a right, another right, but it's a dead end. I focus on the paper with the map on it, but it gets ruined by the hard rain. The positive thing is that my canoe seems to be stable and not too affected by the rain that is increasingly falling. I also can keep my camera dry, even though my seat is already covered in water. I get back my calm and steadily paddle in another direction, where I soon see other people canoeing. They seem to just have started a tour, but they all wear ponchos keeping them drier than I am. I ask their guide for the way back and he's pointing me to where I was already going, and where I soon recognise things again. This adventure literally fell into the water, and unlike Chris McCandless I found my way back, even though the river was rising. I land at the rental place, turn my stuff in and get a good laugh about what I had been doing. The guy was kind of mad, because this is what kills tourists. I'm laughing it away and just thinking of a warm shower and dry clothes. The rain lasts until the late afternoon, and I head out again once it stops, again exploring the trail. I'm renting rain boots now, to not be sucked into the mud, of which the trail now mainly consists. I see wet spider monkeys eating berries, some crabs, and birds. I'm still fascinated by the spider monkeys and follow a troop for a while, before heading back and calling it a day.

Six o'clock seems to be my normal time to head out here, to explore, and to find animals in the best photo light of the day: the early morning. This afternoon I head back to Sao Jose, giving me time to go into the forest one more time. It's sunny today and it gives a very good light on the red-brown fur of the spider monkeys, who are out to eat the red berries from the trees. I walk the trail as far as I can, given the time, and surpass the official end of the trail once more. I spot two very loud spider monkeys, who are playing, I think. I stand still and start taking photos. These monkeys aren't very fond of my presence though and with an enormous noise, breaking branches, making frightening sounds, they seem to come directly at me. I was not expecting this at all, and like the Panamanian howler monkey, I do a step back in order to show my respect. They now throw broken branches at me, and I don't want to be jumped by them. I back off a bit more, seeing their teeth in the blistering sun light. I admit it is quite intimidating, but also realise they will most likely not jump me. I stand ground now and they start hugging each other, making them look bigger, as their arms spread at maximum length. Later I find out this is indeed a ritual of intimidation, to protect themselves. I pretend to walk away now, and they still chase me a bit, but then head off in the forest towards the beach. I follow them from a distance and find them again in a tree right next to the sand. They don't seem to notice me at first, but as soon as they do, the ritual starts again, with them coming at me with big exposure. I now hold still and try to take some good photos of them trying to intimidate me. When they have given up on trying to scare me away, they move away from me with speed, further into the forest, where no trail can follow them. I must say this experience made my heart beat faster, but it was very well worth it to see them in this behaviour. I now head back to the hotel, which is about a two-hour walk, and there I say farewell to my room, the hotel, and the great staff. I head to the docks and await my transport there. The boat is not completely full, and has some nice folks on it, one girl even wearing a 'I heart Amsterdam'-shirt. On our way back to the big parking spot there are again some nice animals to see and even when we are driving in the van we make a stop for some spider monkeys, before we finally get to the highway and cross back to Sao Jose. I get back to the same hotel, which gives me an upgraded room this time, as I seem to be a loyal guest, which of course I am. In the evening I meet up with my friend Anaka, who I met in my first week in Costa Rica, to have dinner.

Costa Rica - San José, San José

I was happy to sleep early yesterday, as I'm deadly exhausted. My body has pushed itself with the long days in Tortuguero, so today I just relax. I visit my favourite shops in Escazu, having lunch, find books about Costa Rican jaguars, get back to the hotel, and rest.

In the afternoon of the next day I get picked up for my first road trip in Costa Rica. My dear friend Adriana picks me up in her car and together we go to Volcán Irazú, outside of the city. This volcano is over 3300 metres, so we're going up high. The sky is smiling at us in blue, and the clouds move by like little white sheep, as we drive towards this dead mountain. The road winds up pretty steep and when we finally think we are there, we end up in a big traffic jam of cars that all want to enter the park on this afternoon. It takes quite a while before we get in, and in the mean time we've bought all the food from the vendors knocking at our windows. We soon get to a parking now, and then it's a small walk into the grey crater. It's freezing up here, and I was not exactly prepared for this. The scenery is magnificent and the views are great. There's grey rocks, while the hillsides are full of bushes and trees. There's a field of what seems to be dune vegetation and it's all waving in the very strong wind. There's colourful flowers, but the best was people laying rocks forming the words of the slogan of Costa Rica: Pura Vida. I'm taking a lot of photos, but never seem to capture the crater's size or its entire beauty. We slowly walk back to the car, not only because we are taking our time, but also because the wind is so strong up here. We then start our drive down, being above the white clouds, gives us another great view of the urban areas in the valley below. We stop at a little restaurant for a drink, and the establishment reminds me of a European Alp hut. We then continue once again to stop at a former hospital, which now supposedly is some haunted place. When we arrive it's just closed unfortunately, so we have to skip this sight. It's still a little drive back to the hotel, and I'm being dropped off after a perfect afternoon of touring.

Costa Rica - San Ramón, Alajuela

After tasting a bit of a drive around Costa Rica, I'm now totally up for the challenge and I have rented a car for the next weeks to see the country by myself, or with anyone that wants to join. I have found a proper deal at a small rental company with a German owner, and I get a small cheap 4x4 car. I sign the papers, pay the fees and the upfront payment, and then I'm off, on to the road. My first stop today is a little town just outside of Sao Jose, where I have a friend, who I will visit. It's about an hour drive to Grecia, and as I leave in the afternoon there's no traffic. It seems Costa Rican traffic isn't that crazy as the other countries I've visited, and the roads are also in good shape. With the help of the application Waze on my iPhone I easily find the centre of this town, which lays a little bit higher than the main valley. It's very small, but has a nice central square, where I park in front of the church. This isn't a very good idea, I hear my friend tell me by phone, as it's a forbidden area for cars. Oops, my first mistake. I'm confident that my 'gringo card' will help me out of all these situations, as I also assume law keepers here don't speak any English. Priscila comes to pick me up from the parking spot I find after circling around the square for a bit, and together we walk to a restaurant where we have a good lunch, great conversation and many silly laughs. We say goodbye after the food, and I head to San Ramon, where I've booked a room in order to visit a nearby park the next day. It's a bit hard to find the hotel, as I run into the problem of street names without numbers, and I have to drive a bit back and forth before I find the small road heading up to the building. I'm warmly welcomed, shown my room, and even cooked a very good dinner, even though the kitchen was already closed. After dinner I crash into the bed and have very good night of sleep.

Costa Rica - Arenal, Alajuela

It's the Tortuguero time schedule again, when I'm sitting at my breakfast at 06:30. I've made a reservation for the 08:30 tour in Villa Blanca, which is also still an hour driving. I make an early phone call to make a last confirmation and then hit the road. I follow my gps system again, and without problems I reach the point where it supposedly is. The only problem is that there's nothing, and I enter a road full of rocks, going down and up, demanding everything from the car. It's not here. I make a phone call again to the Villa Blanca hotel and am informed I'm indeed wrong, and I should get back and drive in another direction. I'm speeding now, as I don't want to miss my tour, and upon arriving on the other road, I quickly see the signs directing me to the park. It eventually leads off the main road, through gloomy green hills, with every now and then a big tree. It's foggy here, because of last night's heavy rain. I'm welcomed at the luxury hotel by my guide Roy and two girls who're also taking the tour. We take a small path into the wet forest, and soon come to a hummingbird feeding place. There's many of them sitting on an artificial rope and they come and go. We observe them for a while and then move on. Roy is explaining a lot about the area and teaching us many things on how these cloud forests work. There's some big toads on our way and also the pink bananas are quite interesting. The absolute highlight still has to come though, as Roy says he's captured a very venomous snake last night, and he will be releasing it after our tour. For me the tour may be over now, as I'm anxious to see the snake, a Fer-de-Lance. The girls are very hesitant, and first don't even want to come. Me and Roy persuade them, although they stay far away when we get it out of the bucket, into the net. We now walk up a trail, away from the cabins, so the snake won't immediately be back to bother the gardeners. The snake's poison is deadly, and can kill a grown man within hours, so I am told. This kind of information makes it reasonable that the girls are a bit scared. Roy says he will hold it back with a device if the snake decides to come at us. He's also bringing his camera and lenses as he's an enthusiastic bird photographer, but doesn't want to miss a chance to shoot this snake. We get to a little open space and he unfolds the net so lifting it will make the snake appear. Slowly the net is moving up, and there it lays down on the pebbles of the path. It's getting adjusted to the surroundings, and I'm taking the photos, which is difficult as it's moving a bit and the light isn't perfect. The pattern on the scales of the snake is black, and brown, its eye the same colour. He suddenly makes a move towards us, showing the fork of its tongue, scaring the girls, and I also feel my heart in my throat, whilst I keep taking photos. Roy calms him down, and is also handling his camera now. Then the snake's done with posing, with being our model, and squirms into the forest, where it perfectly blends in. The girls are some metres behind us asking if the snake's really gone, and after we confirm it is, they finally start breathing again. They are done now for the day, and I walk up with Roy, as he wants to show me some footage they have from a puma, taken by the new (night) cameras they have installed. While walking back to his office, we hear a very sharp sound to our left, and soon see a baby hummingbird laying on the ground, probably fallen from its nest. We take a close look, and then continue to walk. At the office Roy gets some gloves and a little cup, and we walk back to pick the poor animal up and carry it back. Here we feed it sugar water with a small pipette. The tiny bird is hesitant at first, but then starts drinking it, moving its enormous long tongue in- and out. The bird's set up in his cup at the window and we talk a bit. The next time we look, the bird's already flown away. Roy shows me the footage of the camera and it's great to see all the animals passing by at night and during the day. I'm then asked to join him to pick up the footage of the last week of one of the cameras. "Hell yes, I am", is my reply. We take off for this surprise tour, leading us to another trail, where we have to walk steep up. Roy recognises all the bird sounds and even though we aren't seeing them, we can hear there's some special ones around us. We get to the camera, and it's nice to see my guide working on it, and instantly looking at his laptop if there were any animals. Except from some coatis there were none, unfortunately. The memory card is put back and we get back uphill, sweating like mad men in this suffocating heat. When we get back it's time for me to take off, as I have reserved a room in a hotel near the Vulcan Arenal, which is some four hours driving from here. I say goodbye to my new friend and head back on the bumpy road before getting to the main road, which is also just a two lane land road, meaning if you're behind a truck, you're screwed. I'm making my progress, until the sky breaks open and it's starts pouring and pouring. I can hardly see what's happening in front of me, and my wipers are making extra hours. A lot of cars seem to stop at the side of the road, afraid of this tropical rain storm. I'm used to it, and finally make some progress now the slow cars are gone. I get to the main tourist hub here, Fortuna, and here I can finally fill up the tank. I also withdraw some money from the ATM, as the town of my hotel has none and the bill will have to be paid in cash most likely. I still have to drive all around the volcano, which lays on my left, but is covered in clouds and I can only see a little bit of the lonely mountain every now and then. This volcano is unlike many others as it, indeed, stands alone. It could be the famous Lonely Mountain, with gold under it, and a dragon called Smaug laying on top, but it probably isn't. While driving around I pass the hot springs just north of the mountain, which by means is even more popular than the volcano itself. There's some big spa hotels here, but I was already told you can enter the river for free at some point, which I by the way am not planning to do. When I'm around it, I leave the main road for an unpaved one and this one is quite bumpy. The rain stops now, but the water covers the huge potholes that are everywhere. I'm hoping I won't get a flat tire here. I see a first sign of the hotel now, and it says I'm very close. Another signs mark the road steep up a hill where the hotel is beautifully situated. I park the car near the lobby and from here I see the lake nearby. I check-in with a friendly girl who's helping me in English and is very helpful in answering all my questions on things to do in the area. I then drive to my room, park, unload and get back to the viewpoint to take some photos of the sun setting behind other mountains, further away, giving the sky an orange glow for a while. The volcano is still covered in clouds unfortunately, and thus it will have to wait to be seen until tomorrow. When the sun's gone I get some food in the restaurant and then get to my room to make some decisions for the next day.

Costa Rica - San José, San José

The plan has been made during the night, and it starts with seeing the volcano from the hotel deck. It's a big singular peak and the sun is coming up at its right. I'm the first one out, at around 06:00, being in an oasis of silence. Soon other guests wake up to see the sun coming up, and for me then it's time to get the buffet breakfast. I can leave my bags at the hotel while I first go to a park with sky bridges, and then for a hike towards the volcano. It's a short drive to the sky bridges, and I find it quite easily, due to the extensive signs that are hanging everywhere. It's a good road going up, which my car can only manage to do in the first gear. I arrive at a wide parking spot and I get my ticket at the booth, and then start walking the trail, which has, the name already gave it away, many sky bridges. Right at the start it's bullseye, as I see a big group of coati's. I finally have a clear view of these animals, after the two shaking times in Panama. There's some babies with the group, and they move as quickly as the ones on Pipeline Road. When I step closer they all spurt away, and one even climbs a tree very quickly. It's a great sight. I then continue walking the trail, seeing some colourful birds, and also a small group of spider monkeys. The trail's getting steeper and steeper, and I feel like I'm climbing the Mount Everest. It's great to walk over the sky bridges, getting some stunning views. I walk the trail twice actually, and the second time it starts drizzling. When I return at the entrance/exit, I make a start for a third round, but get stuck there trying to get a photo of a black howler monkey, which is hanging in the trees, and is protected by too much green. It's nearly impossible to see it, but I manage to spot it frequently and even showing it to an elderly couple that has just started their hike. When I turn to exit the park after some four hours of walking, I stumble upon a group of wild pigs, and it's my first sighting of them in this trip. Outside the park now is a huge yellow and blue parrot sitting, a tame one. A group of children is trying to talk to him, but he's not very responsive today. The rain is continuing falling slowly, and I drive back in the direction of the hotel, but upon reaching the dirt road, I take one of the first exits to the left, into the volcano's national park, from where I want to do another hike. I pay an entrance fee to a ranger, and then go on yet another bumpy road to a big parking, where there's only a few cars. There's a circular trail here, bringing me to a very old and big tree, and then to a former lava river, with black volcano rocks. The trail is flat this time, and I make good progress. At first there's high grass on both sides of the trail, which is then replaced by small trees, until it changes into very tall ones. Just as I take my right towards the big tree, it starts pouring once again. Shit. I put my camera away, and numbly continue the walk, until I reach a huge tree, the main destination of this trail. I quickly take some photos, and then hurry towards the lava stones. It's really too wet here, and walking on them, makes me slip from them. These rocks are also out in the open, thus no trees to protect me, a bit. Every raindrop now makes me more soaked, and soon I call it a day and head back, walking in a high pace to keep warm. I get back to the car, head back in, and the drive back to the hotel to pick up my bags and also to enjoy a lovely late lunch. I setup my gps to drive back to Sao Jose now, and over a northern route I head back. It's dry now for a bit, and the scenery is great. Green on both sides, and mountains to my far right. This road will bring me over a very high mountain range back to the capital, and this way isn't the easiest one. It's high, very high, and my ears soon sizzle. Besides the rain another problem is starting: darkness. The sun is gone and I'm high in the mountains where there's no street lights. It's hard to keep my eyes focused, but I'm glad the gps is showing me the way and I don't have to think about that too much. I pass some desolated houses, empty villages, before I finally start to descend. Under me I now see million lights of the Sao Jose agglomerate. It makes it worth the hard road I'm travelling. I stop for a pee break and to enjoy the view. It's cold, so I don't last too long outside. I get back to my Sao Jose home, my regular hotel, do my check in and have dinner here.

<u>Costa Rica - Playa Tortuga, Puntarenas</u>

Even though I'm in downtown Sao Jose, opening my window gives me two little parrots sitting on the fence, sunbathing in the early morning sun. I've finally found a travel companion, and Anaka will join me on a little road trip to the southwest of the country, where I hope to see more wildlife. The first important stop is made at the bridge over the Tarcoles river, which has a little secret underneath it: a very big group of American crocodiles. There's tourist facilities right in front of the bridge, where we park, and I nearly run onto the bridge to see if what I've read is true. As Anaka promised, it is true: there are gigantic crocodiles lying in a river bank just under the bridge. Amazing. There's a very famous photo taken here of a cow walking in between these predators without being attacked. I now also see the cows, in a little distance, and I can now put the picture clearly in my mind. The animals are massive and I can't get enough. The road's calling though and we buy some snacks and then continue our way south. We make a stop at the party town Jacó, which is one of Anaka's beloved destinations. The beach is okay, the setting nice, but seeing how touristy it is, not directly my cup of tea. I wander around a bit for some photos and we then take off again. Just outside town we get to a viewpoint from where we see Jacó's bay at its fullest. It's decent from up here. Our next stop is a random one, near the road, as I've spotted an eagle sitting on an electricity wire. I'm taking some photos from the window and we then head on into the national park Manuel Antonio. We park the car somewhere in a parking near the beach and then walk to the ticket booth. There are guides everywhere offering their services and they all carry a telescope to zoom in on the animals. We refuse all the offers politely and go explore on our own. Soon it's quite obvious this park is nearly overrun by tourists, as the road to the beaches is crowded. The same ritual is happening all the time: guide with their groups looking through the telescopes. Every time we see one showing something we just look by ourselves, and most of the time see what is being shown. I must admit we would have missed most of it if it wasn't for these guides, but now we saw the lizards, toucans and crickets. When we take a left to explore some of the trails, we almost immediately walk into two capuchin monkeys, who aren't shy at all, and just scramble right next to the trail. We follow them until they disappear and then set foot on a small beach, where there's some iguanas that remind me of the black ones in the Galápagos. We turn around and head to the main beach, which is situated in a very pretty bay. It's empty now, as we arrive quite late, and even the famous raccoon thieves are not to be seen. We have a talk with a very friendly ranger and then walk through the sand to the rocks at the end and back again. The sun's hiding behind the clouds and we probably don't see it in its full glory, but with a little imagination we can clearly see why this is so popular. We are the last ones to leave here and head back to the exit right after. At the end we see a mother and baby deer near the ranger booth. Like the other animals they don't seem shy, at all. We walk back to the car, and are happy to sit down for a bit. The final part of today's journey now starts and we drive more south, towards Playa Tortuga, where I've made a hotel reservation. We pass another very well-known tourist town, Playa Dominical and then get on a road without any markers, at which somewhere, the hotel should be. Again, having no house numbers here makes it terribly hard to find places. It's also dark as soon as we start our search, which isn't helping us either. Our gps is lost, and so are we, and for a long time we head down the same road back and forth. Anaka asks at another hotel, which gives us an indication, but not a final answer to our question. We finally do find it, and a steep hidden entrance brings us to a house. There's artificial green lights everywhere, and it immediately feels like a hippie hangout. An old American lady comes to welcome us, talking non-stop, and gives us the key to our very big room, including kitchen, and living room. I didn't see this coming. We drop our bags and then head back to the car, so we can find a restaurant for some food. We find a very nice place, but get lost again when returning. Turns out we totally drove in the wrong direction. Eventually we find our way back again and are relieved when we get to our rooms.

Costa Rica - Uvita, Puntarenas

We're extremely lucky as it turns out there's a whale festival this
weekend in Uvita, in the Marino Ballena national park. This means
we can get on a boat to see whales for a very low fare. My morning
starts with a walk around the hotel property to see if there's any
wildlife to be seen. The dog that walks with me makes sure there isn't
any to be seen, but the little river down is quite peaceful. We head
down to Uvita, turn towards the beaches and find a big stand very
soon. The car is parked a few metres from there and we head into the
tent to get our tickets. I can't believe the price difference with the
tour I had in Panama, and now I hope it will be just as good. First we
have to wait until enough people arrive to let a boat get out, and
when there's finally enough of us we walk to the beach, where we
wade to a boat. We all get in and take off. Soon we already see our
first whale, and it's quietly laying in the water, just like the first one I
saw in Panama. It's so amazing though to see a whale. Soon after we
see a second one and this one is blowing water into the air, which I
had not seen before and which is truly amazing. It continues for a
while and it gives me time to take at least one good photo. There's
few other boats out there, and we all circle around the whale until it
leaves us. Then we soon find another one again, and are all
hypnotised by the sight of these power beasts. The highlight still has
to come, and happens right in front of us. A mother and her baby are
swimming to the wide ocean, gaining more speed every time they
come up. And then the baby suddenly jumps from the water, and
again, and again. Wowowow! It's nearly impossible to photograph,
but this baby whale makes the day. Soon they are out of sight, sunken
into the deep ocean. It leaves me behind flabbergasted, thrilled,
excited. The tour continues a bit more, showing some rocks with
boobies, of which later one is following the boat, gracefully carried by
the wind. After about 1.5 hours we make a Normandy landing, and
we safely get to a restaurant near our car, where we enjoy a fine meal,
and delicious juices. I have the idea to do a hike in the afternoon and
I've read about a piece of farmland, where they have made some
trails through the forests, where, supposedly, there is a good chance
on wildlife. We drive there, park our car on the emptier than empty
parking spice and get to the wooden building that serves as tourist
facility and where you can buy the tickets. The guy tells us we have a
very good chance to see all kinds of animals and then walks us to the
start of the trail, which is on the other side of the road. Here we

nearly crawl through some thick bushes and then see the trail. It's not very well maintained, if it's maintained at all, and it leads through a dark forest. There's no sunlight coming down here and it makes it a bit spooky. The trail goes uphill, and at times we have to climb over the fallen trees, or we have to stop to see what is the trail, and what is not. There's no wildlife these hours, and the only thing Anaka is worried about is to see a frog, of which she's frightened to death. We climb and climb, deeper into the forest, our legs soon sore from planting our feet in the soft soil and dragging them out over and over. We pass some streams and take a rest. Then we think we have lost the trail and for a moment we feel lost. A quick exploration expedition makes me find the path back, and we now finally go down a bit. My friend's shoes aren't made for going down and her sandals soon constantly slide off her feet, making her decide to go barefoot. I'm worried, offer my shoes, but she's persistent in walking like this. We now move slower, but steady, and come to a little bit of an open spot where we finally see some capuchin monkeys, far away. At least it's something on this God forgotten trail. The leafs slide under our feet while we think to walk over the trail down to the exit, but multiple times we wonder if it's the trail at all. We manage though, and finally get back to the road. This trail is absolutely not recommendable. We get to the car and drive back to Uvita, where we try to find an accommodation for the night. Through my hotel application on the phone we eventually book a nice room in a German-run hotel/hostel. It has a very pretty viewing deck, and its setting is perfect. There's no light on the trail to the establishment though, creating anxiety with Anaka for her frogs. My iPhone light helps. We find the same restaurant as the night before and then drive back to catch up on our sleep.

Costa Rica - Manuel Antonio, Puntarenas

Yesterday the farm trails were horrid, but today we will try the same thing in another place. Hacienda Barú has some better reviews on the internet, so we're hoping for the best. It's not easily found, and we have to ask some locals, but eventually we get there. The parking is a bit smaller, and again there are no other cars. We buy the ticket and first go to a lookout tower from where we should see some birds. It's nearby and the tower isn't that tall. From the top we see some birds, but soon head down again. We start to explore the main trails, and in comparison to yesterday this is perfection. Everything is well maintained and has information signs with details about the animals and vegetation on this property. And yes, there's even words about the damned jaguar. We take a left to see one part of the trail, and we walk in silence, as I don't want to be too noisy for the animals. It pays off, as soon I see an animal, big as a cat, grey as an elephant, with a very specific head: a racoon. My first racoon ever and it briefly stand still for a moment, before it disappears again. On our toes we now make some process and in a tree to the left we see two sloths, who aren't hiding too much: phenomenal. We follow this trail to the road, and then turn back, to walk back all the way and take another turn, more towards the beach. The forest here has trees at large distances from each other and the branches and trunks are skinny. Here we suddenly see a big bunch of capuchin monkeys collecting their food from the floor. It's nice to see them walk over the ground, instead of them moving in the trees. They are moving in the same direction as we are walking, and we gently follow them for a while. When they are a bit out of sight, suddenly something very weird happens: they all come running back. It's as if they have seen an enemy and the entire troop rushes past us, not even paying attention to us anymore. What the hell have they just seen? We decide to follow them in their direction of escape and reach a little bridge we had just past earlier. Here the second awkward moment occurs: as most of the monkeys have crossed, one monkey walks back to us, holding a green object in one of its hands. I can't believe it, as it turns out to be a dead lizard, with its head completely torn off. It seems to be a warning to us: if you follow us, your head we be cut off as well. I'm flabbergasted and stunned by this monkey's behaviour. I follow them nevertheless for a while, until I can't find any way to go where they went. I head back to my friend who had been waiting for me, and we continue our way. There's a little shack, with some tools for maintenance, and some piles of food here. A giant iguana is resting here. We don't think this is the reason of the monkeys' fearful escape, so we keep looking for other clues. I'm praying for a giant cat, a puma or jaguar, even though chances are zero at this time of the day. The trail now leads us to the share, and there's a small strip of trees between us and the beach. Here's a family having a beach day, and we also set foot in the sand for a while, looking over a dark brown sand surface, covered with pieces of trees. It's an ugly beach and not good for any chilling. We head back to the trail and now see how the family's car got here: it's a road that can bring you all the way here. I look at the wide road and see another group of capuchin monkeys walking over it, some drinking in the rain pools. One monkey is standing on its back feet, showing signs of evolution. I'm trying to quietly get closer, not wanting to disturb the group. At my right there's a monkey fairly close eating a fruit. I take some photos. I continue on the right side of the road, until I suddenly stand face to face with two capuchin monkeys. They aren't friendly, at all, and with two jumps they suddenly are within arm distance. These sudden leaps scare the hell out of me, and I turn and run away, bringing tears of laughter to my friend. I'm persistent however, and turn back to the two monkeys, getting closer step by step. They both hang over each other now, and fiercely and aggressively showing off their teeth. I'm not welcome, and should get away, their obvious message. I'm so close to these two crazy little fucks, that I'm finally taking some good photos. And I know, they most likely won't attack anyway. I show them my teeth now too, and this is what scares them, and they see their behaviour isn't working with me anymore. They climb a tree, cross the road, and blend in with this group of nearly fifty monkeys. We take our time to observe them, to see the babies, and to see their hunt for food. They exactly move in the way our path goes, so we can follow them for quite a bit. They make some pretty sick jumps from tree to tree at times, but I'm too slow in recording it. When they finally lose us, or we them, our trail leads us gradually back to the stationary, from where we pick up the car and drive back to Manuel Antonio, where we finally have a hotel with good beds. It turns out to be one of the best hotel rooms I've been in so far on my entire trip, and its luxury could not be seen from the road. We drop off our luggage, and then head out to find a restaurant, while the rain is falling down on us. We find a place in some dark alley from the main road, and are the only customers who need to be fed. The food's good, and the sleep afterwards even better. The beds are amazing.

Costa Rica - San José, San José

It's the final day of a great road trip, and we have time to visit the Manuel Antonio park once more. Today the sun is shining and we deserve some beach time after hiking so much the last couple of days. We take a very early breakfast, as I, of course, want to be in the park as early as possible. After eating it's only a short drive to the park entrance. We now know the drill, and enter the park before 8am. We soon see our first sloth of the day, and then continue to walk to the far end of the park. It's a lot of steps up the hill, but fortunately we're distracted by some howler monkeys near the top. It gives us some time to breathe before we continue on the descend, towards a very pretty bay. The water is glowingly turquoise blue and the surrounding forest deep green. It's high tide sadly and thus we can't continue to the beach further down the bay, but this amazing view was well worth the climb. We head back to the main beach, again going up first, before making our way down to the sands and green waters. Today is racoon time, and these animals are incredibly cheeky. I see them open backpacks, stealing cookies, and other foods. When I am in the water for a swim, one of these bastards is also reaching into my bag. It makes me rush out of the water to scare the poor animal away. It's in a way hilarious how these beasts evolved in losing their fear for humans, and then how to open bags, and zippers. There's also many of them, and I follow some on their pirate crusade. This way I get to the other side of the beach, where there's another, more hidden, beach. As the tide's high, there's not much sand left to walk on, and there's only few people here. After some sunbathing, chilling and talking, we have had our rest for the day, and head back to the park's exit, to the car and then drive off. Just outside of town we find a big restaurant for a good lunch, and then it's back north, towards San José. We make a couple of stops on our way: the first stop is when I pull the car over at the side of the main road, because I think to see the famous red parrots. I get out of the car with my camera, step into the rain, walk a bit back, and indeed see four of these giant birds eating berries on top of the tree. It's the cherry on my dessert to even see these birds on this trip. I already had started to believe they were part of a fable. The other stop we make at the Tarcoles river, of course, to again look at the giant American crocodiles. They're still there, laying lazily on the sandbank. No action, unfortunately. Back in San José I drop Anaka at her home, and I head back to mine, the same good old hotel. Check in, baggage drop, dinner and then sleep.

Costa Rica - Liberia, Guanacaste

I've set my mind on the parks in the northwest of the country. These are more distant, less travelled, and, according to the books, also have the mighty cats. Anaka's grandfather had a farm there and jaguars were regular visitors to kill the cattle. This story makes me strongly believe I might be able to see one there. After yet another great breakfast in my hotel, I check out, and hit the road. First I make a stop in Grecia again, to see my friend Priscila, have lunch with her, visit her sister's beauty salon, and hang out in the park. Now I'm here I also seize the opportunity to return my purple iPhone cable at the store where I bought it on my last visit. I'm getting a new cable right away, and continue to talk to the sales lady for a bit, asking her what her favourite spots are in Costa Rica and what she would recommend me. Her answer surprises me as she hasn't left this town in the eight months she's here. My tongue is quicker than my mind, and before realising it I've offered her to join me on a road trip one of these days. Maybe I had expected the offer to be turned down, but she accepts it immediately. There's no way back now, and maybe it's not that bad: I get to have someone to talk to again, and I can stop the talking to myself for a bit. We exchange numbers to plan things later. I head out, get the car from the parking, and drive to the west coast, before taking the road north. It's quite a long drive, especially given the fact all highways are one lane only here, and passing other cars is nearly impossible. Fifty kilometres before Liberia there are road constructions, and even slower traffic. I get to the hotel I've reserved in the very late afternoon. It's again some kind of motel, and next to this 'highway'. I drop off my stuff in the fine room I get, and then enjoy a meal in the hotel's restaurant. The driving today made me tired, so the rest of the night I'm just chilling in the room.

The first national park of this northern trip is the one of Santa Rosa, which is about an hour north of Liberia and covers a huge area of land and forest, and reaches out all the way to the ocean. I depart very early, before any other traffic and have the road north of Liberia all to myself, making good progress at a proper speed. When I arrive at the park's entrance there's no one there. I step out of the car, knocking on the station's door, but there's no response. As there's no gate, I decide to just continue. I've read there's a possibility of sleeping in the park, and I'm considering doing so. From the first station until the park ranger's village it's still quite a drive, and there's signs next to the road warning for all kinds of crossing animals. I reach a fork in the road, giving me several options. I take the right and arrive at a huge building. I park the car, and walk in. I find a ranger to whom I can pay my entrance fee and who I can ask my questions. I of course first ask about the jaguar, and he says there are sightings of the elusive animal, yes, but very rarely. He only saw one once in his ten years of duty here. Sigh. This isn't very promising again. I explore the monument at the back of the building, giving me a view over a sea of green trees. Marvellous. I head back to the car and follow the instructions of the ranger in finding information on accommodation. I get into an area with many barracks and knock on the door of one of them. It's the human resource cabin, and I immediately offer them my services. The two girls laugh out loud and the ice is immediately broken. They tell me numerous things about the park, and eventually also point me to where I can find more information on the sleeping. I get to a very big barrack, which is nearly military, and has many dorms, with bunk beds. A young fellow shows me around, and explains me how it all would work. I thank him and take it in consideration. First I will go explore the park. I get to the road which will bring me to the beach, where some trails will start through the forest. The sign at the start is a bit worrying: the road is only allowed to be entered with a 4x4 car. It also says hiking is recommended at the rainy season. It kind of is rain season now, but no one told me to not go here by car, so I start my twelve kilometres drive to the shore. The road is awfully bad, with giant rocks everywhere. I'm so hoping my tires will hold up, as I would have no clue how to change it. There's enormous potholes in the road, and at times I'm almost vertical with my car. The worst is still to come, as there's many pools of water, and I don't have any idea how deep it is. I feel like having to cross rivers at times, but I don't know if they're actually are. The first few are quite innocent. I drive slow, with one side at the dry part, and tilting a bit while moving forward. It gets worse when there's no dry parts of the roads, and I just have to go in. I'm worried I get stuck in these pools, but am determined to get to the beach. One pool gives me a near heart attack: I drive in and soon the water gets as high up as my window, meaning the engine must be underwater. I hit the gas and feel the rocks slip under the wheels, not making as much speed as I want. I'm still moving, giving me hope to make it, and eventually the car seems to break free and rushes forwards at the speed I had expected before. It's hot outside, but the sweat on my forehead is not from that. There's other pools but none as bad as this one. I'm already shooting prayers for the way back. I mostly have to drive in my first gear, second maximum, because the rocks prevent getting at a normal speed. When there's a hill, I have to steer better than any Formula 1 driver, avoiding big rocks, small rocks, potholes, in square centimetres. This drive makes me deserve a long vacation. I finally reach the open space of dunes, and there's more water here than before. If it will start raining I'm probably really screwed. I park the car, and walk over the last unstable wooden bridge to a ranger station where I get some information about the trails. There's two of them, both making a round. I go to the right, and walk through a low tree forest. I don't see much animals, unfortunately. One animal is making crazy sounds throughout my hike however and it takes a while before I find out it's a kind of eagle sitting on a branch and is relatively easy to approach. When I get too close it flies though. There's two of them, and it seems to be some kind of mating ritual. I observe them for a while from a distance, and then head to the river. This river has its connection with the ocean here, and it's quite a spectacle to see how both streams are fighting each other. I continue to walk over the beach, see the famous witch rock, one of the most famous surfing spots of the country, and then slowly head back to the station. There I decide to walk down to the little lake a bit further down. The ranger's told me there might be some crocodiles there, so it's worth a shot. While going there the blue sky is getting covered by grey clouds. I hurry myself to the lake, and then go straight back to the car. I've got to get out of this place. I say farewell to my ranger friend and start driving. Before I'm away, I'm already photographing a big black eagle sitting in the dazzling rain. I'm not thinking for some thirty minutes, only focused on the road and its obstacles. The higher I get, the drier, which allows me to make a couple of stops to walk to some viewpoints. When I come back from one of them, it really starts raining hard. I see another car stop now and three guys jump out, get their surf boards and run to the beach, which is at least some kilometres from here. They've obviously done this before, as they park the car right before the shitty holes and deep pools, which I just had passed again. The rain doesn't last too long fortunately, and the sun is winning today's fight. I invite a guy for the drive back, as he's trying to hike back. His thumb was saying he wanted to get the ride, so why not help him? He's Costa Rican and has an internship at the ranger station here. I drop him off at one of the cabins and then go buy a soda at the restaurant, where I also inform the people I won't be staying for dinner or sleeping. It's quite early, and there's no other trails in the park I can walk anyway. The one to the turtle beach is sadly forbidden and closed this time of the year. I meet a guy walking around the area, and this Argentinian man says to study the spider monkeys here. I was just following a mother and her baby and he says there's a whole bunch around the barracks here. He also points to the lavatories, where the howler monkeys are holding camp. I go there quickly and indeed see a big group of them, including babies. The spider monkeys intrigue me more though and I soon head back to the mother and baby, who are still spending quality time together in the tree. I follow them for a bit, and then head back to the car. At the station I decide to walk the nearby trail once more, even though the twilight makes it hard to see things right now. The trees protect the last sun rays from coming in, and soon I have to use my iPhone's light to make sure I keep on the track. The sound of the forest grows stronger now, and the insects are wide awake. I get back to the car without any snake bites, and drive back to Liberia.

I've had another good meal in the hotel's restaurant yesterday, and today I have my breakfast early in the morning again. I pack my stuff, and walk to my car. When I drive off, I immediately notice something's wrong. I park the car again, step out, and check the four tires. One of them is flat. Damnit. I'm not very good in fixing things, and I've never been taught how to change a tire, nor did I ever have this experience. I have no clue what to do next, and I walk back to the front desk and ask if they have an idea. They tell me to put on the spare tire and then drive to the gas station nearby, and they will fix it in ten minutes. This country's used to cars with flat tires and therefore has tire shops everywhere. The only problem I have that putting on the spare isn't that easy, for me. I ask them for help, and they tell me there's a guy that might be able to help. They call him and an old guy walks up to the front desk now. I shake his hand and ask him if he can help me. I can't even finish the question, because he's already walking outside, and telling me to open the trunk. I do as he requests and help get out the spare tire. We then use the jack to lift the car. I write 'we', but it's the old man doing all the work. I'm just scratching my head. He makes it look easy and within ten minutes the spare is attached. I shake his hand a thousand times, but he just walks off. I ask the front desk what the old man likes, and they say he drinks one glass of cola every day. That is his joy. I know enough and head out to drive the car to the tire shop. It's only a one-minute drive and there's no other cars in line. The three guys working are tough guys, but with my silly jokes and Spanish I break the ice quite fast, and now they laugh while fixing my tire, and then replacing it. They charge me two euros after the twenty-minute work. I give them ten, as I'm happy it's all fixed so fast. With my payment they also seem to be very happy, and they enthusiastically wave goodbye to their 'amigo'. I stop at the gas station's shop and buy five cola bottles of two litres to give to my rescuer. At the hotel I ask the front desk to call him again, and I hand him his bottles. He not only starts shaking my hand thousand times, but also starts hugging me like I'm his lost son, and I think he never wants to let go again. When the hug's over, his eyes seem to be a bit wet. I never thought cola would make a man so grateful. And it's still me who needs to be grateful, not him. After some more talking, I finally hit the road, to the second national park: Rincón de Vieja. This is a park near an active volcano, and supposedly you can see the earth boiling here. I arrive just after midday, and park my car in a meadow, and walk the final metres to the ranger station, where I have to pay for the entrance and register myself. I'm of course asking about the jaguar, as the animal's on the leaflets again that I can check. I'm getting to same reply again, that I might see it, but most likely not. I head off, immediately walking into a playful group of capuchin monkeys, who are chasing each other in the trees. A group of Americans catches up on me and I point them to where the monkeys just went. I follow the trail, and again walk into a group of animals, this time them being coatis. They are on their food search and not backing off when tourists are walking by them. When coming too close they make a little run though, and then gather. I continue the walk, seeing an ever bigger group of coatis further down the path. There's ingenious trees, growing braided, and suddenly a strong sulphur smell. I reckon this is the pits I was told about, and soon I indeed see the smoke coming from a little lava pool. The smell is horrible, and I have to walk through the smoke to continue, making it even worse. It's fascinating to see how it's working though, and from another viewpoint I stand to observe. A sign says the water is the pool reaches up from 75 to 106 degrees Celsius, and is logically mentioned as a dangerous zone. At other pools there's wooden fences to prevent people from coming too close, which makes sense giving these temperatures. I reach a big open spot and now see the smoke rising from the forest at several points, which gives a very nice sight. I don't see much more animals, just another group of coatis, some hummingbirds, and green little parrots. Then I think to have lost track, and I'm not sure what the way back actually is. I make same guesses and they turn out to be right, as not much later I seem to have finished my round, and arrive back at the ranger station. I decide to walk the other trail for a bit, but don't find it that interesting, so I turn back after walking it for some thirty minutes. Once more I head to the station, sign myself out, make a short talk with the ranger, and then get to the car to drive back to Liberia. On my way back I make a stop for passing capuchin monkeys, and a group of howlers, who are seeming to mingle. Then it's a straight drive back to my hotel, and the rain joins me again, crying a river.

Another park lays more south of Liberia, and this is today's destination: Palo Verde. It's again a gigantic park, with multiple entrances, and is also known for its great variety of birds. I don't have a flat today, so I'm on the road before 8am. It's about a forty-five-minute drive over the main highway, and then thirty more minutes over a dust road. It's a flat area with pastures on both sides, some of them full of water, attracting all kinds of birds. At the entrance I overhear a Belgian family discussing a boat trip, and for a fair price they seem to be able to take it, at least if they hurry to the end of the road. I ask them if I can join for the same price, and that seems to be no problem. Both cars then get on the track to the river, which is around thirty minutes of slow driving. We get to a little dock, park the cars and enter the boat, where already two other tourists were waiting. It's a wide river, and we start exploring the northern shore all the way, stopping at various point to spot birds and iguanas who perfectly blend in with the trees. Then there's some commotion in the front of the boat, as they see a huge crocodile lying in the water. As the boat is quite long, the people in the back, like me, don't see it immediately. The ship's captain manoeuvres in a good position and now we can all see the grand beast. Only his eyes and a part of the tail are visible, but you can measure its size by it well. We stick around for a while and then see it swim away, giving us even a better idea of its size. After one hour the boat turns to go back, and we start exploring the other side of the river, which gives us the same animals, including two other crocodiles, again. One of these crocs is lying with its mouth wide open on a river bank, giving us a peek into its giant mouth. When we come closer it quickly moves itself into the brown river water. An hour after our turn we get back to the dock and again enter our cars. I say farewell to them all and head back to the ranger stations in the middle of the road, which I had to pass already going to the river. Before I get there I see a deer as cute as Bambi observing me, at the side of the road, and I manage to pull off some snaps. I park the car next to the buildings, which look like big Texan mansions, and then start the trail. Within five minutes I'm already going totally nuts as there must be a billion mosquitoes here. It's absolutely insane. The trail also goes steep us, and all the markings are soon gone, making me just randomly climb a very steep hill with many smooth leaves, making me feel I'm walking on an ice mountain, slipping and falling. It gets a layer of scary when I walk into a perfect monkey skull, or is it human...? This can be a scene of a horror movie, with mosquitoes being the monsters. I pour nearly all my repellent over my skin in order to keep them away, but these little bastards are persistent in getting my blood. I get to a big rock and start to fight them, smashing hundreds of them by my mighty claws. For every beast I kill, four seem to return, making it an impossible fight to win. I'm beating a hasty retreat, and like Indians attacking cowboys, I now rush off the hill, waving my arms to keep the flies away. I get to escape to my car, lock all the doors and finally breathe again. My arms are reds from the bites and I for sure now have dengue or malaria or any other terrible disease these little insects carry. This should be the moment for the end credits of the movie. I drive away, and look at the map of the park where else I can go. I see a possible right turn in the road, and I decide to take it, not exactly knowing where it will take me. It's just another forest road, with the difference it's not driven so often, as there are plenty of branches blocking the road, which I have to either carry away, or pass with a little curve. I get deeper and deeper into this park, take another right, and then come into what it seems to be rice fields: water grass land, with many birds again. Here I see a beautiful eagle, a laughing falcon, posing on top of a tree. I manage to take some great photos of this tiny predator, as it keeps sitting there, unruffled. He wins the staring match, and I continue driving, soon, but a bit late, realising there's nowhere I can turn my car to drive back, as the road is very small, and on both sides there's water. I hope to find a place more down the road, but the problem I drive in soon, is that the road ends. There's high grass and more water in front of me. Now what? I've been driving this road for twenty minutes, of which at least ten were with the water on both sides. I start to turn my car inch by inch, more careful than I've ever done, focused to the max. I pull it off, and give myself a big round of applause. I step out of the car to see my tracks of turning, and I really did well, even though my wheels obviously hung over the ridge a couple of times at least. I can now slowly drive back to the main road. I make some stops for a couple of eagles and even a big owl. Back on the main track I slowly drive to the exit. I spot a snake in the middle of the road, but it escapes before I can take some good photos. Outside the park I take some bird shots, and eventually also make a stop for a small group of howler monkeys, who're chilling in a tree. The sky is lit by orange light of the sun going down, while the clouds are closing in, and I can hear the thunder roar. Some light flashes at the horizon prove Thor has woken up and is heading my way. I accelerate and drive to Liberia before his hammer hits me.

Costa Rica - Sámara, Guanacaste

There was no mosquito invasion in my dreams, and I wake up rested. I'm going to take a break from the forest hikes, and mosquito stings today, and head for the coast of Guanacaste, the province with some great beaches, so I've read. I say goodbye to my friends of the staff, and hit the road, going west, life is peaceful there, as the Pet Shop Boys would sing. It's only a forty-minute drive, given there's some traffic, to the first beach I visit: Playa Panama. The sand is dark, the bay nice, but it's not getting to my heart. I quickly head back to the car, and drive the hilly coastal road to the next one, Playa Hermosa. The facilities here are totally focused on all the tourists coming in, but the beach's sand has the same thick structure again. It's not appealing to me. I drive away soon again, up a hill, and have a great view to the bay. This is much nicer than to be on the actual beach. My hopes are still high though, as I've always heard Costa Rica has fantastic beaches. The next stop is Playa del Coco, also said to be great. It's again a bit of a disappointment, as even though the setting is nice, the sand is horrible. Maybe, but more likely: I'm too spoiled. I head back to the main road, to go more to the south, towards Playa Brasilito, which was recommended by some friends in Sao Jose. It's over an hour drive, as I avoid the inland road, and go over the main traffic hub. Just before Brasilito, I head to the left, as there's a sign saying Playa Conchal, which I think to have heard of before. Soon the road ends though, and I have to drive over the beach. The sand's hard enough to easily carry the cars, and some are going more to the sea to make some nice spins. It's pretty much one-way traffic, as the road's too small. After this short piece of beach there's a hill that can easily demolish a car, as the rocks are huge and you have to make sure you're the only one heading up. Lower cars stay behind and park here, and these people walk the last metres. I'm going for it and easily make it in my super (old) car. Now I have to go around trees, avoid pools. Many cars are parked here, and to the left there's some luxury resorts. When I see open beach I stop again, as this sand seems to be very thin, and I don't want to push my luck too much. I get out, and finally wander in white sand, that softly falls over my feet with every step. This is how I like beaches, and I'm hooked to this quiet piece of paradise. I sit myself down in the sand and gaze over the sea that is blue at the horizon and light green in its waves splashing to the shore. Of this, I can't get enough, and I spend some serious time here, before heading back to the town, seeing that relative ugly beach, and then more south again, to the tourist hub of Tamarindo. It's only a thirty-minute drive, and I arrive there shortly to indeed see it has a touristy hippie vibe around it. In a way it reminds me of the town of Pipa, Brazil. I enjoy a lunch in a restaurant and then start walking the beach, meeting a young American couple, with who I spend some time talking. I move off beach, back to the car, and think of how I want to reach Samara, where I will stay overnight. There's a coastal road that passes three rivers, and two of them might be inaccessible, as there's no bridges, and when the water's too high, there's no way you can cross the other side. When I arrive at the turn to this road, I hold still for a moment, considering, but decide to avoid this road, and make a big round way to get to Samara. I have a friend in Samara, who has offered me a bed room, so I can finally couchsurf once again. It's a mere two-hour drive, first passing Santa Cruz, then the bigger town of Nicoya, and then it's a road through the mountains. There's some rain and clouds while driving through these mountains, but eventually I get to a dry Samara, where I can just see the sun going down behind the trees. If Tamarindo has already a kind of hippie vibe, Samara doubles this easily. I've never been to Jamaica, but this could be like there. It's all very laid back, and the first smell that comes into the car when opening the window, is the one of weed. Hello Amsterdam. My friend's in Carrillo, and a little drive from Samara. We meet up at a bar, where there are some friends having drinks. As soon as I step out though, I realise again how much my hernia had been killing me the entire day. It was a bit too much of driving, walking, driving, walking, driving, today. I can barely stand on my feet and request a bed right away. It's kind of disturbing to treat my host this way, so I also tell him I can take a hotel whenever needed. No need for that, and soon I get into a lovely home, where I get a spacious bedroom for myself. I lay down and this is exactly what I seem to need. I also pass out in seconds. I was not aware of how tired I really was.

Costa Rica - Tamarindo, Guanacaste

Even though I've visited many beach places, a breakfast with my feet
in the sand hasn't occurred too often so far. Today I sit with my host
in a little restaurant at the Samara beach, having a very fresh fruit
breakfast. My leg's a bit better than yesterday, and I intend not to
walk too much today. The less, the better. My friend takes off after
finishing the coffee, and I stay a bit longer, enjoying the view, and the
orange juices. I then drive back to Samara to see the beach once
more, and spot a crocodile in a river that flows into the sea. On the
beach there's also warning signs for the crocodiles. The weather isn't
very tempting for a beach walk, so I head in the car to drive to
Puntarenas, where my new friend from the Grecia store will join me
for the agreed road trip. It's a drive of about three hours, but it takes
me a bit longer as I make some stops, one of them being quite long
in the south part of the Palo Verde national park. I arrive in the city
in the afternoon, and enjoy a fine lunch at the utmost restaurant of
the land tongue. From this town a lot of ferries leave to Guanacaste,
and this is what I plan to do as soon as my friend will arrive with the
bus. Minutes are ticking away, while I wait for the bus, then it
becomes hours. According to text messages I receive there's insane
traffic and it can take a long time before the bus will arrive. If I check
this with the bus station, they tell me there's no problems, and all
buses are on schedule. I do however keep trusting my friend, but the
waiting becomes a real drag. Fortunately a brass band starts practicing
nearby, and even though it's raining cats and dogs, they pursue their
practice. I'm listening from my car and actually enjoy their
performance, including the girls marching on the music. Then, finally,
the bus arrives. It's been crazy, and my friend's apologising for the
delay. There's no time to waste now, because the ferries have already
stopped going hours ago, and the drive to Tamarindo is still over
three hours. It's a bit of a crazy trip now that the night's fallen, and
we're about the only car on the street. I'm speeding. My eyes are
super focused on the road and weary for any animal that might cross
the road. When there's traffic I slow down, and pass them as soon as
I suspect it's possible. We pass some small towns, and gas stations,
and at one of them is a police control. My friend shrinks in her chair
when seeing the uniforms. The first time I let it go, but when it
happens the second time I ask what's wrong. She then reveals to be
illegal in Costa Rica. I already knew she was from Honduras, but now
I also understand why she had not seen any other place of this

country. I ask her if she wants to go back, if this trip is too stressful. She replies she's fine, and soon we're again singing along with Enrique Iglesias: Bailandooo. When we get to Tamarindo it's already midnight. We've arranged a hotel by phone, and the owner has come out of his bed to open the gate for us. The room's very spacious and could easily hold five people. There's a nice balcony with a hammock and in the patio there's a pool. We ask where we still can get dinner, and we are shown to a nearby restaurant where we quickly have a bite, before returning to the hotel and fall asleep immediately.

Costa Rica - Cartago, Cartago

I can't remember oversleeping an included breakfast so far on my trip, but today's the day. My eyes were so heavy yesterday from the night's drive, that I couldn't open them this morning and I just kept lying down, head in my pillow. My friend's already had her breakfast, and is very eager to see some sights. This enthusiasm gets me going and I get a shower and we immediately check out. I want to show her the beach I like most so far in Costa Rica, Playa Conchal, the one with the white sand. I now know my way and we easily reach the beach. My friend's blown away and adores the place. I take some photos of her there, for the memory and so she can show her family back home. I first thought to also show other places, but it's too nice here. We sit down on a tree trunk and just watch the waves endlessly hit the shore. It's only our appetite that disturbs the peaceful sit-down, and we head back to the car in order to find a restaurant. It's easier said than done, and it takes a while before we find one. Then it's time to already start the drive back to Grecia, as it's probably a four to five-hour ride. My friend seems now more relaxed when seeing police, and I believe this little getaway trip did her well. I've been so grateful to all the people that have been helping me, and even though I had my doubts in the beginning, it's a great thing to give something back to someone. Her eyes sparkle. I did well by doing this. I drop her off at her uncle's home in Grecia and then continue to drive to Cartago where I'll meet another friend to have dinner. Cartago is another 1.5-hour drive and my legs are getting the rest they need, even though they're bent the entire day. I meet my friend at a shopping mall and have a nice dinner there. We mainly laugh about my Spanish, and on how the waitress is totally not understanding any of my silly jokes. I then realise I didn't book my hotel yet, so I right away call them. I'm told there's no availability, and as it gets close to midnight, I wonder if I can find a place. My friend starts to call hotels in the area that I give her after a search on booking.com. None of them is answering. We then just start driving around, hoping to find an open on. The first two we find are closed, but at the third I'm lucky. The night guard lets me in, and I have to do my check in tomorrow, as well as my payment. I then bring my friend to her home, where she lives with her mother and daughter, in a small apartment not too far away. I'm back at the hotel within minutes and have a final talk with the night-watch. Then it's time for bed, and again my eyes close like a guillotine, cutting me asleep.

Costa Rica - San José, San José

I'm planning on a trip to Costa Rica's most rural park, Corcovado and spend today retrieving information from the internet and collecting possibilities. I also meet with the friend I had dinner with yesterday, now for lunch. The Wi-Fi in Cartago is a lot better than in San José, so my work's going pretty fast. I nevertheless change back to my home hotel today, as it's more centrally located and it would save me a lot of time in traffic if I decide to drive off tomorrow. I feel like having a productive day, even though there's no sightseeing involved. I decide to drive south tomorrow after breakfast, and when the decision's made, the burden falls off my shoulder and I feel the sleep coming over me, meaning I can go to bed early and catch up with what I've missed.

I'm ready as can be in the morning, and I eat an extra plate of breakfast today, to be ready for the long ride south, which can take over six hours. After breakfast I get back to my room to pack my stuff. Then there's a change of events, as suddenly my front left tooth breaks, and its filling is in the palm of my hand. Djeez. With my tongue the hole feels enormous and this isn't a good sign. Being abroad and now having to look for medical assistance, was something I really wanted to avoid. I right away walk to the front desk to ask them if they know a good dentist, that has helped Europeans before, and thus speaks English. They tell me something that surprises me: Costa Rica is a very popular destination for Americans to go to for dental care. Here it's much cheaper and the service and quality is as good. I should just take a look on the internet and I will find a place soon, according to them. This isn't a joke, and my research shows hundreds of good results. What to pick if it all seems good? I take one with good reviews, in a posh area of the city, and with helpful information on their website in good English. I call them to make an appointment and to my surprise they can already help me today, in the very late afternoon. The woman on the phone is very helpful and it gives me the feeling I will be in good hands. I spend the day reading more articles about Corcovado, and start believing this park might be my ultimate shot for seeing a jaguar. There's been some sightings there, and not only of this big cat, also of the puma, which of course is also on my list. Then it's time to leave. Waze is indicating there's traffic, so I better leave in time. It tells me to avoid the highway, and just go via the smaller roads, avoiding the big traffic jams. As soon as I get on this road however, there's crazy traffic here too. It's pulling up, and stopping, pulling up, and stopping. I think to know a shortcut, so I get off the road left, and finally arrive at a bridge, which is unfortunately only accessible for pedestrians. I head back to the road, and it's the same snake meandering. I get my car in the line again and slowly move towards my destination, step by step. Then my tooth distracts me for a second, as my tongue moves in, I feel a sharp pain, and close my eyes for, what I think, one second. When I open my eyes I see that the car in front of me suddenly has stopped, and as I was gaining speed, I press the brake as hard as possible. The car seems to break through the breaks, not immediately stopping, and I hear my tires burn its rubber. I'm too late and with a very soft bump I hit the car in front of me. My heart's beating throughout my body now, and I hit my wheel out of frustration. I remember the instruction of my rental company: never move your car after an accident and leave it in the same situation until police has arrived. I step out my car, and walk to the other car. The driver's already stepped out and walks to me with a relaxed face, immediately shaking my hand and then looking at his bumper. There's a big bump in this aluminium thing, and I sigh. I'm glad I've taken the full coverage insurance, but I rather not be in this situation. The guy speaks a bit of English and says it can be fixed, so there's no worries. He calls the highway police and the insurance, who also have to come to the scene to objectively write down a report. I look at my brake trail and it's very long, wow. I also decide to call my friends at the rental company and explain the situation. They don't seem to worry too much and respond relaxed to my news. I'm asked to stop by tomorrow for a quick inspection, which I of course can and will do. Then I call the dentist saying I probably won't make it, and Becky, the assistant, friendly answers my call and she helps me laugh at the situation, and it's good to have the smile back. I now handle the situation a bit easier and when first the police and then the insurance man arrives, I answer the questions and joke with them. It's quite an experience actually to have an accident in another country. When all is done, I shake everyone's hand and return to my hotel, taking a shower to rinse the stress. Then I head to SubWay, to treat myself on a soft sandwich and a big soda. I talk with the staff and seem to make new friends again. I walk back to the hotel and was happy to be able to share my adventure with some real people.

Dentist day. When I was a child it was my worst nightmare to see a dentist, but now I've outgrown that fear already for a long time, and since my sister recommended my current dentist in Amsterdam it almost has become fun to go. But what will happen today? If I blindly follow Becky it will be all good, but she's not the one who's going to actually try to fix it. I safely drive to the building now and park the car in front. I'm early. I get in, walk the stairs and finally get to say hi to Becky in person. She's as caring here as she was on the phone, and lets me sit down to fill out some forms. I get to talk to an elderly American in the waiting area, and he confirms what I had read online: they do come here especially for their treatment. He's here for three weeks to fix it all. Then I'm called in and a real assistant brings me to a room, where I can take a seat in the special chair. The dentist is a very lovely lady that seems to be knowing what she's doing and today she will do some x-rays and inspection to decide what's needed. Upon this check she also notice a hole in a molar, which also requires some attention. We make a plan and today we only do a little cleaning. Tomorrow the rest. I thank everyone for their amazingly friendly service, and drive to the rental office to have them check the car for a bit. This is all smooth and they say insurance will cover the small damage. I head back to the hotel for another chilling afternoon, tongue in the tooth of course.

My fix's ready for today and I will go back to my dentist friends in the late afternoon. I have an extended breakfast again and hang out in my hotel room afterwards. Then I drive to Escazu and make it right in time for my appointment. I have some time to chat with Becky, before I get called in and they start working on me. I'm injected with enough anaesthesia to get through the hour of drilling, cutting and liming. I feel they're doing a good job, but can't really tell now, of course. I'm numb, and feel like my cheeks are balloons. When they're done, I can only thank them for their time. I leave after some more talking with Becky, and head to a nearby sushi restaurant where I had made some friends through one friend of one of my first nights in San José. I take a seat at the bar and take the chef's choices. The anaesthesia has faded by now and I can actually taste the lovely fresh fish food. One thing is bothering me though, as my molars don't really seem to fit. I will see if it gets better tomorrow or else go back. I nearly am the last customer to leave the restaurant and then head back to the hotel.

Surprisingly my clothes do get dirty on my trip, and today is one of those days I pack all the dirty stuff and bring it to a laundromat. It's always a little risky to let your clothes be washed in another country, by people you don't know. Often word-to-mouth brings me to a place, or the hotel has a service. This last option is mostly very expensive, and thus I find myself today driving around to find a place where I can drop off the big bag. I also need to fill my tank and while doing that I ask the attendant, you can't fill your own tank in South America, if he knows a place. He points to the other side of the road and tells me in one of those houses there's a laundromat. I walk over with my bag, up to the driveway of this place. There's a small sign telling it's indeed a lavanderia, but it looks like a regular home. I ring a bell and an old woman walks up. There's a gate with fences in between us, and as soon as she finds out my Spanish is poor, she calls her daughter, who understands me better. She also calls her other daughter and I'm making friends once again. I immediately trust these folks and the price is ridiculously low in comparison to the hotel. I leave my bags and walk back to the car. I drive to a bar to have a tea with Anaka and to catch up a bit. I then return to my hotel, and be a boring dude once more. Friday night, and no party. Wuu huu.

Costa Rica - Puerto Viejo, Limón

Of course there are reasons for me to not go out so much. First of all, I don't party back at home, so I'm not used to it, mostly because I don't like it. As I've again got confirmed on this trip, I'm not a good dancer, I don't drink alcohol, never used drugs, and mostly get my energy from talking with people, which is nearly impossible in clubs and bars where the music is so loud you can barely understand what the other is saying. Now that I'm in countries where people neither speak Dutch, or fluent English, that problem even becomes bigger. Secondly I love South America's nature so much that I want to be fit for my walks and explorations, and parties just don't fit in that scheme. For example, yesterday I hit the sack early, because today I'm road tripping again. Parties may come when the time's right, and right now it isn't. I go with my illegal friend again today, this time to the southeast, where they say is a Caribbean feeling, with pristine beaches and a warm sea. As my trip to Corcovado has been postponed a bit, I'm deadly curious if the east can show me some more decent beaches. It's over a four hour drive and passes the notorious city of Limon, where I'm told you better watch your belongings as theft is happening there all the time. I of course think people are exaggerating, but keep the warning in mind. We first have to take a long detour to avoid the road directly crossings the mountains to the east: big rocks have fallen on the road and have to be removed. In the more northern mountains we stop for a nice waterfall, and take some snacks, so we don't have to stop in Limon. I don't know if it's because of the warning, or because I really see it myself, but it seems a shady city, even though we probably only pass some of the outskirts. From Limon it's only one hour to our goal, and we now drive along a road that runs parallel to the sea. The jungle seems to swallow us, as the trees get higher, the green gets greener, and there's vegetation everywhere. We pass a little town called Cahuita and now are getting very close. While we sing there's a police post. There's an officer checking cars, but most can just pass without even opening their window. There's a speed bump right in front of their office, strategically placed. All prosperity seems to explode when the officer signals me to open my window, and immediately asks for my identification. I quickly look to the right and see my friend's face turn pale. The officer also asks her id, and she hands it without further thinking. The guy walks away with both passports and tells us to set the car aside. I pretend to not understand the situation, and tell him we're just travelling and there's no bad intention. He tells me that my passport is fine, but the one of my friend not. I ask him what's wrong, and he again summons me to move the car, as there's other cars lining up behind us now. I ask him quickly if there's no other way to get out of this mess, obviously hinting to handing him some money. He gives me a smile and tells me that might work normally, but not today. I pout, and give him my saddest face. It isn't working, and I drive to where he's pointing. My mind is spinning, as if it's hit by a virus. I'm still trying to find a way out, but I can't think of anything. If bribing isn't working, what will? I get my passport back and am told I can go on. I oppose, of course, as I'm here together with a friend, and that friend now needs a friend. Her eyes have a glassy stare, while she's talking to the three police officers. First I feel anger, then it becomes a feeling of guilt, which then becomes pity. While she's being interrogated I reach out to some friends, and they all keep telling me it isn't my fault, and that a person of her age has her own responsibility. I get my reason back, and kick the virus out of my mind. I can only support her now, and sit myself next to her, giving the officers my meanest look. In difficult situations I tend to make even sillier jokes, which usually works, as it does today. Soon my friend gets her smile back, when I tell her my plan on how to steal the police hat, then get into their car and escape. When all the paperwork is filled out, we have to wait for a special unit that has to come from Limon. The bureaucracy! I ask what will happen next, and the only thing I understand is 'deportation'. That sounds too harsh. While the police officers continue filing stuff, I ask what she thinks will happen, and what will happen to her job, her uncle, etc. She seems strong and says the future will reveal itself eventually. Wise words. The other car arrives with two people, and there's another filing of paperwork. They don't seem to be interested in the story, more like it's case number thousand today. She gets a statement and they confiscate her passport. In two weeks she has to report to the immigration office in San José. With all this said and done, we may continue our road trip, oh the joy. There's a layer of a fucked-up-situation over this trip now, and I hope time will kill her pain. The hotel's found after some puzzling over directions, but is beautiful situated in the forest, with a big pool. We drop our stuff and head back to the cosy looking village, which indeed has a hippie atmosphere over it. I'm normally not the one of fancy restaurants, but to ease the situation, I just pick the best looking one, and even offer to pay the bill entirely, whilst we normally cut it in two. It's the least I can do, I think, for someone that had only been working these eight months, sending most of the money back home to support her parents. I see it does her well, and she enjoys the food, while I eat my food as any other day. Her bit of wine makes it more loose and she's the first one to clap her hands excitedly for a sloth that comes through the restaurant's roof for a quick peek. After dinner we head to our rooms and today's events have drained all energy, making falling asleep easy.

Costa Rica - San José, San José

Waking up for me is today as easy as it was for falling asleep yesterday. I'm fit and ready to make a great day out of today. I wake my friend, who's not exactly in the same mood, but I manage to get her up and going anyway, summoning her to the delicious breakfast buffet. We sit down, and eat as much as we can. I then ask the front desk if I can make a phone call, as I have to call KLM to again change my ticket. I want to push the date once more, and get into an endless loop of research: my question to change to fly back from another continent seems to be impossible, and this is found out after merely forty-five minutes. I then ask to push the date a bit forward, so I have more flexibility, but I'm told the ticket loses validity after January 21st, so I just decide to set it on that date, with the departure city unchanged: Rio de Janeiro. When I'm finally done, I get a bill presented of nearly one hundred euros. What the hell. I tell him he could have warned me about these costs, and he apologises, then gets his manager and eventually they let me pay a quarter of the amount, which I still believe is too much. I have to cheer up someone today, so don't let it get to me. We leave our bags at the room and take off, to drive towards the Panamanian border and from there move up again visiting all possible beaches. The sand again isn't the most beautiful, but the water is amazing. The colours seem to change every minute and is warm as promised. The strips of sand are very small on these beaches and it doesn't do good for the scenery. What does make it beautiful is all the green around it, and the little bays. There aren't as many people as on the west coast as well, which make you more feel like an explorer; a nice extra touch. After visiting all possible beaches, we get back to the hotel to pick up our stuff and then continue beach hopping on our way to Limon. It isn't get prettier there, so soon we only stick to the road. In a small establishment we get a lunch, and then go straight back to Grecia, first crossing the mountain range, which according to Waze is still locked down, and soon signs tell the same. We don't care, and as long as no one is stopping us, we follow the shortest way back to the urban areas. The road indeed seems to be open, they just seem lazy in removing the signs. We pass Cartago, then San José, before arriving in the hills of Grecia. I drop her at her home and turn back to get to my very own hotel again.

Costa Rica - Puerto Jiménez, Puntarenas

I take it easy this morning, even though I've finally decided to go on my postponed trip south, to Puerto Jiménez and then enter Corcovado from there. I leave around noon and first drive the road west, and then south, and it's the same road along the coast that passes Tarcoles, Jacó, Manuel Antonio, and Uvita, all places that I've visited before. I of course make my stop at the crocodile bridge, and past Jacó I spot a very big group of big red parrots and I take my time to look at them, together with a big family. Then, when I continue, it starts pouring. When it's finally dry, I drive into the mountain that gives access to Puerto Jiménez. It's a small and tricky road, and my car can't really handle it, so I'm using my lowest gears mostly, while crawling up. Upon reaching the 'top', I park the car aside of the road and take some photos of the great view. It's then a long way down, and it's dark when I finally get to town. I've made a reservation for a hotel, and it's of course impossible to find. I ask some folks, and am pointed to the airstrip. Here I drive some rounds on some of the worst 'roads' so far in Costa Rica, before finally finding a small entrance to a wide parking spot, which apparently belongs to the property. There's no front desk at this hour of day, and I have to deal with the night's watch, who keeps telling me winter is coming. So annoying. I do get my key to my tiny room, where the bed just fits in, but I wasn't expecting more knowing it was hella cheap here. I drop my bags, and then get back into town, to find a dinner. I get to a restaurant, sit myself down, and talk to two girls who've been around for a while, but didn't have enough money to get into the park. My restaurant also seems to be some kind of hostel, and they introduce me to some kind of manager, who gives me more information on how to access the park. I tell him I want to go tomorrow, and he says that's nearly impossible because you need a special permit in order to sleep in the park, and that can only be fixed during office hours. I then ask if I can just do a day trip to see if I like it, and then decide if I want to get a permit. He says it's possible, but it might be hard to find a guide that is available for tomorrow. He walks off and comes back with a business card, telling me I can try this guy. I call him and he is actually available. He doesn't speak any English, but it brings the price down significantly. I also don't need transport, as we can go by my car. The other option was the morning 'bus' (big truck), which didn't look too tempting. We agree on going tomorrow very early in the morning so we can have most of the day.

It's also still quite a drive, and the road won't be easy, as we have to cross rivers which water levels might be high after rain. We will see, and he will be at my hotel at 05:30.

I'm not too sharp this morning, as the few hours of sleep haven't done me very well. Ulises punctually arrives at the hotel with his motor, and we put his stuff in the trunk, and then start the drive. The road is extremely bad, with potholes and pools everywhere. My memories go back to that bad road in Santa Rosa, and the flat tire the day after. Ulises doesn't have a driver's licence, but says he knows how to fix cars, so I'm counting on him if things might go wrong. The road leads us through farm lands on both sides and beyond the left side the mighty ocean looms. The first rays of sun are showing now, and it soon gets very warm. The road gets worse and worse. We really do have to pass rivers with the car, and fortunately the first one isn't very deep. Nor is the second, nor the third. We're lucky today. We pass a hill which hosts a forest with enormous tall trees, and even has some housing properties. Beyond the hill we get in a more tranquil area, with even more houses. It's the last resorts before Corcovado, and most of them are expensive luxury getaways. We finally drive past an airstrip and just beyond that we park our car. Here is Carate, the last car-stop before the national park. From now on it's our feet that have to carry us further. We plan to go to the ranger station of La Leona, and from there a bit more up, until we get to a ship wreck. The first obstacle of the trail is quite instant, as there's a fast rushing river just beyond the first row of bushes. I'm not used to crossing rivers, so I properly untie my shoes, roll up my pants, and cross the river on my bare feet. Ulises is doing the same, so it must be the way to do it. Passing the little stream is quite easy actually, even though the water is a bit cold. Then we head onto the trail through the forest, to hopefully see some wildlife. The first eagles we already had seen at the airstrip, where a black one was sitting on a fence drying its wings. We also had made a stop on the road before to see two beautiful little owls, and one capuchin- and howler monkey. The day could have started worse. The long beach that we parallel walk of is dark, and stands in contrast with the bright ocean water. We see some nice birds, frogs, insects, and flowers, before we get to La Leona after about an hour of speed walking. Here we have to register again. I see a paper hanging with a missing person on it, an American, who had gone in and never got out. It makes the people nervous here. My thoughts go to him, and his fate, but soon are distracted by a pale warning sign. This sign instructs visitors how to handle when facing a feline, clearly stating jaguar and puma. My heart starts beating fast now. This must be a sign! I ask the ranger how often he's seen one, and with a grin he answers zero... Crap. Pumas are more often seen here, so I will make a better chance on this big cat. I keep my hopes high though, and more focused than before we start the hike. We first see another eagle, and then a group of loud red parrots. Soon after we walk into a small group of my spider monkeys, which I heartily greet. They are a bit shy, but eventually show their faces to my camera. Ulises then hurries me over, as he's seen something special between the roots of a big tree. I walk to him, and he points to a snake. It's thin, with an orange-golden underside, while its top is dark brown. Around its eyes there's a bright circle of orange with in the middle a big black orb. It isn't exactly posing, and I have a hard time taking some proper photos. The snake then moves quickly away from us and we continue as well. Ulises is doing a great job spotting things and he now sees a footprint of a tapir. We head to a small trail over a hillock, and come in a thicker part of forest, with more down a fast flowing river. Now my guide puts his finger on his lips, and points to our left. A tapir! The big grey animal with his cut-off proboscis, is laying here to rest and we are only steps away from it. It isn't a feline, but this animal had been very high on my wish list. The animal isn't disturbed by our presence, and we even can take some steps closer, always respecting the distance. For a second I think I see a tear rolling from its sad looking eyes, but it might have been snot. I can't get enough of this big creature and I'm totally excited. I high five Ulises and thank him for his tracking. The animal gets into a deep sleep once more, and we walk to the next river that we have to pass. This one looks way more serious as it's flushing fast. Before we even get to try, Ulises eyes see yet another animal, which is moving through the trees at our back. We hurry there, and it's a big Tamandua anteater, another first ever sighting for me. It has amazing claws with which he hangs in the trees, putting his pointy head into small tree openings in order to find his food, the ants. Out of his mouth comes a very thin small tongue that slurps the ants from their hiding. It's awfully good in climbing the trees, and it's also using its tail like a monkey. The yellow-whitish and black coat also gives it enough camouflage, even though it isn't exactly trying to hide itself from us. We follow it as long as we can and then lay our focus on the river. Now it becomes clear Ulises is the experienced one, while I cautiously set foot after foot over the slippery rocks while I balance myself wading through this powerful stream. I make it to the other side dry and we continue our walk, seeing the bananas grow around us, and then shortly see another little snake. Then I get to see the last out of four Costa Rican monkey species: the small squirrel monkeys. There's a small group, but one is an easy prey for my camera, as it lazily hangs over a branch. When I get enough photos we continue to walk a bit more, seeing some howlers, and birds. Then it's time to turn and slowly find our way back. We now walk bigger parts over the beach, seeing the forest as an inaccessible wall to our left. There are some eagles again, and even a white chicken. We pass La Leona, sign out, and walk the final hour back to the car. The drive back is fine too, as it didn't rain, leaving the rivers passable. We get back to the hotel in the late afternoon and then go to the office to sign up for a two-night sleepover in the park. We sign up for tomorrow and I pay the necessary fees for accommodation in the park. Tomorrow we will head out very early again, as tomorrow's hike is over 21 kilometres, so I have my dinner at the typical Dutch time, and hit the sack early. I can't get to sleep however, as all the animals pass my eyes once more.

The rain ticking on the hotel's roof wakes me up, even before my alarm clock would, and makes this room impossible to sleep in. I put my head between the curtains and see a miserable sky. I get dressed, drag my bag to a storage room, and wait in the car for my guide. Ulises appears in his rain cover, and I last minute get one from the night's watch, a bright yellow one, and not black as I would expect. Ulises tells me the rivers are probably too high because it's been raining all night, but I'm stubbornly thinking it can't be that bad. We take off and an hour later we cross the first river. The water is indeed much higher than yesterday, but I guess not a real problem. When we arrive at the second river it appears to be a problem however. It's now wider, and runs much faster than yesterday. I want to give it a go, but Ulises holds us on this side of the water. He finds it irresponsible to go. Even if we would make it to Carate by car, we still have to walk through numerous rivers, and these might be too high to cross. I don't know anything about those rivers, so I can only go with his judgement. In a WhatsApp group of guides soon the news is spread that the big river near the stationery in the middle of the park is indeed inaccessible. People there can't leave, and people also can't come. I head back slightly disappointed but do realise it is a fair call. We go to the main ranger station in town to postpone our entrance with one day, and hope tomorrow's weather will be better. I park the car, and spend some time talking with the front desk, as well as extending the room with a night. I walk back to the car to pick up my luggage and see my second flat tire. I sigh and head back in, to ask if there's a tire shop nearby. They make some phone calls and within minutes a truck pulls up the parking, to help me put on the spare, and drive me back to the garage. Here they fix it, and I'm relieved and happy all people are so helpful. The rest of the day I spend walking around the hotel terrain, seeing some small animals, and in the afternoon some spider monkeys.

Costa Rica - Sirena, Corcovado, Puntarenas

I wake up at 5am today again, and now see a grey, but dry, sky. After yesterday's flat, Ulises doesn't want to go with my car anymore, and we've arranged to go in a van with another group of tourists, and with their guide and driver. We'll be the passengers. We gather at the bakery in the main street, and get some bread and food for today's long hike. The van's pretty packed, and isn't higher than my car. I understand Ulises' concerns though. It's less fun however to be driven there, instead of driving myself. The first river is passed easily again, and at the second one Ulises heads out to wade through and see how deep it actually is. After some measuring all agree it must be doable and with ease we cross the river that had held us back yesterday. We now came over this first barrier and head to the final river. It's a ramp down and then a sharp turn left through the river. At the ramp we all leave the van for a bit, and then head in again to get to the other side dry. Now we drive straight to Carate, and unload all our stuff here. We're carrying food for the two nights' sleep, my heavy rain cover, and some clean sheets. We cross the first river, which runs much faster than two days ago, and then walk to La Leona. It's drizzling, and Ulises already starts using his green cover. I put my camera away, and protect my backpack, but let the rain fall over me. The forest offers fair protection from the heavy drops, and it isn't falling too hard, yet. A dead spider monkey on the trail draws our attention, and at that moment we meet a group of four who are on their way back from Sirena. At that point I think we must be almost there, as it's not even 11am. It's a bit of a mistake, as it's quite some hours more of walking. My guide shows me a group of bats sleeping in a tree, which is nice, as I had never seen these animals this close. A whale skeleton is another point of interest along the way. It's pouring now and my clothes are totally wet. The heavy yellow cover doesn't help anymore. The rain's warm, but sticky clothes clamp to the body, making it annoying to walk. We carry on though, in a pretty high speed. The other group is far behind us, and at our breaks they never show up. We walk over to the high end of the beach, over the hard sand. At times I make some figures in it, to say hi to others that might pass. There's rocks we have to pass, and hills we must climb. The clouds rise up from the forest, giving it a haunting look. Even though I would have preferred sun, this setting gives me chills. We finally arrive at Rio Claro, the last river before Sirena, and also the widest of them all. When I arrive here, at first I can't believe we will really walk through it. The river's water is brown, the rain is still falling down in millions of drops, and now there's this monstrous river. Ulises has done this before and leads the way, making progress fast. I don't care to take off my shoes anymore, everything's wet, so I set foot on the rocky bottom of the river, and surprisingly move fast as well. The river wants to pull me over, but I resist its strength. In the middle I even find time to unpack my camera and take a photo. Then I continue to the other side. River or land, it made no difference in the amount of wet. Even mud pools on the track I now don't avoid anymore. The mud sucks me in though, and pulls at my shoes. Without lifting them too much, I shuffle through them. I don't pay any attention now to animals, the only goal I have is to reach the stationary. On my repetitive question on how much longer, Ulises has found the father's answer, "not too far now", and it pleases me. Then, we suddenly get out of the forest and walk onto a big field of grass, with at the end the ranger station. I now seem to fly, and the ground under me isn't existing anymore. Finally! I kick my shoes off, drop my bag on the floor and sit on the bench. I can't be arsed to move now, after this crazy 7.5-hour hike. I let my breath return to normal speed, and talk to some folks that are also sitting here, hoping for the rain to pass, so they can explore more of the area, in this inner part of Corcovado. While sitting here, looking at the rain falling down, we get company of a big tapir walking at the edge of the forest, crossing the field, putting its nose to the ground, searching for food. Two days ago I had seen this animal lying down, and now I see it walking, amazing. The other group finally arrives some 1.5 hours after us, also totally soaked. In the meantime Ulises has created a lunch/dinner, which tastes incredibly good after today's exercise. I get to talk to Gloriana, a girl who's working here, and who came to tell me my eyes are the only light shining in the misery of today. It's a nice compliment, and once again, it's all in the eyes. We all have a good laugh when we sit ourselves near the only electricity point of the camp. More and more people join, and if there would have been a bonfire, it would have been great. Lights in the camp are only turned on from 18:00 to 20:00, and after that we are left in the utmost dark of this world's far end corner. The clouds hide the stars, even when the rain finally surrenders. It's bed time, and I share my dormitory with two Asian people. I give them tips about Brazil and we all fall asleep in our bunk beds.

Me and Ulises are the first ones at the picnic area around 05:30 in the morning. We want to explore some of the trail, and hunt down those cursed jaguars and pumas. At 6am sharp we head out, and when I see a first bird that I want to photograph I find out my lens seems to be ruined. There's moisture to be seen, and none of the photos are turning out well. Screw this. If I would see my feline today, I would cry. I have had this problem before, but keeping it turned on for a while normally did the trick. Not today, and my battery runs low whilst trying. I take my pocket camera and iPhone, and pretend they can do the same thing, which they really cannot. I walk the trail with quite some frustration about this malfunctioning camera, but my guide keeps the spirit high by showing me some nice flowers, and even a puma footprint. A mother tapir with her baby pass our trail, and we gasp at these animals being so close, and so pure. The trail goes up along the river, and then down in the forest. We make the round, and when we enter the field of grass, the station is lit in sunlight. We head down there to take some tea, and to try to fix my camera. I put the lens straight in the sunlight and let it lay down there while we drink our cups, and have our snacks. Some thirty minutes later the moisture is gone, and I'm back in the cat hunt, even though the morning's moment now pretty much is gone. We walk the other trails around the camp, and see a variety of animals, such as a big group of coatis, a huge grasshopper, a pig family, capuchin- and spider monkeys, and, when we get back at our three-day-home, some squirrel monkeys. The most impressive animal encounter today however, is one with a big crocodile. Now it isn't the first one I've seen this trip, but what made it big, was that it was laying down on the shore of the wide river we had passed yesterday, and Ulises explains that the river's full of them. I'm glad I didn't know this yesterday, ha! I will try to forget when we have to cross tomorrow., I tell him. All in all, we've covered all trails today, so tomorrow we only have to do the big hike back. The other group, who will share the van with us tomorrow, haven't seen it all, yet, and they head out to the other nearby river in the late afternoon. We are asked to join them, and now we join a group ourselves. It's a different experience, to be in a group, and to share your guide. I can define and decide my two-group's-behaviour, but with more it's impossible. People walk slow, or fast, talk, or are silent. Even though I was told they had all paid less money, I'm happy I had my private guide, who's also doing an excellent job. We get to the river and there see the sun going under, in what also seems to be a weather turning point: the clouds are quickly gathering now, and our guides now hurry us back to our dry safe haven. Like horses we are whipped to keep the speed up, but unfortunately the bad weather catches up on us and we all get wet. Wet isn't dead, so we all live another day. Ulises then again cooks a wonderful meal, and we join the story telling and sharing of the other tables, before hitting the sack early again.

Costa Rica - San José, San José

We're out early again, as it is first the long hike back, and then the
drive back to Puerto Viejo. As soon as I wake up, I rush to the only
shower in my block, to let the cold water flush the sleep out of my
eyes. Then I get back to my private dorm, as I had to change my
room yesterday: my Japanese friends got another room, and the
entire block we were at before is now rented to an apparent school
class. We have our final meal in the open kitchen, where ants walk
freely, and where spiders are common intruders. The best thing about
this morning is that it's dry. The rain has been falling throughout the
night, but now finally stopped. We don't hear anything about
impassable rivers, so at 6am we're the first two to leave the camp,
soon followed by the group who we will share the van back to town
with. We soon arrive at the big river, which is running slightly faster
than the days before, but we can cross fairly easy, despite my
crocodile knowledge. Not much later a deer crosses our path, and so
do squirrel monkeys, a woodpecker, hawks, and again a sleepy tapir.
We now walk more over the beach, as the trails are one big mud
pool. The stones we have to cross are slippery as well, but these
cannot be avoided. I nearly fall one time, but manage to keep my
balance. At one estuary I climb some rocks in the middle, while the
stream peacefully surrounds me. Looking from here to the ocean
makes me realise once more how beautiful and desolate this place is.
From what I've heard is that most tourist stick to Manuel Antonio,
and maybe the east coast, but this park is Costa Rica's highlight for
me. We continue our path, seeing capuchins eating their breakfast,
and then today's animal highlight, a big owl sitting high in the tree,
gazing at us with big dark eyes. He's been pointed to us by another
guide, who's just started a hike with his tourists. Back at the first
hotels along the way to Leona we see the red parrots and one other
big eagle. Once more Ulises climbs a coconut tree to cut a fresh one
for me and him. This is the best coconut water I've drank on my
voyage, so fresh. And if we're longing for a snack, we just get a
banana from the trees. Paradise. I've been carrying an extra bag with
me, with some kitchen and sleeping gear, leaving my left shoulder a
bit out of balance in the end. We arrive at the final river after 7.5
hours, having covered over 21 kilometres in total today, through
rough and heavy terrain. At this final river I wash all the sand off my
socks, and we then sit ourselves down in the grass, where our driver
is already awaiting us. We now only wait for the other to arrive,

which only takes about thirty to forty-five minutes this time. We're all satisfied with today's performance, but are also happy we can sit down and relax for a bit. On our way back we have to walk through some of the high water rivers, to ease the car's burden. The car then comes after us and we hop in again. In the late afternoon we get back to the town, and the group is dropped off one by one at their accommodations. Two of the group were also sleeping in the hotel I was staying at, and I offer Olga and Rafael a ride to Uvita, where they are planning to go by bus. My plan is to drive back to San José, and get a good night sleep in my home hotel. We all gather and pack our stuff, and then start the drive. It's pouring again and even before we reach the hills that separates this peninsula from the mainland, the world's covered in night's darkness. There are no lights on this hill, and the view is limited to just a couple of metres because of the rain. I drive a tad slower than normal. Then I flush through a huge pool, slipping the car from left to right, and I have the feeling I have hit something serious. About five minutes later I decide to return there to check it I didn't hit something for real. We get to the place and don't see anything: just a big deep pool of rainwater. Relieved I continue the drive until we reach the normal 'highway', leading us north. My friends haven't arranged any accommodation, nor do they have a phone they can use. I help them, and when we reach Uvita we stop at several hotels to check availability and prices. After about four stops we find a suitable place and I drop them off there. They're Spanish and Swiss, so we might see each other in Europe in the future. From Uvita I cruise my way back to San José, with eventually also leaving the rain behind me, and finally reaching the hotel, checking in, and falling asleep directly.

I last long in bed after these lousy nights of sleep in Puerto Viejo and Corcovado. I do get out in time for the lovely breakfast, but then get back to have another nap. In the afternoon I drive to Grecia to say goodbye to one friend, pick up the other, and then from there to Zarcero, a town with hedge sculptures on the main square, which was recommended by another friend. I spend the day here, and have a very late lunch in a packed restaurant. The weather is miserable today, so there is not much left of the promised views. Clouds are blocking proper sights. After this tour I drop my friend off at Grecia, say goodbye, and then head back to San José, to have dinner with yet another friend. I pick her up in the outskirts of town, and I had asked the hotel for directions, but their first response was to not go to that area at all. I stupidly always laugh at these warnings, as I'm (over)confident nothing will happen. After some navigation I get to the neighbourhood, but then soon get a bit lost. I park my car across a school and text my friend I will be waiting there. I see some shady people walking around, and more police cars passing by than I had seen before in other parts of the city. Then a woman knocks on my window, hand in hand with her son. I carefully open the window and she warns me to lock the doors and not open windows if guys come to my car. I ask her if I should be this worried, and she confirms, saying car robberies are very common in this part of town. I nod my head, lock doors and windows, and again text my friend. Late isn't fashionable here, it's just standard. I'm pretty used to that by now, and even took over this habit many times already, but things do change a bit now that I'm standing here with my car and random people knock on my window to warn me for danger. It doesn't take too long before my friend arrives, and with slipping wheels I take off to a restaurant downtown, where we enjoy a lovely dinner. After dessert I bring her back home, and as soon as she leaves the car, I'm out of there. The front-desk of the hotel seem relieved when I come back in one piece, and say they are happy to see me back alive. I get to my room and sleep.

For today's afternoon I have an appointment at the dentist, as my denture isn't closing too well after they've filled my molar. I don't leave the hotel in the morning, and get to my appointment a bit early, as the accident still leaves me with a little scar in my memory. Besides that, I can have a chat with my friend Becky before the appointment's due. The fix is fast and easy, and I come out reborn. In the evening I head out to Heredia, where there's a casino I had won some money in my first week in this country, and I feel it's my lucky day again. Ever since I won my first 100 US dollars in Las Vegas, I'm hooked to playing roulette. I only play black or red, odd or even, and lower than 18 or higher than 18. I rarely put money on the small numbers as odds are much smaller. I start with the smallest possible amount and continue playing one bet until I win, raising my bet every time I lose. It's a common tactic, and it requires some nerves of steel, but it pays off again. Two years ago I had won over 1000 dollars in another Vegas visit, but today I settle for less. I do win again, and when my two friends come pick me up for dinner and drinks, I happy to have won another free night in the hotel. Outside it's raining, but I'm smiling like always, and we get in one of my friend's car some blocks further to get to a cool bar. Here they drink their booze, me my water, and we have some nice finger food. Later I'm dropped off back at my own car, and head back to my hotel.

<u>Costa Rica - Monteverde, Alajuela</u>

There's been one place in Costa Rica that has been on the to-visit-list throughout my stay here, and today I decide to go, without further thinking, or planning. After breakfast I take my stuff and head to Monteverde, a famous cloud forest, some hours north of San José. Waze is my guide once more, and soon it indicates a lot of red roads. Then also the signs along the road appear, saying there's a detour to Monteverde. A detour is a way as well, so I happily follow the signs. Then I get in an insane traffic jam, that lasts for hours. It's a one lane north, one lane south, but when I finally pass the location of the accident, I see that two trucks have frontally clashed. The scene is horrible, making it understandable why it had to take so long. I'm on the way between Puntarenas and Liberia, but soon take a right, going off the main road into the mountains. I pass a little village, where I fill my tank, and get some money, thinking I'm getting into nowhere after this. This is partially true, when I drive up the windy road into the mountains. The curves are dangerous here, but more dangerous is the local traffic not giving a damn and just rushing up and down. My car can't handle the steepness again, so I go very slow. It gives me time to enjoy the surroundings, and listen to weird Spanish music. Soon the radio signal gives up though, meaning I'm out of reach. My cell phone has also lost its signal, so this means I'm cut off. I reach a little village at the plateau on top of the hills, where I ask for directions and buy some snacks and drinks. It's quite lovely here, and the people are very friendly. I follow their directions, and head over an insanely bad road, where the pointy rocks on the road might stab my tires. I feel like I'm holding my breath and just waiting for this to happen, but it's not. I climb higher and higher with my car, and feel like I'm alone on this world. I get to Santa Elena, which is the closest town nearby the cloud forest, which is part of the same big forest I had seen in Vila Blanca, and in Arenal. I get a signal on my phone and look for some hotels that are mentioned. I don't directly find something and decide to drive to the Monteverde park entrance. Here I see they have rooms too, and I inform at the office to prices and availability. They have a room for me, and the price is equal to what I have seen in town. The only disadvantage is that I'm here in the middle of nowhere, with no facilities after park's closure at 6pm. I decide to take the room, which is very spacious and looks perfect. For dinner I drive a bit back towards town and along the way I find a very neat place where I enjoy a good meal. There's no streetlights at all here and driving back is a bit crazy, given the road's conditions. I see bats flying over my car, and when I get to the property I've arrived at a cacophony of jungle sounds. I stay out to listen to this symphony for a long time, and then head to bed.

Costa Rica - San José, San José

The best thing about my 'hotel' is its location, and as soon as I wake up I put my clothes on and firmly step into the park. Normally visitors are only allowed to enter at 7am, but I can now go at 6, giving all the trails to me, as I'm the only one sleeping here it seems. I walk to a small waterfall, and hear the jungle wake up. The birds are singing, chirping, and the trees seem to come alive when daylight reaches them. The trees are tall, and in between their tops I see the clouds sail, blown by the fierce wind. I start to understand the name of 'cloud forest' seeing this phenomenon. At 8am I have booked a tour, and with a group and guide I walk the same trails I did myself this morning, but now with detailed information about all I see. It's a great tour, and the guide seems to know it all. There's a nice group of Belgians in the group and we share our travel experiences and itineraries. They are biologists and seem to know an awful lot as well. The tour's done in two hours, and I get some snacks in my room before exploring the other unvisited trails. One leads to a marvellous view point, where I spend some time overlooking the green sea of trees. Besides some birds there's not much wildlife to see this day, despite being given a heads up by the possible presence of a puma in this area. I talk to numerous other people walking the trails, and when I'm out of breath climbing to a sky bridge, I walk into the Belgians again, giving me the necessary break of climbing. We talk a bit and then head in our own directions again. I cross the sky bridge, and then slowly walk back to the park's exit. There I first pack my stuff, load them in the car, and then chat a bit more with the staff, before telling them farewell. I start the drive back, and on advice of my ranger friends, make a stop at a big special tree in Santa Elena: a hollow braided one, which I climb to the top and from there get a great view. As it begins to rain now I carefully take my steps back to the ground, hurry to the car and then head out, back to San José. The rain isn't making it an easier drive, but I manage in the end. I trust my Waze again, even though it brings me through another way back, then that I came here. At times I wonder if it's roads at all, or just dry river beds. I pass some farm houses, and finally get back on the main asphalt road which will bring me back to the highway. Now I do recognise my way again, and as the rain's stopped, I get some great views from over the mountains. I cross the mountains, get to the main road, where today there's no traffic jam, and I get just north of Puntarenas, where I see the sky in orange, because of the sunset. I park the car, sit down on the shore's rocks, and take some photos, while I get in a zen mode. In San José I get another hotel, as 'mine' is fully booked for the rooms I like. I get to the hotel, check in, and see my room has a great view over the city. At night I have dinner with a friend in the proximity of my hotel and when I'm full and fat, I roll myself back to the hotel, to get a good night sleep.

My choice of hotel is bullseye as I find a channel the next day that live broadcasts Feyenoord's home game versus Standard Luik. So far all of the games I've been watching were through illegal (Russian) streams, mostly leaving me with frustration over the connection. My team wins and I could not be happier today. I don't do much the rest of the day, except for planning my next step. I think I've now seen all places of Costa Rica, and I might be ready for my next destination: but where to?

It's this question that keeps me busy the six days, and in between meeting all my friends here in San José and surroundings, I'm doing research on the internet, sending mails with KLM, investigating the countries north of Costa Rica, and discussing all these options with many friends over WhatsApp. I change my hotel again, not to my home hotel, but to another one, at the other side of the park, which now becomes my residence. The staff's great here, and they soon become friends too. On their advice one night I decide to go out to party in a nearby club they have recommended. When I get there I park my car at the next door's parking, stand in line a bit, and then get in. It's in ways a deja vu. Here people dress to impress and mainly look at each other, instead of talking. People are mainly talking to their companions, and I'm just standing at the side observing the party. As time ticks, people get happier, crazier. Alcohol is doing its job. Even though I'm still the same, now people walk up to me and ask where I'm from. Soon word seem to spread there's a Dutch gringo here, and I'm introduced to more and more people. I'm liking it, and even move my feet now on the dance floor. Bailando. Then I get introduced to two girls who soon become my friends, as we keep laughing about silly things. When they leave I still hang around for a bit, getting to talk to some other folks, discussion world politics. It's a five-minute drive back to my hotel when the club closes, and my old body is in dire need of a bed, and of sleep, a lot of sleep.

My days continue in the same speed now, mainly over thinking my next step. I meet up with Becky and her family a couple of times, getting myself back to being a kid while doing children's games with her daughter, while I get the best food in a hospitable surrounding. Also other friends I've made during my long stay in Costa Rica are visited, met up with, wined with, dined with. Then finally the bomb in my head drops, as I have made up my mind on my next step. What is it I really want to see in these parts of America? The answer is easier than the question: a jaguar. What is the best place in the world to see a jaguar? This answer's also easy: Brazil's Pantanal. And thus I change my ticket to Managua, Nicaragua, back to Panama, and from there a one-way flight to São Paulo. Now that I've made my decision, I reach out to tour agencies in Cuiabá, that can bring me to see jaguars, and one easily stands out, Ailton's organisation Pantanal Nature. As all other trips into the rural Pantanal it's extremely expensive, and it's the biggest price I will have to pay for any of the tours so far. I don't confirm to Ailton yet, as I will have to rethink this for a bit longer.

Costa Rica - Liberia, Guanacaste

As it takes some days before my flight is departing to Panama, I decide to go to Nicaragua to cross the border and get it off my country list. I once more book my hotel in Liberia, and drive north. It's quite a drive north, and I leave early. On Google Maps I've found a route at the utmost northwest of the country, far from the main road, and far from the big traffic hub I expect there. I don't find any information about this road on Google though, so it's another step into an abyss. When I get to the most northern town, the last before the border, La Cruz, I take a left and head to the coast on a very small road. My gps isn't recognising this road either, so I switch to Google to find it. When I reach the sea, I know I'm too far, so I head back to the mountains. Now I see a small dirt road, that most likely is the one Google Maps is talking about. There's a small 'house' at the entrance of this road, and I get out to ask if this is a road I can use. I have no clue what the boy is telling me, so I repeat my question a couple of times before I have to give up. I walk down the road for a bit, and slide all ways. The rain has hurt this not well maintained road very badly. I cancel my idea, and decide to go on the main road. From La Cruz it's another hour drive north, and soon I see the enormous lines of trucks waiting. I follow some other cars passing this line and for kilometres these trucks are on my right side. At times I'm driving at the wrong side of the road, and even driving on the opposite shoulder. Then there are some buildings and finally I arrive at the border area. It doesn't look too good here, with all these truckers. Near the actual border there are soldiers, and as soon as I've parked my car I'm approached by a dozen people who want to sell me some kind of visa. I don't understand any of it, and walk to two policemen and ask what I need to cross the border. They tell me I need the immigration form, which these people are selling, and that I can then walk around, to get out, and then get in again. I make sure this is the procedure by asking another person as well, and then head to the border crossing, leaving my car and belongings in Costa Rica. I walk over the border, and then it's said I'm in Nicaragua. I continue to walk a bit further, and then turn again. I don't like doing this too much. It reminds me of my nerve wrecking hour passage in Tijuana, Mexico. I soon head back to the Costa Rican post, and get at the booth. I show them my passport and papers, and am then asked for proof I will leave Costa Rica again. Oops. My airline didn't email me any ticket, and my physical tickets are in my luggage in Liberia. I tell them I just was on the other side, and my car's parked there, but they are numb to my arguments: I need proof to leave the country. They advise me to go buy a bus ticket at a booth further down, so I can buy a ticket back to Nicaragua. This doesn't make any sense to me at all, and I keep opposing this ridiculous measure, which will cost me around thirty bucks. Eventually I do what they tell me, get the ticket, and then return to the booth, now easily getting through. This sucked big time. I walk directly back to my car, and leave this wretched place as soon as I can. Soon I'm stopped by a road block though, and the interrogation starts all over again. Now I get through without problems though, and the road to Liberia is wide open. I make a stop at the Santa Rosa's park entrance, drive a bit into the park, and then head back again. I drive to Liberia and arrive there late in the evening, quickly grabbing food and then sleep.

Costa Rica - San José, San José

On my way back from Liberia to San José I make a stop at an animal shelter, called Las Pumas. I've told myself I can't leave Costa Rica without seeing a jaguar, and I've read there's one or two here. The park is very small, with big cages for a variety of animals. There's pumas, spider monkeys, and yes, a jaguar. It's laying behind a fence. It's kind of a sad sight, as its eyes seems to have lost all hope in life. These animals are rescued though, and could not survive anymore in the wild, so it's a good thing in a way. I walk the small area twice, and then get back into my car to drive to San José, where I hang out with friends in the evening.

On my final day I meet up with Johanna and Nickole, the girls I had met on my party night, and we have dinner in some shopping centre, before going for drinks in a bar near my hotel. Then I realise this is my final night of sleep in a country I have started to like very much, and where I have made so many great friends in the last eight weeks. I'm sad I will have to miss all these fantastic folks, but my jaguar mission is calling.

Chapter XI

PANAMA II

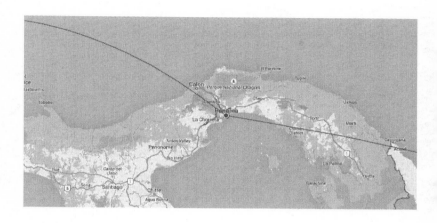

Panama - Panama City, Panamá

I leave in the early morning to return my car to the rental company and from there take a taxi to the international airport. I'm welcomed in the VIP bar there, and get some food and drink for free. I'm not feeling too well today, and I think it's a part of my mind that really wants to stay in Costa Rica longer. I don't regret my decision though, as I'm moving forward to chase the dream of seeing a jaguar. I again fly over the Panama Canal, which in my eyes is more beautiful from up in the air, than it is to stand next to it. I've booked the same hotel again, and the front desk is very surprised to see me back. Within minutes they all come to listen to my stories, and all welcome me back. In the evening I meet friends and their cute son.

My two full days in Panama are spent very relaxed, and I'm mainly meeting up with old friends, and meeting new ones in the most random places. I don't do anymore sightseeing, I just keep considering paying that sick money for a Pantanal tour. I just can't make up my mind about it.

Chapter XI

BRAZIL II

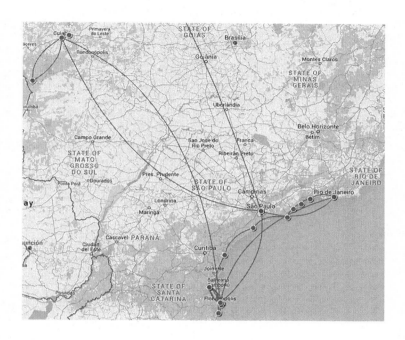

Brazil - Guarulhos, São Paulo

Then it's already the final of three nights in Panama, and I have a long flight to the international airport of Guarulhos, Brazil. At the Panama airport I get to meet new folks again, and I'm invited to come to Colombia once more. My flight unfortunately will go over it, so I won't be able to visit that lovely country just now again. In the plane I get to sit to a very nice Brazilian couple, and they are helping me to start-up my Portuguese once again. It makes the flight go pretty fast after all. After about seven hours we land at the airport, and I wait for a hotel transport to bring me to the hotel I thought to have booked close by. The drive however takes thirty minutes, and making me already realise how big this city of São Paulo must be. The hotel itself is fine, but the area seems to be not too good.

I find this out properly the next day, when I make an afternoon walk through the dirty streets. I'm again very much looked at. Panama and Costa Rica had unlearned me that this happens, as in those countries Western people are more than common. Here I'm the white gringo once more. I sit myself down for acai, even though my stomach's rumbling. The first taste is as good as ever, and I think I'm getting addicted again. This food gives me the required energy however to finally decide, and I email Ailton to confirm I will join the tour, if still possible, and I book a flight to Cuiabá, departing tomorrow. Ailton soon mails me back that he had kept my spot free, and I'm more than welcome to join. Great! Now my mind is only focused on this elusive animal called the jaguar. I might finally see it, or not...

Brazil - Cuiabá, Mato Grosso

At the hotel's checkout I have an issue with my phone bill, as again an enormous amount appears on the check, even though there was no warning that interstate calls would be this expensive. I file a complaint, and eventually a manager solves it by offering me 50% discount, which I take, even though I feel treated badly. Then I take the same little hotel transport back to the airport, and wait for my flight north. São Paulo was already hot, but I'm told Cuiabá will be an inferno. I'm eager to find out. I land in the early evening, and then take a taxi to the hotel I've booked in the centre of town. It's a grand hotel, and I especially took this one, because I need to have some good nights before being dropped in the jungle in two days. This hotel also had the best reviews, so even though I pay a little bit more, I'm happy doing so. After a smooth check-in, I arrive in the luxury room. After a quick shower I head out to grab some sushi in a nearby restaurant. Here I make friends with the chef, who offers me a seat next to his kitchen, even though there's no table. While waiting for a table, he gives me some free sushi, making me feel almost satisfied. When I get my table I order just one other dish, which is like the earlier samples, excellent. After paying the bill, I walk to the hotel. Even though it's 9pm, it's hot here, very hot. Upon arrival in the hotel I get a text from my friend Patricia that she will come pick me up at the hotel, and I await her arrival to go for a drink together. When her car pulls up in front of the hotel my expectations of seeing just her are immediately shattered, as she's brought two friends, Joeslayne and Mariana. None of them speaks English, and their Portuguese is so fast, and in such dialect, that my ears are flapping the first thirty minutes. The only thing I do understand is that they constantly say "amiga, amiga", which, to my ears, is hilarious. This Cuiabá Portuguese also makes the 'r' much different than what I have heard before, except for my two days in São Paulo. It sounds more like a posh 'r'. We go to a very nice restaurant, where there's plenty of food served, and the girls are liking their drinks. The longer I talk to them, the better I seem to understand them, and these ladies are really amazing company. We talk and laugh all the time. After dinner they bring me to the city's world cup stadium, which is huge, and stands in quite a contrast of what I've seen from the city so far. We take some photos before I'm dropped off back at my hotel, not having expected such a great welcome here. Forever grateful, again.

The next day is now fully booked as well, as Patricia and her awesome son Victor pick me up in the afternoon to have lunch at a natural food place, and then to a shopping area where we walk around and get some of the things she needs to buy. Then we head to her place, where I get injected with the gaming virus again, and play video games with Victor all afternoon. It's great fun, and Victor's English is better than that of all the other folks I have met so far here, and he also seems to understand my baby Portuguese. Besides that, gaming language is universal. After game time's over me and Patricia drive to a very nice restaurant where we have dinner with her sister and husband. It's a great dinner, and the sister's husband is fluent in English, helping me say what I want to say today. The food's delicious and the company great, and time goes to fast when you're amongst great people. After dinner we drop off the other two, and head to Mariana's birthday party at Valley Pub, very close to my hotel. I just go in quickly to congratulate my friend and hand her a Dutch postcard as a gift. I need to wake up extremely early tomorrow for the tour and don't stay too long today. The bar's staff doesn't agree at first that I just go in and out, as they want my fingerprint, photo, and whatever more. I can skip it, for now. After the congratulations, and one photo, I walk back to the hotel and get my stuff ready for the trip into the wild.

Brazil - Pantanal, Mato Grosso

I'm being picked up at my hotel in the very early morning, and I do my second part of my payment. I enter a Mercedes minivan with a nice Dutch couple, a guide and driver. It's some 80 km to Poconé, then 150 on a dirt road on the Transpantaneira to Porto Joffre. There's much wildlife on and besides the road, but we make few stops; time is ticking and lunch will be at the flotel (a boat hotel). We see many birds, capybaras, and even a group of black howler monkeys (one running along the road, then climbing a solitary tree and jumping out to the floor again). At Porto Joffre we are being awaited by our boat driver, Manuel, and Fisher, the guide. It's around fifteen minutes by boat to the flotel, where the baggage is dropped off in a tiny room with one single bed and a bunk bed, all for myself. There's a tiny bathroom as well, completing all I need. There a really good lunch is served. At 14:00 we're starting the tour in our small boat. Going up to Cuiabá river and then to Black Bay river. Two minutes after departure we see a group of Giant otters already! We parallel follow them upstream for a few minutes. They are really big and look like sea lions. We stop following them after 15 minutes and then see them cross land to a smaller river. We stop at a river bank to see a group of very colourful butterflies (yellow, green, and orange ones). The boat continues and we go slow speed over the wide river. At one shore we spot two capybaras and their baby. The vegetarian animals jump into the bush when they see us. Around 14:25 we are entering Black Bay river; this is a smaller river with much green floating around, which we have to push away at times to pass. Then, at 14:41 Fisher whispers loudly: JAGUAR! He's pointing to the left river bank. I wear my sunglasses and the shade of trees block a clear sighting. I grab my camera and aim to the spot and see it. Lying there, like a king, a big male jaguar. Wow! I shoot the same photo fifty times. What an excitement! Then our guide confirms what Gerard, the Dutch guy, already said; there is a second jaguar two meters to the right, a female. Wow again! I can't see it from my position in the boat and only spot it after a while when it lifts its head. Magnificent! We wait for things to happen. I can only gaze, mouth wide open. For nearly nine months I've been telling everyone I want to see a jaguar, at almost every national park I had introduced myself as Jort who is here to see a jaguar, and now finally, I'm facing one. The adrenaline is flushing out the lack of sleep, making me forget I'm sitting in the burning sun. All the wait, so worth it. It even gets better when the female stands up, walks up to the male and they mate. They mate! Right in front of our boat. We can see their scars. We can see into their eyes that twinkle in the light. Like golden stars flickering. Their sounds, their moaning. High above all other sounds around us. Our guide is excited too and shows a big smile. We are all happy. Other boats have come too, but I don't notice them too much. All focus on those divine animals. The male is much bigger than the female, but in this case the female is being the dominant one. The pattern of their fur is captivating. Their scars of war intimidating. Wow. My highlight. We observe them for a bit over three hours and see them mate four times in total; the other three times more out of sight. We see the female go drink twice. She lays down on the lower bank at one point and the male can't reach her. He stays and lays on the upper part and it gives a very pretty scene. Even more boats have arrived and a total of seven are now observing the two felines. Until 18:30, when the sun is going down like a red ball on fire, we stay there and then return to the flotel. When I step out of the boat I feel tired. The search that lasted so long came to an end. But the search for more jaguars has only just begun... I take a quick shower and then a good meal is served. Two Brits join our group and we share some of our backgrounds before hitting the sack at 21:30. All the excitement passes in my mind and I don't fall asleep until 00:30.

I think I wake up at 05:30, but when I go to the restaurant at 06:00 all is closed. It is super dark outside as well, and I can see millions of stars. I'm one hour too early. The breakfast is served one hour later and then we head off on the boat. We first head to Black Bay again and get into a big group of otters there. They seem pretty used to boats as they eat their caught fish not far from us repeatedly. It's a beautiful sight. Then we continue seeing many different birds. We get to the spot where we saw the jaguars yesterday but now they are nowhere to be seen. Just as we approach the end of this river a radio message comes in that there is a jaguar spotting in the Three Brothers river. High speed we turn and head back, into that river. Here we quite soon see three boats in front of a big male jaguar. A different one than the ones yesterday. We stay awhile to observe. Some boats leave and out of seven only three remain. Then we see the jaguar look. First we think it is looking at us, but we find out there's a caiman and also some capybaras behind us in the river corner. Not much later the jaguar gets up and disappears in the thick bush. About 15 minutes later he arrives at the river beach, where the caiman has already left, probably aware of the danger. The capybaras stay and one is making danger sounds, looking in the jaguar's direction without seeing it. The jaguar is taking it easy and lays down in the sand and sleeps. Then two capybaras and three of their babies jump into the water apparently afraid of something. They swim a couple of rounds before returning to the shore. Things change in a worse way when rain starts coming down. The jaguar stands up and walks towards the capybaras, into the bush separating them. We anxiously wait in boat for the jaguar to jump out, but as the rain pours harder and harder, it never happens. After waiting one hour we decide to accept our loss and return to the flotel, where we arrive at 10:45. After lunch at 12:00 I take an hour nap before we start our search for jaguars again. In Black Bay river we find none, so we head far up Three Brothers river, seeing many animals but zero jaguars. We head back to Black Bay around 17:45 and put the boat at Bay to see the Giant otters play. Not much later an incoming radio messages tells us the mating couple of yesterday has been seen. We hurry to the spot, search the area, but unfortunately don't see them. We return to the flotel and arrive at 19:00. Dinner is then served at 19:30, and I head to my room at 20:45 for hopefully enough hours of sleep.

Today I wake up at the right time. Breakfast is at 06:00 again, and departure at 06:30. There is a beautiful sunrise today. The light in the morning is now very good for some bird photography, and we make several stops to observe the animals. There's no jaguar in Black Bay, and we then go up to Cuiabá river. Nothing. We get a call of a sighting in Three Brothers and hurry there. No jaguar again. Not much later there's an incoming call for a jaguar in Cuiabá river, but again we see nothing. There's at least eight boats looking for it now. We go upriver until we get a call it is seen again. We hurry there once more without success, and then back to Three Brothers, circling this area hoping for a sighting. We head into a side river and only see a frog, besides the usual birds. Then I think we head back for lunch, but passing Cuiabá river we get a third call for that jaguar there. We rush there, slow down and see the head of a jaguar in the high grass. Before we get closer it vanishes. We decide to wait a bit, together with the only other boat there. On my photos I see a huge collar on the cat. The guide explains it is a cat that was in farm's territory and instead of it being killed it is used for research. I think it's very sad. Just when we stop looking at the photos we see the jaguar start swimming to the other side. We rush over there, and we get a few photos, until the other boat cuts the passage of the cat on high speed. We are all flabbergasted by the disrespect for the cat. Just after that all other boats arrive and the cat just climbs up shore through insanely thick bushes. It vanishes and there's no further sighting of the jaguar and so we head back to the flotel. There we have lunch and some nice conversation. I don't take a nap today even though I'm pretty tired. Just before 14:00 we take off again for the second part of the day tour. Almost immediately we see a guy in another boat point at the water and we see a head moving in the water. It climbs on the shore and we see it is an Ocelot! Wowsers. We try taking some good photos but this cat is fast. We all are very excited with this kick-off. With smiles on our faces we head to Black Bay and Fisher spots a hidden jaguar there, probably eating a dead caiman we had seen earlier today. Wow again! It is very hard to see this jaguar however, but it's another cheer in the group. We circle around that spot for a while, before heading to one of the other rivers. There we search for a while until we get a radio call for another jaguar at the island in the Three Brother river. We speed up there and are the third boat to arrive. In the thick bushes we see a tail of a jaguar, but it is too dark to see it well. The jaguar is eating a caiman. A couple of minutes later it stands up and moves; right in the line of our boat, but still behind too many branches. Many other boats arrive and all tourists gather for this cat, that apparently is not too shy. Again some minutes later it stands up and slowly walks. The grass moves quite near us and it seems he's heading straight at us. We see its head come over the grass, peaking at the thirteen boats. Then it moves again, and all boats strategically place themselves at another position too. We do too but then Fisher decides to get a bit back as he expects it to return. And yes, he's right. We see the cat laying down in other thick bushes and our boat is the only one to see it. All boats move back again in this small creek/river. When it moves again a couple of minutes later we also move more up, to a little open area at the shore. And yes, the jaguar comes there and lays itself down right in the middle of it. Wow. The king ascended its throne and is looking down at the crowd. A crowd of 88 (!) people in thirteen boats. It lays calmly and observes its audience. It is a juvenile cat, six to twelve months old, and still curious to the world. We look at it for an hour. Other boats depart after a while as the jaguar is not doing too much and it is getting closer to sunset. With six boats left it moves into an attacking position; there is a caiman right under it. We all hope he makes the leap, but eventually he doesn't. At 17:45 we leave the scene, being the second last boat to depart. What a treat, this jaguar! We arrive back at the boat around 18:15, after observing the sunset for a bit. Then the evening ritual: dinner, talk, sleep.

The next day it's the same morning routine, and then dropping of my new Dutch friends in Porto Joffre. At 07:15 we start touring Black Bay, but no jaguars. We head up Three Brothers and there get a call for a jaguar, further upstream. We take off high speed but when we arrive in the area the jaguar is long gone. We take a canal connecting Three Brothers to Cuiabá River, which was narrower than other rivers. We arrive at Cuiabá river and head a bit more upstream, until entering an even narrower creek called San Lorenzo back to Three Brothers. We get another call when we are there and speed there. When we arrive we see many tourist boats, but no jaguar. Around 10:45 we start heading back and arrive at 11:35 back at the flotel for lunch. At 14:00 we depart again skipping Black Bay, and immediately heading up Three Brothers. There we make some stops for howler monkeys and birds. We also explore the creek near Ilha, the island in the river where we saw the juvenile jaguar yesterday. Now there is nothing and I'm falling asleep. I'm brutally woken up by Fisher again after a few minutes, when he says 'jaguar' out loud, while there's none to be seen. We then go more upstream until we meet two boats that are observing a whitish corpse: the dead body of a caiman laying belly up at a river bank. With a quick look in my camera I see the jaguar responsible for this kill. A vulture arrives too and then the jaguar gets up and scares off the bird. This meal is his. Then he starts laying around, napping. More and more boats arrive and we're all there in the end. Then the jaguar walks up to the caiman and starts feeding on it. Wow! It slurps out the intestines and the blood is dripping from his mouth. Although the light is super bad I try to take many photos. After eating for about fifteen minutes it lays itself down in the sand again, sleeping and licking its paws. This continues until sun is setting and we have to hurry back. I wave farewell and off we are. Just before arriving at the flotel we see another boat lying still and pointing to the shore: another jaguar! One with a collar again, walking across the steep river shore looking for a place to ascend. All photos I take are a disaster due to the shimmering, the movement, and my lack of skill. Too bad. The jaguar finds its way and we continue ours. We get to the flotel at 19:00, I take a shower, and then dinner and talking until 21:15. Fifteen minutes later I'm asleep, deadly exhausted...

Brazil - Cuiabá, Mato Grosso

I have had dreams about the words Manuel, the boat driver, is using all the time: "postivo" and "negativo". Whenever he has radio contact these are the words mostly used and it has penetrated my ears. In the morning I'm saying goodbye to the British couple and Fisher at breakfast, and then I go on a tour with Ailton and Mauricio (a cameraman who is exploring the Pantanal for a BBC documentary next year). We directly go upriver of Three Brothers and there get a report of a possible sighting near Ilha. We head there and unfortunately see nothing, so we slowly head up river a bit more where we run into two boats at the same place where we saw the jaguar eating a caiman yesterday. I assume it is the same jaguar, but then I see a person putting up three fingers. Three jaguars? I can't believe it! I quickly spot two: a collared father and a cub of around two years old. Then a bit later also a third one: another cub! Wow. And they are feeding themselves on the dead caiman, which makes it likely the jaguar yesterday was their mother. We observe them for a while and see the cubs one after the other eating and then sleeping. Also one of them climbs in a tree further in the forest. The father leaves shortly after our arrival, while the cubs stay there hidden in the shadows of the forest. We also stay another hour and then head a bit more upstream where we see another jaguar! A big male totally blended into the forest, sleeping. It is hard to see and after some photos we head back, where we pass the other spot again and see the two cubs in one shot together for the first time. Amazing! Such fascinating animals. They walk to the meal and then head back into the forest. After this we speed back to the flotel where we arrive thirty minutes later. The right place, but no flotel. Oops. It apparently went back to Porto Joffre for supplies. Off we go and another twenty minutes later we are back to pack and have lunch. After that Mauricio, Ailton and me get in a car and start the four-hour journey back to Cuiabá. I return back to the fancy hotel, which I think I deserve after the little bed for four nights, even though sleeping was perfect there. I go out for dinner, and return to the hotel early, ready for a good night of sleep.

My camera's memory cards are full once more, and I haven't been able to back it up properly lately. So I walk to a market where Patricia had taken me before in order to find new cards. Back then the stand I needed was closed, and today I find it open. I buy two new cards, and another device to connect to a computer directly. For lunch Patricia picks me up again to go have lunch at the natural place. The food's so good there, I'm loving it. After lunch we head to her place where some other friends and her mom are hanging out. We're supposed to all go out later tonight, but they need some girl time before to prepare themselves, so I'm being dropped off at the hotel, where I take a nap and shower. Then word arrives that there has been broken into Sara's car, and the party is cancelled, unfortunately. I spend the rest of the night thinking of other plans, now that the jaguar's finally spotted.

At breakfast these thoughts continue, and I decide I want to see the third Chapada of Brazil, Chapada dos Guimarães. Now all I need is a way to get there, and I'm talking through options with Patricia, Sara, and their friend, at a nice lunch, where there seems to be unlimited food. It's a food madhouse. After finishing the food, I play some (video) games with Victor at the special area for children, and from now on also gringos. After lunch I'm dropped off at the hotel again, where I chill and await yet another pickup, as Mariana and Priscilla will take me to Garden Nuun, which is also right around the corner of my hotel. Mariana seems to know everyone in this place, and I'm introduced to an endless line of great people. All are now my 'amigos' and 'amigas'. It's also the night before the elections, and I get explained more about the difference in candidates and parties. My new friends all dislike Dilma, the current president, and from what I know, even before tonight, she's the worst possible option. Besides the politics we dance on some great electronic music, and when the rain comes, the roof closes for a while, before it's being danced off again. It's a great atmosphere, a great party, with again great company. When the feet start to hurt, and the stomach's calling for food, the three of us head out to find good snacks at Getulio's once more. Mariana and Priscilla make me laugh with their hilarious conversation, and Mari's fanatic singing of sertaneja songs is the best there is. Late at night I get back to the hotel, exhausted.

The breakfast buffet in this hotel is amazing, and there's such a wide variety of things to eat. Back in the Netherlands breakfast was my least favourite meal, but things change here in South America, and the fresh fruits and pastels all are so delicious here. And if my breakfast wasn't too tasty today, Mari's picking me up again, to have lunch with two other friends, Vanessa and Mariella. After Mari's picked me up we drive forever and ever to find Vanessa's place, and I don't recall where about in the city this was, but it seemed to be in a galaxy far far away. Then we drive to Mariella's place, but she's driving herself, and the two cars head for the fancy restaurant called, Avec. Of course there's valet parking, as this seems to be the way it's done, or at least with these friends. The food's delicious, both entree and dessert are picked from a widely varied buffet. After dinner the cars are brought to the designated drivers and we all head to Getulio's once more: election day! The place is packed, but we find a table outside, from where we just can see the television, that's broadcasting the entire day about exit polls. This entire bar's supporting Aécio Neves, and not one seems to like Dilma Rousseff. Today's the second round of the election, as in the first round none of the then three candidates got the required >50%. Voting in Brazil is obligatory, but with a relative small fine you can dash it. Alcohol is drunk non-stop, and the atmosphere's getting better and better, all confident the nation will finally realise it's time for change. Dilma, the sneaky rat according to my friends, just handed out a new bill, saying all people get 50 reais (about 17 euros) per child, per month. For nothing, to raise living circumstances, but to all people here, it seems to be a bribe to get the poorer people's votes. Besides this, it's also a pure short-term solution, as for those people that benefit from this the most, the poor people, still will lack education, or good health care. I do think however that there also has to be an instant solution for the current situation, but the long term should not be forgotten. The more I talk with all my friends here, the more I oppose this woman. I run back to my hotel to change my clothes, and quickly take a shower, as the party will continue in Valley afterwards. The result of the election isn't what the people have hoped for, and Dilma wins again... Some Dilma fans pass the bar in car, making noise and taunting the opponents here. Politics is just like football here. The party however continues until late, and deadly tired I again hit the sack in the early morning.

The current hotel is super fine, but also quite expensive. I've therefore decided to change it for a while, and I find a very cheap one in the centre of town. This area is as shady as most other Brazilian's downtowns, but I've again lost my worries about safety. It'll be fine. I spend the day chilling, doing nothing. All my friends are at their jobs, and it gives me time to recover. Old men need recovery time after a party.

Like yesterday, also today's a day of chilling. I head to a mall. The city's university has a department in this shopping mall, and while I have lunch I get in touch with some new folks. It's great how I can meet all these different kind of people, and like always my gringo appearance, and my baby Portuguese might have done the trick. The rest of the day I prepare for my trip to the Chapada the next day.

Brazil - Chapada dos Guimarães, Mato Grosso

I've found a travel agency through Ailton to bring me to the mountains north of Cuiabá. I'm being picked up very early by Nidelci and her husband. He's the driver, she's the guide. We have a big hike today, but first start at the park's biggest waterfall, which is situated at the start of a lovely valley, and all is surrounded by a sea of green. The rocks of the mountain are red with gold, and the sun makes it a perfect view. We then drive further into the park, open a gate that is locked for public, and drive into the road beyond it. We drive a fair amount of time, and then me and Nidelci are dropped off. It's warm again, but not as hot as it is in the city of Cuiabá. Today we do a trail along a river, where we will see several waterfalls. The first one is the biggest of them, and we have to walk down dilapidated stairs to get to the pool. Here I don't think twice, and head in the fresh water and head to the fall where I let the powerful falling water hit my head, and make some handstands for the camera. I could be in this pool forever, as it's so peaceful here. It helps that there are absolutely no other people here, which makes it feel like these mountains and falls are all ours. We continue and walk up the stairs again, and head for the second waterfall. It's not very high, but it's a nice pool to have a second swim. The freshness of the water is perfect in these temperatures. My guide stays out of the water, but I'm like an otter, feeling one with the water. We move ourselves to the next waterfall, where a tree hangs over the water. Today I'm not only an otter, but also a monkey. I try to climb the tree, and when I finally manage to do so, I take a dive from there into the water. Except for some spiders and birds, we unfortunately don't walk into much wildlife today, but given all the fun I have in the water I can't be bothered. We finish the waterfall series at one of my height and I can stand in it for a while, before we walk down to a big rock house. This is the last stop of the hike, and we then go up and down the trail again, where we meet up with our driver again, and we head to the town with the same name as the park. Here we make a stop at the travel agency's office, where I can make my payment, and we then head for a late lunch in town. After eating a fine meal, I'm brought to my hotel, which is quite decent. I tell my friends goodbye for now, and chill a bit in the room before I head out to eat some pasta in an Italian restaurant, not too far from my hotel.

Brazil - Cuiabá, Mato Grosso

My alarm clock wakes me early once more. At 07:30 my tour will start, and I will have breakfast before at the buffet. I pack my stuff, and my ride's perfectly on time. We first drive to a viewpoint over the great plains around the city of Cuiabá, which skyline can be seen at the horizon. Then we follow the main road for a while, until we take a right exit, and now cross big farm lands on both sides, until we drive up a little hill, where there's a restaurant, and from where a trail will start to the caverns beyond. First we have to attach protection to our shins, which at first I thought was a joke, but it's damn serious: snakes are plenty here, and can be deadly. I so hope we can see a snake, but Nidelci rather stays away from it, far away. We take off, and make a first stop at a big bridge made out of a rock. It's quite fascinating to see the formations here. We continue our path, through a very snake likely area, with low bushes. Unfortunately, we don't see any. Then we arrive at the first cave. We enter and I push us forward, beyond what my guide would really like. There's two flashlights, and I admit that going deep in, worries me a bit, as there's no one else out here, and if we would need help, it would certainly come too late. Nidelci wanted to go back long ago, but step by step we move further into the darkness. It's wet down here, and there's a very small stream of water here. There's some bats, but besides that we don't see a thing. When there's a fork, we decide to go back, not wanting to get actually lost here. It's cold in the cave, and I'm happy to see the sunlight when we get out again. We follow the trail through the forest, and arrive to a big rock that has only three resting points, with the rest floating in the air. It's a rock with a name (which I have forgotten), and for the photo I will pretend this rock is the earth and I'll be the Greek God Atlas, carrying that burden. Just when I put my back to the rock, and spread my arm, suddenly I feel like I'm being shot down by a bullet. BOOM. I'm hit by a killer bee, or whatever insect it is. I only know it hurts terribly. Such a small nasty animal giving me such pain, insane. I directly jump off the rock, and run some metres away. When I was little I once walked through a wasp nest, and got over fifty bites over my body, and they were even under my clothes. I can't remember that pain, fortunately, but I do know the pain now is crazily intense. My guide has a medical kit and puts some stuff on my finger, where the bee hit me like a bomb. My spine is trembling, brrr. I walk back and see a big nest of wasps hanging under the rocks. If only I had seen this before... The pain slightly fades after some thirty minutes, and in the mean time we have already reached a second cave, which we again enter. This one is higher, and less deep. We do see more bats here though, and at the entrance little green parrots nest in the dens around. A next cave is one with amazing blue water, just like the ones I had seen in the gorgeous Chapada Diamantina. The sunlight makes it so amazing, and it's so transparent, and so calm. I take some steps to the edge, and then in one second all those steps back, as I see an anaconda in the water. It's a young one, only about two to three metres long, but it's laying there, and I was only inches away. I tell Nidelci what I saw and we had a short discussion about the exact kind, but I'm pretty sure it's an anaconda. She doesn't dare to get closer, but I get back to take some photos. The pattern on its scale is perfect, and things get better when it awakes, and starts swimming. We see the snake gallantly move through the heavenly blue water, and in this moment I can't see why God made this the symbol of evil. It moves to the side and there tries to get into some underwater holes. We don't know where these holes will lead, but it might be just behind us, so we try to see some exits, but there's none. The snake is now gone for 90%, and only a small piece of tail is visible through the water. This is the moment we leave and continue down on the trail, to a narrow cave passage. The walls on both sides are steep and high, and there's a little stream under us. The sunlight gives a nice effect at the tall openings on both sides. When we get through it's the end of our line of the day, and we head back from there. On our way back we make some short stops at the day's highlights, but mostly firmly step back to the restaurant. There we have a nice lunch, and some chats with the owners. With the car we then drive back to the main road and then to a series of rapids a bit more north. Here we go for a swim, and walk behind one of the falls, making it a movie scene. At one point when I try to climb through a waterfall to the next level over the slippery rocks, my legs slip away and moves to a huge hole under me. I pull my leg up, but opening my shin, removing most of the skin, and making the river red for a moment. I don't feel the pain as the cold water eases it, but when I get out, it's seriously hurting. I get numb to it soon enough, and a quick inspection by my friends makes it clear it's nothing serious, and it will fix itself easily. Heading back to Cuiabá we make a stop to see the South American ostrich, and some land owls, and finally one at the great viewpoint and now see the sun setting behind the clouds. From there it's the same drive back to the city and I let them drop me off at the fancy hotel, leaving the cheaper one for what it is.

My body's not made for so much hiking, and the next day I feel I need to rest all the time. In the afternoon I drag myself out of bed to visit a barber, and have a haircut. It's super cheap to go in Brazil, and most of them are pretty good, so I've made a custom to go every three to four weeks, cutting the few hairs I have left. Upon return in the hotel I book my flight from Cuiabá to the south, to Florianópolis in four days. When all's said and done, I walk to a sushi restaurant nearby and enjoy the fine meal, creating a solid foundation for a party night. Mariana's going to take me out, but the place we are supposed to go to stays empty, and a girl's a girl, and it takes longer than I thought it would. My outside waiting is cancelled when Mari texts me she's in her second home, Valley Pub, so I head over there, and meet up with her and Renata, who takes me to the dancefloor to teach me some sertaneja moves. This is of course hilarious, as my hips don't lie once again. Everyone's getting pretty wasted and I'm once again introduced to half the pub by Mari. Some guys come to me to talk about girls, which is mostly showing off photos on their phones to see what girls they have had, and then letting me know they're married or have a steady relationship while they're at it. Maybe this happens in my country too, but I don't think anyone would brag about it the way these guys seem to do it. I keep my discretion in order to reach world peace. The evening's pretty wild, and I'm among the last ones to be kicked out. I feel drunk, without having drank a drop. The stars smile at me, the moon makes some winks, and I drift back to the hotel. They have a great service there to serve an early breakfast for people who arrive in the middle of the night, and so I find myself eating sandwiches at 5:30 in the morning.

The curtains in the hotel are so good that even when I wake up I believe it's night. It's past noon when I finally get out, and my 'drunk' feeling of yesterday has made me hungry like someone with a hangover, and I don't excuse myself for going to SubWay to have a big sandwich and talk with the friends I've made there during my stay these weeks. In the evening I take a cab to meet up with two other friends in some weird neighbourhood, almost unfindable, but when I do we're all having a great time talking and laughing. When this party's over, I move on to the next, and head to Nuun, where yesterday there was no one entering, today it's pretty packed. I skip the lines by playing the gringo card, and even skip payment, saying I live on water, and I don't need registration. It all works out well, as inside I don't see any people I know, but soon am invited to join a big group in their V.I.P. section, and get the water I need for free. The house lights are moving fast; I'm moving in slow motion. The crowd's jumping on the music beats, and more than once there's some kind of group hug and we all shuffle left to right, right to left, until one breaks free again and we can all continue with what we're doing before. There's one long buzz in my eyes, a combination of house beats and Portuguese, of some English, and screaming ladies' voices. I'm having a blast. Women in Brazil dress to impress, and tonight's another example of that, leaving my eyes spinning. It's another late/early finish and I get back to the hotel around 6am, having my breakfast once more in between the drunk and wasted.

I'm craving for acai when I finally wake up, and I will have it for lunch, as snack, and as dinner. I need energy. If my body's not made for hiking, it's certainly not for so much and long partying. It has not ended yet, as tonight there's one final night in Valley for me to attend. There's a live band playing sertaneja once more, and even though it's a weekday the place is packed. I don't know how they pull it off, but Brazilians always seem to party. It's another great night, and I really start to like the music: the worse it gets, the better it sounds. It's late again when I lay in bed, and I'm praying I will get back to a normal rhythm soon again.

My final full day in Cuiabá is spent with a lunch with Subway friends, and then a final dinner with Patricia, Mariana and Victor. I'm touched by the care of all my friends, and even though Cuiabá as a city is just another example of Brazilian chaotic architecture, the people are making the difference, and their hearts can't be bigger, and my gratitude can't be either. One day I will be back here, to meet all these fantastic folks.

Brazil - Florianópolis, Santa Catarina

For now it's time to pack my stuff and leave, and in the early morning I grab a taxi to the airport, from where a plane will take me to São Paulo Congonhas, and after a short waiting time, another one to Florianópolis. I have booked an Ibis hotel in downtown Floripa, from where I want to explore the city a little bit.

Yesterday I only chilled, and today I take a walk through the city's shopping streets and eat acai. In the afternoon I meet up with my friend Patricia who I had met in Amsterdam some years back. With her I have dinner in the hotel. I had changed to another hotel as I had only booked the Ibis for one night and when I wanted to extend this morning, everything was fully booked. Actually everything seemed to be booked as there was an event going on this weekend, and after some phone calls I did manage to find a room in a tad more expensive hotel some blocks away.

Patricia's working nearby as a police officer and the next day we meet up again shortly for breakfast. For lunch I meet one of Tete's friends, Luana, who lives in this city and with whom I have a nice walk and great talk. In the cafe we're being joined by an American guy, who overheard us speaking English, and obviously is in dire need for company. Me and Luana then pay and go for another walk, to a very nice viewpoint of the city's bridge, that connects the island with the mainland. I then rush back to my hotel to see Feyenoord play for the Europa League, and they manage to get another win, leaving me in excitement. I get to bed early as tomorrow another part of my trip will start.

<u>Brazil - Garopaba, Santa Catarina</u>

Today my friends Fernanda, Tete and Téo, will pick me up at my hotel and together we will go to the beach town of Garopaba, where Tete's family has a vacation home and where we will spend over a week together. My friends have left their homes at a crazy hour in the morning and arrive at lunch time in the city of Floripa. Here we first have lunch together in a nearby restaurant, and we then go south for the one to two-hour drive. The clouds on our way aren't very promising for a sunny day, but in the car the sun is shining as we talk, laugh and sing our way south. It's been seven months since I had left from Passo Fundo, so I have quite some stories to share, even though most of them are already shared over the digital highway. From the main highway we take the exit to the coast and through some smaller roads we reach the cute little town. After dropping off our luggage our first stop is the supermarket, where we buy the stuff we need, and even get some acai. When all is stored in the nice home we head to the main beach of Garopaba for the first time and get our first swim in the freezing water. At night we have dinner together and then sleep. I've gotten a wonderful room for our stay here, and things can't be better.

Garopaba is home of one of the surf brands from Brazil, Mormaii. Besides the factory there's also a cafe here with a big store, and outlet. As I need some proper swimming gear instead of the five euro one I'm using now, in the morning me and Téo head down to the store, and get me some colourful shorts, and a shirt. Now I'm beach ready, and so is the sun, shining in a cloudless sky. We head to the main beach once more, and from there me and Téo walk to the beach past the cliffs. Here there's beautiful sand dunes, and we climb some of them to get a nice view. The grass is pointy and our bare feet can't really stand a long hike here, so we head back to the girls who are sunbathing and sleeping in their chairs. We take a lunch at a buffet restaurant nearby, and then chill a bit at the home. In the afternoon we head out to another beach, Silveira. Here we sit ourselves down in the sand, and they soon have to let me go into the ocean, where I spend a lot of time playing with the strong waves. The water is much better today and I can't seem to get enough of it. Swimming makes me hungry, so a perfect ending of the day happens in Mormaii's Surf Bar, with a big bowl of acai with granola and banana. We chill here for a bit, and continue doing so at the house, before we walk to a restaurant to eat Brazilian pancakes for dinner. These pancakes taste slightly the same as the Dutch ones, but here they are wrapped around a normal plate of food, meaning my chicken with vegetables is hidden inside a pancake. It takes a while before my mind is understanding what's happening, but I'm really eating a pancake with warm chicken. After dinner we walk back to the house, and then by car to a bar where we meet Tete's cousin Rafa, and a bunch of their friends. The live band doesn't make us stick around, and as soon as we've finished our one drink, we're headed out again. We head home and all fall asleep soon after.

Surfing hadn't been high on my to-do-list, and I had never done it, or even considered doing it. Neither on this trip, or before. Today's the day however my opinion on surfing changes and I will be laying on a board for the first time in my life. We take it very easy in the morning, having a late lunch. Around noon we take the car and drive to a beach a little bit further away, Ferrugem. Here we unload the board, chairs and stuff from the car, and walk to the lovely beach. It's situated in a little bay, and just behind a small line of dunes, there's the hippie village. It's not busy here today, and we soon find a spot to lay down. At this moment I don't think of going into the water with a board yet, and me and Téo first head to the rock formations that is splitting this shore in two, making it two beaches. Here we climb the rocks, and head to a top, which gives a nice view over the beaches. The water has a perfect colour of green and blue, and now I really want to go in there. We first take some photos and then we walk back to our spot. Here I take the board and take it into the water, into the strong current of waves. I have no clue what to do, or how to surf, but I try to look at other people doing it, without getting close to them. Téo also gives me some tips, even though he doesn't really know how to surf either. Balancing on the board laying down is already a big challenge for me, and the first times I keep waving my arms and legs in order to not fall off. I manage to lay down, and then the next step is paddling, which is easy. My arms are too weak though to go very fast, but I move forward, which is what counts. How to get the right wave remains a mystery to me, even though I make some nice rides on them, laying down. I think I can try to stand up now, but have no clue how to do this. I'm continuously trying to put my knee in front of me, and stand up from this position, but I'm failing miserably. I'm having great fun nevertheless and I love to be out in the ocean, being carried by the waves; it's super fun. I do get tired from it though, and I bring back the board, and get to walk around the beach with my camera taking some photos, and talking to a crazy drunk woman. I get back to my friends, and we all go to the bar at the far end of the beach where we have a drink. We head back home, freshen ourselves up and for dinner we meet up with Rafa and his wife Solange. It's another great night out with friends, and this surf life could be perfectly mine; if only I could surf...

My hopes for learning more the next day are a bit higher, as Rafa, who works for Mormaii, will meet up with us at yet another beach, Praia do Rosa. Earlier than we are used to we have our breakfast, load our car, and drive to Rafa's home, from where we will drive south to the beach in two cars. When we get there we first get to a road that gives us a great lookout over the bay, and the great beach is down, with a big stripe of green separating us. The cars are parked, and we walk down with all our stuff, and then take a left to the more rural part of the beach. To our right there are some bars, which can be packed with parties during the right time of the year. Today's main goal is surfing, and Rafa even borrowed me a special surf shirt, as the board's paraffin scratched my skin open the days before, and this should protect me a bit from that, and from the cold that might happen when staying in the water for too long. There's quite some people laying in the water and they are all awaiting their perfect wave. After some struggles with the waves I also get to their spot, and I lay among these people as if I also know how to do it. I just hope I won't be a wave-blocker for any of these people. Rafa and his friend give me tips and tell me when I have to start paddling for my life when the right wave comes. I fail continuously again, and even though sometimes I really feel I'm being carried by the wave, even for longer times, I just can't manage to stand up. My body's too fat for my arms to push up. I keep trying though and spend the entire day in the water. Even though I keep failing, I'm absolutely loving it, being here, in the great ocean, being part of nature, it brings peace to the mind. The girls also want to use the board though, so I let them have it for a while. Tete manages to stand up at one of her first tries, and she seems to know what to do, without having any prior experience. Rafa's friend's wife had given Tete and Nanda a speed course of surfing in the sand, and it directly pays off. Also Solange is pulling it off, better than Tete, but with more experience. She says it's the result of two months practicing, but it perfectly shows what I once hope to achieve. I have a new dream now, and it can be added to the list. We spend the entire day on this great beach, and when the sun starts setting slowly, we pack our stuff, head to the car, and drive to the more touristy part, where we unfortunately don't find any bar that's open. We head back to the cars and then drive back to Garopaba. To see the sunset, we head to a hill overlooking the town, and here we just see the twilight coming, and the last bit of sun disappearing behind the hills, giving an orange glow to the sky. At dinner time we meet up with our friends again and today we have some good burgers at an American burger restaurant: great food.

It's awfully cold the next day and the wind is blowing very hard. It's more weather for windsurfing than it is for regular surfing, but we're heading out to try anyway. First we head to Rafa's and we install the boards now on the car's roof, so we have a comfier ride to the beaches. Today we head to the beach next to Garopaba's, but at the far end of the dunes. We have the beach to ourselves as the weather really sucks too much. Setting up the parasol is impossible and it's only me heading into the very cold water. It's not doable to grab any wave today, as they don't go in a straight line, and trying doesn't even make sense, but here I still am, in the bumpy ocean with the board. We call it a day pretty soon though, and head back to the house for some chilling. In the evening we go to Tete's favourite burger bar, and all get sick from the food they serve. It was a nice effort going there though.

Tete and Téo are knocked out because of yesterday's food, and stay in all day. Me and Nanda go out for lunch at the beach side's kilo restaurant, and after that take a walk up the hill, to oversee the town from a different perspective. We are also tired and head back pretty soon, and have some hours of chilling at the house before we walk out again for dinner. The other two are still out, so it's just the two of us. We find a decent restaurant and have some good food there.

A dream came to visit me during the night and whispered that I have to create a movie in order to get the ideal job: a surfing traveller, that promotes the brand of Mormaii. The name of the project I make up in the morning, and is called 'Everyone can be a surfer'. I'm not adding the '(except for me)' just yet, as this hopefully is not needed. The idea is to create a movie about a gringo coming to Brazil, not knowing how to surf, and then learning it, step by step. From the moment he'll be able to stand on the board he would travel through Brazil to explore the finest beaches and eventually becoming a better surfer. Ideally it would be with me being that surfer, but if I can direct it's also fine. Today we head out again with the group, and go to the main beach, where I film some silly shots for my movie. For lunch we get to our favourite kilo restaurant, and dinner is later that night consumed near the video store, where we're renting movies to see at night.

Rafa and Solange join us the next day again when we go to Rosa. Today we bring wetsuits, as the weather is letting us down again. Me and Tete are heading in as soon as we get there, and even though the waves aren't very good, Tete manages to stand again, leaving me scratching my head. It's a matter of talent, I think, or it's just because I'm stupid. I keep trying for some hours, even when Tete is long back on the beach, and I only get out because my friends signal me they are leaving for lunch. I quickly get out and join them to a restaurant in the little town of Rosa. Our stomachs are filled when we leave with the cars to checkout Silveira, and see the sunset from there. At Silveira there's a famous surf spot near the rocks, called Mike Tyson: the waves come at you right away with fierce power, punching you like the name giver. We observe some surfers on the low waves there, and walk over the grass, waving the Brazilian flag. In the evening we eat at a temaki restaurant.

After yet another lazy morning, we head to Silveira in the morning. Here me and Téo finally go to where it is called Mike Tyson, and we paddle, paddle, paddle, at the rhythm of Jason Derulo's 'Wiggle'. We're making some friends here in the water, but the waves aren't really punchy today. There's not much excitement, and we go for lunch and then head to Ferrugem, where also Rafa and his entourage are chilling. Rafa gets in with me and helps me today by pushing the board, giving me a little extra speed. Again I nearly get to stand, but it's another day of failure. I get awfully close, but don't pull it off. Rafa then takes off, and the four of us hang around a little bit more. In the evening we have food and ice-creams for a change. I hit the bed fairly early, as tomorrow I take a bus back to the city of Florianópolis, as my friends will have to return to their homes, and Téo is expected to be at work again tomorrow as well.

Brazil - Florianópolis, Santa Catarina

It's very early today as I have to catch the darn bus. My friends bring me to the bus station, and together we wait there for it to arrive. It's been a blessed week, with amazing friends once more. The bus takes about 2.5 hours to get back to the centre of Florianópolis, where I've booked a hotel nearby a shopping mall. I'm a real mall person now, and love to hang out here... It's kind of okay to be next to one, but it's not really a necessity. I have pizza at night, and stroll along the boulevard, thinking of where to go next. I'm considering renting a car and finally see something of the European (mainly German) influences in this state of Brazil. I get online, and look for options, do some research, and make some decisions, also based on my quick browse on couchsurfing, and get surprisingly fast accepted to stay at someone's home in the centre of German Brazil: Blumenau.

Brazil - Blumenau, Santa Catarina

I had not expected to get a response on couchsurfing so fast, as most of the times I had written to Brazilians the answer took forever, or, in most cases, never came. The only thing I need to get moving is a car, and my police friend helps me allocate a good rental company, and I even get a lift to this place near the airport. I believe everyone's getting money for everything, so there must be a reason for this kindness from the police. I negotiate a fair price with the vendors, and for that I get an okayish car. All I need is it to work, so I'm fine with anything. The bigger adventure is to see if I can handle Brazilian traffic, which seems to be fairly easy, as here in Santa Catarina it all seems very calm, and even the roads are well maintained. I take off, saying goodbye to my friend, and drive towards the big bridge, and from there north. It is as easy as I thought it would be, and I have no annoying dent that can distract me from driving now, so it should be all good. I find the right directions, as the gps is very helpful, and when I get to Blumenau it actually feels a bit German. The city is advertised as 'Allemao sem passaporte' (Germany without passport), and this actually makes sense. It also hosts the second largest Oktoberfest in the world, after Munich. Finding my host's apartment is a big pain in the ass though, as there's no signs indicating where to enter. I finally manage to find it though, and meet Roseli, who's just chilling at the pool. Even though there's the language barrier, we seem to understand what we're all saying, and she's a very laidback person. Later we bring my stuff to the guestroom, and we head out to have tremendously delicious sushi.

Roseli works as a hairdresser, and leaves at a crazy early time, leaving me behind in my luxury life, in her nice apartment. I head out quite early myself, trying to make as much of my days with a car as possible. I first drive to the town of Pomerode, where every school teaches children German as second language. I get through the town's gate, which has a German tint over it, but the rest of the village I find totally uninteresting. I get away as soon as possible, and hit the coast, as I plan to visit some of the beaches at the Ilha de São Francisco do Sul, a bit north, towards Joinville. I go all north on the island, until the road seems to end. Here I visit 'Praia do Forte', and park the car in order to walk to the beach. The beach isn't too much, but the view to the other side of the bay is pretty nice. From the beach I have a good view of the military base that is situated here at the fort, and when I get back to the car, I drive up to the gate, as it seems you can enter so you can drive to the top, where there's a viewpoint. I have to pay a little entrance fee and can then take the small road up. There are quite some young soldiers working here. At the top there's a bunker with some bigger cannons. Quite impressive for a country that never went to war. I absorb the view and head down again, just in time, as there's a big group of children walking up, disturbing the sound of silence. I follow the long road along the coast, along a very small beach, with fancy houses along all the way to some kind of centre. I make one stop to photograph the ground owls that are here too, and then continue into town, and from there to two other beaches. Here I meet some local school kids and they take me for a small walk over the cliffs, treating me like a very old man. Which I just might be. Around the cliff I see the small bayed beach, and in the water now many surfers. The waves seem to be good, for as far I can tell. I walk back to the other beach, leave the rocks, and then walk around a bit there. All in all, these aren't my favourite beaches, but they could be nice to hang out on with friends. I now head back to the island's town, and have a late lunch here, and then speed back to Blumenau, to be in time for dinner with my host.

In the morning I head out on my second beach expedition, and this time I head for the northern part of the island of Florianópolis. I first drive back east to the coast, and then over the main highway south, towards the island, only separated by one bridge. After crossing this junction, I head north, where I drive into the posh town of Jurerê, where I visit the beaches, before heading more east to Canasvieiras. Here I visit Ponta das Canas, Lagoinha Norte (which I probably liked most of all northern beaches), and Praia Brava. From there I drive south again, and then to the eastern part of the island, through the seemingly ugly town of Ingleses, where there's tourist hotels everywhere. It's a huge area of concrete, and deep behind there's the beach with the same name, which isn't that pretty, and a bit more south is Santinho, which is also very wide, and seems almost like an artificial beach. Out of all places so far the Ingleses area is the least appealing to me. I get back to the main road and drive south, towards the island's biggest beach, Moçambique. It takes a while before I finally find an entrance to this beach, as it's right behind a big forest, which is a protected area. I drive a little bit over a forest road and then park in the dunes. It's an openly wide coast here, with a beach that mostly reminds me of a Dutch one, especially with the sand dunes. The sand strip is much smaller though, and there's no Germans digging holes. I sit down for a while and let the wind blow up my three hairs. I head back to the car and drive further south, to Barra da Lagoa. This beach isn't too pretty either (it's the ending of Moçambique with a lot more structures), and I make a quick stop at the TAMAR project, where they, like in Noronha, help sea turtles. From here I get over the hill, with a great view over the island's lake, to Mole beach, which is recommended for its surfing, and has all facilities for it. It's more like a hippie atmosphere here, with some street vendors at the entrances, and a lot of surf people. The wind's too strong however today, and there are no good waves. Only some wind and kite surfers are headed into the water. I've seen enough of this nice beach, and drive to today's final beach, Joaquina. Here it's packed with surfers, and at the very left it seems to be a perfect spot to learn how to surf: two rocks break bigger waves into faster smaller ones, and seem to launch the surf class practising there. With my eyes closed this could be me... I take some photos, walk back to the car, stop at a big sand dune on my way back to Lagoa, where I have some acai, and then start the long drive back to Blumenau. I of course exactly end up in rush hour and it takes forever to cross the bridge and get to the highway. It's late when I get back 'home', and food is picked up from across the street.

Brazil - Canasvieiras, Santa Catarina

The weather is horrible when I wake up, with the rain falling down noisily. This is not exactly a good day for going to the beach again. I stay in in the morning and in the afternoon, when the rain's stopped, I head out to check out the city of Balneário Camboriú, and then the peninsula of Porto Belo and Bombinhas, and I will sleep in the Floripa proximity in order to get out early to see the parts of the island the next morning. I have passed Balneário on all my trips north of Floripa, and have seen the city's skyline laying as an ugly grey monster blocking the view of the sea. Today I head in, and it's monstrous indeed, even though the weather has a big influence today. Maybe sun rays would brighten this place up, but while driving through the overcrowded streets, looking up the tall skyscrapers, I can't find too much beauty. I drive along the boulevard, seeing many tourists, expensive cars, fancy restaurants, and I can see parties are probably extravagant here, but beach life's a thug. I head to a hill overlooking the city and the beach, and overseeing it all. There's still rain drizzling and there are thick dark clouds hanging over the entire bay with its high buildings. I've got to get out this place, and cross the hill where I find a smaller community, with low buildings, and a more peaceful appearance. Here I have lunch, and then head out to the highway again, aiming for the Porto Belo exit. When I'm at the toll gate I ask the helpful lady, and she tells me I've missed it, and I could make a turn, pay again, and then take it, or go more south, into a village called Tijucas, and then north over smaller roads. This last option sounds like an adventure and I head there, and with the help of my phone's gps, I find the small road going north. Only problem is that there a sign saying the road's closed due to road constructions... I see another car enter the road, and if he can do it, I can do it. He's going much faster on this bumpy road, so I lose sight of it pretty soon. There's no construction yet, but this starts just after I cross the river's bridge. It's not inaccessible, it's just one-way traffic, and it probably said 'blocked' to avoid a mass of cars here. I'm greeted by the workers and I happily wave back. I now soon enter the town of Porto Belo, and from here I have a great view of the other skyscraper town, Itapema. I walk around a bit, and sit on a bench enjoying the view and the sun that's finally making her appearance of the day. I then drive to Bombinhas and visit the beaches here, none of them impressing me too much. No beauty, no reason, and I decide to continue to the island of Florianópolis where I have booked a hotel for the night at the town of Canasvieiras. At tonight's dinner at a sushi restaurant, which took forever to find, in Jureré I complain about the weather to the staff, and they all seem to agree with me.

<u>Brazil - Blumenau, Santa Catarina</u>

The complaints might be overheard by the weather gods, as the next day there's no rain, and only sun. A perfect day to explore the southern part of the island of Florianópolis. I take breakfast before 8am, and then get in the car and head south. My first stops are the beaches of Mole and Galheta. I climb the dunes and overlook both, and then the big rocks separating the two beaches. From here I have a perfect view over the surfers at the Mole part of the ocean, who are there in big numbers. It's interesting how some climb the rocks, jump off at the far end, and quickly paddle to saver haven, just avoiding the huge waves smacking on the rocks. If you're squeezed, you'll probably die or end up in the hospital. I drive more south to Joaquina, and then visit Campeche's wide beach, and then more south to Morro da Pedras, which is quite nice. Then to Matadeiro, which is a bit hidden behind a river, and I have to park my car in an area where there's a lot of car theft, so I am told. I eventually get to talk to a local and she offers to watch over my car if I park it in front of her house, as she had confirmed these theft rumours. I only walk to the hill separating Matadeiro from the little town, and from there get a good idea of what the beach is like, and it's not too tempting to walk all the way. I get my car and head to the last beach on the southeast that I can drive to: Acores, near the community of Pântano do Sul. Here the sea is very calm, and there's no waves, at all. It's like a lake, and it's amazing. The sand's also white, and there's fisherman's boat in different colours laying to rest. It's an oasis of tranquillity here, and I just sit down in the powdery sand, and let my ears, nose and eyes suck it all in. When all is processed in my mind, I drive as south as I can to Solidão beach, but this is not much. I head back north, take a left at Campeche and head to the western part to see how far south I can go there. Here is a chain of small communities, villages, and beaches aren't existent, except for some one metre pieces of sand. I drive until the end of the road, and then I have to turn, as there's no more road going south. I head back to this one metre beach I saw, park my car, and sit for a bit on a bench. I get to talk to three tourists, who I had seen being dropped off by a taxi just before, and one of them even lives in Maastricht, in my home country, even though she's Bulgarian. They share some of their french fries with me, and I offer them a ride back to civilisation. I take them until the road splits to downtown Floripa and Lagoa, and as I head back to Blumenau, and they are on their way to their hostel in Lagoa, I leave them at a bus terminal from where they will take public transport for the rest of their journey. I then slowly cruise back to Roseli's apartment, where my room is awaiting me.

Some days doing absolutely nothing are the best of days, and after all this road tripping, I decide to give my car, and mostly myself, a day of nothing. While my host's working, I'm just chilling and doing nothing, except for running some errands. I also arrange a hotel at Joaquina, for two reasons: to treat myself on some surfing lessons on my birthday tomorrow, and to thank my host for all she's done for me, and taking her out on a well-deserved beach trip.

Brazil - Joaquina, Santa Catarina

Thirty-five. I wake up with a new number behind my name, 35. I'm walking the earth for a long time now, and I hope the wandering isn't over soon, and I may add much higher numbers behind my name in the future. Roseli even hands me a gift, a nice cap, which is extremely sweet. We then take off for a 'weekend' trip to Joaquina, where we arrive in the early afternoon. We quickly check into the hotel and get to our rooms. I'm getting an upgrade, because they see it's my birthday, hooray. There's a surf class starting in an hour, and tomorrow there's none, so it is the only chance I have. I sign up for it, pay the fee, which is a great birthday gift from my sister, and then get some acai to be full of energy for the 1.5 hours in the ocean. I get a big wetsuit, showing off my big acai belly, and I'm joined by two Finnish girls. We first go for some dry exercises, and situate ourselves in the middle of the beach crowd. Everyone's looking on how we first loosen our muscles, and then are taught how to stand up on the board. I don't know why, but all those days I've been laying in the water, I had always tried to put my knee down first, and from such a position stand up. As it turns out, I was horribly wrong. What I learn now makes more sense, and I'm dying to try it out in the water. We head out, and the first tries are with help of the instructor, but soon he's only giving attention to the girls, and sometimes shouting at me. The board is much bigger than the ones I had used before, and it's more stable in the water. On my third try I already pull it off, and I'm standing on the board, and riding the wave: yes, yes, yes, finally! The adrenaline's pumping through my body and I'm running back into the ocean to try again. Unfortunately it's not that now I have pulled it off once, it's a guarantee all other tries will be successful too. I'm falling a lot of times, but those few times I manage to stand up gives me some things I need: hope, faith, confidence. For over an hour I'm having the best of fun, and this surf lesson is the best birthday gift I could have gotten. Roseli in the meantime is manoeuvring through the crowds and taking photos of all my tries. I had given her a quick lesson on how to use my camera, and she has taken at least one photo with me standing, so the proof's there. The instructor has to kick me out of the water, as I really don't want to leave. He manages to get me out though, and I saunter back to the surf school. I'm immediately asking if there's no lesson tomorrow, and he confirms what was already answered before: nothing will happen tomorrow. I take a shower, put some clothes on, and together with Roseli I drive to Lagoa, to do some shopping, then sushi for dinner, and the evening's ended with Mexican fruit ice cream. We head back to the hotel, and I fall asleep after reading the hundreds of messages I've received today. I'm far, but not forgotten.

Brazil - Blumenau, Santa Catarina

The day after my birthday we spend the morning observing the
surfers at Joaquina, from the rocks at the side, taking many photos.
We continue taking photos in the big dunes behind Joaquina, making
crazy jumps and poses. Then I drive the car back to Blumenau, where
we arrive in the evening. I'm having pizza, as my friend heads out to
have a friends' night out.

<u>Brazil - Florianópolis, Santa Catarina</u>

I book the Ibis hotel in Floripa again for my last two nights in Florianópolis, as after that I will fly back to Rio de Janeiro. I've said goodbye to my fantastic host the evening before, and after a self-prepared lunch I pack my stuff and drive through the rain back to the city of Floripa. I do my check in at the hotel, and then chill for the rest of the night.

I'm having my haircut the next day, and the rest of the day I just drive around a bit, and hang out in the Beira Mar shopping area. In the evening I meet my previous couchsurfing host's friend Daiana, who lives in Campeche. We have dinner together in Lagoa, and then I drive back to my hotel.

Brazil - Rio de Janeiro, Rio de Janeiro

I have to return my travel companion today at the rental company, which is close to the airport. My flight's in the late afternoon, and I spend the day being lazy and not doing too much. I've booked a room in Sonho do Papagaio, which is a bed & breakfast in Santa Teresa, a former villa neighbourhood, close to the infamous Lapa district. Before I arrive there I have turned my car in, and taken the two-hour flight to Rio. I take a taxi to my accommodation. It's quite hard to find the place, but my driver finally manages to find it, and I ring the bell of the big house hidden behind the trees, and laying even higher than we're standing now. A guy walks down, opens the door and carries my big bag up the stairs. When we arrive in the house my tongue is hanging under my flip flops as I'm exhausted. The house is amazing, with a great decoration, and I'm being welcomed like a king. I'm walked to my room, which is another stair up, and it's very spacious. Only downside is that there's a shared bathroom and toilet. I put away my stuff, and head down to talk to the friendly guy, and his wife. His name's Fabio, hers Angela, and they run this house, that is owned by a wealthy Italian. They've just recently started renting out rooms; before that it was mainly used for parties and ceremonies. I'm getting some instructions about how it all works here, and also how I can get in at night, without having to wake them. I get a key of the gate, and the front door will be open. When I've absorbed all the information, I head out to meet my dear friend Jessica, whom I met at the Flamengo match back in April. We have agreed to meet at the Arches of Lapa, but as her phone is not working on the streets, it might be slightly difficult to meet each other. I head out and walk through the empty streets of Santa Teresa, take the stairs down, and then into Lapa. These streets are quite dodgy, and maybe not too safe. In Lapa I directly walk to the Arches, which are close. Here I am for some minutes before my friend with the golden locks and brightest smile gracefully walks to me, her long dress flaunting. It is as if there's no seven months in between our first meeting and now, and we soon are laughing tears again. We sit down in an organic restaurant, where I get my daily dose of acai, and some delicious fruit juice. We then take a walk through the streets, to the Arches again, and then to the street corner of her home where we say goodbye. I then head back up the hills of Santa Teresa, leaving me completely breathless by the time I finally get to the house. I'm so sweaty that I take the coldest possible shower, and pass out as soon as I hit the bed, soon entering the world of dreams.

The house interior is as beautiful during the day as it is at night, and I'm having a perfect breakfast in the big living room. There's all kinds of fresh food and fruits, and it's all very tasty. This is beyond what I could have dreamt of, and I feel like royalty. I then talk with Fabio about extending my stay, and trying to get a better price, as I can't afford the same room longer. He offers me a room a bit under the house, with private bathroom, and after a short inspection I decide to take it. There's only one extra hurdle, and that is that the entire house is rented out for Saturday night, because there will be a wedding tomorrow, and most guests will sleep here. He offers me to sleep on the couch, for free, and this makes me accept the deal. The couch also looks comfortable enough. I get my bags from the upstairs room, and bring them downstairs, as I can sleep one night in the bed downstairs, before I move to the couch. In the afternoon I head out to meet other Flamengo friends, Dado and Alex. They are having after work drinks in the (business) centre, and I walk there in about thirty minutes. I see their crazy faces in a bar where they have a table with nothing but beers on it. They've been going on for a while now, it seems. There's a third friend of them, also Flamenguista, and we catch up about life, about football, about Flamengo. I'm their mascot and they would love to see me in the stadium all the time, so they can finally win the championship again. We all laugh about it. Rain ruins the open terrace, and everyone needs to move their tables under the canopy. All tables are now super close to each other, and we soon have laughs with the neighbours too. The drinking ends when they seem to be too drunk to walk, and with big smiles we split our ways again. It's dark now, and the streets are a tad dodgy. I've agreed to meet up with my friend, and host in Brasilia, Renata and her boyfriend Hélio, who are here on a weekend trip. They are planning to go with Renata's cousin to a restaurant in the Flamengo neighbourhood, which is not too far. I'm grabbing the metro there, and then walk to the address she's given me. I'm earlier than my friends, and decide to ring the doorbell. A guy working in the apartment block's lobby ask me for who I'm here, and I tell him the house number. He heads off to make some phone calls, but while he's doing that Renata tells me I'm not supposed to go there, as her cousin's sick, and they won't be coming. I get the name of the restaurant and walk there. It's packed, and there are no free tables, yet. I give my name and then wait until I'm called for seating. I get a nice table in the overcrowded, thus popular, establishment. Here I wait for my friends to arrive, and the three of us have a very nice dinner. Then they ask me to join them to a party on the other side of town, in Jardim Botânico, and after some first doubts I decide to join them. It's quite a taxi drive there, and it brings us through streets I had never seen before. We get to the party called Bagunca, and I can buy my ticket at the entrance. An expensive ticket, so the party better be good. It's pretty packed when we enter, and there's a live band playing funky music. We explore the venue, which is great, with coloured lights shining on the big palm trees, giving it all a surrealistic feeling. We then hit the dance floor, where I don't move, just bounce a bit from left to right, right to left, just enough to make it look like I'm dancing. My friends do know the moves, as everyone else here. The music gets catchier the later it gets, and the people crazier, due to the huge amounts of alcohol. Vodka with energy drinks seems to be popular here too. It's nice to see how people are changing over time due to the use of alcohol, and only looking at this is already giving me a great night out. The music is the cake's cherry, and even I get more loose at the end of the evening, probably because of all the litres of water I drank that is now bulging through my body. It's late when we finally head out, and there's a long battle for taxis happening outside. There's no rules, everyone for themselves, and we soon reckon we won't get one here, so we head down the road, and manage to stop one on its way to the venue's parking. The taxi drops my friends off at Copacabana, and then drives me to Santa Teresa. I climb the stairs, and get down to my room to sleep deeply.

Even though Fabio had told me there'll be a wedding today, I have no clue what to expect. From what I've been hearing while lying in bed, there's quite some people arriving, but I can't get my imagination to bend around it. I figure out I've already missed breakfast when I take my shower and get my clothes on to head out. I silently walk up the stairs and as soon as I stick my head out over the floor I see that the wedding ceremony is going on and the bride and groom are standing in front of a table to give each other their vows. I stand here frozen like a deer captured in a car's front lights, until Fabio passes, sees me, and gestures me to come. I feel like an intruder, and tell this to my host, who's immediately dismissing all these kinds of thoughts. I'm being placed at a stylish little table at the back of the big balcony, with a table full of the best foods once again.

I'm looking out at the last rows of chairs of the guest, and shyly wave to them, making a gesture to excuses myself for being here. Some of the children from now on have more attention for me, than for the ceremony, and I try to look as much to my plate as possible, hoping to let their attention slip away. I overhear them talking and it's mostly in Spanish, as it's guy from Argentina marrying a woman from Brazil. It's all beautiful words from what I understand, and at times I feel the goose bumps over my body, especially when they finally say 'yes', and the people I do see are clapping and crying. Now some guests come to me and talk with me too, and I get to speak to a father and son, who came all the way from Spain for this wedding, and the cousin of the bride, who's from Santa Catarina. She's quite funny, but also a bit intimidating, which I don't know how to handle well. Then I'm introduced to the newlyweds, and I congratulate them, and excuse myself for intruding their wedding. They are lovely, and apologise back for disturbing my stay in Rio. For me this is the other way around, and we play the apology game back and forth until we all can't stop laughing. I'm now offered drinks and food, and get totally invited to this wedding. Did I just crash a wedding? Wait... I talk with all the people, and also the photographers, who are incredibly impressed by my footage of the mating jaguars. When the entire crew goes out for sightseeing, I also hit the road, as I've been invited for another visit to the Maracanã by my good friend Ingred. I walk the twenty minutes to the metro, and then hop in to go north to visit my friend who I had met in the group of guides at the Cristo monument back in April. I get out, walk to the stadium, notify the security of my arrival, who then call my friend, and I can walk past them with no problems. It's great to see my friend again, and even though we had kept in touch through WhatsApp, we have a lot of things to talk about again. She gives me a tour through the stadium, introducing me to all her co-workers when we pass them by. After the great tour, I get to talk with her friend Cínthia about the Vasco-Flamengo rivalry, her being a Vasco fanatic, and the only thing I've been taught so far by my Flamengo friend is that this team always comes second: sempre vice. We have a good laugh about it. As their work continues I decide to visit the same shopping mall I had visited with one of the other 'guides', Juliana, who had helped me with a Flamengo ticket back in April, and with whom I ate delicious acai here. I easily get to its metro station and get swallowed by the crowds there. Here I'm for sure the only gringo, and more than once I get waved at by little children, or winked at by very old women. I find my acai, sit down to eat it, and after that get to the Flamengo fan store, where there's salespeople all over me, getting me to try on all kinds of stuff. It's fun, but not worth the money. I can't believe how ordinary people can pay these prices, but I soon realise they can't, and this is why the fake shirt business is so big here. I take the metro back to the Cinelândia stop and from there walk back to Lapa, where there's a big stage built up at the Arches with a band playing live music. I spend some time listening between the drunk, the crazy, and the insane. After this I continue back to my room, take a shower to get the day's sweat off, and then walk back to Lapa to find a place to eat, and I get myself a table in a small sushi restaurant, where I eat deliciously. I feel like going to party again, and I ask Renata where she is, and they apparently are in some pizza place nearby where there's a band playing the smooth rhythms of samba. This music fits my dance style perfectly, of course.... I head in, meet my friends, and eventually get dragged to the dance floor, where I conquer all women's hearts by my great moves. This means that I'm mainly laughed at. We leave late, saying goodbye for now, and I head back uphill to sleep on the couch.

The sleep wasn't that bad, and when I finally wake up, or get myself dragged from under the sheets, all the wedding guests have already left the building. I can directly reclaim my room, and then sit myself down for another delicious breakfast. In the afternoon I head out, as me and Ingred have bought tickets for today's match of her favourite team, Fluminense. They have to play the notorious Corinthians from São Paulo, and in the metro I see many fans of this club, and almost none of the home team. The metro's packed, and Ingred nervously messages me that I should hurry, as there's an entire family waiting for my arrival. I walk as fast as possible and then see them already behind the fences. I enter, and get introduced to them all. It's all Bruna's (Ingred's best friend) family, and they have a passion for the 'tricolores' running through their veins. We sit down on the long side of the stadium, near the away section, which is packed and loud. The crowd here is mixed, but mainly has Fluminense fans. The stadium however stays very empty throughout the fantastic match, which is won by the Rio team with 5-2, making everyone jump for joy. One guy behind us is totally going mental; he was taunting the away section before, and now he's like a mad man, screaming, yelling, running back and forth. For us it's a funny sight, but fans for the opposing team don't seem to appreciate it too much. After the match our ways part again, and I head back to my home, where I can recover from the late party nights, and the intensity of today's match. I only head out for dinner at night, and the rest of the time I just chill.

Social media isn't that bad, as is proven today. My very good friend Alan from Amsterdam had posted a check-in at a place in Rio de Janeiro yesterday, and I immediately reached out to say hi, and see if we can meet up. I head to Ipanema in the late morning to have lunch with him, and where we continue our talk as if they've never ended. This is what friendship is: take off as if there's no time in between, as it's been awhile since I last saw him. After the lunch we walk to the beach to find his co-worker, as he's here on a semi business trip. His co-worker's started an organisation many years ago that helps Dutch people in foreign prisons, and Alan's been doing work for them for many years now. After some time, we do find his friend/colleague, and we talk shortly. I then leave them sunbathing to say bye to my other friends, Renata and Hélio, who will fly back to their homes today. After a long stroll over Ipanema beach, and then Copacabana beach, I head to their friend's apartment to say bye. I join them in the taxi to the city's central airport, and there we say goodbye. It was a great surprise they were in Rio at the same time as me, and it was even better to catch up with them, and spend time together. The same taxi driver then drops me off back in Santa Teresa, where I get ready to go back to Ipanema, to have sushi with Alan and Rachel. Their daily sushi getaway is closed unfortunately, so we end up at a tapas restaurant in Copacabana, where we eat, talk, laugh, thus have a great evening. I take a cab back to my home after midnight, satisfied from the food I fall asleep soon.

I hang around the house most of the next day, talking to my friends Fabio and Angela. Fabio shows me a tree full of bats, and it's amazing how they sleep in the sunlight. In the afternoon an awkward photo shoot happens in the house next door, and Fabio and me have a good laugh about it. In the evening I head out for dinner, and directly head back after. I'm loving these empty days.

I take it slow the next day, and have my breakfast around lunch time. I then head out to finally see the famous stairs of Lapa, and walk them to the top. It's one of the iconic images of Rio, but I don't like these stairs too much. From the top I head back to the Arches, and have an acai at my favourite natural food place, to which Jessica had introduced me days before. After this I head back home. At the top of the house property is a fantastic pool, which I hadn't been enjoying until today. I take my bathing suit and head there for a perfect afternoon. As the sun's burning hot, the water is a splendid distraction from it. In the late afternoon I head out again, meet some friends near the Cinelândia metro station, and then head out for sushi by myself in my favourite sushi bar in Lapa.

I'm becoming some local here in Rio, with so many different people I know. Real Dutch locals though are Diana and Gerard, who I've met in the Pantanal, and have been living in the Copacabana area now for some years already. I envy them for being abroad for such a long time, as before Brazil they have been in Qatar for many years. After a very lazy day today I meet up with them in a sushi restaurant near their home. The sushi boat we get here is excellent, and long after I'm satisfied I continue taking for what has been served. We talk about a wide variety of options, and tell them Fabio thought of me to run the home for a while, when he gets back to Minas Gerais. They are thinking about a career change as well, so we brainstorm a bit about possible bed and breakfast ideas, which is incredibly inspiring to do. After a long night of talking I take a taxi back to the house.

December fifth is the best family day of the year for me that I usually celebrate with my parents and sister. Today is the first year I can't be there, so when we found out we already thought of postponing the traditionally Dutch celebration of 'Sinterklaas' to a moment when I get back. My sister Aline however came up with the bright idea to celebrate it with webcams, over FaceTime. It's a great solution to celebrate even though there's this big distance. Traditionally we buy each other some three to five gifts per person and every gift is accompanied by a rhyme, in which we anonymously deliver a message to the receiver. This can be a hymn, or a piece of criticism. We've agreed to write one rhyme for every participant, meaning I have to write three. I write four though, as I have a continual prank with my mom about collecting stamps. My mom has also written four, as she yearly creates a world class masterpiece: one rhyme covering normally more than ten pages giving an overview of the family's year. It's brilliancy, and also this year she's done it again. We get the connection to work perfectly and emotionally I hear my dad read my mom's fantastic year rhyme first. Then we take turns, reading out the given rhyme, and unwrapping the gifts. Normally this evening takes about five hours, today we're unfortunately done in 1.5. It's amazing though how the technique brings us together and we can celebrate this night together. I can't taste my mom's 'speculaas' (a typical Dutch ginger cookie filled with anise), and not drink the hot chocolate, but this afternoon brings a tremendous joy to my heart. After disconnection with my parent's home I walk to Lapa, strolling around, reminiscing about the celebration, and then having dinner at a terrace near my sushi bar. At the terrace I get to talk to a couple, and we join tables and talk until deep in the night.

I sleep in the next day, and stay lazy again throughout the morning and afternoon. I get the breakfast as a lunch today, and talk with Angela. It's only at night when I feel it's worth getting out of the home to meet Jessica at my favourite sushi place. My stomach hurts from laughing with her, and I can barely get my food in. After dinner we stroll the streets once more, and walk to the Arches. After sightseeing at this former aqueduct, we sit ourselves down at a bar, and have some drinks until it's bed time again, and I walk her to her street and walk myself up the hill after securing her safe homecoming.

I don't get out until the afternoon once again, and today Jessica will take me to see the sunset at the rocks of Ipanema. We head down there with a taxi and then walk along the boulevard until we reach the rocks. There's a massive crowd on the beach, and a lot of them slowly start occupying the rocks, all to see the sun setting. We find ourselves a place somewhere high up and wait for the sun to do his thing. It starts as a ball of white and yellow, slowly turning into orange, until it becomes nearly red. The sky's changing colours and there's no blue to be seen at the horizon when the sun is nearly hitting it. I'm taking many photos and we heart the sun. Something unexpected happens when the sun finally starts falling behind the horizon, as people massively start clapping. Oh yes, the sun will be very grateful for this gesture... I can't believe people are doing this, but find out this is a tradition. It must have started with some crazy folks who thought the Sun was their god, and lasted for thousands of years, as I can't believe modern people would come up with this. I'm the only one thinking like this as all others are excitedly putting their hands together, continuously creating a wave of sound. Jessica hasn't put her hands together either, and fortunately she laughs about it as much as I do. Great minds think alike. We now head back to the boulevard and then walk to the sushi restaurant Alan had wanted to take me to but it was closed. Now it's open and we get a table to eat Rio's finest sushi so far. Hell yeah. After dinner we walk out to find an ATM as I might need some money for a cab. We finally find one after some serious minutes of walking. Here the machines don't seem to work however. One machine says to have given me the money, but as nothing came out, I'm pretty annoyed. With Jessica's phone I call this bank, and they don't seem to have any solution. Later I will find out the money was 'withdrawn', and directly refunded, but right now I'm pretty pissed off. Jessica knows how to calm me down though and we then stop a taxi to bring us back to Lapa, first to her home to drop her off, then to mine.

In next day's afternoon I meet up with yet another member of the guide's group, and again I meet up at the Maracanã. Kelly's practicing English, so I help her with her practice on our walk to a bar, and then over a drink. Like many other Brazilians I notice what I've seen much more extreme in Japan: people are very afraid to make mistakes, and most of the time they know more than they actually give themselves credit for. I hope to leave her with more confidence and some tips to continue improving. I head back to my home, and in the evening I end up at the Copacabana sushi restaurant once more.

Malls are everywhere in Brazil, and today I spend the afternoon in one in Botafogo. There's a cinema too, and I plan to see a movie. After some walking around, trying on some clothes, not buying them, and a lunch, I buy my tickets, as I plan to see two. Horrible Bosses 2 is the entree, and Interstellar is the main course. Both are subtitled in Portuguese and today there's no Colombian mistakes. The first movie is kind of funny, but the second is just absolutely mind blowing. It leaves me flabbergasted, stunned, amazed. This must be this year's best movie for me, and it's been long since a movie left me like this. I keep sitting gazing at the screen until the cleaners kicked me out, and I then hurry myself in a taxi back to Santa Teresa. I've made a friend in the neighbourhood, Mara, and we shortly meet up; she brings me to a viewpoint which gives a sea of lights. I can't believe how good people are to me, and how friendly they all are. It's a repetitive, but plausible thought, I think. At this moment I sincerely hope all my friendships will last forever.

"Do not go gentle into that good night, Old age should burn and rave at close of day; Rage, rage against the dying of the light." I can't get the beautiful poem of Dylan Thomas out of my mind since yesterday's movie. I had come across it while reading Thomas' work when exploring Bob Dylan's influences, but it now has gotten a way deeper meaning to me. The movie indeed left me with a deep impact. My sight's today is endless, and I stroll around the Carioca area, having a juice at a bar there, and then walk back again, for dinner in the terrace bar I had been before. Back at the house I book a flight to São Paulo, and hotel in the Morumbi area.

Brazil - São Paulo, São Paulo

I tell Fabio and Angela I will be back before my flight back to
Amsterdam and I ask them to keep the downstairs room free for me.
These two people have been so great to me, and even on this last day
Fabio drives me to the airport, without accepting a payment for it. At
the airport I pay a lot of money to use a computer with internet to
see Feyenoord play the away game against Standard Luik, which ends
in another great win. I board the plane and then fly to the economic
heart of the country. I land there late in the evening, and my
couchsurfing friend Samantha picks me up from the airport and
drives us to Brooklin, where we go to a very nice bar, have drinks and
food, and have a great night out. After this I'm delivered to my Ibis
hotel not too far from there, and I get the same standard Ibis room
as everywhere.

My hotel is near two big malls, but far from all other interesting stuff
in São Paulo, it seems. I have my breakfast in the hotel, and then
lunch in a quite nice restaurant in the mall nearby, recommended by
Samantha, who's already been a great help so far. After lunch I go see
a movie in the cinema, and after that I stroll through the bookstore,
and for the first time this trip actually missing a book to read. At
Starbucks I order a chai latte, and this must be my first one in a year.
After tasting it, it's clear I haven't missed it at all, and I will stick to
fresh fruit juices. I have a little dinner then too, and then head back
to the hotel. Connected to the Wi-Fi I now see a Facebook check-in
of my dear friend Cassia and her boyfriend Ismael, the ones who
took me out for this great trip to Chapada dos Veadeiros. They are in
a bar called Delirium, and I get a taxi to take me there. It's great to
meet up with these two great people and we talk and laugh for some
time. They then hit the road again, as they're tired, and I stick around
for a bit before leaving as well, back to the hotel.

I spend another morning in the hotel, enjoying my breakfast and
reaching out to friends. In the afternoon Samantha picks me up for a
lunch at a natural food place, where I eat a salad. A salad, and not
acai, I'm proud of myself. This acai isn't as good for me as I thought
it was, making me gain many kilos since I started this purple diet.
After lunch Sam drives me to the famous Avenida Paulista, from
where I take a giant walk over this overrated street that is well

prepared for Christmas. It's a grey area, and even though it seems to have some nice museums, and important buildings, it's not appealing to me, at all. It's good that I've seen it myself though. Trying to find a taxi to my hotel is harder though, and I have to walk some blocks before finding one. In the evening I have yet another meal in the mall next door, and then sleep early.

Focusing on my next step is again a goal. Christmas is coming up, as is New Year's, and I'm not sure what I want to do. The entire day I spend thinking, and talking to people. By far my best option is to return to Garopaba, and spend this family days of the year with my friend Téo and Tete, and her family in their vacation home. I decide to confirm my arrival there, and just stay a bit flexible in my final arrival time. Having decided on this, I spend some time in the mall, and being lazy most of the day.

Samantha has another afternoon trip planned for today, and she picks me up to see downtown São Paulo. We first head to a market hall, where there's a wide variety of the most delicious food. She has me eat a typical Paulista dish, Pastel de Bacalhau, which is extremely tasty. We stroll through this magical place and even though I'm not a foodie, such a place might convince me into it. If I would drink beer I would probably already be sold, as I also find a place where they sell a special acai beer. From here we walk through the more or less dodgy streets towards the centre, and there see various older buildings, and if it would not have this shady atmosphere, it would be actually very nice. Too bad there's so many crazy people here, and people that probably have no other intention than to rob other people. We head to another mall, that is full of rock and tattoo shops. Some five floors only dedicated to this subculture. It's amazing, even though I don't find much Bob Dylan stuff. We then walk back to the car, which is now a pretty long walk, and we have to hurry a bit, because Sam's (illegal) timer is running out. We make it in time, and then hit the traffic, as São Paulo is a traffic jam the entire day, the entire week, the entire month, the entire year, its entire existence. It must be so frustrating to commute here. Sam again very sweetly drops me off at my hotel, and it's late at night when I head out again, this time to eat some good sushi.

Another one of Sam's great recommendations is where I head for the next day, and is called something like "Batman's Cave" (Beco do Batman). I take a taxi to the street name she's given to me, and with some help of Google the driver manages to drop me off exactly in the middle of this modern city phenomenon. When I step out I immediately notice Sam was not exaggerating. There's graffiti all around me, and all the different brushed walls are amazingly done. On the sidewalks there are many figures of Batman's signal, hence the name. I walk this area back and forth for a long time, and find new details every time. This is the first time the suit called Brazilian's biggest capital seems to fit me, and I start to forget my first negative observations of the city. After a lunch in a very small, but very good, kilo restaurant, I walk through the neighbourhood and visit some art galleries. I end up eating a Mexican ice cream, and get to talk with the staff. The manager offers me a table, and sits with me, and we have some nice talks about this area, about São Paulo, and about Brazil in general. It's also a good moment to give my feet some rest, as these hilly roads aren't ideal for strolling around. I walk a bit more after the energetic ice cream and then call a taxi with an iPhone application. I ask him to bring me to the shopping mall in Jardims, which is amongst the most luxurious in the city. As soon as I walk around I see why, as all the big rich brands are represented here. Informing to prices make me dizzy, and it seems even more than what people have to pay for this in Europe. The best about this mall however is not what is sold in these shops, but what can be seen from the top. The roof offers a stunning view over this endless city of concrete. I spend quite a while here, and it's sad that the clouds block the sun, otherwise the sunset would have been great from up here. No sun, less fun, and I head back to my local mall, where I finally eat the famous São Paulo pizza, which is indeed delicious.

My final full day in this city is again spend with my great friend Samantha. She first picks me up for lunch, which we consume at a lovely sushi bar near her home, and after that we take her two dogs to the big central park, Parque do Ibirapuera. Her dogs are amazing, and there's a big appearance contrast between Mel, the lazy looking sausage dog, and Valentino, the bad ass pit bull. They join us in the little red car and we head into traffic. The car lacks air conditioning, and soon the dogs breathe rapidly and drool. They're cute, and it makes me miss the dog that was once part of my family, and has already passed away many years ago. We park the car at one of the many entrances, and walk in. Dogs are obligated to stay on the leash in most of the areas in the park, but when they can finally go loose, they run and play, like little new born sheep hopping around in the grass. I'm taking some photos of these sweet dogs while we make a big round through the park. I really like this park and I now have forgotten my bad thoughts of São Paulo. This dog walk might last forever, as both dogs as human are showing to be perfect company. We head back to the car when the circle's complete and I'm again dropped off at my hotel. Here I say farewell to my Paulista caretaker and tell her I'm forever thankful.

Brazil - Blumenau, Santa Catarina

It's a hell of a distance from my hotel in Morumbi to the international airport of Guarulhos, and it seems my cab driver, who I had hired a couple of times before, is slightly wrong in his time indication. Even though there's traffic every day, he had thought it would not be this bad at noon. We are stuck in traffic and I have a plane to catch. He brought a friend today, and the three of us fall silent when it seems I'm going to miss my plane. Then suddenly traffic's gone and the driver speeds to the airport, where I actually easily seem to make it. I drop my bag, get through customs and then even have time to sit down in the waiting area. It's only a short flight and in Florianópolis I now know how to walk to the car rental place, where I again have arranged a car. Today I will drive to my friend Roseli, who again has made her guest room available for me. It's just a bit more than a month before my flight back to Amsterdam is due, and I'm seriously considering heading back sooner. I have the feeling I've seen what I've seen, done what I wanted to do, and the spirit to explore new things has faded. This feeling is confirmed by the idea I'm not revisiting an area I've already seen. My drive to Blumenau is also an example of how my ideas for new things have slowly vanished, and also that maybe celebrating family days like Christmas alone isn't really appealing too. Before I go mingle with family business though, I head to my friend, who is still working as hard as always, giving me some time at her apartment to think about my last upcoming month. When I arrive at my friend's apartment, after yet another drive through the pouring Santa Catarina rain, I'm once again heartily welcomed, and some of the negative thoughts about things being repetitive disappear immediately as snow for the sun. We talk again and laugh again, just like before.

When Roseli's gone for work I do some grocery shopping, so her fridge is full again for the next couple of days. I then head off to Vila Germânica, a sight I had not visited last time, but when I arrive I see I have not missed a thing. I leave as soon as I arrive and head to a nearby shopping mall to see a movie. Back home we order sushi and it tastes nearly as good as eating it in the restaurant.

Again I head to a mall after being lazy in the morning, and here I spend some time on a computer, playing silly video games, and talking to some fanatic gamers. It seems ages ago that I was a fanatic as well, and upon seeing them play I feel like doing it again too, but I resist the temptation. Back home I buy some forgotten supplies for my host, and then order pizza once more.

Brazil - Garopaba, Santa Catarina

It's been only two days, but I'm already leaving Blumenau. I leave
with a big smile on my face, as what I thought to have lost, has come
back during these peaceful days: the spirit to travel, to see places, to
meet people, to reconnect with friends. I now head south to my
friend's family home. The road's quiet today, probably given to the
rain. The result of the weather today is I see a thick blanket of white
clouds slowly crawling over the hills, which is truly fascinating. I
continue to Garopaba, and find the house without any problems.
Here I'm welcomed by Téo, his daughter Victoria, Tete, and her
lovely parents, Desiree and Silvano. Desiree speaks French very well,
but my French is non-existent at this very moment. I do understand,
but formulating sentences get all mixed up with Portuguese. I'm
therefore managing in their mother tongue once more.

It seems I've brought bad weather, as it's raining all the time and
there's no way we can have fun beach days now. We spend some
time in bars, and go out for dinner once more.

The next day we have a game day, and we play Monopoly and some
different card games. Tete is owning Victoria and me, and this is to
be heard forever, most likely echoing through the times of the future.
If I would have won, the same probably would have happened. It's
nice to do some board games again though, and we're having good
times. Another good thing happens today as Raymond, another
Dutch friend, who I've worked for the last decade, is coming to
Florianópolis, and we agree to meet up when I get back there.
Téo's friend Gabriel is in town, also spending Christmas here with his
family, and in the afternoon we decide to go on a kayak trip to an
island in front of the coast, where to Silvano will swim. We take the
car to the beach and then our ways split: Silvano goes left and walks
to a point where the distance is closest to the island, and the three of
us walk to a kayak rental office at the beach to the right. Here we rent
the kayak for two hours, and then immediately hit the seemingly calm
ocean. I'm in the back of the kayak and after the first few waves
there's so much water in my seat it isn't possible anymore to get it
out. I don't mind being wet, but we also have to carry this water
every paddle. Beyond the first set of waves suddenly the waves also
become much bigger and it isn't a calm sea anymore. We are peddling

against the waves, and it's not easy at all. In a straight line we head to the small island, in the meantime looking everywhere for Silvano's white hair. He's not to be seen, and I start to worry. The waves have white tops too, and the tide is extremely strong. We then reach the island after more than one hour of paddling, and we manoeuvre our kayak into a small rock bay, where we barely manage to get out. We climb the rocks and stare over the waves hoping to find Tete's father. Nowhere is a swimmer to be spotted and we walk to the far end of the island, passing many birds' nests in order to get a view from all angles. At the nearest shore I see a man standing and I ask Téo if that isn't Silvano, but the idea is put aside as absurd. Now we all worry that something might have happened and we decide to start paddling back. The two hours of rental are also long past now, and I wonder if we will be fined. The waves now are again against us, making it very hard to move at all. Very slowly we get closer to the beach again, and then I see a ship coming towards us. Téo insists we move aside, but I already tell him we're being picked up. Gabriel in the meantime is closer to crying than to smiling, because Téo told him some crazy shark stories. The boat rapidly heads to us, and there's fishermen telling us they've come for us. One by one we are being lifted over the high railing, and then also the kayak is brought in. Now it's a piece of cake coming back, even though the kayak turning in is a disaster, as the guy makes a huge fuss about us being so reckless. Now I see Silvano coming over the beach, running, and it becomes clear he was indeed standing on the beach, and never started his swim, as he made a different agreement with Téo about us picking him up and then starting, instead of meeting at the island. We now laugh about it, and head back home, for a warm shower, as we're all cold and exhausted. The shower makes us feel much better, and in the evening we head out for sushi at the regular temaki bar.

Today it's Christmas eve, and this is the only day they celebrate in Brazil. In the Netherlands Christmas Eve used to be not that big, and we celebrate Christmas Day 1, and Day 2, which are the days after the mentioned evening. The family is preparing a food fest, but first we finally can go to the beach and into the ocean. We go to the town's beach and have some fun in the low and slow waves. None of us manages to stand up, unfortunately. The water's filled with little jellyfish today, and there are more of those than there is water, and it is extremely weird to fall in the water and then get out on the board again and have all these slimy little creatures in your ears and all over your body. It's not the perfect day to stay long, and we soon have lunch at our kilo restaurant. In the afternoon the weather is bothering us once more, but Téo and me keep being at the beach, now joined by Téo's friend Mario, while Tete and Victoria are preparing a huge salmon at the house. Mario and Téo are drinking some kind of strong alcohol, and I'm splashing in the sea with the surfboard. When I get out, Téo's completely wasted, and his eyes are like the ones of a fish: very glassy. It's hilarious to see how he can't keep a grin from his face. Mario still has to drive, but I will be driving Téo's car, as I did during my last visit to Garopaba as well, when Téo's was feeling sick. We all safely arrive back at our house. The table is already prepared and looks lovely. To my surprise there's gifts at the little Christmas tree, and even a package for me. It makes me feel being part of this family today and the given havaianas fit perfectly. Desiree's sister also joins us, and then it's time to attack all the delicious dishes and we eat until we fall silent as our bodies can't process so much food and talk at the same time. It's a perfect evening, it's a perfect dinner. After cleaning up our mess we head to bed for a good night of sleep.

The day after starts with a slow morning, and we hang out around the house. After lunch we head to Ferrugem, where me and Téo climb the unexplored rocks nearby, overviewing the bay this time from the other side. There are a lot of surfers in the water, and as soon as we get back, me and Tete head in, to catch some waves. Again they aren't really made for us, it seems. We don't feel like going in the mass, where probably the better waves are, so we stick to fast crashing small ones near the beach, which also make us crash fast. After the beach we head to the Surf Bar for some fresh juices, and as I can't get enough they leave me behind, and I chill there with my banana shakes. I walk home alone and we then together head out for dinner.

It's my final day in Garopaba today, and I chose Silveira as the beach destination of today. I once more want to take the waves of Mike Tyson, or better its punches. The weather's lovely today and we head out the far end entrance and from there walk our stuff through a small nature area, over a little bridge, and then through to dunes to arrive at the beach. We set up our camp, and I make my own in the water, plunging through the strong waves. They are very good today, but my skill level is way too low to crack them. At times I catch a wave, but it's so high and so fast, that when I try to stand up and fall, the wave is totally demolishing me, and I'm being spun like a piece of cloth in a washing machine. It makes me kind of dizzy, but I'm not giving up just yet, and I keep entering the waves, passing through the wall of its breaks, and ending up in quiet water to try to grab a next one, and a next one, until I finally take a break at the beach. Here I regulate my breathing and get a good rest, before going in again. I keep trying, but keep failing as well, so at one moment it's enough and I head out, and we head back to the house.

Brazil - Campeche, Santa Catarina

I've been offered a place to sleep by my couchsurfing friend's friend, whom I had met briefly on my last visit to Florianópolis, and I'm accepting the offer happily. She lives in a nice spacious apartment in an unfinished complex in Campeche, just south of Lagoa. Before getting there I have to drive from Garopaba, and say goodbye to all these great friends. They have all been great to me, and like many times before there's not enough words to express my gratitude to Téo, Tete, Victoria, Desiree and Silvano. They've made me feel like part of this family, like a brother and like a son. I load my stuff in the car, and head back north, to the urban areas of Florianópolis' island. I arrive in the early afternoon and am welcomed by my friend who's having a day off. We have some lunch together, and I then head out to find a cybercafé to start uploading my photos from the last couple of weeks. After doing this for several hours, including organising some emails, I drive back to Lagoa, where I meet Raymond, who's in a hostel near the town's centre. He directs me to a free parking spot, and we then head out to eat sushi. It's very good seeing him again, and we discuss past and future travels. He might be spending New Year's in Floripa too, and we decide to keep in touch. I head back to my friend's home and find my bed quietly and fall asleep soon after.

Now Raymond's here, I'm organising two nights out, and I've got Tete and Fernanda to join us to two big show events here in Floripa: a concert of David Guetta first, and the day after one of Hardwell. Today I'm picking up tickets for us all, and it's good to have some prospect. I head to a mall where there's an office of the ticket service, as the website isn't working too well. Tickets for men and women often differ in price here in Brazil, and it makes me wonder how about inequality that many women in this country (justly) complain about. It obviously also has an upside. I buy two times four tickets for these two shows, and also buy two tickets for tomorrow's party at P12, a club in fancy Jurerê, where Dutch DJ Chuckie will come and play a set. All in all I spend a small fortune on all these tickets, awaiting the refund from my friends. I also talk to the girls working here and ask them for tips for New Year's eve, but besides one big party in the Pacha, they don't come up with much. I head back to my friend's place and we then go out for sushi at a very good buffet place.

Raymond already went to this club with the name Parador 12, which is the name of the twelfth beach pole, measuring distances along the coast, but is mainly used for coordination, and today will be my first time. In the afternoon I drive from Campeche to Lagoa, where I pick up Raymond at his hostel. He's bringing a Colombian girl, Claudia, he's met in the hostel, and the three of us then go north. We get to Jurerê and drive as far west as we can go, until people are offering us free parking spaces, for which we of course will have to pay. For five reais they will look after my car, but I'm only paying it to prevent them destroying my car instead. We then walk in, show our tickets, and enter the venue. There are several bars inside here, good toilet facilities, a covered area for a DJ, with tables on both sides, and a big outside pool at the far end, close to the few dunes that separate the property from the beach. Here there's a DJ booth and one is already playing some house beats. We get our drinks through a prepaid bracelet system, and then find a spot to enjoy the scenery and the music. The sun is shining, all the people are very relaxed, and the music is getting better and better. I shyly start my dance moves and eventually get sucked into it, throwing every dance move I know. This is mainly based on Dutch rave parties I was a frequent visitor of in my younger years, and now this dance attracts Brazilians to talk with me. Even if they had a doubt I was Brazilian, it is now totally taken away. There's camarotes ("cabins") on both sides, meaning beds to chill at, and we soon get in touch with two girls from a big group from São Paulo to our right. Tita and Natalia are our new friends and we bounce to the beats together. I bounce a little bit too hard, as one of my non-maintained nails crushes deep into the toe next to it, making it bleed like hell. I slowly shuffle to the first aid post and let them band aid me. I can re-enter the party and go crazy again. In the meantime, all the pillows from the beds fly through the air and land in the pool, frustrating the staff, who's picking them all out. The crowd's gone crazy and having the best of times. When the sun's gone, the party moves to the covered area, where also DJ Chuckie makes his appearance. His set is below our expectations however, and what could have been the highlight, isn't. The party now never explodes. It's too soft and too monotone what he's playing now, unfortunately. On this packed dance floor, I however make other new friends and therefore the party's never really dull. When Chuckie stops playing the party's over and we head back to Lagoa, where me and Ray have some wraps for dinner. Exhausted I then head back to Daiana's home and find my bed to finally get some well-deserved sleep.

I wake up by my legs making dance moves, which obviously is a sign to go back to P12 again. I text Ray and he's up for it, so after a lunch I go pick him up again. Claudia's game again too today, and she's joined by her friend Riikka, from Finland. I drive the four of us to Jurerê, park the car, and then we enter once again. It's packed today, and the atmosphere seems to be as good as yesterday. We find our spot again, and Raymond then ascertains that there's a lot of men today, a lot. I look around and confirm his observation. It seems to be gay day. Less women, more men, means less eye candy for us, unfortunately. Our friends from São Paulo fortunately are here once more, and they're even more wasted than the day before. Within minutes of our arrival I get approached by a gym type of guy, asking me where I'm from. As soon as I answer from the Netherlands, he excitedly replies he's from there too, and by the way his jaws are moving I suspect he's on dope. He takes me with him and introduces me to all his friends, also from the Netherlands. I try to have a normal conversation, but it seems to be impossible. They're from the south of my country, their accent is different, and the drugs seem to numb their tongues. I make my conversation and then try to walk away again. My new 'friend' joins me because he wants to meet Raymond too. Ray now too has to undergo the introduction and he's handed a pill in his first handshake. He politely refuses the gift and returns it. I ask them what they do here, and one of them answers they run a small hotel in the south of the island here and that he's been living in Brazil for almost fifteen years now. That is at least one thing I like about him, but when I ask him how he's done it, it becomes a completely vague story, and both Ray and me suspect some drug trafficking, and money laundering. We manage to free ourselves from our new buddies and then join our other, real, friends again. The only one getting upset now is Claudia, as she wanted to have that free pill for her and Riikka to use today. Riikka has never used drugs before, and today she thinks is a perfect opportunity. They start a drug hunt now, leaving me and Ray behind laughing. It should not be too difficult for them, as there's barely people here not using drugs. At times we feel we're the only ones. The party's pretty wild today, but the pillows mainly remain in their places today. When it's dark we all head inside and listen to the okayish set of today's main act, Deepdish. It's again not very booming, but at least already better than yesterday. When the set's over we find Claudia and Riikka, get to our car and drive south. The eyes of the girls are nearly popping out, telling us their mission was a success. We find a pizzeria where we have the finest pizzas, and we have great fun with our dopers. Then we drive back to the hostel, pick up Riikka's stuff and we bring her to the airport, as her plane to Rio leaves in the very early morning. Me and Ray are bit concerned how she will manage, as she's totally high on drugs for the first time in her life, but Claudia ensures us she will manage. We trust her and then drive back to Lagoa, and after dropping them off I continue to Campeche.

Brazil - Lagoa da Conceição, Santa Catarina

My host will receive her family for New Year's, so I have to get out. I'm extremely thankful I could stay so many nights, especially because I wasn't around much. Raymond has a private room in the hostel fortunately and he says there can be an extra mattress placed on the floor. I pack my stuff and then head there. It's the last day of 2014, and we're told that all the roads on the island will turn into huge traffic jams. We are still undecided where to go. As soon as I've unloaded my luggage into the room, we list our opportunities and decide to go with the wind. At a supermarket we buy some snacks and drinks, and then go in the car to Canasvieiras, and then to Jurerê. At Jurerê we first drive to P12 to see what kind of event they have, but the price makes us turn around immediately. At several beach clubs we make a stop, but all the prices are insane. We then park our car in a street full of villas, and decide to take a walk on the beach to see what's going to happen there. People from the hostel will be taken to this beach tonight, as it's said to be a happening. Both me and Ray are dressed in white, as people have suggested us, and we soon see many others in white too. Maybe indeed something will be happening here. Just in front of us four girls unload their vehicle and start carrying their stuff to the beach, and we slowly walk behind them. I consider offering my help, but I'm too shy today. We also reach the beach, see the girls build their camp, and pass them on our way to the far end. Everywhere people are setting up tents, and hanging up plastic roofs, as they will sit here and await midnight. At the end there's P12, and from here we walk back again. We don't have a tent, nor do we have other people we know here. Now we stop at the beach clubs again, and ask for prices and availability. Most is sold out, and when they do have tickets, the prices are sky high. Cafe de La Musique tops the price charts with around 800 euros per person, for a night with unlimited booze and food. It's kind of a lot for someone that only drinks water... We head into a small shopping street and have a seat here. All restaurants are closed, so we head back to our car and sit here eating the snacks we've brought. Then we head out to the beach again, and some two hours before midnight I tell Ray we should go to the tent with the four ladies, but again we're too shy. We're actually discussing on how we can approach them, and finally I find the guts to go. Three of the ladies just left, probably in search for a toilet, as they've been drinking, so there's only one now, which is maybe less intimidating. I leave Ray standing in the sea, take a deep breath and walk up to her. She's extremely friendly, laughs out loud because of my Portuguese, and almost instantly offers me a chair. Me and Nadine chat and talk, and surprisingly connect very well. When the other ladies return and I ask them if me and my friend can stay, upon which they reply they would love us to stay with them. I now gesture Ray to come, and we sit ourselves down in the sand, having great laughs with the girls. Nadine and Michelle are friends, and Michelle's sister Aryane is there together with her friend Evellyn. They all are super fun and nice, and even teach us some more Portuguese. Later other people will come: the more the merrier. When they do come, we introduce ourselves, but there seems to be absolutely no connection between them and the girls. Me and Ray kind of sit in the middle, being the bridge in contact. I try to figure out the relation, but I don't succeed. We keep laughing however, with whoever we talk to, and it's a great spontaneous night. At midnight there's a small countdown between all the tents, but it's not really in step, so when the first start screaming "Feliz Ano Novo!!!", the rest automatically follows. There's no big fireworks here, just some rockets fired from the beach. Behind us though at one of the beach clubs there's a slightly bigger show, that lasts longer as well. We wish everyone the best for 2015, and continue talking with our new friends. Then another group of their friends comes over, and for us it's then time to walk over the beach for a bit and see what's happening in other places here. We walk over the beach, but it's more difficult to make good progress as it's now packed with people, mostly drunk people. We find out way forward though, and then walk into two girls and a guy, with who I immediately start talking to, for some reason. It's Elias, Andreza and Raquel, who are all from the state of São Paulo. It takes a while before we all understand each other, but then they take us for a typical Brazilian tradition: jump the ocean's waves. You have to do this seven times, and only while there's still fireworks in the air. Even though most of the fireworks are long gone, every now and then there's a rocket fired into the air, perfect for our needs. We make the seven jumps, and now are blessed for the upcoming year. Hurray. We continue talking a bit more with our new friends, and I of course exchange details, and then head our own ways again. We get back to the tent, sit a little bit more here, and then say goodbye to our new dear friends. Slowly we walk back to the car and then slowly drive back to Lagoa, where we sleep our first night of 2015.

The Dutch drug dealers in P12 had told us the first day of the year is the most crowded one in the club, so we of course head out there as soon as we've had our lunch. Claudia is also coming again, and I've also persuaded Nanda and Tete to come to this place today, as they should not miss out on the crazy parties here. We hit the club, park the car, get inside, and party hard once more. The São Paulo group is here once more, and Flavio is now their spokesman, and he's the one going crazy with us, and offering us the widest variety of drugs, which we politely refuse. He can't believe how I can go on and on and on, day after day, without the use of drugs and alcohol. Even though my feet are slightly tired, my mind is getting motivated by the beats and kicks of the music, and of all the new people I'm meeting. All the staff now seems to know me, and I talk with them all the time. We're getting famous. Natalia's not here today, but an Asian looking girl, and another friend of hers from São Paulo, have taken her place, even though these two are totally lost in the use of alcohol. The Asian girl is totally passed out, and is a puppet in her friend's hands, while the other girl, who I get to know is Caroline, makes the biggest fall of them all, by slipping over the watery beds, making half a loop, and then landing on her back, while she keeps having a smile on her face. I help her get up, but she insists on laying on the ground a bit more. When she's done laughing, I lift her up, and only then see that her legs and arms are completely bruised, being purple and blue. I tell her friends to take her to the first aid post, but it seems the party can't be abandoned and the hands go up in the air once more. Me and Ray look at each other, and roll our eyes of how crazy people can be. We continue our dancing and singing along again, until our other two friends finally arrive. It took them quite some time to get ready, but now they're here, they immediately get into the grooves. There's no special act today, so the party keeps going on outside, in the dark, barely lit by house lights, but this is better than the two main acts we've seen before. The party also lasts a bit longer tonight and we head out when all is done. The five of us then go to a nearby sushi restaurant, which just closes as we arrive, so we sit ourselves down at the restaurant next door, where we have some good food. Claudia is spacing and not eating, as she's taken some acid today and all light hurts her eyes. It's quite interesting to see how she's experiencing the world, and how open she is now about everything. Everyone's tired though, and as soon as the food's in our stomachs, we hit the road. The two Gaucho girls leave for Tete's cousin's home, and we head back to Lagoa, to get some sleep.

David Guetta's show is tonight, and I've heard it will only start far past midnight. What to do with the rest of the day then? Right, we go to P12. I head to another hostel where there's a guy selling tickets for a much cheaper price than the door price. He's not here, so I'm helped by Sofia, who's planning to go to the Netherlands to study there. We have a nice chat about my home country and it makes the wait for the tickets a very nice one. I head back to the hostel, and me and Ray get to a restaurant for a nice lunch, while we await the girls' arrival. They arrive when my plate's nearly done, and also still have to fix themselves for tonight. When we come pick them up at Tete's cousin's place they're not ready, yet, and we decide to go ahead, so they'll have to take their own car today again. We arrive at P12 in the late afternoon and almost directly walk into Andreza and Raquel, our New Year's wave jumping friends. Together we party inside, as the rain is ruining the actual pool party. We're now all packed on the small dance floor, where we nevertheless make our dance move, go crazy, go wild. Natalia's here too again, and she joins our spot for a while, right in front of the DJ booth. After the regular DJ it's time for Otto Knows, and he's giving a class act. It almost seems to a good build up done by the organisation bringing better DJ's every day. Our other friends finally join us hours after we were at their place to pick them up, so they're only there for about 1.5 hours of today's asylum. They nevertheless join hard, and despite all the pushing by passing people we have a great warmup for the David Guetta show later. When P12 is closing we head out, get the cars and drive to Canasvieiras. The road to there is packed and we have to wait in line quite some time as we pass some hip hop party that's about to start in the Pacha. When we get to Canasvieiras we park our cars in front of the supermarket, as passing the venue the line before parking there was quite insane. We decide to grab a taxi from here and await arrival of one of the yellow vehicles. As none is arriving we are reconsidering, but just then a guy walks up to us and he says he wants to bring us there for a small fee. After a short consult we decide to seize the moment, and step in his small car and let him drive us there. Some fifteen minutes later we have past the traffic line and he drops us off when he also gets stuck in some traffic. From here on we walk, and from the road the venue really seems like a random party tent in the middle of a meadow. This feeling gets stronger when we walk through the mud and cow shit. We can't bring our own snacks and drinks inside, so we leave it tied to a fence, hoping maybe we can pick it up later. Then we enter and this tent is really massively big. We walk in a bit, and quickly find out how the bar system works and we queue up in the long line for the machines. I then see a guy paying with a card to some random guy with a machine on his back, and bluntly step up to him, and he indeed confirms I can pay with him too. Within minutes we've passed the line and now get our drinks smooth and easy. Then we walk to some spot in the crowd and wait for what's coming. Other DJ's are there to warm up the audience, but that's not really necessary with the temperatures in this tent. Despite this the atmosphere is good, the people great, and we've enough space for our moves. The waiting just takes a little bit too long, and most people seem to lose a lot of their excitement. When David Guetta finally makes his appearance some of it seems to get back to the thousands in the crowd, and the start is promising. Everyone's bouncing and going nuts on his popular records. When my favourite comes by I also jump high, higher, until I feel I'm floating, "why does it feel so good, so good to be bad?", and finally landing back on the ground to be one with the bass. It's more or less the same songs that are being played in P12, but in this crowd, with its creator, makes hearing them extra special. Guetta's making a hell of a show, and it's not only his music, but also the light show that's quite impressive. My feet have carried me a week from party to party, jumped to the beats, but are still strong to go on. Mario, Téo's friend, has also joined us, and he's just like us, just like the tens of thousands here, sucked into the big show. And when the artist finishes his show, the party isn't over yet, as another DJ takes control of the wheels of steel and pumps some new vibes into the hall. We'll never go home. When we finally do however, it's quite a challenge to get back to our cars. There's no taxis, and we decide to walk along the highway, and hope to maybe find one that stops. The female friends are slightly complaining about the walk, but we keep the positive spirit. When we're on 75% of the way finally a little bus stops for us, and we gladly pay the handful of reais to bring us back to the supermarket. Here we get into the cars and take off, back home. Me and Ray escort the ladies as far as we can, and then point them to their direction. We drive over the hill and make a stop just after 6am at the viewpoint at the top, where we can see the first rays of light, as the sun raises. Then it's only a short drive down to the hostel, where we park and rush to our beds. Our feet may finally rest, in peace.

Our party marathon has almost come to an end. Foreseeing that we would party hard for some time, and that the hotels were pretty much booked this entire week, I've made a reservation for a slightly better hotel in downtown Florianópolis for tomorrow. Today though, is our final finest hour, our final full party day. There's not even consideration, it's certain that today we will go to P12, and then for the final aftermath see our fellow countryman, and world's number one DJ, Hardwell. Once again I get to the other hostel for my P12 tickets, and together with Ray I after that enjoy a lunch, and then directly head to our second home. Before we enter Raymond buys us upgraded tickets for tonight's show, and gets 'camarote' access for better view, and better comfort. It's a great gesture of my friend. Then we enter the club, and it's crowded again today, and we of course find our spot outside again. There's a lot of new folks, and except for the crew we don't see many familiar faces. Flavio is there of course, with his wild bunch, and his weird cans of smoke giving them their kicks, but our other friends are not to be found. The outside house DJ is now almost becoming predictable for us, but it's doesn't ruin the fun at all. New people, old people, we don't care, we go, and go hard once more. The best then is still to come, as at prime time Nervo enters the covered area, and these Australian twins, tear the roof off. These chicks know how to build up the party and then let it boom at the right moment. I had never heard of them before, but Tete even made sure they were on time for this act, and just in time she and Nanda entered the arena. We have to endure a lot of elbows today, as the place is packed, and again we're not put down by this. The hands go up in the air, and there's some serious fist pumping going on. The evening here is coming to an end, but for us the night has just started. We escape the crowds now quickly as Tete is nearly passing out, hyperventilating, and we sit her down outside on the curbs. I keep talking to her, and making sure she gets back to normal breathing. As soon as this happens she's totally ready again, and we drive our cars to the sushi restaurant that was closed some days ago. Now we shortly wait in line and then get floor seats, which is not very supporting for our backs. It also takes quite a while before the food's served, and when it finally comes we attack it like starving wolves. The food is eaten as soon as it's served, and we all get our necessary energy for the aperture. We now take an alternative route to the venue, which is the same as yesterday's, and we park at a parking on the other side of the highway, which is much quieter, and easy accessible. From here we walk to the venue, but I soon head back, because I still have our old tickets, which I want to sell. There's a whole black market going on, and it takes a while before I know what these tickets are worth. I think we arrived a tad too late, as the prices are at a dump level already. The professional traders seem to stop all the people coming in and buying up their tickets to sell it for more some steps later. I then also aim for the new arrivals, and as soon as I do that, the traders finally pay me some decent money. Still less than that we had paid for them, but it's more than nothing. I've already received a text that I have to hurry as the party's about to explode, so I urge my feet to carry me as fast as they can. I pass security, get my camarote bracelet, and rush to the stairs taking me to the deck. Here my friends have taken their positions, just behind the people that have also paid for chairs. Two of these booths stay empty however, and as soon as the lights dim, Ray, Nanda and Tete walk to the rail and start filming and photographing the appearance of tonight's star. Below us there's a sea of cell phone lights, and there's a big silence when Hardwell comes to the stage. "Oi Braziiil, who's ready to party, let me see your hands in the air", he screams in the microphone, and the beat's building up, building up, building up, until it drops, and the bass kicks in, and the crowd goes mental. I've found another guy on the deck who's a crazy dancer like me, and to the delight of his friends, we entertain the others. This guy is totally wasted however, and me? I don't have an excuse, I'm just like this, and on every drop I jump up and down, making the floor bend a bit, and launch me in the air again. This deck is not build for people like me, and they must be happy I'm one of a kind. "Yes I'm an alien, when I'm touching the earth, call me a spaceman, when I travel universe", when this Hardwell original is played, the non-lyrical version, it must be about me, and I'm spacing away in my very own universe. This is the climax of one week of partying hard, and I can't recall the last time in life doing a full week of parties. My friends are also losing it, and the four of us are having a fantastic time. Dutch do know how to party as Ray and me have proven the last week and now also Hardwell is taking everyone on a trip to lala land. The DJ proves to be a master of build-up, and he knows how to get the crowd going; he proves to be number one for a reason. Hardwell leaves us then, and is replaced by a lesser star, but the party is still going strong. As it continues, something else is up in the air, and me and Tete know when it's our time to leave the scene for a bit, and giving some space to our friends. It's not that it's needed actually, because things will happen as they happen, but for our sanity it was good to go. Tete however suddenly tells me that Nanda wants to leave, but when I ask both her and Ray, both deny to have said something about permanently leaving. It's kind of awkward Tete is being Nanda's conscience and deciding for her feeling tired is a reason to go. It makes me frown a bit, but I can't be arsed to discuss it, as maybe things should be left at the highlight, avoiding disappointment. We now wait a bit for things to calm down, and then walk to our cars. Tete sits herself down in my car, as the lovebirds take some time to themselves. We then drive back in this setting to the fork of roads in Floripa, and there Tete and Ray switch places again, and we're both heading to our beds. We lasted until the final moment and this week couldn't have been any better.

Brazil - Florianópolis, Santa Catarina

Our final night in the hostel was as good as the ones before. When I'm this tired it doesn't really matter in what kind of accommodation I sleep. We are a bit lazy in the morning, pack our stuff, and then do our checkout and say bye to the people that have been great to us here. We now drive to the hotel I have reserved, and park our car in front. I have to wait in line before I can check-in and when you're ready and have to wait every second can be annoying. I keep breathing though, and when it's my turn things are fixed pretty quick. We have to wait though for our room to be ready, and we decide to have a lunch in the hotel's restaurant. The best of this establishment was the view, as the food was certainly not top of the bill. High price, lousy food. When we get back down to the front desk, we get our key card and then head to our room, which is spacious and has two perfect beds. In the late afternoon we then head out to go to the beach, but most of the beaches are overcrowded it seems. We finally find a quieter beach at Praia Brava, and there sit down in the sand. Nanda and Tete join us there, and there's some nice, but also awkward conversations. One misunderstood word has led to confusion, and this is cleared at the rocks, once and for all. I took a swim earlier, and now we're all just lazily lying in the sand, listening to a car's audio system playing an album of David Guetta. The sun sets, and we then find ourselves a nice pizzeria and have a good deal of pizzas, even a pizza dessert with ice cream, strawberry and chocolate.

The next day Tete and Nanda head back south, and me and Ray will wait for the other part of the group to pick us up for a road trip to Rio de Janeiro. Me and Téo have planned a road trip for a while now, and he's told me he would bring two other friends, but when I told him Raymond would be happy to join, he's made a spot free in the car. In two days he and his friend Cassiano will come pick us up for a drive along the coast. For now me and Ray have some time to recover though and today we spend solely at the hotel, and in the nearby mall for our lunch, and in a nearby restaurant for our dinner. It is in this dinner me and Ray have a great conversation about past, present and future. Ray's meal is gigantic though, and by talking a lot, he can consume it all, to my surprise. We then walk back to the hotel and sleep again.

On our final day we do want to see something more from the island, and by advice from the guy who talked to us at the lavanderia some blocks from our hotel. we decide to go all the way south, where we can drink 'caldo de cana', which is a sugar cane water. The best of this is sold in the corner of Ponta das Pedras, at a parking near aside of the road. We take off, and drive there, and enjoy a truly delicious drink. The guy was right about it in all his praising words. We then continue further south, past the town of Armacão, and then see two girls with their thumbs up, hitchhiking. Quickly I ask Ray yes, or no, but he just shrugs his shoulders. Alone I would have thought twice, but now I put the car aside, and let the girls in. The girls are from Argentina, but Manu (I love her name, as she shares it with a Feyenoord player) lives in Montevideo, while Carolina still lives in Buenos Aires. Both are students and are having a little vacation at the Brazilian coast. When we arrive at the beach, one I had already visited before of course, we walk up together, and then also jointly make our beach camp. I take a quick swim, and Manu and Ray stay in a little longer. There are few waves here again, making it more a lake than an ocean. When they come out for some reason we start singing songs, and surprisingly the girls fantastically pick up the Dutch song we teach them: Vader Jacob (Brother John). I told them this would be a song that exists in every language and soon after me and Ray are introduced to the Spanish version. For some reason this serenity and singing is as good as the parties we've been having last week. It's a truer connection, which might lead to real friendship. All tales come to an end though, as Téo and Cassiano will arrive and we will have dinner with them, and before that I have to return the car. When we head back we help Manu get a Brazilian chip for her phone and she eventually gets it activated. We bring them as far as they want, and then say goodbye, for now. We drive back to the hotel, dump our stuff, and then drive to the airport where I deliver the car. A taxi then brings us back, and this surf dude driver in the end gives me his card and tells me to look him up to catch some waves together. If only he really had understood how bad I am at surfing. At night we then meet up with Téo and Cassiano. I had not met Téo's friend before, and soon find out why: he's not the type of guy that normally leaves his house, let alone his hometown, and this is actually his first trip out of there without family. He's an extremely nice, and smart guy however, and this first meeting promises to make our trip with all four unforgettable. The dinner is eaten in a sushi restaurant, which is quite nice. The two Brazilian friends then return over the bridge to an Ibis hotel where they had found an available room, while me and Ray head back to our room and pack for the next morning; we will leave early, very early.

Me and Ray have an early breakfast and are then picked up in Téo's speedy car. We take the bridge out of town and then head north, past all the places I've been visiting lately. Our destination for today is Ilha do Mel (Honey Island), of which Téo has very fond memories and has been one of the highlights for him in Brazil. The weather sucks today, but as we're in the car listening to music, and talking, it doesn't matter to us. We drive around Joinville and I'm then in an unvisited area. Scenery doesn't change too much though, until we leave the highway and take a smaller road to the coast, towards the town of Guaratuba. It is at this little beach town, with a big estuary, where we drive the car onto a ferry and sail to the other side, where the road then continues north. Téo had let me drive his car before, and now Ray makes his entry as a driver. Only Cassiano lets the opportunity pass. We now drive parallel to the beach, in a continuous urban area, with plenty of vacation homes and hotels. This is clearly where the people from the state's capital, Curitiba, come to escape from the city. We literally drive to the end of the road, and then a lot of parkings appear, and even guys trying to get us in theirs. Téo knows the first ones are quite far from the boat we have to take, so we pass them, and end up at a parking lot that's in one-minute walk to the ticket booth and to the dock from where a boat will bring us to Ilha do Mel. This island has no cars, no roads, and is only accessible over the ocean. We have not organised a thing, so we literally go with the flow. At the booth we find out a ferry is leaving shortly, so we're lucky. We quickly buy some stuff in the nearby supermarket, and then line up for entering a primitive big fisher's boat. I'm the only one with a huge suitcase, and it's put on the roof of the boat, while my other two bags come with me, and are put under the long wooden benches where we take our seats. The water is very calm, and waves are not to be discovered as we sail out the river and enter the open sea. It's only a forty-five-minute slow boat ride, and at a big pier at the island we disembark. Here trouble begins, as I'm wheeling my suitcase over the last piece of hard underground, and then I'm dragging it through the beach sand, as we go lookout for a place to stay. Téo has some ideas, but first we sit ourselves down for a lunch. It's a buffet, but the food's not too good. After finishing our meal, we head out to find a place and again I drag my suitcase over beach and then unpaved jungle trails, bumping it and letting it falling over again and again. It's tiring. The place my friend had in mind is full and some other properties we walk into are also fully booked. Finally we find a place, but it's two bunk beds in a very small room, without any air-conditioning or ventilation. Before we take it I ask Téo to continue his search for a bit, and fortunately it pays off. We find another place with a bigger room, and air conditioning, right at the main beach. I'm relieved but this search kind of stressed me out, and it left me even unaware of the rural pure beauty of this island. After dropping off our stuff we go explore the island, and walk on a trail to the other side, where there's no buildings, but only the purity of nature. There's a very tall small cave on a beach here, and we look at it for a while. Then we look at the ocean and what we see blows all our minds. In the air the pure black clouds are slowly swallowing the little white ones and at the horizon there's thunder flashing. There's no light at the horizon anymore, and we can see how the rain falls down very hard there. Despite this weather coming our way we enter the ocean, and take a swim. The waves are now getting bigger every minute as the darkness closes in on us, but we stay inside the warm sea water. This must be the apocalypse, and I see myself standing in one of the Dutch master's paintings about sea battles, where the waves are higher than the ships. We let it come to us, brave young men, and the deeper we walk into the ocean, the more the darkness surrounds us. The ocean water is now as dark as the sky, with a deep dark blue colour, and there's no white tops on the top of the waves. The sky is roaring, lightning is coming closer, and we feel the first drops of rain. To our left is heaven, to our right is hell, and we are about to enter the Hades. A lifeguard appears on the beach, removing a flag, and then heads to the next, bigger, beach, not giving us a warning to leave. We all know that if lightning hits the water near us we are screwed, but we push the moment until we think it is really irresponsible. This moment comes when the rain starts pouring down on us, as the heaven splits open, and falls down on us with all its weight. We don't care, we feel so alive. We walk out, grab our wet shirts, and slowly head back to town. On this finest moment I didn't bring my camera, but I know I will never forget. We walk back to the posada to get some dry clothes and then walk a bit over the main beach until the sun sets, as the storm has past us entirely, and look for a restaurant to eat, which we eventually find, and where we are helped by a funny and good staff. Before midnight we lay in our beds and fall asleep.

Brazil - Peruíbe, São Paulo

I get the same breathing problem as I once had in the cabin in Tayrona, when the room was more like a sauna. Our air conditioning isn't working how it should, and somewhere in the middle of the night I stick my head outside a small window, trying to catch some fresh air. I now know my sleep for tonight's done, even though I keep trying. When the others wake up I find out I was not the only one having problems sleeping in this room, and what looked pretty good, turned out to be pretty bad. We head out for a breakfast and then prepare for a hike over the island. There's a slightly bigger village on the north side of the island, and to get there we have to walk a pretty long distance. I'm bringing my camera (bag) today, and I hope there will be another wonder of nature like last day's afternoon. We start the walk at the same point as yesterday and hang out a bit on the main big beach, which we then cross to get to the other side. Yesterday we had climbed one of the rocks here to get a view, but now we walk on the stairs on the other hill and cross the first (easy) obstacle. On the other side there's a little bay with a wide beach, and we decide to take a swim here, sweaty from our first hour of walking. The sea is very refreshing, and it makes it a perfect pit stop. We then continue and come to the most serious of all obstacles: we have to find a way over a small rock area, with the sea on our right hand. We're not the only people crossing, but it's not as easy as it seems, even though we all make it without any problems. There's a small den where we have to go through, or as Ray does, it, climb high over it, ignoring simplicity. We reach the other side and now are at a big beach again. At first this beach is very empty, but the closer we get to civilisation, the more crowded it gets. There's a beautiful thing happening with our first steps here, as the water being carried from the waves leaves a mirror in the sand, reflecting the blue sky and white clouds. It's perfect for some photos. We then continue to the beach, and cut through a forest trail to indeed enter the village, where we walk to a beach from where we can see a big white lighthouse. Then we turn back, and walk into the town to find a place where we can fill our engines with the purple fuel, acai. We are kind of on a time schedule as our checkout time from the posada is noon, and we already know we're not going to make it. A fine is what we want to prevent, but it doesn't make us run back. Calmly we eat our acai and then start our journey back to the south. As we now know what to expect, we move faster than before, and soon reach the big beach on

354

the south. Me and Ray move very fast over the rocks, and then the hill, and we decide to take a swim in the ocean until the others arrive. When they do they join us, we use our bodies as human surfboards, and we fly with the waves. For around thirty minutes we enjoy the water, and then head back to our room, to do our check out. Just then a loud horn sounds and apparently there's a boat leaving. Cassiano and Téo are soon there, and are trying to hold the boat for me and Ray. I arrive first and not much later Raymond's also there, and we allow the boat to leave. It's packed though, and the only spaces left are at the back, in the burning sun. Me and Téo sit down there, wrap clothes around our heads, while the other two decide to keep standing. From the pier we walk back to our car and then cruise shortly west, and then north until we reach the main highway. Here we can make some good progress, as we are heading to the state of São Paulo and somewhere at its coast we hope to find a place to sleep tonight. Ray and Cassiano fall asleep, while I'm driving us over the empty roads. At a gas station we make a stop, and buy some snacks, and then Ray takes over the wheel. We drive some kilometres and then the sky cracks open again and the rain falls down heavily. Then one scary moment occurs as a truck is coming at us, through a pool, and the water is all over our car, while we with relative high speed move through this pool, and we don't see a thing for nearly three seconds, while Raymond manages to keep a straight line, even though this pool pushes us both left and right. We have all hold our breath in the seconds that seemed to last for minutes, and our adrenaline levels all go up high. We thank Ray for keeping the control, because we all know things could have turned out pretty bad if he had not. Soon after the rain stops falling and we drive towards a pink horizon, where the sun is going under. We take the exit to Peruíbe, and on the internet I try to find a hotel, but there's no options listed. We drive through the centre, and ask at a fairly okay looking hotel. They don't have availability, so he directs us to a hotel further down the road, far outside the town's little busy centre. When we finally arrive there, Téo heads out to check if there's a room, and if yes, what it will look like. He comes out with his thumbs up, and we then dump our stuff in the room. All we need now is a restaurant, and now the internet is helpful as we find a nice place not too far away by car. We park across the street, enter, and indeed find a nice place with very good food. After dinner we look at the full moon from the boulevard near the hotel and then get to bed.

<u>Brazil - Ilhabela, São Paulo</u>

There's no plan for today, only that we want to see some nice beaches along the way. I've been doing some reading and consulted Téo and we aim to reach Maresias today, a buzzing party town. We're not the only ones on the road today and it seems there's an exodus from the city of São Paulo to the state's coast, especially when we finally pass the harbour of Santos. The road to Santos was just one straight line with no variety of beaches at all. We did make a stop at Monagaguá though, so I can send Tita a photo of us visiting the town where she has a beach house. We then avoid driving through one of the country's biggest harbours, Santos, and take the highway around it. We get to some hills and from there see the harbour in its full glory. From this point it looks pretty big. We keep following the 101 through the mountains and then we see the ocean getting closer once again, and the first town we hit on the more rural coastline, is Bertioga. Now we hit traffic jams of all the weekend escapers, and we only slowly make progress. The road winds through nice scenery though, with mountains to our left, and the ocean to our right. The sun's shining today and we keep the mood up with our collection of songs. We finally arrive in Maresias, and as a town it's not much more than we've seen along the coast already. It's lunch time, so the first thing we do is find a restaurant. The car is parked in a paid parking lot, and adjacent to it is a nice place where we can sit. A quick look at the beach shows us besides the normal sea, a sea of parasols, in all kinds of colours. It's not even weekend and this beach's already packed. While we eat our meals, I'm looking online for accommodations but again find nothing. Our waiter points us to a neighbourhood a bit down the street and tells us we should look there. We walk there, and indeed find a variety of posadas. I'm a bit ahead of the other three and talk to a woman who's renting rooms to budget travellers and tells me she has some places in a hostel, without air conditioning. I'm still this spoiled traveller and politely refuse the offer. In the meantime the others have also found a place, and they want me to inspect it. I'm again extremely worried about the heat of the room, with only a small van to keep us cold. Today's a bad day to have no air-conditioning, I reckon, as temperatures hit nearly 40 Celsius. We have a small discussion, and it's my vote to cancel this opportunity and to decide to continue driving, as this town maybe is also not the paradise that we're looking for. We head back to the car, and continue following the coastal road, now again up to the mountains, where we now pass a big waterfall. We make a short stop to take some photos and then continue again. While sitting in the car we decide to take a ferry and head to Ilhabela, which is supposed to be a very nice island, and we're not far from the town where the ferry leaves, São Sebastião. There's one more stop to be made, as we find a point with a gorgeous view over the bay below. The town of São Sebastião is much more industrialised than any of the towns we've seen after passing Santos, and from what we see it's not an award winning community. Me and Ray have to withdraw some money, and as we're stuck in a crazy traffic jam we decide to walk and then meet our friends back at the gas station. We do some speed walking to the ATM, get our money, and head back to our meeting point. Téo and Cassiano are not to be seen here however, and we walk up and down the jam but don't find them. After some phone calls we manage to get back in the car, escape the traffic and head for the ferry. Téo's a bit pig-headed here, as we say he has to enter a line, but he refuses to do it. We now drive the wrong way, and we are at the wrong side of the ticket booth, and the line is blocked by orange cones. I then ignorantly walk to the woman and at the ticket booth and she removes to cones for us to enter the line. This ferry is much bigger than the one we had to take in the state of Paraná, with four lines of cars on it. We keep seated in the car until we reach the other side. I now have booked a room for us through the iPhone application, as it states is has air-co. We drive to the place, and its entrance is kind of hard to find, and to drive into, as it's steep and small. We're being welcomed and then brought to our room, which is up some steep stairs, and with my big bag it isn't too much fun to carry it there in this heat. The room has one bunk bed, a big bed, and the guy provides a single mattress on the floor. The air-co also seems to work to my relief. The property has a very nice view at the mountains in the middle of this big island. We ask the guy running the place where there's a good area for food, and to party, and then we head to the given direction, which appears to be the old centre. We pass the club the guy's mentioned, Sea Club, and we park the car so I can inspect it. It's super closed and there's nothing going on tonight, unfortunately. We then find a very nice restaurant, where we have to wait in line first, and then have a fine meal. Next to it is supposedly a bar to party, which was recommended by one of the guys organising stuff for tomorrow's party at Sea Club, but when we are done with our meal around midnight nothing is going on. We sit ourselves in a boteco across from it and wait for things to come, but even though some people come check it out, no one really enters. We walk a bit more down the street to hopefully find another place, but it all stays dead as can be. We decide to go to our room and sleep and see what tomorrow will bring.

I'm quite picky in what I do and see, and now that I'm travelling with other people, it's mostly me making the calls for where to go. Others don't seem to care so much as I do, so in a way I'm becoming some kind of organiser. I've heard about a series of waterfalls on the island and I would want to check them out. As soon as we wake up we get ready for some touring, and first stop at the big waterfall that we already saw from our room. It's not really accessible, so after some quick snaps we head to the real deal, for which we have to drive over a dirt road into the island's mountains. At first Téo's a bit concerned to drive on this road, as we don't know how far it will get us, and what the state will be around the next corner, but we keep pushing our luck. Ideally this road will bring us to the other side of the island, where there supposedly are pristine beaches, saved from people. We however hit a road block, which is the entrance of the national park, and where we can either continue by foot, or by motor. Given we don't have a motor, we decide to walk, and here we stand at the start of the waterfall trail. We write down our names, and then walk the trails. It's crazy hot, even though the trees provide enough shadow. I'm mainly concerned about the mosquitos, but fortunately we don't hear, feel or see many. As the trail's small and we're not the only ones, we end up in a human traffic jam, behind a family that isn't too fast. We finally pass them and head out for the furthest fall at first, which is also the one that was recommended by the rangers as being the best. When we arrive we first only see a stream and the water gradually falling down over the rocks. Téo walks all the way down and let the water run over him, while Ray is taking some photos of the fast running water. I notice a young couple that is being photographed on the other side, near the pool that leads to these rapids. I shortly talk to the two women organising this photoshoot, and wave to the newlyweds. We then walk around this pool and discover the real waterfall. There's more people here, and one guy is totally willing to show us how to get under this very strong waterfall. I haven't brought my swim shorts for some stupid reason, so I first only take photos of how Téo enters the cold water and then slowly heads to the fall. There's a group of three women he has to pass and it gives a funny sight on how Téo finds his way under and around them. He screams for joy like a little child when the waterfall is crushing his bones and he is like Atlas carrying the world's weight for some moments. He is enjoying himself and it convinces me to go in as well. I take off my clothes and head there in my boxer shorts. The water however is freezing, and I'm having second thoughts. Then one of the women starts splashing water on me gently, making my body to adapt to the temperature. An extreme nice gesture that was just needed to keep me going. I now also get to the two waterfalls, together with Raymond, and we experience the same pleasure that Téo just did. Like him we also go into the even stronger one, but this one is unbearable, and in seconds I give into its power, escaping again to the smaller one. Raymond leaves now again, and Téo comes back, and we try the bigger one again, this time with a bit more success. We then head out of the water, pack our stuff, and head back, making two more stops at two other small waterfalls on our way. We drive back to our posada, quickly grab our stuff and check out. The only thing we know now is that we will go to Sea Club. Nearby the venue we find a parking lot, where I immediately make friends with the group of people running the place. Even though it's valet parking, they let me park for a bit, so I can change my clothes. The others also change their shirts, and we walk to the club's entrance. Here we have to pay our tickets, and me and Cassiano get the cheapest one, excluding any drinks, and Raymond and Téo get one with some booze included. We then walk in and walk in a little circle around the pool, and past the stage, where there's a DJ, but not (m)any people yet. It's still relatively quiet, and we get a table near the entrance, looking at the back of the stage. I see a girl at the table next to us with a big camera, and this give me the idea to pick up mine as well. I walk back to the car, make fun with the crew at the parking again, and then head back. Téo and Raymond have now started drinking seriously and soon the infamous glassy eyes of Téo appear once again. In the mean time I have met Bia, who's working here, and is in charge of our table. We have fun chats, and she's being very great to us from the first moment on. As Téo is already too wasted I ask her if she knows a place on the island where we could sleep tonight, she immediately runs off making phone calls for us. It is this kind of big heart that makes me love Brazil so much. She keeps me informed all the time about the progress, and I have no doubts now it will all be taken care of. In my first round with my camera I'm at the dance floor, when suddenly a beautiful girl beckons me to come to her. My first thought that she's not meaning me, so I look around to see who she is beckoning. As I'm the only one there, I walk up to her, and she very sweetly asks me for a photo. I tell Paula that I'm just a tourist finally bringing my camera to a party and trying out some party photography, and she lovely responds that my Portuguese is so good and asks me where I've learned it. I tell her it's just picked up on the road, and she excitedly claps her hands. Then I take her photos, and some of us together, and we hang out a bit more. I then move on, back to Cassiano, as Ray and Téo have now brought their drinking into the pool. Every time I walk around with my camera from now on everyone seems to think I'm the party photographer, and they all start posing, or ask me to take photos of them. The party's now crowded, and there's a nice build up in music. My camera and my gringo appearance make me meet about everyone in this club, and in a way I like the attention. I also get to talk with the real party photographer, and we exchange our lenses for a moment, and she tells me she's been doing this here already for several years. It seems like a fantastic job. Through her I meet her friends, and I come across them regularly on my rounds. Caro even fixes my flip flop when it breaks during my endless circles. Another group I keep running into is the one of another Paula who's having her bachelor party here. They also keep asking me for photos which I happily take for them. Bia's also introduced me to her friend Thayna, who's in control of the ice creams, so she moves around less often than my other new dear friend, and regularly I come around for some fun talks. She also understands English, but is too shy to speak it. Cassiano in the meantime has become the king of his first ever real party, and his chair has become a throne. Once he has to escape because he thinks a lovely lady that approaches him is a transgender. It's hilarious as she absolutely isn't, and Cassiano just got nervous. I walk around with him a bit and introduce him to more people. The party's absolutely booming now, and then Bia also brings the best news that she's arranged rooms for us in the south part of the island. I'm delighted and do a little dance to celebrate. Bia's amazing! Now this burden is off my shoulders and I continue to party hard. Téo's become a bad drunk though and I try to avoid him as much as possible. Ray's been drinking too, but he remains his calm self, and keeps being fun to be around. The DJ is now playing the records we've been going crazy on at P12, and because I know so many people now, it seems to be topping it. Everywhere I go and look are familiar faces, and they all have small talks with me when I pass. I'm loving this gig, and it seems everyone's having a blast. I now want to live here. Forever. Like any party the longer it takes, the more wasted people are, and the less I seem to understand them. A guy and his wife offer me to take photos of the Brazilian national team because they believe I'm the best photographer in the world. And I have to come to their house for an after party. Okaaay, I nod my head often saying I understand, but I try to get out of this conversation as soon as possible. There's more of these kinds of talks, and I'm happy when I get to talk to my sober friends Cassiano, Bia and Thayna, who are not only sober, they're also much nicer than most of the other folks anyhow. Téo is now totally lost and he sits with his head bowed staring in the bottom of the pool. Ray, like me, is walking circles, and Cassiano is sitting on his throne. The party's coming to an end, and people start leaving now. We stick around longer though, as we all can't get enough of it. When the DJ's gone though, and the crew starts packing up things, it's also for us time to leave. Once more I run through the directions with Bia, and I get her phone number in case we need help. We get to the car, and I drive us there, but as soon as we get to the neighbourhood we get totally lost. We're supposed to be at Bia's house to let her father drive us to the place, but we can't seem to find this house. We ask a lot of people, and they all seem to point in different directions. We are in the right street, but the number doesn't exist. Google isn't helping either, so we're lost, horribly lost. I call Bia and she tells us we have to drive to the main road and then to the right, but we all think there's only sea there, until we give it a final try, and indeed find a little street going to the right, which is also that street name where we've been desperately walking around. Humbly I ring the bell and Bia's energetic father comes out to welcome us. I do the talking as I want Téo to stay away from people with his evil glassy eyes. We now follow Bia's father's car and head down to the property which we had already passed several times. We wait for the gates to be opened and then head in, where we are welcomed by an amazingly hospitable woman, called Luzia, who shows us the bungalow where we can sleep in. It's much more than we ever expected and it's absolutely perfect. The only thing now we lack is dinner, as it is pretty late. We talk a bit with the woman and her two children, get introduced to another Téo, which is their dog, and then get directions to a restaurant that still might serve some food. We decide to walk, but unfortunately take off in the wrong direction and soon we are climbing a hill, and getting even more tired than we already were. Halfway we turn and walk back to either pick up the car, or to order food to our house. There's one small problem and that is the gate to the property is now locked and we can't seem to notify the woman. I tell Téo to not climb over the fence, as I think we need to respect our host's property, and I head to the other side of the road to ask in that posada to call ours, and it seems to be working. When I walk back though, baby Téo still has climbed over, opened the gate, and then apologises to the friendly woman who had just came to open it. I'm pretty annoyed for a second, but as soon as the pizzas arrive thirty minutes later all is forgotten. The lady has helped us once more, and this was the only thing separating us from sleeping. There's two fine bedrooms, and six beds, so we have plenty of choice. Few minutes pass before we're all knocked out.

Brazil - Ubatuba, São Paulo

We're taking it very easy the next morning, and don't leave the lovely property until after noon. We say goodbye to our great hostess and her two adorable children and then head for Bia's home again, to invite her to lunch so we can thank her properly. Now we find the house without any hesitation, but ringing the bell doesn't bring her to the door, but her two small cousins, who do understand my Portuguese, but tell me Biatriz is not here. Just when we leave again her father pulls up his car, and we tell him we wanted to surprise his daughter with a lunch invite, but he tells us she has to work today, at Sea Club. Another afternoon at Sea Club? Maybe not a bad idea! We get excited about the idea and after driving to the far south point of the island to see if we can find some nice beaches, we head back north, merely because we need gas. We head back to civilisation, fill up the car and drive to Sea Club. The parking is now completely empty, and it doesn't look too promising. We head to the back door, and see it's just a pool day here, and there's no party coming up. We ask the door guy if he can call Bia for us, and she comes to say hi, and after a short talk, also goodbye. Next to the parking we get into a restaurant and have our lunch. When we're stuffed we drive to the far north of the island and explore the beaches there. At one bay there's a beautiful view, but the parking is full, paid, and still far from the beach, so we decide to just turn and drive back. It's time to leave this great island, and we take the ferry back to the mainland. Ray then decides he indeed is going to follow up his promise to meet two French friends he had met on a trip, in São Paulo, and we find out there's a bus terminal in Caraguatatuba, from where he can travel there. We drive him there, buy a ticket with him, and then wait on a 'terrace' in this shady hood. Ray is then escorted into his bus, and we continue our drive to Ubatuba. It's dark now, and we don't see any of the scenery. I've booked a hotel somewhere in Ubatuba, which is also said to be a prime tourist destination and it's surrounded by many (hidden) beaches. The first sights of town are horrible, with big tourist hotels, and masses of people. It gets a bit quieter when we get more into town, and the area where our hotel is, is very quiet. We get a gay welcome at our hotel, which was easily found, but entering our room I notice the third bed is missing. I get into a discussion with the front desk, and after some thirty minutes they offer me a second room, but I'm fine with them placing an extra mattress on the floor. Sorting this thing made me hungry, and the three of us walk to the town's downtown, and find a restaurant on the main boulevard, which is crazily busy and is one street with only restaurants. It's extremely hot in this restaurant despite all the fans. Even though Téo has a huge hangover today, he's drinking another beer again. From previous experience I know this normally gets him going again. Cassiano joins him drinking some beers, but nothing crazy today. On our way back to the hotel we stop at an ice cream shop, and the guys eat some ice cream before we walk the final metres and fall asleep soon after.

Brazil - Paraty, Rio de Janeiro

In the morning we're just in time for breakfast. The hotel had a bad
start for me, but has made it up by its service, and this breakfast. I
have the terrible urge for always wanting to know everything, and
now we're in Paraty I want to see all the beaches, to get at least an
idea of them. After breakfast we pack our stuff, and start in the
southern parts, to one by one see the beaches that were
recommended to us. We go, walk out, take some photos, and drive
off, and repeat this trick on several beaches. None of them are really
appealing to us however, mainly because how they're situated, and
even more because of how they are all packed with people. I believe
there's a quieter beach just north of town, with the name of Praia do
Cedro, and I share the idea with my friends. They're up for it and we
drive there, even though the road after the last houses is extremely
bad. It's going uphill, and there are so many holes, that our heads
nearly stick to the car's roof by the time we finally arrive to what
seems to be a parking. There's a line blocking the entrance though,
but soon a guy comes to remove it and lets us pay the ticket. From
the parking there's a small road going down to the sea, and when we
arrive a lovely small beach appears. There's even a little restaurant,
and of course there are many parasols, and tables. We dump our stuff
at one of these tables, and then rush to the water. I wasn't planning
to rush, but as soon as my feet hit the sand in the sun, I have to run.
This is the hottest sand ever, and my feet are literally burning as I try
to reach the sea. I believe some skin must be still at the beach, as I try
to cool off in the sea. The water however is nearly as warm as the
sand, and it's like a hot tub. Me and Téo swim a bit, while Cassiano is
watching over our stuff. Later Téo and Cassiano switch, but I'm the
one constantly in the water. Then me and Téo go walk the rocks at
the side, and climb as far as we can. It's a dead end soon though, and
the tide seems pretty strong to go into the water from here. We head
back to the beach and then swim to the rocks, from where I take
some dives into the water. If only we would have an underwater
camera... There are big boats coming into this small bay, constantly
dropping off tourists for a dip, and the water gets crowded at these
moments. Téo and I get to talk to a mother and daughter and then I
notice a girl with a GoPro. If only she would borrow it to me. She's
snorkelling with her two friends, and actively using the camera, so it's
not the moment to ask, if I will dare to ask at all. We're hungry now
and head back to the table and join Cassiano again. We order three

cups of acai, and eat this as our lunch. I then want to head out again to take some photos, and see the snorkelling ladies just returned. I ask Téo if I should go ask, and he thinks I should, so I walk up to them and offer my camera to trade with their GoPro. They're very friendly and sweet and without hesitation they tell me I can go take their GoPro into the sea. I beckon Téo and together we run again over the hot sand and swim to the rocks to do some more cliff diving. We take some crazy videos and many selfies. Having a GoPro rocks, and it makes me want to kill myself for not bringing one myself since day one. It's great fun in the water with the camera, and when we're done we head back to the ladies, and after some more talking we join Cyndi, Ivaneth and Mirina at their table. We continue to talk about travelling, beaches, locations, and surfing. They say they all surf, and I wish I had met them earlier so they could have taught me some skills. These girls are very sporty and it's cool to hear them talk about all their activities. We're all taking some photos together, and then jointly walk back up the steep hill. They are on their motors, and soon cross away, leaving us behind in the dust. Our car awaits us, and we get it moving, and drive north, to see some other beaches. We make a stop at a nice beach at Itamambuca, where we sit down on a dead tree trunk, and overlook the ocean, and then continue to Prumirim, which is our final stop on our way towards Paraty, where I've booked a posada for the night. It's quite a drive through some mountains before we reach that town, and there are no street lights whatsoever, making it a very dark road. We listen to loud electronic music again, and I'm steering the car over the curvy road. Then, just when I'm about to enter a curve to the right, another car is driving towards me on my lane. My hands tighten around the wheel and I focus my eyes for what's to come. The other car then luckily sees he's doing something wrong and steers his car to the correct lane, preventing what would have been a horrible accident. My heart's beating in my body entirely, and also Téo's a bit shocked because of the event. We safely get to Paraty, but it takes a while before we find the hotel I've made a reservation for. It's some kind of motel in the Jacaquara area, which is across a hill from the old centre, but then not on a normal road. There's no adult at the front desk, and a child of ten years old or something is helping us. Later a guy comes to bring us an extra mattress. We drop our stuff in the room and then take the car to find a restaurant. We find it close by on the beach side and wait a bit before our table is ready. A packed restaurant is generally a good restaurant. The best thing happening however is the lightning choreography at the horizon. Flashes come down and light the sky beautifully. I try to snap some photos and magically capture one strike in a photo. The staff is even impressed by my photo and asks me to email it. This same staff is extremely friendly to us and also serves great food from the kitchen. After we're satisfied we head to bed, to go to sleep relatively early.

<u>Brazil - Angra dos Reis, Rio de Janeiro</u>

Some mosquitos kept us awake longer than we expected, but after a
small massacre it was a calm night. At the small breakfast area, I walk
into a very pretty girl, which I greet with a shy "bom dia", and then
sit myself down at the table. She sits with a guy behind me, and her
beauty is striking. When we have loaded in our car and checked out, I
see her enter a car next to us, apparently with a family. She gives me
one huge smile, and then sits down. I think I'm silent for a while,
repeatedly seeing this smile again in my own stare. We now drive to
the centre of Paraty which is extremely nice, and old, for a change. Its
historical buildings are preserved and not ruined by random modern
buildings in between. It's a nice change from all the other towns
we've seen on this road trip so far. We snap some photos and then
head out to find the town of Trindade, which was recommended to
us. It's a bit south of Paraty, so we're driving back the way we came
and now see the route by daylight. We're surrounded by green hills
and head up a bit before we find the exit; a small road that will lead
us to our destination. This road is much smaller and soon we make a
stop because there's a burnt down car at one of the two lanes. Téo
stops the car so I can take some photos, but leaving the car in the
middle of the road, both us and the burnt car resolves in a traffic jam,
so after some tooting of another car, Téo pulls the car to the side, to
clear the way again. I take my photos and then head back in. We
drive all the way to the ocean, and then there's suddenly no road
anymore, and the way to town leads over massive rocks, over which a
stream calmly flows. Téo's a bit hesitant at first to drive past this, but
as other non-4x4 cars are doing it, we're doing it too and simply
reach the other side. Now we pass town, and find a big parking area
where we park the car, grab our stuff, and then take a walk to the
beaches. There's a bay here, with a rock separating a first small beach
from a wider beach more north. Supposedly there's a great waterfall
in the jungle somewhere and beyond the big beach there should be a
natural swimming pool. We first decide to go into the jungle and
follow the trail to the waterfall. It goes steep up, and on the way we
see many other folks. It's quite a walk, and this normally isn't a
problem, because you will be rewarded. When we reach the end of
this trail we can't discover a serious waterfall in the few drops of
water falling from the rocks. There are many people sitting on the
rocks here though and we even continue up a bit to see if this is really
it. I even ask some of the folks if this is it, and after being confirmed

what I was already suspecting, we disappointedly start our way back. This hour of hiking sucked. Going down is again harder than going up, merely because we run into other people who are much slower than we are and the path doesn't leave room to pass. Eventually we do get back to the beach and as the small beach is quite full, we cross the big rock in the middle to the other side. This rock is even steeper than the trail before and I feel like I'm leaving a trail of sweat, like snail slime. When I reach the other side the only thing I want is to get into the water as soon as possible, and after waiting for my friends, the three of us dump our stuff, ask three Argentinian ladies to look after it, and then take a swim in the warm ocean. It's only at these moments I wish for cold water, as this temperature of water is not very refreshing. We act like human surf boards again, and hang out a bit in this big shallow part of the ocean. Then we get out, talk a bit more with our neighbours and then I persuade the other two to also go check out those natural pools. We head down the beach first and then enter a trail into the jungle, which is going steeply up and down once again. Upon arrival there it's full of people, even more than at that small beach. There are boats delivering packs of tourists and there's no spot in the water unoccupied. I wade through the water to the rocky other side and there explore a bit of these huge rocks. It's not very interesting, or beautiful. We head back then and we take another swim when we reach the beach again. Then we walk back, over the beach, over the rocks, and at the small beach we treat ourselves on fresh coconut water, which is the refreshment we were looking for. Drinks aren't enough to keep us calm, as our stomachs are screaming for lunch. We walk towards the parking, but before we are there we see some establishments, and head there for our well-deserved meal. If only they would have not forgotten us, this meal would have been great, but our waiting time runs up to over an hour, and then finally the huge fish we've ordered is served to our table. A misunderstanding between staff and kitchen, leaving us like whining children. It makes the fish not taste as great as it could have, but our hunger is appeased for now. We tiredly walk back to our car and when I want to take my seat, I realise my swim shorts are still carrying the water of the entire ocean. Before I started this big journey I would have cared about changing my shorts in the middle of a parking lot, now I can't be arsed to be bothered anymore, and I drop my shorts, step out of them, and for one moment the world is blinded by my extremely white bottom. Téo then tells me I'm being watched, and still only dressed in a shirt, I turn my head to the mentioned car and I see two girls laughing out loud. While stepping into my boxers, I ask them how big it was what they've seen and start with two fingers closed, until arms wide, making them crack up even more. I bet this is the whitest they've ever seen. It's a great non-verbal interaction though, and it makes me and my friends laugh a lot. They then drive off, with big smiles on their faces, and we finish changing our clothes and then also hit the road. Things soon continue to be funny, as in the village we pass the girls' car and we honk to them, and they honk back. They now follow us, with two cars in between. I urge Téo to let them pass again, and our cat and mouse game has now started. Cassiano is repeatedly saying it's bollocks what we're doing, and even though we know it indeed is, we keep it up all the way to the big road. There Téo signals them to stop, and when they do he runs over to their car and has a small talk with them. He's forgotten to put on his flip flops though and soon me and Cassiano see him create a hilarious dance, whilst he tries to be focused on talking with the girls. After a few minutes he returns and tells us we're going to meet them later tonight. I directly oppose this late time, as we've to continue to Angra dos Reis tonight, in order to still have a chance to hit Ilha Grande for one or two nights before reaching Rio. I ask Téo to make them stop again, and it takes a while, but eventually we stop them near a gas station just outside of Paraty. Now I also get out, and make some proper introductions, and also get their names: Thais and Paola. They work on an oil platform, as a nutritionist and personal trainer. I manage to get the time pushed back by two hours and we will meet a bit earlier now in the old town. We head directly into town and kill some time by walking around, and eventually sitting ourselves down in the bar where we will meet. Cassiano and Téo have their first beers of the day, while I slam some waters. I also head out to buy a new iPhone cable, as mine's again broken. We then wait for our new friends' arrival and together we enjoy talking, laughs and drinks. Then we head out to find a restaurant for dinner, and we walk through the cute streets. I'm walking ahead as always, but then Cassiano calls me back. I stop, look around, and see the beautiful girl from this morning again, but now it seems she's a bag vendor. She's talking with my friends, and I take some photos of them and 'the bag vendor', before I walk up to them. I then directly find out she's not selling bags, but she's a friend of Paola, and her name is Aline, just like my sister. Isn't this a coincidence? She's an architecture student and we add her to our group, and jointly walk to find a restaurant. It takes a while before we finally find something, and now the group totally splinters; Téo and Thais head out to eat some kind of waffles, Aline heads back to her family for dinner, promising she will be back, and me, Cassiano and Paola sit down in a very nice living room alike Italian restaurant. The three guys are a bit on a time schedule as we still have to drive over 1.5 hours to our next destination, and we don't want to arrive when the sun's coming up again. The food's ordered and served quickly and we immensely enjoy it. Aline soon joins our table again and the time then stands still for a bit longer, as our conversation seem to take place in vacuum. It's not until Téo and Thais return till this bubble explodes. The six of us now walk to our car and there we say goodbye...

Yesterday's night drive brought us in intense darkness to the ugly urban city of Angra dos Reis, where we've found an ordinary hotel. My mind's not here, it's still in Paraty, and I wonder why I wanted to travel on so badly yesterday. I regret the choice, but accept the decision, and now try to focus on things to come, instead of things that might have been. We're quite lazy today, but manage to be in time for both breakfast and lunch. Then we go into town, with all our stuff, to find a way to get to Ilha Grande. First we head to a parking nearby where the ferry should leave. It's damned empty though, and I go ask when it's leaving. This won't be until late afternoon, so we take the time to explore other options, and walk to a travel agency that offers tours to the island. Here we sit down and talk with the lady and she doesn't do overnight tours, only ones that go for one day. There's a tourist office just across the street and we decide to check that out before making up our mind. Here they say it's possible to go to the famous tourist destination with their transport, leaving every hour, and then get an accommodation to sleep. They hand us a book with properties on the island, and we can also use their phone. Téo calls more than ten of these posadas, but they are either full, or they don't answer at all. Even though we agree there's most likely a place to be found when we arrive there, just like on Ilha do Mel, we decide not to take the risk, and head back to the woman selling the day tours, and make a reservation for the next day. After all this hesitation today we are happy to have organised something. At the hotel we then spend some time in the pool, and in the evening we search for a sushi restaurant, don't find it, and end up at an entirely different one, which is quite good actually. We then head to bed, which doesn't take too long for me, as my stomach is crying, and the bathroom calling...

I barely slept this night and a war seems to be happening in my stomach. I know myself well enough to know this won't be good for any travelling, and I tell the guys I won't join them on the tour, but insist they go, after they nearly decide to also bail. They now leave for the departure point, walk there, and leave me at the hotel. Here I spend most of the time in front of the computer, uploading photos, while drowning the enemies in my stomach by drinking litres of water. When my friends come back I jealously listen to their stories, and see their amazing photos and videos. It's certainly a place that I want to go to some other day. Dinner is now taken at the hotel, and I mainly eat rice and cooked vegetables.

Brazil - Rio de Janeiro, Rio de Janeiro

We wake up late, missing breakfast, but just in time for lunch. I'm
again on rice and vegetables, even though it's tempting to taste all the
other delicious choices at the buffet. Today we will drive the final
stage of this memorable road trip to the city of Rio de Janeiro.
Raymond is also arriving there today by plane from São Paulo, and
will join us for the time the guys have left before having to return to
their jobs in their hometowns. Reaching Rio is crossing highways
with an endless amount of cars, and with hitting traffic at almost
every exit, accident or narrowing of the road. It's like any big city
here an ostensibly chaos. Téo now wants to logically drive himself, so
he can drive his car into safety. I'm good with navigation, so it's a
good deal. Cassiano entertains us with anecdotes, and the three of us
hit the traffic's black hole after some hours of driving, exchanging the
beautiful coastal road, for immense urban areas. Finally I start
realising the size of this city. The outskirts are enormous and there's
so much more than I see as a tourist. Even though it's not gorgeous,
it is interesting to see all this. Being in this traffic is also better than to
read or hear about it. It's actually not that bad: just avoid other cars,
and find your own way from A to B. We do have some trouble
finding our hotel though, which is in the area of Catete, but our
navigation application isn't showing the right point on the map. With
some asking we finally do find it though, and from the outside it kind
of looks like a brothel, but the inside doesn't have the ladies, just
modern newly furnished rooms. Ray then already shows up with a
taxi from the airport, and the four of us do the check in. Me and Ray
take a room, and Téo and Cassiano share another. We quickly
arrange our stuff, and then walk out to find a place to eat. We walk all
the way to Flamengo, and then back again, not finding anything
suitable (acai). We finally find a small fruit bar selling it and sit down
for a big glass of the purple gold. This is the base we need for some
serious drinking (water for me) in Lapa. We take a cab down there,
walk around a bit, and go to the hostel Ray's previously stayed to get
some information on parties. The guy with this information is not
there though, so we walk back to the bars of Lapa and sit down on
barstools at the curb, letting the waiter bring us beer, beer, beer, and
more beer for my friends, and occasionally a water for me. I'm clearly
watching Téo's eyes, hoping they won't be glassy tonight, and I think
he will finally manage to be in control of the alcohol's influence.

Around midnight we head back to the hotel, unable to find any other good party.

Téo deservedly summons us to do something touristy the next day, as he's not here every day. It's now my third time here, and I'm lacking initiative, so Téo gets us moving to a place where we can buy tickets for the Pão da Açúcar (Sugarloaf Mountain). He knows a place where we can buy tickets, so we walk after him to this booth, which turns out to not sell any tickets at all, only for Cristo. So far for Téo taking the lead, and we democratically put him aside as today's tour guide. We now take a taxi directly to the foot of the two mountains, who like camel humps rise up at the south of the city. Here's a smaller line than we've expected and the tickets are rapidly bought, and then it's only a fifteen to twenty-minute wait before we get into the cable cart bring us to the first hump. Téo and Cassiano only have been here once on a school trip together when they were very young, but it all seems to come back to them. Both me and Ray more recently were on top here, but are still impressed by the marvellous views from this altitude, overseeing the beautiful situated city at our feet. Its hills, its high buildings, the Copacabana, the favelas, and Cristo all looking down on it with an eternal same expression. I overhear two girls talk Dutch, with an accent betraying they're from the eastern side of the country, even though at my first sight they don't really look like they come from our little country, nor from the west, nor the east. I play the game 'spot-the-Dutch' with Ray, where he has to walk closer to what he will think are Dutch, unfortunately not coming close to these girls' table. My entire trip I was very happy to avoid other Dutch tourists and today's not an exception. If I want to meet other Dutch people, I will stay in the Netherlands. Abroad, I want to meet different nationalities, different cultures, and not people on wooden clogs. We now take the second cable cart to the top, and walk around a bit, exploring the little trails at the eastern side of the second hump, which has trails covered in the shade of trees, making it a bit easier to endure today's heat. Even though this park is quite small we manage to lose Téo and we don't see him anywhere. We walk back up, but again don't find him, now thinking he's joined the monkeys in the trees, looking for a different life. Us three now go to a viewpoint which is perfect for a photo, and as there's no one here but an old lady we wait for the next to appear. And the next to come are the two Dutch girls, who I then approach for taking a photo of us, seeing one of them is carrying a big camera as well, thinking she knows what to do with it. Too bad the railing can't be removed, making the photos not as good as they could have come out. Cassiano now joins me and Ray in the photo and the girls happily shoot many photos of us. We then get to talk to them, while the monkeys pass us on the railing. Malena and Tatiane are in Rio for a short vacation together. Malena's been living in Perth, Australia, for the last three years, and now is on a trip to enlighten her brain, and passing and stopping in Rio made it a perfect moment for her friend from Deventer to come to visit her. Tatiane actually is Brazilian, born in Belo Horizonte, Minas Gerais, but adopted by a Dutch family at a young age. This is her first trip here since leaving her motherland at the age of five. It's actually great getting to know these two ladies, and my prejudgement about meeting Dutch people is again proven wrong. Just like with all the other Dutch people I had met during my trip: all great experiences. Téo now also finally showed up, and we're complete again. The talks shift from Dutch to English and we decide to stay up here together for the sunset. We first have some drinks and snacks at the bar, and then find a viewpoint from where we think to see the sunset at its best. Malena and Tatiane have experienced Rio as dodgy so far, but up here they are in their element, and when we've told them it's tradition to clap when the sun sets, they are, together with Ray, the first to clap very loudly, making the rest follow. Photos are taken by the hundreds here, and soon the ladies are posing for my camera making the craziest faces, making me laugh a lot, which is not a good thing for keeping the camera still. Continuously laughing and talking we see the sun disappear behind the hills, leaving the sky in our national colour, orange. It could not have been a better ending of a great afternoon with old and new friends. We all head down together, and then decide to have dinner with the six of us. It's a bit hard to find the taxis we need, but eventually we're on our way to the Copacabana, and there end up in the girls' local Lebanese restaurant. The food is great here, and looking around at the table, seeing an old Dutch friend, two amazing Brazilian friends, and two new Dutch friends, I can bless myself with the company too. After dinner our paths separate, and we take a taxi back to our hotel, and then to my bed and breakfast, Sonho de Papagaio, where I had promised to arrive again this day. It's great seeing Fabio and Angela again, and I'm welcomed as a dear friend once again. We drop the stuff off, and then head out again. Cassiano's not with us tonight, as he's a bit tired from today and last night, so the three of us head into Lapa once more, but don't find any good parties. We try, but fail to find anything. just sitting ourselves down once more at barstools observing the passing people. We call it a night early, and this is the moment for me to say farewell to my friends; they'll drive back together, southward bound. Téo and Cassiano to their jobs, Ray to Nanda. They will drive south in three days, leaving me behind in Rio for my final nights before this big year of adventures will come to an end.

I wake up late in my good old room, and at breakfast/lunch am welcomed to the table with Angela and Fabio. I get to hear great news: Angela's carrying a baby, and I'm extremely happy for my friend. We together eat a very fine lunch, and I spend the rest of the day around the house, after Malena and Tatiane cancel our afternoon Lapa meeting. Over WhatsApp we do agree to go to tomorrow's David Guetta show and I promise to get us tickets. Online I don't get it to work, and thus decide to go to a vending point tomorrow. The rest of this day passes and I get my needed rest, charging my battery for one final night of partying.

I get out of my room way too late, making me need to rush to this shop, instead of having time. I've taken a late breakfast again, and then walk to this shop in about a thirty-minute walk. Here I line up and when it's my turn they say they only accept cash. I now rush back out, trying to find a Banco de Brasil, which is the only bank with which I guaranteed can withdraw money. I find the bank, but the card's being refused. No, not again! It's so frustrating. I immediately call my bank over Skype, thus over 3G, which means the connection isn't that good. The card is blocked, but the call keeps failing. I head back to my room in a taxi, and then call again over Wi-Fi. I get the card unblocked again and now decide to call the ticket website, to see if I can work that out, instead of returning to the shop once more. Now I get to talk to a very friendly woman who helps me and gets the ticket reservation. I just need to pick them up at the venue tonight. All's fallen into place now, and I'm just ready in time to meet up with my Dutch friends at the Lapa Arches. I walk the stress off and minutes after I arrive their taxi stops. Their eyes are ominous today, unlike two days ago. They're extremely wary and nervous about the city's dangers. I'm here now for the third time and Lapa and Santa Teresa have become neighbourhoods I know quite well, thus I'm not worried at all anymore. I try to calm the girls down, and at our first stop, the famous stairs, this helps, and they happily take their photos, and Pharrell-like video clip, making some slick dance moves. We walk all the way up now, and then into the streets of Santa Teresa. Here they don't feel very comfortable and they rather go back to the crowded streets, leaving these abandoned cobble roads behind. We walk down and then get to the fruit bar, to get some acai, and juice. Then I walk them past the crazy cathedral and to the famous club Rio Scenarium, before we find a taxi, as our next stop will be Ipanema, for today's sunset. When we are dropped off at the boulevard we make our way to the rock, and find a place in between the massive crowd. There's a photo shoot happening for a program that seems to be something like Geordie Shore, soon making us talk in a weird British accent. This shooting is also blocking a big part of the rocks, leaving other places even more crowded. The sun is slowly setting and like all the times, the crowd bursts into an ecstatic applause, with my Dutch friends being among the most fanatic once again. It's funny to see their happy faces and their posing for their thousands of selfies. For dinner we of course head to the Arabian restaurant and once again have some good food, even though I stick to a bowl of rice with vegetables. Then we walk back to the girls' hotel, and they are going to prepare for a night's out. I wait in the lobby, give them my phone to get charged, and without that device of communication I get in a great conversation with the bell 'boy', an old man with great historical knowledge. We talk for longer than the hour the girls said they needed, and when it's nearly two, they come down and we get into a taxi which has to bring us to Barra da Tijuca, where tonight's venue is situated. I immediately question the driver about the route, as he's taking an obvious longer route. I demand he will follow my directions, and with a grin on his face he accepts these terms. When we hit nightly traffic jams, I set him loose from my regime, so he can find a way around it. It's quite a long drive, and eventually this driver turns out to be pretty cool. Time's ticking however, and for a moment we're worried to get there too late. Needless worrying as it turns out, and even though the traffic's really crazy we managed to be dropped off nearby, and walk the final metres to the place where I can pick up the ticket. Another line, which moves quite fast, and then the tickets are in our possession. Now it's another walk to the stage, and we all have to go through ticket control and a body search, which isn't actually happening. Then we get into a massive hall, which reminds me of the RAI in Amsterdam. We have premium tickets, meaning we can be in front of an even bigger crowd, even though the thousands of people in front of us still separate us from the DJ who's warming up the party people. While getting drinks Malena gets into a discussion with the bar keeper as she gets a pure vodka, instead of something to mix it with, and the problem can't be solved easily, only with buying different tokens. These people here are weird. We find a spot in the midst of the people, and await David Guetta's arrival. As soon as he enters the stage the crowd goes wild, and it's much more massive here than in Floripa, as there's seemingly twice the amount of people. We join the craziness and soon are bouncing to the beats. There's a group next to us who are incredibly nuts, and even annoying eventually when they start swinging shirts, hitting people passing by, and also Tatiane in her neck. The good vibes conquer these incidents though, and Guetta seems to be playing a way longer set than he did in Floripa. All the hits of course come by, but also some slower less popular records, during which sleep tries to infiltrate my mind. We've had a long day and the moment Guetta ends his set we head out, looking back on a great show. Getting away from here isn't that great, as soon thousands of people try to stop the same taxi. It's hopeless and after walking up and down the street a bit, we decide to walk a bit further off. The first taxi that's standing to wait for its client Malena however asks if he can't swap his other clients for us, and surprisingly he gives a positive answer. My friend's persistence is getting us out of this place. The girls soon close their eyes for a bit, and I fight to keep them open in order to make sure we're being brought to the right place. After about an hour we drop my friends off at their hotel, and we say farewell here. Tomorrow I fly back home already. Then the taxi brings me back to Santa Teresa and it is also day again when I walk the stairs to my bed.

I don't want to believe it really is my last day of this epic trip, but this evening a plane of KLM will bring me back to Amsterdam. Once more I enjoy the great breakfast and lunch in this fantastic house, with my two great hosts. While having the lunch, Angela's cousin comes in, together with her boyfriend and another couple. They quickly also start talking to me, and we're having very nice conversations. They are all fans of Vasco da Gama, the club I had learned is always to come in second place, but now I finally get to hear the other side of the story and hear about their love for their club. While they go hang out at the pool, I go back to my room to pack everything and prepare myself for my return. Then I also head to the pool, find the dogs, and then again talk to Jéssica, Hugo,

Melca, and Igor. Hugo's offered me to drive me to the airport and I can't believe these people do that for a guy they had just met. It's my final example of the amazing Brazilian hospitality and their friendliness. Not much later we load in my stuff, I say goodbye to Angela and Fabio, thanking them for all they've been doing for me. I also say goodbye to Melca, whose English by the way is excellent, and Igor, and then I get into the car with Jéssica and Hugo for the drive to the airport. I see the city of Rio passing by me, but now realising it will take some time before I can see it all again. I continue to have great conversations with my new friends, and I find it sad I meet these awesome people only on the day I'm leaving. They drop me off at the airport, and it's yet another farewell, with my hope to see them again soon. I check in at the booth, and then head to customs. There's no one to be seen here, so I pick my own attendant, this time it being an older woman, who I have a nice short talk with. I'm a bit worried as I've stayed a bit longer in Brazil this time than the allowed three months, but the woman isn't even mentioning it. When I'm through, I let her know to look behind, as the sun is beautifully setting. This leads to a longer conversation, where I learn that she's lived in the Netherlands for 1.5 years, and she's giving me tips on how I can stay in Brazil longer next time. All left to do now is to wait for the flight to board, and to depart. With a heart aching I sit myself in my designated seat and then feel the plane moving, accelerating, until its comes off the ground, and I see the billion lights below me become one as I reach the sky.

EPILOGUE

It's a long and comfortable flight, and soon I stand on Dutch soil again. I wait for my luggage and then walk through the doors into the arms of my father, mother and sister, who very sweet, are waiting for me, holding a balloon 'Welkom Thuis' ('Welcome Home'). For 366 days my home was the road, and even though physically separated I've never felt apart from the people who are my dearest, my family.

As the room in my own apartment is rented for some ten days more, I take residence in my old room in my parents' home, and these ten days eventually become five weeks, as the love and care of a mother knows no boundaries, and I adapt back to life and to the Dutch cold in their town, whilst the snow is covering the world around.

Back in Amsterdam I decide to continue renting my second bedroom to my friend Mirjam, and she becomes my first ever flatmate.

I start with sorting my pictures and on March 30th I start writing down my memories, which now are written down in the pages before this one, spreading out like a pyramid: from few memories of the start of my trip, to plenty at the end.

Life in the Netherlands isn't the same anymore as it was, as things do have changed for me. I had been earning good money, materialising the things around me, collecting cd's, books, DVD's, all of which have near to zero meaning to me now. All I care about is the connections I've made, the memories created, as written in this book. And all I want is to create more. I want to break free from the chains of expectations, keep my body free from the chronic problems that stress gives me, and live the life I want. I guess this all will again be up to me.

WORDS OF THANKS

Even though this trip was up to me, it would not have been the same if I wouldn't have made the hundreds of connections with all the people I've met. All the people who gave me shelter, who helped me, who shared time with me. A special thanks for my father Nico, who's also helped me with sorting all photos of this trip, my mother Loes, and my sister Aline, who even though separated always were there when I needed them.

I also want to thank Sylvia for proofreading my manuscript, all editing help and supplying me with feedback, and Daniel for both his feedback and amazing cover. I'm extremely grateful to both of you.

I thank you all:

Abel, Adamey, Adriana, Adriana F., Adrihanna, Agda, Ailton, Alan, Alaor, Alejandra R., Alejandra, Alessandra, Alex, Alexandre, Aline, Amanda O., Amanda T., Ana, Ana, Ana I., Ana Carolina, Ana Catalina, Analía, Analu, Andrea R., Andrea M., Andrea, Andrew, Andreza, Andreza C., Angel Fernando, Angela, Angelica, Angie H., Angie F., Ania, Anita, Anja, Anye, Anyela, Aryane, Ashley, Beatriz, Becky B., Becky A., Betina, Bettina, Bianca, Biatriz, Bruna, Bruno S., Bruno, Buddhinha, Carlos, Carlos Alberto, Carolina, Carolina M., Carolina F., Carolina G., Caroline O., Caroline B., Cassia, Cassiano, Catia, Chris, Cid, Cinthia, Cintia, Cissa, Claire, Claudia Z., Claudia S., Claudia A., Cláudio, Cleusa, Consuelo, Cristiana Sara, Crystall, Cyndi, Cynthia, Dado, Daiana, Daniel, Daniela, Dar, Darnely, Davi, Dayanara, Denise, Desiree, Deusa, Diana I., Diana G., Diana N., Diana Alexandra, Diego, Dineyis, Diogo, Douglas, Edilania, Edinho, Edipo, Eduard, Elaine, Eleazar, Elena, Elias, Élida, Endor, Endor Sr., Erica S., Erica R., Estanislao, Esteban, Estefania, Evan, Evellyn, Evert, Eyda, Fabi, Fabiana, Fabio C., Fabio S., Facundo, Fatima, Fatima R., Felipe, Fernanda, Fernando, Fisher, Flavio, Foek, Franci, Franciele, Frania, Gabriel, Gabrielle D., Gabrielle M., Gaby L., Gaby E., Gaby, Genesio, Gerard, Gercy, Gesiane, Giovanny, Giseth, Gloriana, Graça, Grace, Greyci, Gris, Guery, Gui, Hadila, Helena,

Helio, Helo, Helô, Hilda, Hugo, Igor, Ilse, Indy, Ingred, Isabella, Ismael, Ítalo, Ivan, Ivaneth, Ivannia, Jaciele, Jainen, James, Jana, Jeniffer, Jennifer, Jenny, Jessica A., Jessica C., Jessica O., Jimena, Jocelyn, Joeslayne, Johanna, Jorge, Josè, Ju, Juddy, Juliana, Juliana B., Juliana M., Julietta, Junior, Justa, Karen, Karla, Karla Patrícia, Karol, Katerin, Kathy, Katia, Kattia, Keila, Kelly, Kenia, Kim, Laura, Lauren, Layne, Leonela, Leticia, Lewina, Lianne, Liege, Lilian, Liliana, Lo, Lu, Luan, Luana V., Luana A., Luana M., Luciana A., Luciana L., Luisa, Luiz Alberto, Luna, Luzer, Luzia, Mabel, Maiara, Malena, Manolo, Manu, Mara, Marcela, Marcelo A., Marcelo S., Marcia, Maria Paula, Maria Teresa, Mariana T., Mariana B., Mariana G., Mariana A., Mariel F., Mariel N., Mariella, Marina, Mario, Mary, Marylin, Mateus, Mauricio, May, Melca, Melisa, Melissa, Micaela, Michal, Michele, Michelle, Midian, Miguel, Milena, Mirina, Morgana, Nadine, Nadna, Natalia R., Natalia B., Natália, Natasha, Nicholas, Nick, Nico, Nicole, Nidelci, Nina, Nito, Olga E., Olga A., Pâmela, Paola N., Paola S., Paola Z., Patricia C., Patricia A., Patty, Paula A., Paula E., Phil, Philippe, Priscilla, Priscilla C., Rachel, Rafa, Rafael, Ramon, Raquel C., Raquel G., Rayana, Raymond, Reinaldo, Renata, Renata A., Renata R., Renata C., Ricardo F., Ricardo G., Ricardo M., Riikka, Rodolfo, Rodrigo C., Rodrigo B., Rogelia, Roman, Ronal, Rosa, Rosario, Roseli, Rosiline, Roxi, Roy, Rudi, Ruth, Samantha, Samara, Sandy, Sara, Sarah, Selma, Sem, Seth, Shana, Sherida, Shoji, Silvano, Silvia S., Silvia M., Simone, Simone D., Simone L., Sindy, Sofia, Solange G., Solange B., Solange C., Soledad, Stela, Stephan, Stephanie, Tainan, Tania, Tatiana L., Tatiana B., Tatiana M., Tatiane, Taynara, Téo, Thais, Thamyris, Thayna, Tita, Tomas, Toni, Tony, Toto, Ulises, Valentina G., Valentina E., Vane, Vanessa A., Vanessa D., Vanessa C., Vanessa, Veronica S., Veronica C., Vicky, Victor, Victoria F., Victoria C., Viktor, Virginia F., Virginia P., Vitória, Vivian, Viviani, Vivianne, Waguinho, Wellington, Wim, Xavier David, Yana, Yendry, Yohana, Yolanda.

Until we all meet again.

LIST OF ACCOMMODATIONS

Date	Nights	Accommodation	City
01/22/2014	3	Queens Hotel	Paramaribo
01/25/2014	3	CS: Raquel	Belem
01/28/2014	8	CS: Ana C.	Sao Luis
02/05/2014	7	Pousada Surfing Jeri	Jericoacoara
02/12/2014	3	Hotel Praia Centro	Fortaleza
02/15/2014	1	Hotel Caminho do Mar	Natal
02/16/2014	8	Casa de Fatima	Fernando de Noronha
02/24/2014	3	CS: Cristiane	Natal
02/27/2014	2	Pousada Tamandua	Pipa
03/01/2014	3	Pousada Portomares	Porto de Galinhas
03/04/2014	2	Best Western Manibu Recife	Recife
03/06/2014	4	Hotel LG Inn	Recife
03/10/2014	2	Pousada Colonial	Salvador
03/12/2014	7	Hotel Vila Guaiamu	Morro de Sao Paulo
03/19/2014	1	Ibis Salvador Aeroporto Hangar	Salvador
03/20/2014	7	Pousada Canto No Bosque	Lencois
03/27/2014	1	Ibis Salvador Aeroporto Hangar	Salvador
03/28/2014	2	Hotel Pousada Alfa e Omega	Alto Paraiso de Goias
03/30/2014	6	CS: Familia Araujo	Brasilia
04/05/2014	11	Ibis Botafogo	Rio de Janeiro
04/16/2014	3	CS: Simone & Felipe	Porto Alegre
04/19/2014	4	CS: Familia Luft	Nao-Me-Toque
04/23/2014	1	Novotel Porto Alegre Aeroporto	Porto Alegre
04/24/2014	5	Hotel Iberia	Montevideo
04/29/2014	1	Pousada Boutique Las Terrazas	Colonia del Sacramento
04/30/2014	2	Duque Hotel Boutique & Spa	Buenos Aires
05/02/2014	4	CS: Familia Figueroa	Rosario
05/06/2014	2	Gran Hotel Espana	Sante Fe
05/08/2014	2	Hotel Felipe II	Cordoba
05/10/2014	2	Villa Bacuna Hotel Boutique	Salta
05/12/2014	2	Terrazas de la Posta	Purmamarca
05/14/2014	2	Hotel Iruya	Iruya
05/16/2014	1	Villa Bacuna Hotel Boutique	Salta
05/17/2014	4	Stannum Boutique Hotel	La Paz

05/21/2014	1	Tierra Viva Cusco San Blas	Cusco
05/22/2014	1	Waman Hotel	Aguas Calientes
05/23/2014	3	Tierra Viva Cusco San Blas	Cusco
05/26/2014	2	Ibis Larco Miraflores	Lima
05/28/2014	3	Hotel Boutique Portal de Cantuna	Quito
05/31/2014	3	Hotel Santa Fe	Puerto Ayora
06/03/2014	3	Gran Hostal Tintorera	Puerto Villamil
06/06/2014	1	Hotel Santa Fe	Puerto Ayora
06/07/2014	6	Hotel Unipark Guayaquil	Guayaquil
06/13/2014	5	Hotel D'Barros	Quevedo
06/18/2014	2	Hotel Puerta del Sol	Banos
06/20/2014	3	CS: Familia Espinel	Quito
06/23/2014	1	Hostal Coturpa	Papallacta
06/24/2014	3	CS: Familia Espinel	Quito
06/27/2014	6	Urban Royal 93B	Bogotá
07/03/2014	5	Casa Abril II	Cartagena
07/08/2014	2	Hotel Boutique Casa Carolina	Santa Marta
07/10/2014	1	Bukaru	Tayrona
07/11/2014	19	Hotel Boutique Casa Carolina	Santa Marta
07/30/2014	1	Hotel Nueva Granada	Santa Marta
07/31/2014	4	Hotel Boutique Casa Carolina	Santa Marta
08/04/2014	1	Old Town San Diego Hostel	Cartagena
08/05/2014	3	Ivan's Bed & Breakfast Birding Lodge	Gamboa
08/08/2014	11	Hotel Principe	Panama City
08/19/2014	1	Hotel Villa Los Candiles	Santa Ana
08/20/2014	1	Hotel Valladolid	Heredia
08/21/2014	4	Hotel KC Colaye San José	San José
08/25/2014	4	Cabinas Balcon del Mar	Tortuguero
08/29/2014	3	Hotel KC Colaye San José	San José
09/01/2014	1	Casa Amanecer Bed and Breakfast	San Ramon
09/02/2014	1	Hotel Linda Vista	Arenal
09/03/2014	1	Hotel KC Colaye San José	San José
09/04/2014	1	Villas de Oros	Playa Tortuga
09/05/2014	1	Cascadas Verde	Uvita
09/06/2014	1	Hotel Plaza Yara	Manuel Antonio
09/07/2014	1	Hotel KC Colaye San José	San José
09/08/2014	4	Hotel Las Espuelas	Liberia
09/12/2014	1	CS: Family Parker	Samara

09/13/2014	1	Domus Kahuna	Tamarindo
09/14/2014	1	El Guarco	Cartago
09/15/2014	5	Hotel KC Colaye San José	San José
09/20/2014	1	Hotel Cariblue	Puerto Viejo
09/21/2014	1	Hotel KC Colaye San José	San José
09/22/2014	3	La Choza del Manglar	Puerto Jiménez
09/25/2014	2	La Sirena	Corcovado
09/27/2014	3	Hotel KC Colaye San José	San José
09/30/2014	1	Albergue la Casona	Monteverde
10/01/2014	2	Tryp Hotel	San José
10/03/2014	6	Palma Real	San José
10/09/2014	1	Hotel Las Espuelas	Liberia
10/10/2014	2	Palma Real	San José
10/12/2014	3	Hotel Principe	Panama City
10/15/2014	2	Monreale Hotels Guarulhos	Sao Paulo
10/17/2014	2	Hotel Deville Prime Cuiaba	Cuiaba
10/19/2014	4	Jaguar do Pantanal	Pantanal
10/23/2014	4	Hotel Deville Prime Cuiaba	Cuiaba
10/27/2014	2	Getullio Hotel	Cuiaba
10/29/2014	1	Hotel Turismo	Chapada dos Guimaraes
10/30/2014	5	Hotel Deville Prime Cuiaba	Cuiaba
11/04/2014	1	Hotel Ibis Florianópolis	Florianópolis
11/05/2014	2	Hotel Valerim Plaza	Florianópolis
11/07/2014	9	CS: Tete & Teo	Garopaba
11/16/2014	1	Blue Tree Towers Florianópolis	Florianópolis
11/17/2014	3	CS: Familia Gomes	Blumenau
11/20/2014	1	Fragata Apart Hotel	Canasvieiras
11/21/2014	2	CS: Familia Gomes	Blumenau
11/23/2014	1	Cris Hotel	Joaquina
11/24/2014	1	CS: Familia Gomes	Blumenau
11/25/2014	2	Hotel Ibis Florianópolis	Florianópolis
11/27/2014	14	Sonho da Papegaio	Rio de Janeiro
12/11/2014	7	Hotel Ibis Budget Morumbi	Sao Paulo
12/18/2014	3	CS: Familia Gomes	Blumenau
12/21/2014	5	CS: Familia Weidlich	Garopaba
12/26/2014	5	CS: Familia Carvalho	Campeche
12/31/2014	4	Tucano House Backpackers	Lagoa da Conceicao
01/04/2015	4	Majestic Palaca Hotel	Florianópolis

01/08/2015	1	Pousada Mar e Cia	Ilha do Mel
01/09/2015	1	Vida Mansa	Ilhabela
01/10/2015	1	Chalé de Bia	Ilhabela
01/11/2015	1	Recanto Domus	Ubatuba
01/12/2015	1	Pousada Raiz da Cajaiba	Paraty
01/13/2015	3	Hotel Acropolis	Angra dos Reis
01/16/2015	1	Elegance Hotel	Rio de Janeiro
01/17/2015	4	Sonho do Papegaio	Rio de Janeiro

Made in the USA
Charleston, SC
20 September 2016